DERRIDA'S DECONSTRUCTION (
WRITING, SELF AND

THEA BELLOU

DERRIDA'S DECONSTRUCTION OF THE SUBJECT: WRITING, SELF AND OTHER

PETER LANG

Bern · Berlin · Bruxelles · Frankfurt am Main · New York · Oxford · Wien

Bibliographic information published by die Deutsche Nationalbibliothek
Die Deutsche Nationalbibliothek lists this publication in the Deutsche Nationalbibliografie; detailed bibliographic data is available on the Internet at ‹http://dnb.d-nb.de›.

British Library Cataloguing-in-Publication Data: A catalogue record for this book is available from The British Library, Great Britain

Library of Congress Cataloging-in-Publication Data

Cover illustration: Natalie Aschwanden (aschart.ch)

ISBN 978-3-0343-1425-1 pb. ISBN 978-3-0351-0639-8 eBook

Hochfeldstrasse 32, CH-3012 Bern, Switzerland
info@peterlang.com, www.peterlang.com

Printed in Switzerland

Acknowledgments

There are many people to whom I am grateful for their help, support and encouragement. It is impossible to name them all here. They know who they are and how important they have been in my long and, at times, very difficult journey. However, special mention should be made of my son Alexander and my colleagues in France. I owe particular gratitude to Professor Michel Prum at Paris VII who has been a great mentor, and has given me the opportunity to pursue my research interests. His unshakable belief that academic scholarship and excellence in research are valuable activities has been inspirational for me and everyone in the research group.

This work owes its origins to my numerous teachers, including Professors Anthony Giddens, Heinz Schütte, Agnes Heller, Michel Foucault, Jacques Derrida, Cornelius Castoriades and Ken K. Ruthven, who have given me intellectual inspiration and opened up the broader field of theory. I would like to thank my many colleagues across the globe who have contributed, in numerous ways, to my intellectual and professional journey.

Thea Bellou

December 2012

Table of Contents

List of Abbreviations

Works by Derrida

AF *The Archeology of the Frivolous, Reading Condillac*, trans. and intro. by John P. Leavy, Jr, University of Nebraska Press, Lincoln and London, 1980.

CAS *Copy, Archive, Signature: A Conversation on Photography*, edited by Richter Gerard, trans. Jeff Fort, Stanford University Press, CA., 2010.

CF *On Cosmopolitanism and Forgiveness*, trans by Mark Dooley and Michael Hughes with Preface of Simon Critchley and Richard Kearney, Routledge, New York, 2001. (e-book)

CIR *Circumfession*, in Geoffrey Bennington, *Jaques Derrida*, trans. Geoffrey Bennington, The University of Chicago Press, Chicago and London, 1993.

CP *The Post Card, From Socrates to Freud and Beyond*, trans. Alan Bass, The University of Chicago Press, Chicago and London, 1987.

D *Dissemination*, trans., introduction and additional notes by Barbara Johnson, The University of Chicago Press, Chicago and London, 1981.

DR *A Derrida Reader: Between the Blinds*, Peggy Kamuf ed., Harvester Wheatsheaf, New York, 1991.

EOa *The Ear of the Other, Otobiography, Transference, Translation*, Christie McDonald ed., trans. Peggy Kamuf, Schocken Books, New York, 1985.

EOb *The Ear of the Other, Otobiography, Transference, Translation,* Christie McDonald ed., trans. Peggy Kamuf, University of Nebraska Press, Lincoln and London, 1988.

EW 'Eating Well,' or the Calculation of the Subject: An Interview with Jacques Derrida, in Eduardo Cadava, Peter Connor and

Jean-Luc Nancy eds, *Who Comes After the Subject?* Routledge, New York and London, 1991.

FK Faith and Knowledge: the Two Sources of 'Religion' at the limits of Reason Alone, In Derrida Jacques and Gianni Vattimo eds, (1998), *Religion*, Polity Press, Cambridge U.K.

GOD *The Gift of Death*, trans. David Wills, The University of Chicago Press, Chicago and London, 1995.

GTC *Given Time: 1. Counterfeit Money*, trans. Peggy Kamuf, The University of Chicago Press, Chicago and London, 1992.

GTK 'Given Time: The Time of the King,' trans. Peggy Kamuf, *Critical Inquiry*, no.18, Winter 1992, pp.161–187.

LI *Limited Inc*, Gerald Graff ed., trans. Samuel Weber and Jeffrey Mehlman, Northwestern University Press, Evanston, ii, 1988.

LMI Jacques Derrida: "I am at War with Myself", Interview given to Jean Birnbaum, Le Monde, August 19, 2004, Studio Vision, New York, 2004. (e-resource)

MP *Margins of Philosophy*, trans. with additional notes by Alan Bass, Harvester Press, Sussex, 1982.

MB *Memoirs of the Blind: The Self-Portrait and Other Ruins*, trans. Pascale-Anne Brault and Michael Naas, The University of Chicago Press, Chicago and London, 1993.

MPM *Memoires for Paul de Man*, rev. ed., trans. Cecile Lindsay, Jonathan Culler, Eduardo Cadava, and Peggy Kamuf, Columbia University Press, New York, 1989.

OG *Of Grammatology*, trans. Gayatri Chakravorty Spivak, The Johns Hopkins University Press, Baltimore and London, 1976.

ORG *Edmund Husserl's Origin of Geometry: An Introduction*, trans John P. Leavey Jr., University of Nebraska Press, Lincoln and London, 1989.

OS *Of Spirit, Heidegger and the Question,* trans. by Geoffrey Bennington and Rachel Bowlby, The University of Chicago Press, Chicago and London, 1989.

PF 'The Politics of Friendship', *Journal of Philosophy*, no.11, November 1988, pp. 632–644.

PO *Points..., Interviews, 1974–1994*, Elizabeth Weber ed., trans. Peggy Kamuf & others, Stanford University Press, Stanford, 1995.

POS *Positions*, trans. and annotated by Alan Bass, The University of Chicago Press, Chicago and London, 1981.

SM *Specters of Marx, The State of the Debt, the Work of Mourning, and the New International*, trans. Peggy Kamuf, Routledge, New York and London, 1994.

SN *Spurs Nietzsche's Styles, E/perons Les Styles de Nietzsche*, trans. Barbara Harlow, The University of Chicago Press, Chicago and London, 1979.

SP *Speech and Phenomena, And Other Essays on Husserl's Theory of Signs*, trans. David B. Allison, Northwestern University Press, Evanston, 1973.

TAT *The Animal that Therefore I Am*, edited by Marie-Louise Mallet, translated by David Wills, Fordham University Press, New York, 2008. (e-book)

TP *The Truth in Painting,* trans. Geoff Bennington and Ian McLeod, The University of Chicago Press, Chicago and London, 1987.

WD *Writing and Difference*, trans. introduction and additional notes by Alan Bass, Routledge and Kegan Paul, London and Henley, 1978.

Works by other authors

OA Ricœur Paul, *Oneself as Another*, trans. Kathleen Blamey, The University of Chicago Press, Chicago and London, 1992.

MHF Ricœur Paul, *Memory, History, Forgetting*, trans. Kathleen Blamey and David Pellauer, University of Chicago Press, Chicago and London, 2004. (e-Book)

I. Introduction: The Strategy of Deconstruction

I.I Exiting phenomenology and the critique of Western metaphysics

Numerous thinkers have sought to reformulate, transform, correct or break out of Western metaphysics, especially since the eighteenth century. Hume's empiricism and Kant's critical rationalism began this process in the eighteenth century, and their legacy – Kant's especially – cannot be ignored. The most influential thinkers, however, are Hegel, Marx, Kierkegaard, Nietzsche and those of the phenomenological tradition, especially Husserl and Heidegger. Derrida, like Levinas, comes out of the phenomenological tradition. Like Heidegger, he tries to make a radical break with that tradition even as he remains within some of its intellectual categories. Derrida exits the phenomenological tradition by deconstructing its philosophy of consciousness as self-referential presence, and breaks out of Western metaphysics by deconstructing its central principle of identity. In order to achieve this, Derrida reduces phenomenology (and especially Husserl) to a philosophy of consciousness, and Western metaphysics to a series of variations on the theme of identity as presence.

Derrida's attitude to Western metaphysics is more ambivalent, however, than this simple but exact statement suggests. Deconstruction is, as we shall see, an immanent reading of Western metaphysics which traces the way in which the systemic closure that the concept attempts 'deconstructs itself'. Hence, Western metaphysics is also a history of the failure of the theme of identity as presence. The idea of Western metaphysics, therefore, is not a simple one: there can be no single definition of it, because each philosophical reading is both a 'singular' approach to it and an 'event' of deconstruction within it. Although the use of the term may seem to contain both a totalising and a pejorative gesture – in so far as it convicts the tradition of succumbing to a particular reading of being – Derrida's philosophy assembles the elements of its deconstruction out of the tradition itself, and can not do otherwise. Derrida accepts, therefore, that there is no such thing as a single Western tradition, even as he suggests that deconstruction makes a step – a moment of transcendence – out of it. Such a step, however, is quite different from the Heideggerian return to the pre-Socratics and the question of Being (*die Seinsfrage*).

Derrida's philosophy belongs to the post-humanist, post-structuralist tradition which questions the sovereignty of a self-reflexive subject. Derrida wants both to deconstruct the idea of an authentic self in his critique of the subjective idealism of Husserl and also to maintain the anti-subjectivism and anti-humanism of structuralism and its variants. Derrida deconstructs the subjectivism of Western metaphysics in his early writings by critiquing the philosophy of consciousness, and in his later work through the quasi-transcendental concept of the other. He targets the construction of the subject based on ideas of identity and, ultimately, self-referential presence. He reads the construction of the self in the Western tradition as resting on the principle of identity, and as excluding, absorbing or neutralising the other. This, he argues, results from the underlying principle of presence upon which subjectivity is constructed. Ultimately, what Derrida wants to deconstruct is the concept of Being as presence. Hence, by substituting the idea of proto-writing or trace for presence, Derrida attempts to construct a 'new' kind of thinking, as a moment of transcendence, based on the concept of the other.

'Deconstruction' is the accepted term for Derrida's intellectual project (or strategy, as he calls it) of radically reinterpreting and questioning those texts and modes of thinking which are characteristic of Western metaphysics. With deconstruction, Derrida institutes a kind of impersonal reflexive mode; having neither actor nor subject, it aims at a kind of reflexivity that does not entail self-consciousness in the subject. In other words, Derrida wants to avoid the pitfalls of a philosophy of consciousness in the construction of subjectivity and reflexivity, and of intersubjectivity as subjective co-presence. His first target is phenomenology and, more specifically, Husserl. In Husserl's phenomenology, the ego is 'transcendentalised' in order to differentiate it from the 'psychological' ego, and this 'transcendental ego' is the source of the *noemata* of pure consciousness (Husserl, 1962). Intersubjectivity, on the other hand, is a result of each individual monad empathically constructing the other. Intersubjectivity is constructed not through interaction but through each individual monad coming to recognise the other in terms of its similarity to itself. The other, therefore, has no independent existence (Husserl, 1960). The other as Ego is a product of my empathic capacity to experience the other.

In Husserl the inner subjective world of others is a product of empathic consciousness as explicated through the process of transcendental reduction. Phenomenology takes the objective world, which is in part also the world of the other, and brackets it or reduces it through *epoche*. Phenomenology's primary aim, therefore, is to describe the structures of pure transcendental consciousness rather than the relationship of the self to the other. The self is constructed by ascertaining what is peculiarly my own, and this 'own-ness' originates in the fact that the world is a product of my own intentionality. The monadic ego relates to the other – including other egos – by means of analogy. What Derrida is seeking is a thinking of the other beyond any possible analogy with the ego. His goal is not the kind of 'otherness' that is merely projected from an ego, but irreducible 'otherness'. Hence, one of the most constantly and strongly re-iterated themes in Derrida's work is the untenability of 'own-ness', 'ownership' and those 'appropriating' gestures by which the ego annuls the 'otherness' of the 'other' through analogy.

Derrida aims therefore, to construct a post-subjectivist and (in his later work) post-deconstructive thinking, based on the conception of the other as an *a priori* for the emergence of subject and self. The transcendental other becomes a category that determines the relationship between self and other(s) as well as how the subject relates to itself. Thus, for Derrida, both the subject and all the categories associated with it become a problematic that needs to be overcome through the radical rethinking of the construction of the subject and alterity. The notion of *arche-écriture* constitutes the beginning of a mode of thought whose aim is not only to demonstrate the fate of irreducible alterity within Western metaphysics, but also to herald Derrida's radical rethinking of the other. These initial deconstructions mark Derrida's departure from, as well as his indebtedness to, phenomenological thought. They also signal those aporias which result from his 'writing off' of the subject, and his attempt to use writing as an opening towards the other.

I.II The problematic of writing and the subject

In his early work, Derrida seeks to extricate writing from its subordination to *phone,* and at the same time use it to deconstruct the logocentrism of Western thought. Derrida aims to deconstruct identitarian philosophy, and to make the 'other' constitutive of a new kind of writing or thought that does not eliminate alterity by conceiving of Being as full presence, whether through Hegelian *Aufhebung* or phenomenological inner self-consciousness. By introducing such 'non-concepts' as *différance,* he attempts to demonstrate the limitations of interpretative paradigms which reduce difference to oppositional binarisms. These binarisms master 'otherness' by subsuming the 'irreducible' to the order of the same, of the identical. Within these schemas, both interpretation and the production of meaning hinge on those concepts of truth, intentionality, and origin which derive from that conception of being as full presence which determines Western metaphysics.

Derrida aims to go beyond these limitations of Western metaphysics by introducing through deconstruction a kind of thought not based on their premises. Derrida's focal point is the irreducible other, rather than any totalisable forms of identity or subjectivity. In 'shaking' the internal coherence of logocentric concepts, deconstruction reveals their internal inconsistencies, paradoxes, and inability to delimit their own boundaries. The treatment of writing within Western metaphysics represents, for Derrida, the entry-point into the problematic of the other. His early deconstructions establish his anti-subjectivism by focusing on the problematic of the sign and the place accorded writing. In short, deconstruction can be seen primarily as a deconstruction of the subjectivism of Western metaphysics. This preoccupation informs almost all of his writings.

It is my contention that Derrida, in his early writings, either eliminates the concept of the self or deals with it only in terms of textuality. Thus, he accords the self no fixity because of his fear of self-presence as a principle of complete closure. For him there is no possibility of 'writing the I', of 'writing off' or 'out of' or 'from' the self as a partly self-defined identity. As soon as it is written or spoken, the 'I' becomes part of writing's own erasure, and therefore never constitutes itself as 'I'. This impossibility of writing the 'I' is evident in Derrida's deconstruction of the phenomenological concept of 'voice'. The philosophy of consciousness, which finds its most sophisticated expression in phenomenology, constructs the 'voice' as fundamental to the revelation of inner self-consciousness. By linking self-consciousness with the self, the voice constitutes the 'I' as the signified of undivided identity. As a result, writing as being the 'other' is bracketed out. An important element of this deconstruction is to show that 'being-for-itself' is structured according to the logic of the voice, of *phone,* and that the simultaneity of thought with voice effects self-presence. This conception results in the debasement of writing by rendering it external both to *phone* and to the construction of the signified. The signified comes to be thought of as a transcendental concept which fully contains the signifier-writing. Writing takes on a representational function that neither affects nor contaminates full presence. No conception of the subject, therefore, escapes this identification of the subject with the voice that 'hears itself speak'.

The impossibility of writing the 'I' is equally evident when Derrida deals with the confessional mode in writing. Until his later work, mainly in the 1990s, he has avoided in his own writing that autobiographical and confessional mode which he conceives of as involving risk. In a footnote to his essay *How to Avoid Speaking,* however, which discusses a tradition of thought that is neither Greek nor Christian, Derrida calls this lecture 'the most "autobiographical" speech I have ever risked' (Derrida, in Budick and Iser, 1989: 66, n.13). The project of 'writing the Self' is taken up further in his *Circumfession,* but in a way that emphasises the materiality rather than the 'spirituality' of the self. Heterography, not autography, is Derrida's claim: the self is determined by heterogeneity and heteronomy rather than by homogeneity and autonomy.

Consequently, Derrida deconstructs not only that confessional mode which has been the privileged entry to writing of the self, but also all modes of thinking which are based on notions of identity. Instead, Derrida valorises a prophetic mode that gestures toward the other. This prophetic mode valorises the message and the unknown sender, rather than the receiver who waits patiently for a message that might never come. Both confessional and prophetic modes, of course, are irreducibly religious. If the confessional mode depends upon presencing and presenting, then the prophetic mode requires a future presence or presencing – the promise of an unveiling, of revelation to come, but one that is forever deferred and delayed. The prophetic mode is structured as a promise, and shapes notions of politics and responsibility in a way quite foreign to

Western metaphysics. The prophetic mode stages with the other an encounter based on asymmetry and dissymmetry rather than on co-present engagement.

Whereas Heidegger is preoccupied with the unconcealment of Being as an originary but occluded possibility, Derrida defers such a prospect *ad infinitum*. Unlike Foucault, he prefers not to deal with technologies of the self and resistance to certain forms of subjectivation. Instead, Derrida emphasises the event, the giving, the promise, the silence that is always and already contaminated with writing, and which cannot be collapsed into those categories of presence and absence which constitute Being. There can be no self that writes the self, because both the self and subjectivity have already been written, and are already contaminated with a 'conception' of writing that makes possible both the production and the writing of the self. Derrida makes clear his position by arguing that the discourse on invention states 'the inventive beginning by speaking of itself, in a reflexive structure that not only does not produce coincidence with or presence to itself, but which instead projects the advent of the self, of the "speaking" or "writing" of itself as other, that is to say, *in the manner of the trace*' (Derrida, in Attridge: 1991: 318). The identity of the self is infinitely differed and fissured by the other. 'Inventing the self', whether in writing or speech, involves 'inventing' the other.

If writing is freed from those categories of presence and absence which constitute Being and all its concomitant categories of interpretation, then the self becomes yet another category that has to be deconstructed by using the very medium that it employs, namely writing. Thus, the self is a term in that binary oppositional logic which has to be 'liberated' by going beyond what is constitutive of this oppositional logic. If self-presence is a category that the self requires for its very emergence, then Derrida denies the subject this self-presence. Instead, he anchors the self in that space 'between' binarisms which contains both absence and presence while remaining irreducible to either of them. The self is subsumed under the larger, all-encompassing but (he argues) non-totalising concepts of writing and the trace. There is no self-presence that has not been already in the past, in the past present. The trace, the graft, the *pharmakon*, and the *arche-écriture* all make the self an artefact of a quasi-ontological structure of difference. The self is decontextualized as it becomes part of a concept of writing that denies the self its own writing. It becomes a disseminated self, within a disseminating subjectivity whose dissemination is without end. For Derrida, the self always requires the supplement. Yet supplementarity is what denies the self its creativity, its originary capabilities. Derrida's 'non-concepts' of writing and trace develop a notion of the subject as self-identical presence. The deconstruction of it leads not to a reformulation of the subject in non-epistemological terms, but to a radical turn toward a thought of the other. As a result, the reconceptualisation of the subject as an ontologically and ethically grounded self is precluded.

I.III The problematic of writing and the other

Derrida's deconstructions focus, therefore, on the notion of Being as presence, and on the privileging of the nexus between presence and subjectivity within Western metaphysics. This strategy links the construction of subjectivity in Western metaphysics to the voice; and its deconstruction to absence and writing. Any attempt to deal with the writing of the self thus entails a careful exposition of the concept of writing in Derrida, and how he attempts to deconstruct the metaphysical privileging of the voice. Moreover, Derrida's own conception of the subject is embedded in his various deconstructions as well as in his concept of writing or textuality. The notion of *arche-écriture* or 'proto-writing' which informs his construction of the self and subjectivity enables Derrida to deconstruct that conception of subjectivity and the self which prevails in Western metaphysics and other dominant intellectual traditions. Derrida employs the concept of writing to deconstruct the Husserlian phenomenology of inner self-consciousness and the notion of coherent intentionality, as well as conceptions of origin and representation. Derridean 'writing' counters various empirical, psychological and psychoanalytical concepts connected with subjectivity, such as desire, need and imagination, living memory and the unconscious. It also deconstructs various linguistic and hermeneutical notions associated with subjectivity and authorship, such as addresser, addressee, destination, genealogy, inheritance, text and reading. These deconstructions of idealism, empiricism and hermeneutics all converge in displacing the assumption that subjectivity and the self rest on identity and self-referential presence.

Derrida argues that, within Western metaphysics, 'otherness' becomes external to identity – that is, the other is constructed through its dependence on an unfissured, conscious and fully self-present subject. Derrida's notion of the 'other' or irreducible otherness calls for a radical abandonment of subjectivity, and all the notions associated with, it in order to institute a 'new' kind of thought and a 'radical' relationship with the other. It is a 'thought' that works at the limit, where 'limit' does not mean 'inherent form', but an 'asymptotic borderline' (Zizek, 1997: 101). This borderline destroys the universe of subjectivity and points to what lies beyond, namely, the thought of the other that is initially conceived as writing. The notions of *différance*, trace, supplementarity, play, graft, etc. – as variations on the theme of *arche-écriture* – become constitutive of being as that which is 'beyond being' (*epekeina tes ousias)*. The 'non-concept' of writing becomes the intellectual tool through which Derrida deconstructs the binary oppositional logic of Western metaphysics, which gives rise to an identitarian conception of subjectivity and the self expressed in the opposition Same/Other.

Derrida's concept of the other, however, does not fully escape Husserlian phenomenology and its concept of transcendental reduction. Whereas in the early Husserl the *epoche* of the natural attitude leads back to the intentional structure of consciousness, in the late Husserl it leads back to a historico-transcendental subjectivity that must be recovered if the theoretical attitude, to which the natural attitude gives rise, is to be validated (Husserl, 1970). It becomes a 'quasi-transcendental' other that does not escape the aporia of identity in difference. What Derrida wants, however, is the thought of pure difference. Difference becomes the quasi-transcendental source of the binarisms that owe their existence to the quasi-transcendental structure of the n/either-n/or that originates them. The 'other' in Derrida cannot be constructed intersubjectively, since it precedes empirical otherness on account of its ontological character. This position gives rise to an ethical position in *stricto sensu* that depends heavily on the notion of injunction and a relation of asymmetry between subjects and otherness. The call of the other and the answer to the call of the other are doubly affirmative *yes* that inscribes the subject *a priori.* The answer to the call does not depend on a subject that can institute itself within any framework of identity.

In this book I argue that Derrida's critique of Western metaphysics falls short of its aim to go beyond subjectivism, and instead reifies 'otherness'. By doing away with or relativising questions of agency, the narrative self, recognition, reflexivity and identity, Derrida's concept of 'irreducible alterity' ends up neglecting such questions or answering them in a way that reduces the problematic of identity to that other reified pole of the oppositional binarism which splits the 'same' from the 'other'. This approach to the self and otherness is pursued by Derrida through various deconstructions which he performs on ideas and metaphors in some of the key philosophical and literary texts of the Western tradition. Thought of in terms of *arche-écriture*, the self acquires the structure of the trace, graft, supplement, play, *différance*, spectre, cinder, etc. The possibility of the self within writing and other media is thought of in terms of the 'non-identical', of alterity, and not of a more complexly conceived notion of 'identity'.

Thus, because the self writes or speaks of itself as other; it is structured like the trace. In other words, Derrida tries to avoid the binary opposition that results from conceiving of the self as the self-identical entity that can fashion itself only by an act of excluding the wholly other. Instead, the self is irredeemably 'contaminated' or inescapably 'inscribed' by the other. In the early works, the writing of the self becomes part of what Derrida terms textuality, while in his later works it is subsumed under the problematic of the other and the Wholly Other. Yet, as we shall see, this is a quite different idea from that which views the self as being embedded within narrative constructions, which is what Taylor, MacIntyre and Ricœur maintain. In short, in Derrida's early works the relationship of 'otherness' to identity (which is central to his thought) is mediated by the idea of proto-writing, *différance* and other 'non-synonymous substitutions', while in the later works it becomes part of the 'new' thinking of the other. Although the thought of the other becomes the focus of his later work, I will argue that the early problems associated with Derrida's 'writing off' of the subject nevertheless remain. In the later work, the other heralds a post-metaphysical, post-deconstructive, post-subjectivist, meta-ethical kind of thinking that leaves behind the sort of reflective engagement that generates notions of exchange, reciprocity, mutuality, symmetry and intersubjective co-presence. For Derrida, our prime engagement is with the other: it belongs to and comes from the other; and inscribes all relations between self and other as non-relations. The notion of the subject and the self is subsumed under the notion of the other.

This 'writing off' of the subject comes at a time when the nation-state's identity is being questioned; when the citizen as a political subject is being reconstituted in some places as the vessel of a seemingly pre-political and 'ethnicized' identity; when Western thought is being accused of Eurocentrism by post-colonial theorists; when identity politics has become implicated in practices of exclusion; and when morality and ethics are being viewed increasingly not in universalistic or proceduralist terms, but through the notion of ambivalence and in relation to our responsibility for the other (Bauman, 1991; 1995: 2). In a world dominated by the emergence of new and more diverse media and technologies – a world in which so many are announcing the death or the return of practically everything, and where the representational or the symbolic image becomes the dominant medium of relating and interpreting – Derrida's thought comes to question the very ideas of identity and representation and their connection to subjectivity. Can we announce 'anew' the death of the subject in this historico-political context? Or is it not time to begin, however tentatively, its rethinking or reconstruction?

Derrida's deconstruction of the subject relativises the division between life and death, animal and human, even as he paradoxically announces the death of identity and self-referential presence (Derrida, 2005). On the one hand, the rise of techno-culture at the end of the millennium makes a concern with self and other(s) less central in its preoccupation with the self as simulacrum and the construction of 'virtual identities' (Derrida 2005a; Turkle, 2005; 1997; Baudrillard, 1983). On the other hand, there has emerged a concern with the body and various forms of gendered, sexual, and hybrid subjectivities (Moghissi, 2007; Hutnyk, 2005; Canclini, 1995; Grosz, 1994). In this context, Derrida's thought appears more sympathetic to the former than to the latter, in so far as *différance* is a disembodied and quasi-transcendental virtual system which, as Taylor astutely notes, has residues of Cartesian intellectualism (Taylor, 1995: 295–296). The modern self that rejected difference is being replaced by the post-modern self, which pursues a simulacrum composed of hyper-individualisation and hyper-subjectivisation. The post-modern self tends to valorise the idea of difference at the expense of the modernist idea of abstract identity.

In addition, the phenomenal and ongoing developments of the digital communication revolution, as well as the fusion between biology and computing, pose new challenges for the notions of subjectivity, self and other, which give rise to new problematics that demand new questionings. A number of scholars, including Derrida, have tackled some important aspects of these problematics (see Baudrillard, 2000; 2008a; Baudrillard in Clarke et al, 2008; Mattelard, 2007; de Rosnay 2006; Derrida 2005a; Castells, 2000; 2000b). The preoccupation with these new challenges, especially the issues associated with the dominance of cyber-communication and accelerated virtualization, and their multiple and ongoing impacts on writing, self, the book, and archiving, is evident in Derrida's later work, including *Archive Fever: A Freudian Impression* and *Paper Machine*, as well as in his last interview where he deals with his own legacy within the contemporary context of an all pervasive mediatized and digital techno-culture (Derrida, in Hill, 2007: 126; Derrida, 1996a, 2005a; Derrida and Vattimo, 1998: 24).

The processes associated with globalisation enjoins us to celebrate difference while cannibalising the exotic through infusing the 'native' into Western models and vice versa, and thus offering up hybrid models for mass consumption within virtual global communication environments (Kraidy, 2005; Chun et al, 2004; Mathews, 2000; Appadurai, 1996; Featherstone, 1990). The hypostasis of otherness and difference leads inevitably to the self-trivialisation of these concepts. Baudrillard goes as far as to argue that 'even the traces of the destruction of the Other have disappeared', in our pursuit of the 'artificial synthesis of otherness' (Baudrillard, 1996: 115). At the end of the millennium, the process of othering appears to be dominated by media images and digital global media networks in a way that makes it difficult to discern how subjects relate to one another and to themselves, and how the other can retain its alterity within such relations. In the new millennium these processes are accelerating and some scholars have raised the spectre of electronic autism and cyber-*imaginaire*, and what I term the solipsism of screen narcissism (Castells, 2009: 66; Flichy, 2007: 107). Can the other as a quasi-transcendental category provide an answer to the contemporary valorisation and liquidation of otherness?

It is against this background that Derrida's anti-subjectivist thought, and especially its turn toward the thought of the other, becomes a challenge. It opens 'anew' the question of the relationship of self and other. Derrida offers the optimistic scenario that the other is the source and destination of practically everything: its irreducibility is given in advance and *a priori*. Derrida's transcendentalism inoculates his thought against any empirically grounded pessimism. As a gesture of emancipation from both psychologism and idealism, Derrida is happy to break away from the subject of Western metaphysics by introducing a futural radicality to all aspects of the thought of the other. On the other hand, Derrida's reluctance to construct the other outside a framework of transcendentality, which has theological overtones, results in an attitude to Western metaphysics which is problematic, given its seeming devaluation of subjectivity and intersubjectivity.

In this book I try to take up the challenge presented by Derrida's thought and to come to some kind of understanding of the role of the other in the deconstruction of subjectivity. I maintain that Derrida's deconstruction of the sign entails also a deconstruction of the subject, and that this results in an anti-subjectivism which runs throughout Derrida's thought and depends upon a one-sided notion of the subject in Western metaphysics. This one-sided notion also influences and determines not only his construction of the relationship between self and other but also his political, ethical, socio-economic, cultural, epistemological and philosophical concerns.

I.IV The problematic of writing and literature

Derrida's early works engage in a dialogue with philosophy and literature. Most of his early deconstructions are based on either philosophical or literary texts, which he treats always as both philosophical and literary. Indeed, Derrida's work can be seen as an attempt to overcome such a problematic opposition. What attracts him most is, of course, the conceptual and supposedly non-literary character of philosophy. His work is a constant polemic against philosophy's blindness to its own characteristic 'literariness' as a kind of 'writing'. Philosophy's treatment of writing accordingly becomes the major focus of Derrida's work, and it is this field that provides him with the locus for the work of deconstruction. However, it is when considering the case of Paul de Man that Derrida defends deconstructive critical approaches to literature and literary works most forcefully, and tries to answer criticisms of deconstruction (*MPM*). For Derrida, to deconstruct literature or literary criticism cannot be a separate project from deconstructing logocentrism and going beyond logocentric principles. This remains for Derrida the basic strategy of deconstruction.

Consequently, deconstruction is 'at work' on texts whenever there is a 'logocentric' denial of the 'literariness' of writing, and where attempts are made to reduce writing to the discipline of the self-identical concept. For Derrida, literary works are better able to circumvent and at times subvert the logocentrism of Western culture than philosophical works, which are seemingly locked into an identitarian philosophy. The same argument applies to the interpretation of literary texts. Some interpretations are 'logocentric' and others 'deconstructive'. For Derrida, all logocentric interpretations (whether thematic, intentionalist, semiotic or structuralist) relate the text back to a transcendental signified. In doing so, they repress and eliminate the literariness of writing (the signifier) by making the signifier a derivative of the signified. By emphasising the thematic unity of the text, thematising approaches, for example, reduce both textual interpretation and the text to a determinable context, and by emphasising structure they produce the dualism of form and content. Since his project is to deconstruct the interpretative paradigms of logocentrism, Derrida attempts to construct an analytic process capable of discerning the effects of *différance*, dissemination, trace, or that which eludes the construction of Being as presence. This process translates into a number of 'non-concepts' for dealing with the interpretation of texts and writing in general.

Classical analysis or interpretation works through the exposition or elimination of contradictions, paradoxes, binarisms, etc., so that a resolution can be achieved without remainder. Derrida's interpretative strategy, however, is based on the concept of remainder – that is, on whatever cannot be eliminated, resolved, fully exposed, or completely appropriated by any general theory or interpretation. Logocentrism constantly disavows or represses the quasi-transcendental necessity of the remainder. With the concept of remainder, Derrida attempts to construct another discourse which, although it cannot wholly escape Western metaphysics, nevertheless suspends, decentres and goes beyond it. It aims to include the exclusion, the parasitical, and the graft. It prevents and prohibits a discourse from appearing to close itself off, from being fully present to itself, from leaving no remainder. It is a discourse beyond the concept and its principle of non-contradiction.

In order to avoid the problem of the binary oppositions of structuralism, in his early works Derrida attempts a new interpretive strategy which joins the two oppositions by means of the 'remainder'. The remainder is what they exclude, that which is irreducible to any dialectical or transcendental strategy which aims to suspend or eliminate the spacing of the two oppositions. In this way, Derrida allows for binarism without closure, deferring the closure of any binarism *ad infinitum* while allowing for the endless possibility of *différance*. Moreover, Derrida argues, this non-totalising, non-unitary effect is inscribed in language itself, and at the same time makes possible language in all its forms. Thus, for Derrida, language is simultaneously both a product and constitutive of what gives rise to the possibility of its emergence. Although the origin and telos of language have been considered insurmountable problems, Derrida's notion that they are transcendental signifieds suggests an alternative analysis of the 'emergence' and its 'effects' of language.

According to Derrida, any conception of language that is based on the binary opposition of signifier and signified results in both the signifier and writing being treated as accidental and external to the signified. Interpretations based on this idea always lead to the unveiling of the transcendental signified through the *phone*. Narratives hinge on the idea of a unitary, conscious, intentional subject whose identity is the identity of identity and difference. In order to conceive identity radically, it is necessary to treat both language itself and writing (as the embodiment of the *phone qua* transcendental signified) as part of a logocentric system of thought that has to be deconstructed. For Derrida, however, language as such cannot be deconstructed if it remains within the binarism of *phone*/writing. His project is to overcome the binarism inherent in logocentrism by radicalising the notion of a subjectless transcendental field out of which such binarisms arise. These 'notions' have an indeterminate structure. They contain a 'both/and' and not an 'either/or'. These are what Gasché calls 'infrastructures': the 'non-originary origin' of those binarisms which structuralism focused on exclusively because it was unable to question the 'structurality' of the structure itself (Gasché, 1986).

Derrida begins his deconstruction of logocentrism by arguing against a phonetic writing that has been conceived of through the binarism of speech/writing, as a result of which writing is rendered secondary to living speech. Deconstruction challenges the primacy of language as living *phone* conceiving of language as writing produced by *différance*. This breaks with the assumption that the living *phone* is connected directly to thought and, ultimately, to a *logos* unaffected by writing. Thus, Derrida places the problematic of writing at the centre of his philosophy, and associates the erasure of writing with the very basis of Western logocentrism. Derrida constructs a new notion of writing as *arche-écriture* or proto-writing. This is a 'trace' inscribed in language conceived of as both phonetic writing and speech, and as such it becomes a non-originary, quasi-transcendental, and infrastructural concept. The trace – like a number of non-synonymous substitutions of this non-concept – is both being and non-being, absence and presence, since it is anterior to each set of oppositions. This trace or *proto*-writing is not reducible to any of the binarisms of Western metaphysics. By encompassing both differing and deferring in language, it is that which produces *différance*.

Derrida's deconstruction of logocentrism radicalises the conceptualisation of language by critically examining the theory of the sign, especially the written sign and writing in general. Here Derrida demonstrates the weaknesses of Western metaphysics in general, and of any philosophical system which rests on the principle of full presence. If full presence is accorded only to *phone*, then the written sign becomes that part of language which is either secondary or even dangerous to the living voice. Although Husserl, Rousseau, Plato and other philosophers recognised the importance of writing, they were at pains to safeguard the principle of full self-presence against the menace of writing. Thus, writing could not be conceived of as being anything other than a representational and mnemotechnic tool of *phone.* Derrida sets out to re-examine and question the treatment of writing within the Western philosophical tradition in order to deconstruct the idea of an identitarian philosophy. Furthermore, he questions the phenomenological concept of the sign by investigating the problematic of signification, and (more specifically) Husserl's attempt to account for both meaning and non-meaning in language by distinguishing expression from indication within signification. Since only expression retains a living relation to the *phone,* once again writing *qua* indication is devalued.

Although Derrida began by deconstructing philosophical texts, he also works on literary texts, and in *Glas* he attempts a parallel reading of both. His interest in literature, however, informs his entire intellectual project, beginning with his postgraduate studies of the ideality of the literary object. As Derrida himself states: 'my most constant interest, coming even before my philosophical interest I should say, if this is possible, has been directed towards literature, towards that writing which is called literary' (Derrida in Montefiore, 1983: 37). What interests Derrida, then, is the 'literary' character of writing rather than the 'conceptual' character of philosophy, which always denies its literary character by subsuming the literary under such notions as content, intention, theme, etc. Such notions relegate the literary signifier (writing) to the representational, to what is external to the signified. Derrida conceives of the question of literature in terms of 'what it is to write', and 'how it is that the fact of writing can disturb the very question "what is?" and even "what does it mean?"' (Derrida in Montefiore, 1983: 37). Writing, then, is that which opens up and at the same time dislocates the ontological question of 'what is'. Writing also becomes part of the hermeneutical question, 'what does it mean?'. To relate writing to these fundamental questions is to disturb and unsettle the ways in which Western metaphysics has dealt with these problematics.

Derrida further argues that the question of literature, philosophy and writing can be put in the following terms: 'when and how does an inscription become literature and what takes place when it does? To what and to whom this is due? What takes place between philosophy and literature, science and literature, politics and literature' (Derrida in Montefiore, 1983: 37–38). The whole issue of debt, restitution and promise in both language and in writing – as well as the presumed polarity of philosophy and literature – become part of Derrida's deconstructive project. The binary opposition between literature and philosophy comes to be questioned through a kind of thinking that frees both philosophy and literature from the shortcomings of Western metaphysics.

Derrida's relationship to philosophy, however, is ambivalent: while not wanting to abandon it, he does not want to contend with it on the established terrain (see Hartman, 1981; Bloom et al, 1979). This is why he claims that he needed a 'non-philosophical site, from which to question philosophy' (Kearney, 1984: 108). That non-site was provided by literature, whose distance from and otherness to philosophy provided him with a 'free space from which to interrogate philosophy anew', and 'to discern the problematic of *writing* as one of the key factors in the deconstruction of metaphysics' (Kearney, 1984: 109). Literature, then, is taken as the other of philosophy which, although it is never 'totally free from the marks of philosophical language', nevertheless 'produces and presents itself as alienated from itself, at a remove, at a distance' (Kearney, 1984: 109). The literariness of literature, therefore, provides Derrida with the means for deconstructing and thus questioning philosophy anew. Literature becomes the other of philosophy by reacting against the exclusion of writing from philosophy. As an alterity constructed as the wholly other, literature threatens philosophy's privileging of identity as full presence. Derrida aims to institute this other as constitutive of philosophy. An expanded concept of the other becomes the main focus of his later work.

Derrida, however, acknowledges his debt to philosophy, and insists that his search for a non-philosophical site or non-site 'does not bespeak an antiphilosophical attitude' (Kearney, 1984: 108). The task of deconstruction is to discover the other of philosophy in literature. Derrida formulates this task in a question: 'Can literary and poetic language provide this non-lieu or u-topos? I think so; but when I speak of literature it is not with a capital L; it is rather an allusion to certain movements which have worked around the limits of our logical concepts, certain texts which make the limits of our language tremble, exposing them as divisible and questionable' (Kearney, 1984: 112). Thus, for Derrida, literature is what questions the limits of concepts that derive from the logocentric principles of Western metaphysics. Philosophy, then, can neither deny nor eliminate its other; it cannot be blind to the literariness of its own writing, to the whole problematic of writing. If literature's other is philosophy, then that other cannot be eliminated by literature, and *vice-versa*.

Derrida demonstrates the limits of both philosophy and literature in *Glas* where he tries 'to compose a writing which would traverse, as rigorously as possible, both the philosophical and literary elements without being definable as either' (Kearny, 1984: 122). Literature alone, therefore, cannot provide the basis for overturning the hierarchical opposition Philosophy/Literature. Nor can deconstruction aim to make philosophy out of literature or vice versa, since it aspires to go beyond the traditionally accepted separation between philosophy and literature. What interests Derrida is where philosophy and literature meet, where they 'cross each other and give rise to something else, some *other* site' (Kearney, 1984: 122). That site is where the contradictions and exclusions of each can be challenged by the deconstructive process of 'katachresis', which

Derrida defines as a 'violent production of meaning' (Kearney, 1984: 123). In *Glas* and in other recent works, he argues, he is trying to produce new writing which 'stakes out the faults (*failles*) and deviations of language' (Kearney, 1984: 123). Derrida understands writing as the other of logocentric conceptions of language. Thus neither the literary nor the philosophical text can be conceived as a homogeneous and autotelic entity. Instead, each is constitutive of a new kind of writing that does not presuppose a totalisation of either language or text as book.

Deconstruction, in this sense, cannot be used to construct a methodology or a theory of either reading or writing as they are commonly understood, for that would constitute an attempt to establish it as a determinate signified. 'Deconstruction asks *why* we read a literary text in this particular manner rather than another', writes Derrida (Kearney, 1984:124). It 'teaches us to read literature more thoroughly by attending to it *as language*, as the production of meaning through *différance* and dissemination, through a complex play of signifying traces' (Kearney, 1984: 125). What, then, has to be conceived of is language's *différance* and dissemination, which is at work irrespective of the classification of a text as literary, political, philosophical, etc. From a deconstructive point of view, literature and philosophy can be both read as languages whose writing must be thought of structured by the trace. Literature and philosophy are, therefore, equally subject to *différance* and the disseminatory power of the text.

I.V The strategy of deconstruction and 'double writing'

Derrida's deconstructive strategy is to demonstrate that most interpretative paradigms rest on the pivotal organisational and orientational principle of full presence in Western metaphysics. Being-as-full-presence gives rise to both a genealogy and an evolutionary archaeology in which difference is constructed in terms of hierarchical oppositions without remainder. Western metaphysics thus becomes a project of suppression, exclusion, neutralisation, assimilation or resolution of irreducible difference. In this respect, deconstruction is a polemic against the Hegelian *Aufhebung*, defined as a *restricted economy* in which the remainder is always reabsorbed into the concept through the dialectical negation of opposites. By contrast, Derrida is interested in a *general economy*, produced by the general strategy of deconstruction (*WD*). This is constituted on the one hand by avoiding that neutralisation of difference entailed by the construction of binary oppositions in Western metaphysics. On the other hand, it is effected by not '*residing* within the closed field of these oppositions, thereby confirming it' (*POS*: 41). A *general economy* is always, as Bataille maintained, an economy of surplus, of excess (Bataille, 1991; 1985). For Derrida, writing is that excess. It is not a *restricted economy* of recuperation or reconciliation, in which every expenditure is recompensed.

The deconstruction of oppositions begins with what Derrida calls 'a double gesture', 'a double writing that is in and of itself multiple' (*POS*: 41). This involves a 'phase of *overturning*' and disrupting the hierarchy embedded in any structure of opposition, a phase which never completely eliminates the possibility that the hierarchy will re-establish itself. Deconstruction must therefore continually guard against the re-emergence of the oppositional hierarchical structure, while simultaneously using the dislocating power of double writing in order to deconstruct the very process of its construction. Double writing acts as a means of dislocation, and of marking the interval between the inversion of hierarchy and 'the irruptive emergence of a new "concept", a concept that can no longer be, and never could be, included in the previous regime' (*POS*: 42). Thus, the deconstruction of each binary structure effects the emergence of a 'new' concept which both exceeds and at the same time comprehends that structure, but without being reducible to it. Through double writing deconstruction marks the interval which engenders its own field by deconstructing the closed field of binary oppositions.

The double writing which marks this interval can do so only in what Derrida calls a '*grouped* textual field', which cannot be designated as a 'unilinear text' (*POS*: 42). This interval is delineated by the setting 'to work, *within* the text of the history of philosophy, as well as *within* the so-called literary text [. . .] certain marks' which Derrida calls 'undecidables' (*POS*: 42–43). He borrows the term from Gödel's logic in which it refers to the fact that mathematical statements do not and can not rest on other statements or axioms internal to the logical system, but on non-axiomatic principles or undecidables. Simply put, this means that mathematics is incapable of logical self grounding, and that therefore logical self-consistency is impossible (Hofstadter, 1979). If mathematics does not constitute a logically self-enclosed system, then neither does philosophy. For Derrida, undecidables are 'unities of simulacrum, "false" verbal properties (nominal or semantic) that can no longer be included within philosophical (binary) opposition, but which, however, inhabit philosophical opposition' (*POS*: 43). In this category Derrida places all those undecidables which dislodge, overturn, displace, or deconstruct binary oppositions, such as the *supplement*. These become the undecidable in the hierarchical binary opposition of speech and writing. Hence, the *pharmakon* is 'neither remedy nor poison', but a spacing which is 'neither space nor time' (*POS*: 43). These 'undecidables' deconstruct the very foundations upon which Western thought rests. Like a number of other undecidables – such as dissemination, *différance*, *iterability*, and *parergon* – they become those 'non-sites' or 'non-concepts' by means of which the undecidability of the text as a field of finite differences can be demonstrated.

I.VI The strategy of deconstruction and the rejection of method

'Deconstruction' is a controversial term which has attracted arguments and counter arguments, claims and counter claims, in both academic and journalistic circles. Its suspicion of the concept has led to its being accused of not being properly philosophical. 'Deconstruction', it is argued not only treats philosophy like literature but even writes philosophy like literature, that is, without due regard for rigorous conceptualisation and sequential argumentation (Thomassen, 2007; 2006; Norris, in 1990: 17–36; Ferry and Renaut, 1990; Habermas, 1987). Furthermore, both the philosophical and literary content of those works which are loosely classified as 'deconstructive' have come under attack for being nihilistic or ahistorical or both. It is further claimed that because 'deconstruction' lacks a cohesive theory of political and intellectual praxis it results in a kind of anarchism (Badiou, 2006; Ryan, 1982). Some critics have even charged deconstruction with providing the intellectual justification of totalitarianism in all its forms, be it Nazism or antisemitism or other forms, since it dispenses with notions of intentionality, truth as either a cognitive or normative concept, and moral and ethical responsibility. (See bibliographical appendix on these issues and on the Paul de Man controversy).

Proponents of deconstruction respond by implicating their critics in that Western logocentric tradition of repressing what is 'other'. The 'other', for Derrida, is what cannot be subsumed under the Hegelian *Aufhebung*, the phenomenological and semiotic concept of the sign, the structuralist concept of structure, or that unbroken nexus between *logos* and *phone* which is thought of as the origin and telos of meaning and truth. Moreover, while critics target various forms of deconstruction, and its defenders emphasise its 'radicality', practitioners of deconstruction argue the merits of its 'applicability' to diverse disciplines and fields. Thus, American deconstruction refers mainly to literary criticism as practiced by Paul de Man, whereas French deconstruction is associated with the works of Jacques Derrida (Haverkamp, 1995:1–13; Johnson, 1994). These two thinkers are seen as exemplars of what deconstruction is, and for many they represent the 'original' model to be followed. Yet the idea of an original or exemplary deconstruction is a contradiction in terms, in so far as deconstruction is an intellectual project that deconstructs such notions as origin, originality and exemplar. Derrida, especially in *Truth in Painting*, sets out to demonstrate that to preserve the idea of a dichotomy between the exemplar or model and either its good or bad imitation is to remain within Western metaphysics and its principle of identity – in other words, to remain within the very logic that deconstruction tries to question and go beyond. No reading of deconstruction can simply re-instate a distinction that deconstruction so radically puts into question. And yet, deconstruction continues to be discussed in terms of Derrida's original articulation of it.

There are even 'methodological' advocates of deconstruction who seek to extract from it a methodology that can be used as a tool for the deconstruction of texts (Culler, 1983). This is an unattainable goal, since deconstruction is a polemic against the very idea of 'method' as a procedure based on principles and techniques whose main outcome is always apodictic certainty. Deconstruction avoids such claims in so far as every deconstruction is further deconstructable. Thus, deconstruction subverts those positivistic tendencies which have dominated the human sciences in the twentieth century, while at the same time questioning that interpretative paradigm of literary studies whose aim has been to determine meaning through the discovery, or re-covery, of the 'lost' authorial intention. Deconstruction sees both gambits as part of logocentrism. Since its entire project is to deconstruct *logos* by decentring its privileged status within Western metaphysics, deconstruction aims to deconstruct both method and *logos*. There is no right road (*odos*) for reason (*logos*) to discover. Deconstruction's dislocation of truth and method parallels Gadamer's, with the significant difference that it rejects the notion of a hermeneutical fusion of horizons between reader and text (Gadamer, 1975; Michelfelder & Palmer, 1989).

Deconstruction, therefore, cannot be reduced to a methodology without denying its radical claims to be a critique of any system of thought which is directed toward totalisation, that is, toward establishing a centre in which the play of *différance* and dissemination is arrested. As a consequence, deconstruction should not be mistaken for an analytical tool or a set of tools, in the Foucaultian sense, because analysis is based on the idea of a system whose complex structures are discovered and simplified. On the contrary, Derrida affirms the complexity and irreducibility of language, and especially the disseminating power of writing. He does not aim to establish those clear-cut definitions or rule-governed procedures which are a function of analysis and logical exposition, since it is this function that Derrida deconstructs (Derrida, in Attridge, 1991; Derrida, 1995a: 43; Derrida, 2001:4). He has maintained this position consistently, and he reasserted it when arguing that because 'deconstruction doesn't consist in a set of theorems, axioms, tools, rules, techniques, methods' it therefore 'cannot be applied and cannot *not* be applied' (Derrida, in Brannigan, Robins and Wolfreys, 1996: 218). Consequently, he went on, 'we have to deal with this *aporia*, and this is what deconstruction is all about' (Derrida, in Brannigan, Robins and Wolfreys, 1996: 218). In a recent assessment, Richter re-confirms that deconstruction is not a method and for Derrida 'there can be no single deconstruction but only multiple deconstructions, singular deconstructions, singular and each time idiomatic operations that are related to each other only in their radical difference' (Derrida, 2010: xiv).

This rejection of methodology also leads exponents of deconstruction to claim, in reply to complaints about the absence of clear definition, that deconstruction is not a singularity but a plurality, since every text suggests its own deconstructions. The strategy of deconstruction is to

> impose its necessity, if at all, only to the extent that [. . .] it accumulates within itself those very forces that try to repress it. But it accumulates these forces without being able to totalise them, like those surplus values from which a victim of aggression always profits; for here totalisation is exactly what an account, a story, and a narrative are denied (*MPM*: 13).

Since deconstruction works on those elements which, in every discourse, resist totalisation, no analysis or interpretation of deconstruction can claim to be total. Deconstruction must carry within itself the possibility of its own deconstruction. As Derrida points out, one must not forget 'that deconstruction is itself a form of literature, a literary text to be read like other texts, an interpretation open to several other interpretations' (Kearney, 1984: 125). In this respect, deconstruction aims to move away from conventional considerations of philosophical rigour as manifested by traditional standards of argumentation which hinge on questions of justification and self-evidence. This orientation has brought upon deconstruction the wrath of Evans and those analytical philosophers who issued the now (in)famous *non placet* when Cambridge proposed to award Derrida an honorary doctorate (see Evans's critique of Derrida's argumentative strategies, 1991). Furthermore, Derrida claims that deconstructive interpretations, as literary texts, 'are written in a language which has no centralising power of mastery or domination, no privileged meta-language over and above the language of literature' (Kearney, 1984: 125). In short, both deconstruction's rigour and its politics of non-mastery rest on its avant-garde approach to language and literature.

Hence, the only definition of itself that deconstruction can entertain is the paradoxical one of being '*plus d' une langue* – both more than a language and no more than *a* language' (*MPM*: 15). Deconstruction, furthermore, can be neither located nor temporalised. As Derrida argues, 'one cannot and should not attempt to survey or totalise the meaning of an ongoing process, especially when its structure is one of transference' (*MPM*: 17). Although the meaning of deconstruction cannot be totalised or objectified, its possibility and effects are inscribed in language itself: 'there is no sense in speaking of *a* deconstruction or *simply* deconstruction as if there were only one, as if the word had a (single) meaning outside of the sentences which inscribe it and carry it within themselves'

(*MPM*: 17). Because deconstruction is not a concept, it is not susceptible to the principle of identity or non-contradiction. Deconstruction is an effect of a text, and has as many 'inscriptions' as there are texts. Furthermore, the idea that it is structured by transference suggests that the textual is as metonymical as desire. Just as desire exists only for that 'obscure object of desire' that Lacan called the '*objet petit a*', deconstruction also slides toward what escapes it, namely, the satisfaction of stabilisation in an irrevocable definition.

Stories have usually been thought to involve a singular or total narrative with both an origin and a destination, an *arche* and a *telos*. But origin and destination are two of the basic tenets of Western metaphysics that Derrida tries to deconstruct. What one needs to keep in mind, however, is Derrida's claim that deconstruction is a kind of literature. Thus, as we have seen, deconstruction disclaims any relation to theory, methodology, analysis or systems of thought. It is often termed a 'happening', an operation, a cultural event, or a radical and ongoing process whose effects cannot be contained. It aims to dethrone logocentrism, and the cultural and interpretative paradigms based on it, without itself becoming a new paradigm upon which other foundationalist discourses or practices can be based. Being anti-foundationalist, its only role in foundationalist discourse is to deconstruct it. Deconstruction is the parasite which preys on the host that receives it in order to unsettle it. Its practice is aesthetico-critical, rather than normative and political, though his later work deals extensively with the political and ethical (see Thomassen, 2007; 2006). More precisely, it sees the political effect of its aesthetico-critical radicalism as residing in its ability to dissolve hierarchical binarisms such as those of speech/writing, same/other, presence/representation, and culture/nature.

I.VII Scope and structure of the book

This book does not purport to 'solve' the problem of subjectivity and its relation to alterity. Instead it seeks to critically examine and evaluate Derrida's thinking about these problematics. It aims to demonstrate that his concept of the other, and particularly its relationship to the subject and the self, fails to answer adequately the questions and issues they raise. The book aims to provide alternative ways of dealing with the problematics identified in this introduction. It does so in order to point towards a direction that does not 'write off' the subject, but instead reinscribes it within a framework that allows a more complex concept of the self and identity to emerge, one that both radicalises these concepts and frees them from the confines of the same without 'writing them off'.

The book is a contribution to the new fields of cultural studies and social theory. These are 'hybrid' fields that contain elements of philosophy (mainly continental European), sociology and anthropology, both classical and contemporary. The pertinent difference between cultural studies and social theory here concerns their treatment of the 'normative'. Whereas social theory (and particularly critical social theory), sometimes contain both normative and descriptive elements, cultural studies tends to naturalise the normative through recourse to a theory of techniques, institutions and power. This is eschewed here in favour of an approach that captures the 'normative' condition of the self by theorising it as embodied, embedded and identity-laden. While this theory contains both normative and empirical dimensions, it does not seek to be a work of 'pure' normative philosophy. In particular, it does not pretend to obey those protocols of conceptual and relational clarity which characterise analytical philosophy. This is because what the author fears is not clarity but that false exactitude which leads to its opposite. This book operates in the continental European tradition of critical social theory, where a hybrid discourse of empirical and normative elements brings a mutually self-corrective perspective to the theory of the subject. This tradition presupposes that the 'relations' that may pertain between two terms do not necessarily conform to the strictures of formal logic, and hence that such 'fuzzy' terms as 'embeddedness' and 'connectedness' are apposite to the object of analysis. The most famous example of this characteristic is, of course, the problem of a 'dialectical relationship', which cannot be gone into here because of reasons of space and relevance.

Dealing with the work of Derrida is a difficult task, not only because of the complexity of his thought, but also because he was a prolific writer whose work continues to generate much debate, analysis and critique. Derrida's influence also continues to resonate in multiple fields ranging from literature, philosophy, politics, law, ethics, religion, cultural studies, and communication, to name just a few. Moreover, a plethora of secondary literature deals both directly with issues raised by his thought, and also uses his thought as a kind of methodological tool that can be applied to various fields. It is not my intention in this work, however, either to deal with all aspects of Derrida's thought or to take account of its reception in a voluminous secondary literature that has emerged and is still emerging especially since Derrida's death (see Davis, 2010; Irwin, 2010; Houppermans, 2010; Noys, 2010; O'Connor, 2010; Reynolds, 2009; Mjaaland, 2008; Fagan et al, 2007; Hill, 2007; Thomassen, 2006). The materials I have chosen to discuss deal with the central optic of this book, namely with the problematics of writing, the subject, the self, and the other, and also of course with their complex inter- and intra-relationships. I have not attempted, therefore, a critical genealogy of Derrida's ideas. There is thus no separate and independent treatment of thinkers who have influenced the development of Derrida's thought, such as Hegel, Nietzsche, Husserl, Heidegger and Levinas, to mention only the most important. Neither is there a separate and independent treatment of all of Derrida's intellectual interlocutors, such as Condillac, Lévi-Strauss, Plato, Mallarme, Lacan etc. A comprehensive account of these matters is beyond the scope of this book.

In this work I will be mainly concentrating on texts published up to and including the mid-1990s. These texts, including some of Derrida's later work, incorporate a turn towards a transcendental, more theological, and more messianic concept of the other which is still marked by a radical break with subjectivism. This phase of Derrida's thought encompasses the philosophical, political, socio-economic, and cultural critique of the subjectivism of Western metaphysics. It points towards the firm establishment of a 'new' thinking based on his concept of the other. By this stage, the other is not simply an epistemological or ontological concern, but an ethico-political one. The thought of the other offers a 'new' mode of thinking that is both emancipatory and futural. It represents an opening towards a future that is yet to come, which no longer dreams of full presence, but instead dispenses with all forms of closed systems and subjectivism.

The strategy of my exposition is to focus on those aspects of Derrida's thought which deal with writing, self and other. In this introduction I have touched on both the problematic of writing and the strategy of deconstruction, partly to clarify questions pertaining to issues of metaphysics and epistemology, and partly to ascertain deconstruction's claims to radicality on both epistemological and philosophical levels. I deal in chapter one with significant moments in the reception of Derrida's work in order to illuminate the central issues of the book, examining the approaches used by other scholars in order to identify which matters have been taken up and which overlooked.

In the second chapter, I analyse Derrida's treatment of, and exit from, phenomenology in order to emphasise the importance of the deconstruction of the sign – and its resultant concept of proto-writing, *différance* and trace – in deconstructive thinking. This early deconstruction, I believe, demonstrates the anti-subjectivism of Derrida's thought, and opens the space for his thought on the other. I argue that Derrida attempts to radicalise the concept of subjectivity and the self through his rejection of phenomenology's construction of subjectivity and, more specifically, the subjective idealism of Husserl and its resulting notion of intersubjectivity. Derrida avoids the solipsism of Husserl by making alterity, the other and otherness constitutive of Being, identity, subjectivity and the self. Derrida substitutes the concept of writing for phenomenology's privileging of the *phone* in the construction of subjectivity. His concept of trace, which he links to his concept of writing, replaces Being as full presence. The self is linked back to the category of writing, and the other comes to replace the construction of the subject in terms of self-identity as well as in terms of subjectivity conceived of as self-referential presence.

In the third chapter, I examine critically Derrida's deconstruction of empirical, narrative, representational, romantic and structuralist notions of the subject in order to establish the 'writing off' of the subject of desire, imagination, memory and representation. This further demonstrates not only Derrida's anti-subjectivism but also the firm establishment of his post-subjectivist thinking as the solution to a problematic of the self which is based on the notion of identity as an origin that admits no alterity.

In the fourth chapter, I map out the critical points of the development of Derrida's thinking on the subject, and demonstrate both its radical departure from Western metaphysics as well as its weaknesses and inherent aporias. In this chapter I maintain that the solutions Derrida offers to the problematic of the subject are determined to a large extent by his construction of the relationship between self and other. I also explore counter theories of the subject and test them against Derrida's critique of the Western metaphysical tradition.

In the fifth and sixth chapters, I re-examine critical developments in Derrida's thinking on the other, and demonstrate both its radical agenda and its aporias. I argue that Derrida's concept of the other becomes imbricated with his philosophical, socio-economic, political, ethical and cultural concerns, and that the questions of self identity and self reflexivity are both overdetermined by the other. The transcendental other becomes linked with messianic and futural thought that radicalises the philosophy of presence. Because the relation between subject, self and other is asymmetrical, notions of intersubjectivity, self-reflexivity and horizontal engagement between self and other have to be abandoned.

In the seventh and eighth chapters I deal with the last phase in Derrida's work to demonstrate his shift towards a preoccupation with the modalities of the 'violence to the other' within diverse spheres. Derrida in this phase constructs the other as ahuman and beyond being and within a more asymmetrical and injunctive framework. He aims to construct a radical philosophy of *limitrophy* and the concepts of hospitality, forgiveness and *animot* become integral to his project.

By way of conclusion, I review again some alternative formulations of the problematic of self and other which retain a place for the subject that is not totally determined by the other, and which allows for the self to be reinscribed within a theoretical framework that takes into account issues of narrativity, reflexivity, recognition, normativity and intersubjectivity. I argue in favour of a more horizontal relationship between self and other that does not collapse the problematic of the self within the concept of the other, and which does not make the other the source of all relations, be they ethico-moral, socio-political or cultural. I further argue that to subsume the notion of intersubjectivity and reflexivity within the thought of the transcendental other does not present us with a viable philosophical or sociological solution to the question of what or who the other is and how we are to relate and live with otherness.

1. The Reception of Derrida's Thought

Derrida's work has influenced many fields and disciplines and has become the rallying point for various intellectual concerns. Several tenets of deconstruction have become the basis of postmodernism and have entered, directly or indirectly, into many other intellectual movements. We can classify the thinkers who concern themselves with Derrida's thought into the following broad categories: those who appropriate his thought and try to turn it into a kind of methodology (Culler, 1983); those who are sympathetic to it and even vaunt its radicality (Houppermans, 2010; Davis, 2010; Irwin, 2010; Van Zilfhout, 2010; Royle, 2009; Wood, 1987;1992; Bannet, 1989; Hill, 2007); those who are critical of his intellectual project and its potential outcomes (Noys, 2010; Habermas, 1987; Taylor, 1992; Ryan, 1982; Dews, 1987; 1995; McCarthy, 1990; 1991; Wolin, 1992; Eagleton, 1981; Lentricchia, 1980) and those who trace the sources and linkages of Derridean thought through a genealogy that reveals its indebtedness to the phenomenological and other traditions (Van Zilfhout, 2010; Sneller, 2010; de Bloois, 2010; Lewis, 2008; Mjaaland, 2008; Howells, 2007; Rappaport, 2002; Lawlor, 1992). A more popular and politically tendentious group sees Derrida's thought as big on style but thin on ideas, or as 'French fog' that lacks the 'masterful precision' of analytical philosophy (Evans, 1991; Ellis, 1989).

The major discipline areas that have appropriated Derrida's thinking are philosophy, theology, politics, literary studies, legal studies, social science, feminism, cultural and communication studies, the fine arts and architecture. The basic idea that underlies all these appropriations is difference and its irreducibility. The idea of difference and the deconstruction of logocentric philosophy and, more specifically, the concept of identity based on a philosophy of consciousness, comprise the central direction of Derrida's thought. His critique of the centrality of the transcendental subject allows Derrida to develop both the epistemological and ethical implications of the notion of irreducible otherness. Derrida opens up this problematic in his earlier work with his concept of writing. In this earlier phase, the problematic of writing and irreducible alterity are interlinked through the emphasis on the deconstruction of the sign and the privileged quasi-epistemological status accorded to difference. In Derrida's later work, however, the concept of the 'other' becomes more central. This does not involve abandoning the connection between writing and the opening of the space of, and for, the 'other'. Rather, the 'other' is perceived as the ethico-political pendant to the earlier epistemo-phenomenological concept of difference.

Derrida focuses, therefore, on the 'addressable identity' of the singularity of the other (Gasché, 1994: 2), and in doing so raises many questions. Can the subject be written out or written under erasure? What is it in the subject that allows it to respond to the other? Is the subject in the subordinate position of an asymmetrical power relationship that over-privileges the injunctive power of the other in the ethical constitution of the subject that responds to the call? The non-relational concept of identity is one-sided in so far as all relations are engendered and determined by the pre-originary relation to the other. Although the other opens up all relations, in itself it is non-relational. For Derrida would have us believe that the other – by resisting all absorption, neutralisation and exclusion by the concept of identity – is irreducible and, therefore, outside the relation.

In order to frame this problem more clearly, I begin by examining some influential approaches to Derrida's thought, particularly in relation to the questions of writing, politics, and ethics. Although my review will include some of Derrida's fiercest critics, it will focus mainly on his two most perceptive interpreters, Rudolph Gasché and Manfred Frank, who address the question most pertinent to this book, namely, what is the status of the subject after its purported deconstruction? I will also look at Richard Rorty's idiosyncratic appropriation of Derrida for pragmatism.

1.1 Derrida and the question of writing

I begin with some important works that deal directly with the question of writing. Writing is important for two reasons. First, the ideality of the literary text was Derrida's earliest philosophical research project; second, and more importantly, his critique of phenomenology resulted in the development of a concept of writing that questioned inherited distinctions between writing and speech, and between literary and philosophical texts. Jean-Luc Nancy analyzes Derrida's essay '*Ellipsis*' from the standpoint of a French Derridean who co-directs with Derrida and others that philosophy series which is their main publishing outlet, namely '*La philosophie en effet*' (Galilée). In 'Elliptical Sense', Nancy equates *différance* and writing with the passion for and of the origin (Nancy, in Wood, 1992). Nancy sees writing not as a vehicle of meaning, but as 'the condition of possibility of the origin or of meaning' (Nancy, in Wood, 1992: 37). Because Derrida's concept of writing has no limit 'it *is* the endless inscription of the end itself' (Nancy, in Wood, 1992: 40). Nancy thus divorces both writing and *différance* from semantic fixity. Consequently, the question of writing becomes the quasi-Kantian one of that condition of possibility which encompasses a 'transcendental experience' of writing, characterised by 'its non-self-identity' as a non-empirical object of experience. For Nancy, passion exemplifies this 'transcendental experience' of writing. The idea of passion will be also taken up by Derrida in his later work on religion (Derrida and Vattimo, 1998).

Nancy also connects the concept of writing to the question of being. He argues that 'the question of writing – as the question of the letter of meaning and of the meaning of the letter (or as the question of a body of language lost on the limit of language itself) – re-inscribes the question of the meaning of being: ellipsis of being and of the letter' (Nancy, in Wood, 1992: 43). He interprets this to mean that Being is itself differ*a*nt, or subject to effacement not simply withdrawal. The differ*a*nt is not simply ontico-ontological difference, but has the aporetic messianic structure of an unfulfillable promise. The differ*a*nt, therefore, is structured by 'having a *to come*, in its advent […] a *coming* which would be equal to the infinite retreat it at the same time traces and effaces' (Nancy, in Wood, 1992: 44). Nancy therefore proposes that being is not a Heideggerian gathering but instead something that marks the limit. This absolute limit 'is seen as a limit with no outside, a frontier without a foreign country, an edge without an external side. It is therefore no longer a limit, or it is the limit *of nothing*' (Nancy, in Wood, 1992: 44).

In this context, writing is an endless digging at the limit of nothing: 'writing is the excavator digging a cave deeper than any cave philosophy has ever dreamed of, a bulldozer and a Caterpillar to break up the whole terrain, passion's machinery, mechanical passion, a mechanical machination' (Nancy, in Wood, 1992: 44). Unlike the Platonic cave, this is a place where 'the machine works by a gutting, which is itself hysterical. This hysteria in writing would bring to light, to an unendurable light, by a genuine simulacrum of disembowelling and parturition, that limit of being which no bowel contains. Writing goes to it with a passion and to the point of exhaustion' (Nancy, in Wood, 1992: 44). Despite all this activity, however, 'writing does not *do* anything; it rather lets itself be done by a machination which always come to it from beyond it, from being's passion in being nothing, nothing but its own difference to come, and which always comes *there*, there where out there is there' (Nancy, in Wood, 1992: 44–45). This characterisation of writing as both anti-logocentric (*différante*) and messianic (à *venir*) leads Nancy to describe Derrida as a 'drunken rabbi' (Nancy, in Wood, 1992: 40). Nancy interprets Derrida's concept of writing, therefore, as an attempt to do away with the idea of *thinking* in writing, because 'writing is the coming, and its call' (Nancy, in Wood, 1992: 45). What Nancy overlooks, however, is how the call is connected to the concept of the other. The one that calls is the other, and the call comes from the other. The connection with writing is this: that just as one writes for the other and in the place of the other, so too one answers to the other and for the other. Once the question of writing is connected to the coming 'the question of the meaning of being is altered *as* question, [and] can no longer appear as a *question*' (Nancy, in Wood, 1992: 45). Nancy connects writing to an anticipatory concept of difference, and to a Derridean concept of being as trace rather than presence. This means that because the question of being cannot be posited within the Heideggerian 'there is' or *es gibt,* it cedes its place to the question of writing. According to Nancy, writing is the lost body of the passion of writing, conceived of as a metaphysical material and spiritual presence. Writing inscribes this lost body beyond the metaphysics of presence:

> [t]o inscribe presence is not to present it or to signify it; it is to let come that which presents itself only on the limit where the inscription withdraws itself. Derrida – under the name of Derrida or under some alteration of this name – did endlessly inscribe this presence of the lost body . . . he always did play . . . *the body which is lost on the limit of all language* . . . (Nancy, in Wood, 1992: 50).

This conclusion goes against the main drift of Derrida's later work on confession and circumfession, which makes it clear that writing on the body is connected to the question of the other rather than the lost body of language.

If Nancy is preoccupied with the philosophical and radical aspects of writing in the deconstructive paradigm, then Christopher Johnston's *System and Writing in the Philosophy of Jacques Derrida* (1993) points in a different direction by studying the concept of writing from a perspective external to that of deconstruction proper. Johnston links developments in other disciplines (such as biochemistry, biology and the life sciences) with shifting conceptions of structure and language. He sees analogical links between Derrida's concept of writing and an epistemic shift towards the scriptural and the informational. He argues that although Derrida's theory of writing still operates within philosophy, it has strong parallels with the discourse 'of modern biology, cybernetics and systems theory' (Johnston, 1993: 7). Derrida uses bio-genetic metaphors which are structuralist in origin, but appropriates them in an unstructuralist way. Johnston locates Derrida within the 'open system' model of systems theory in order to 'extend our understanding of Derrida's work' (Johnston, 1993: 10) and to see Derrida's general theory of writing in materialist terms as a 'fundamental structure of phenomena' (Johnston, 1993: 8).

To situate Derrida within the atomistic or materialist tradition of philosophy involves placing great emphasis on the biological character of Derridean metaphors. Derrida becomes a kind of neo-structuralist, whose categories of system and writing are embedded within a formal structure. Johnston argues that this formal structure is 'expressed in system-cybernetic language', and that Derrida's 'discursive system is itself highly overdetermined or equifinal' (Johnston, 1993: 188). Derrida's concept of writing is seen as both a metaphor and more than a metaphor, 'because for Derrida writing in its common sense is not only a useful model for the differential structure of systems, it is also in its general sense the fundamental structure of systems' (Johnston, 1993: 190). To assimilate the notion of difference to that of system in Derrida's readings of Freud and Lévi-Strauss 'would be impossible without the modern development of cybernetic and information theory, even if he does not appear to make any direct use of the concepts and technologies of these disciplines' (Johnston, 1993: 76). Johnston's systems-theoretical style of reading, however, cannot connect the notion of difference to the ethico-political concept of the 'other'. It misses the transcendent aspect of Derrida's critique of the idea of an equifinal system that tries to contain the disseminatory power of writing. Hence, Johnston fails to see that the concept of writing is linked to the problematic of alterity. The result is a one-sided and cognitivist reading of Derrida that is unaware of the experience of the limit *qua* 'asymptotic limit'.

David Wood's work also raises questions pertinent to the radicality of both Derrida's concepts and philosophical project in general. He questions the claim that Derridean *différance* is able to 'displace the foundational language of metaphysics', and argues instead that if this is achievable then it will be so only if 'terms such as produce, constitute, etc., are understood out of erasure' (Wood, in Sallis, 1987: 147). Furthermore, Derrida has shown 'the threat writing poses to life', Wood argues and attempts to explore 'the relationship between writing, death, and the Other' (Wood, in Sallis, 1987: 155). Wood interprets this as the question of the '*vulnerability* of the writer'. By merely raising the question of reading, however, he falls short of exploring this relationship (Wood, in Sallis, 1987: 156). In a later work, Wood goes further when engaging with the question of what he calls the status of a '*strong reading*' of Derrida's work. But his conclusion is disappointingly weak: 'the paradox of *strong reading* is that it is strong precisely to the extent that it is not a reading, but the use of a sacrificial victim to exhibit one's own position' (Wood, 1992: 2). For Wood, deconstructive readings 'do not conquer from the sky' and Derrida's readings represent '*a new space of reading*', which suggests a deconstructive logic and the ethical space of responsibility (Wood, 1992: 3). In other words, Wood heralds a new logic of deconstruction and a new ethics. As he puts it, Derrida 'is engaged in a theatrical re-animation of the textual space of philosophy's passion' (Wood, 1992: 3).

It is clear from this brief survey that while some scholars emphasise the anti-logocentric, radical and messianic aspects of the concept of writing in Derrida, others question the radicality of such concepts as *différance* and trace. There is a marked tendency to appropriate Derrida's thought (especially about writing) in order to radicalise both reading and writing within literary, interpretive and philosophical paradigms. The connection between writing and the other remains undertheorised, and its relation to the opening of irreducible alterity tends to be overlooked. In other words, the quasi-transcendental function of writing within Derrida's thought is still to be explored adequately.

1.2 Derrida and the question of politics

The political implications of Derrida's thought are two-fold. On the one hand, the critique of logocentrism leads to complementary critiques of phallogocentrism, Eurocentrism and fratrocentrism, in which many see the radical core of Derrida's deconstruction. On the other hand, the notion of a weak Messianic impulse without Messianism is the more transcendent aspect of his critique of contemporary politics. Robert Magliola, for example, draws a comparison with eastern forms of thought, and argues that logocentrism is equated with power and European ethnocentrism in the work of Derrida (Magliola, 1986: 53). This is a 'postcolonial' argument that acknowledges deconstruction's usefulness in unmasking the ethnocentrism and the Eurocentrism of Western metaphysics, and takes seriously the claims that it is a radical system of thought. For Krupnik, the radical agenda of deconstruction is feminist, in so far as it 'enables a return of the repressed, unsettling the law that gives priority to voice, patriarchy, rational consciousness, and the Greek-Christian logos. Deconstruction unsettles the idealisms that provide the ideological justification for relations of power', while questioning if the 'old, bad (metaphysical) order can be transcended' (Krupnick, 1983: 3, 2). What Krupnik neglects in his remarks on the 'Greek-Christian logos' is the fact that, for Derrida, what cannot be transcended is the entire legacy of Greek philosophy and the 'religions of the book'.

Spivak also praises deconstruction as a critique of phallogocentrism and its discourses. However, there is a trace of Irigaray in her argument that deconstruction safeguards the irreducible 'sexual *differential* between man and woman' (Spivak, in Krupnick, 1983: 184). This is to ignore Derrida's critique of feminism, and his thinking about the other, which is not limited to a concern for the other as woman (*SN*: 65). Spivak appropriates deconstruction for a feminist practice and discourse by keeping man and woman as separate categories in order to maintain the notion of female subjectivity. She even goes as far as to claim that deconstruction, as a practice and a questioning, 'restores to us the position of the questioning *subject* by virtue of the question-effect' (Spivak, in Krupnick, 1983: 186). Her argument ignores the fact that, for Derrida, the question comes from the 'other'.

The issue of radicality, however, is emphasised, underplayed or questioned most often by scholars who compare Derrida's work with that of other thinkers. Roy Boyne, who connects Derrida explicitly with Foucault, constructs their radicality as a product 'of an aesthetics of existence oriented to the careful (in the fullest sense of the word) destabilisation of hierarchical determinations of otherness', which 'at least provides the possibility of an exit from the anti-social snares of liberal individualism' (Boyne, 1990: 170). Hence, Boyne concludes that the

> ultimate lesson of the Foucault-Derrida debate is that there is no pure other, that ontological difference is a chimera. This means that there is no bright promise on the other side of reason. It also means, if all is on our side, that there is no reason, outside of our reach, why we cannot generate our own bright hope for a different future (Boyne, 1990: 170).

Boyne locates the construction of the other within historical specificity and links it to the regulation of the self. This 'Foucaultian' argument tends to reduce the complexity of the construction of the other in Derrida to the notion of reason and the problem of exclusion. It ignores the futural orientation of Derrida's thought, namely as a future encapsulated in the concept of promise, event and anticipation. It needs to be emphasised here once again that the notion of a future promise traverses most of Derrida's thought. Furthermore, although his concern for the 'other' is connected to the question of ethics and politics, it is independent of historical specificity and deconstructs the notion of a subjectivist ethics. This, of course, sharply differentiates Derrida's conception of otherness from that of Foucault, for whom truth was once thought to be located on the other side of reason (Foucault, 1973).

Irene Harvey takes up some of the challenges posed by Derrida's thinking on the other, and (like Rapaport) explores its connections with Hebraic rather than Foucaultian thought. Harvey has done important work on the problematic of the other in both Derrida and Levinas. Dealing with the concept of writing in Derrida, she argues that it represents a shift 'from the *is* structure of *Logos* to the *as* structure of that which founds it' (Harvey, 1986: 155). Although this assessment correctly emphasises the deconstructive function of writing with regard to the *logos,* it does not explore adequately the interconnections between writing, self and other. Nevertheless, she makes some important points about the construction of subjectivity and the other in Derrida. According to her interpretation of *The Scene of Writing,* for instance, the movement of the trace in Derrida is unlike Freud's, in so far as it is not synonymous with memory, but exhibits two aspects 'as it a) inscribes itself and b) therein effaces itself' (Harvey, 1986: 175).

Yet this formulation underestimates Derrida's later critique of autobiography and confession, which confronts more directly the concept of memory and autobiography, and tries to 'de-spiritualise' the Western metaphysical concept of memory that Freud only partly escapes. Harvey concludes that in Derrida's model the subject is 'necessarily a "victim". Its actions are always already inscribed by the "other"; indeed by otherness itself' (Harvey, 1986: 179). She puts this even more emphatically when suggesting that the subject is a victim in Derrida's work because it is 'comparable to the Master, to the Father, to the author, to the agent, indeed to an ultimate causality and, in this sense, does not exist' (Harvey, 1986: 181). This argument is important because it signals, without really developing, a critique of the fate of the subject in Derrida. For Harvey, Derrida's thought rests on 'a fundamental identity between the "subject" and the machine in terms of nonresponsibility' (Harvey, 1986: 180). The accusation that Derrida's notion of the subject abrogates its own responsibility is one that has been leveled before against Derrida. However, it is an argument that cannot be sustained if one takes into account his later work, and especially his development of an ethico-moral dimension to the concept of the other (Beardsworth, 1996).

Most scholars accept that the politics of deconstruction is radical, and various attempts have been made to trace the sources of Derrida's work. It is important to emphasise, however, that the question of how the subject – and in particular the self – relates to the other is under-theorised. Some point to the problems with Derrida's construction of subjectivity, but do not fully explore the fate of the subject within the Derridean project. There is a reluctance to deal with the anti-subjectivism of deconstruction, and to explore its various implications especially with regard to the politics which ensues from the asymmetrical relationship between self and other.

1.3 Philosophy and the question of ethics

Derrida's work on ethics is at the core of his concerns during the 1990's and beyond, although it is possible to read it back into some of the earlier essays. It has also been prepared by the earlier work on difference, in so far as that 'non-concept' was devised as an alternative to the Heideggerian escape-route from European subjectivism. But the concern with the other and the notion of responsibility, as stemming from the other, constitute the necessary ethical complement to the earlier epistemological anti-subjectivism. It also raises another perennial concern of Derrida's thought, namely the relationship between Judaism and Greek philosophy.

Herman Rapaport's work on Derrida is relevant to my concerns because it analyses the connections between Heidegger's notion of temporality and Derrida's. Rapaport sets out to make Heidegger more Derridean and Derrida less Heideggerian. This is evident in his attempt to interpret the Heideggerian turn in Derrida's thought as a movement 'from Christianity to Judaism by way of re-examination of the philosophy of Emmanuel Levinas' (Rapaport, 1991: 17). The encounter with Levinas, therefore, results in a Heideggerian 'turn' which proves insufficiently radical for Derrida. What proves decisive is Levinas' notion of temporality and its relationship to Being.

Rapaport locates this radical break in Derrida's work in the period after *The Post Card* (1987) and closely examines the notions of event and apocalypse. Rapaport argues that Derrida transforms the Heideggerian *es gibt,* which keeps open the coming by withholding the present in the coming, into a kind of withholding which is not only

> marked by an absencing but by another directedness or exteriorisation of one's consciousness of Being such that Being in its openness or coming can be intuited in its *Ereignis* in that granting constituted by tone. In terms of the correspondence of tones and times, the coming of the sent dispatch, the withholding of the self as that which is present-to-self, we can make the transition or translation from philosophy to theology and back again, a translation which demystifies Kant's absolute difference between the voice of reason and the voice of the oracle (Rapaport, 1991: 209).

This reading, which emphasises correctly the withholding of the self as that which is present-to-self, is influenced greatly by Levinas. Derrida's concept of the other, however, is formulated in a less theological manner than Rapaport's reading suggests.

Rapaport's assertion that Derrida's 'I shall come' is conceived of as 'an other that is truly Other in the sense formulated by Levinas' overlooks the differences between the theological concept of Levinas's other and Derrida's idea of the other as trace or as a non-originary difference (Rapaport, 1991: 216). For Levinas, as we shall see later, the encounter with the other is a 'face to face' encounter, while the other in Derrida is beyond being and beyond any subjectivist or theological conceptions of the other. As Rapaport rightly points out, it is connected to ethics and responsibility. He asserts that Derrida's deconstruction of the dichotomy between event and apocalypse is not 'what some Christian readers will suspect' – namely the expression of 'a deep seated atheism' – but rather 'an interpretation of Christian apocalypse from the standpoint of the *au-delà de L'Etre* as developed by Levinas in a Judaic context' (Rapaport, 1991: 220–221). This remark subsumes Derrida's thought once again within Levinas' concept of the other. As a consequence, it underplays the anti-subjectivist consequences of Derrida's critique of Levinas' notion of the face and its centrality to his ethics of responsibility.

Christopher Norris, who has consistently addressed such issues, has tried to locate Derrida's concerns within the history of philosophy. Norris has defended Derrida against attacks not only from analytical philosophers but also from Habermas, who fails to recognise those aspects of Derrida's thought which move away from 'a generalised "postmodern" or post-structuralist discourse' (Norris, 1990b: 50). Norris sees Derrida and deconstruction as part of that development which wrestles with the problematics of Enlightenment and post-Kantian thought, rather than as part of the counter-enlightenment tradition. According to Norris, Derrida wants to maintain the critical force of the Kantian tradition even as he remains critical of it. Pointing out rightly that both Levinas and Derrida emphasise the primacy of ethical concerns, Norris also emphasises the importance of Derrida's early critique of Levinas in his essay on 'Violence and Metaphysics' which contains 'some crucial (though hitherto neglected) implications' pertaining to the 'question of ethics as the recognition of absolute alterity' (Norris, 1994: 50). Norris, however, does not take up the issue of differences in the ways that both Levinas and Derrida construct the 'Other', and therefore does not consider the implications of these differences.

Simon Critchley also links the ethical dimensions of Derrida's thought to those of Levinas in order to correct what he calls an impasse in Derrida's work, in so far as it 'fails to offer a coherent account of the passage from ethical responsibility to political questioning and critique' (Critchley, 1992: xii). Critchley therefore links the practice of deconstructive reading to ethics and, more specifically, responsibility. He argues that an 'ethical moment is essential to deconstructive reading and that ethics is the goal, or horizon, towards which Derrida's work tends' (Critchley, 1992: 2). He emphasises correctly that both Derrida's and Levinas' textual encounters not only centre on the issue of responsibility for the 'other' but also attempt to answer the question, How does deconstruction concern itself with the other? According to Critchley, Derrida fails to see the ethical dimension of the indicative sign in Husserl, which Levinas takes to be a relation of non-identity that maintains the unassimilable and absolute difference of the other.

In order to bring out the ethical dimension of Derrida's thought, Critchley shows through a reading of Derrida's texts *Of Spirit* and *The Other Heading* that the 'Other's' significance is ethical, and argues that ethics for Levinas is a relation of the subjection of the subject to the other, and is 'enacted at the level of skin' (Critchley, 1992: 180). Critchley underplays, however, both Derrida's critique of Levinas and his rejection of Levinas' subjectivism, especially in his later work. Derrida calls for a relation between self and other that not only differs from subjugation to the demands of the other and responsibility for the other, but also engenders the subject within a relation of asymmetry. This asymmetry goes beyond Levinasian ethics enacted at the level of skin, and aims to deconstruct any vestiges of subjectivism in Levinas' thought. Hence, unlike Norris, Critchley fails to see a crucial difference between Derrida's and Levinas' philosophy of the 'other' (Norris, 1994).

A more extreme interpretation by Caputo of the ethics of Derrida is subtitled significantly, 'religion without religion' (Caputo, 1997). For Caputo, Derrida's thought is governed both by a lost or 'broken alliance' and the promise of a 'new *alliance*'. Deconstruction is not a two-step event that contains both overthrowal and transcendence, but a thought dominated by the 'movement of transcendence'. According to Caputo's main thesis, 'deconstruction is set in motion by an overarching aspiration, which on a certain analysis can be called a religious or prophetic aspiration' (Caputo, 1997: xix). This aspiration is specified further as being centred on that '*tout autre*' which seems to function as the most elemental religious relation that we can maintain to something else in the modern world. Although the '*tout autre*' is, of course, a complex notion, it refers clearly to the 'promise' of something ethical which is qualitatively new, as well as to the experience of this promise throughout history, and the possibility of this promise today. It needs to be conceived of, according to Caputo's meticulous reading of Derrida, outside all institutionalised religion and it is a visceral rather than spiritual experience. This makes Derrida's texts enactments of faith. Derrida's point is 'more performative than constative' and because 'it is religious without a theology . . . it hangs on by a prayer' (Caputo, 1997: 328). Although Caputo manages to prove his point that Derrida's thought is not nihilistic, but increasingly religious, his book does not display much critical distance from Derrida. Caputo accepts all those one-sided characterisations of the subject, self-consciousness and the *logos* which are key parts of the argument for messianism. He is too entranced by the insistence of Derrida's faith to recognise the extreme fragility of those paradoxes – religion without religion, faith without a Church, an alliance without allies – on which it rests.

1.4 Gasché: Variations on the theme of difference

Early interpretations of Derrida's thought are located mainly within its methodological appropriation by literary and cultural studies, and failed to fully explore and then incorporate the philosophical aspects of Derrida's thought. Formed against this background, Gasché's work has attempted to rescue Derrida's thinking not only from a literary-oriented methodology, but also from any attempt to reduce the complexity and singularity of Derrida's thought. Gasché investigates the German philosophical traditions, particularly idealism, from which Derrida's thought both emerges and departs. Unlike Habermas, therefore, who emphasises the literary dimension of Derrida's project, Gasché argues that Derrida's thought 'can be adequately understood only if approached philosophically – that is, shown to be engaged in a constant debate with the major philosophical themes' (Gasché, 1986: 2). Moreover, Gasché places Derrida's thought both within and outside the tradition of reflective philosophy. He views Derrida as opening up the space which makes possible a philosophy of reflection without, however, permitting his thought to be reducible to the problematic of reflexivity. By divorcing Derrida's thought from the constructivism which places it within American New Criticism, he underplays correctly the significance of the American reception of deconstruction in the understanding of Derrida.

Subsequently, Gasché has attempted to establish a relationship between Derrida's *différance* and Heidegger's ontological difference concerning Being and beings. However, because he sees *différance* as a cluster of concepts, he regards it anterior to the Heideggerian ontological difference. The radicality of *différance* rests on the fact that it is perceived as thought which encounters 'the very limit of limitlessness' (Gasché, 1994: 106). Gasché still retains from his earlier work the concept of infrastructures to describe the nature and the operations of Derrida's 'non-concepts' such as *différance*. Nevertheless, he opens up the problematic of the other in Derrida's thought by arguing that the *arche*-trace (as indicative of what he calls infrastructures) is to be understood as 'the minimal structure of *reference to Other*' and that this structure of

> generalised indication points incessantly away from itself even when its 'own' minimal identity is in question. The structure of reference to the Other, *necessarily*, deports itself away from itself, toward the Other-infinitely (Gasché, 1994: 141).

Consequently, self-reference always contains a reference to what is foreign, namely its supplement. In other words, in order to exist it must always refer back to, and be contaminated by, that non-present difference which constituted it. Self-reference requires difference but not self-closure. The myth of self-closure is the myth of absolute identity. It is myth because the notion of identity must contain a reference to that difference or otherness which constitutes it. As Gasché argues, 'we face *a structure of self-reference* which, instead of producing a coincidence with self, always-and endlessly-gives rise to a supplementary turn' (Gasché, 1994: 142).

Gasché emphasises the fact that all Derrida's quasi-transcendental structures (rather than concepts) depend on a structure of referral that refers ceaselessly to an other. Deconstruction is a call by the other 'to respond to thinking's attempt to coil upon itself in a gesture of auto-affective self-positioning' (Gasché, 1994: 203). This call necessitates an affirmative response, since

> there remains the essential risk of failing to genuinely respond to the call by the Other which renders a genuine response possible at all. Indeed, just as the *place* of the Other in a text or work of thought is nothing but a referential vector, a gesturing, pointing toward and calling upon the Other, which cannot avoid determining itself as for-itself, and hence give itself a self, or identity, so a genuine response, which is at first nothing but a *yes*-saying to the Other as Other, cannot altogether escape the risk of saying *yes* to itself, and hence of opening the annulations of its own identity (Gasché, 1994: 204).

Having identified this very important issue, Gasché proceeds to draw attention to the paradox of the concept of identity in Derrida. While identity as self-closure is denied to the self as 'I' within Derridean thought, it is this 'I' which answers with an affirmative Yes to the call of the other. Here Gasché raises the possibility of failing to respond genuinely to the call of the other, and attributes this risk to the possibility that the other may form itself as an identity which says 'yes' within a structure of identity. Gasché argues that, under deconstruction, identity 'is a concept that testifies to Hegel's impressive efforts to overcome the difficulties in articulating a philosophical monism freed from both subject and substance' (Gasché, 1994: 206). What Gasché fails to think about, however, is the position of both the subject and self-identity beyond the deconstructionist rejection of absolute self-identity.

According to Gasché, Derrida's thought is based on a 'deconstructive "operation" on identity itself', rather than a critique of identity 'in the name of the nonidentical' (Gasché, 1994: 218). Gasché tries to free Derrida from accusations of nihilism, negative theology, and (in Adorno's sense) negative dialectics. He wants to place Derrida firmly within the camp of German idealism, even though Derrida deconstructs its positing of the question of identity. Gasché points out that the 'deconstruction of speculative identity does not consist in opposing a non-identical (either in a Hegelian sense or in one determined by a critique of identifying thought and of the thought of absolute identity) to identity' (Gasché, 1994: 222–223). He proposes that 'only a *relation without relation* to absolute identity can escape or resist it' (Gasché, 1994: 223). This he takes to be the remainder that 'a deconstruction discerns *in* a speculative totality and identical whole', a '"remainder that is both quasi-transcendental and supplementary"' (Gasché, 1994: 223). Gasché stresses that Derrida's concept of the remainder '*resists* the meaning of both the identical and the non-identical, and cannot be questioned within their horizon', either in terms of negativity or in terms of positive identity or infinity (Gasché, 1994: 223). It is anterior to, and escapes all, dialectical reversals and inversions. The remainder remains and this '*remaining* is the structure of that which simultaneously adds itself to and withdraws from a self-identical and self-present totalisation' (Gasché, 1994: 223–224).

What Gasché calls infrastructural *remaining* is what allows the remaining to 'play the role of a condition of possibility *and* impossibility for absolute identity' (Gasché, 1994: 224). Gasché argues that an affirmative *yes* is required as a response to the call of the Other, and that this *yes* to

> the speculative *yes* of reconciliation is one such instance of undecidable infrastructural *remaining*. It is a response demanded by the very fact that even the most absolute, that is, self-inclusive, totalisation involves, as a performative event, the Other and, hence, the request to say *yes* (Gasché, 1994: 225).

This affirmative *yes,* required by both the speculative and the reconciling *yes*, is outside speculative affirmation and negation, since 'it is not of the order of a non-identical Other *of* the system of identity' (Gasché, 1994: 225). As a result of its undecidibility, this *yes* 'can always slip, turning into the affirmative *yes* itself or into mere repetitive affirmation of Hegelian reconciliation' (Gasché, 1994: 225).

Although Gasché cautions against a tautological response to the *yes*, he nevertheless sees this response to the *yes* as being singular, due to the possibility of it both occurring and not occurring. Its response can recede

> out of the reach of that to which it consents . . . [as] . . . these intelligible structural traits of the deconstructive *yes*, all by the mselves and alone, explain why and how such a *yes* makes absolute identity tremble. In answering the call to say *yes* to absolute identity, *yes* has, indeed, deconstructed it. In responding to the call, the *yes* of deconstruction opens the space of the Other without whose consent absolute identity as event could not spiral upward, encircling itself and the Other, and re-descend into itself. By the same token, however, an outside of absolute identity has become marked, and *remains* (Gasché, 1994: 226).

It is clear that this deconstructive *yes* is seen as an affirmation and a response to both identity and the other while remaining outside their construction. The affirmative *yes* is a precondition for the opening of the space of the other. How this *yes* which is both affirmative and deconstructive relates to the other is of special importance to my own study. Gasché argues that the consent of the other is necessary for absolute identity as an event to occur. In other words, Gasché is reluctant to abandon the notion of absolute identity in the Hegelian sense, rather he sees it as spiralling upwards while encircling itself and the other only to redescend into itself. Only through this process is the concept of remainder marked as an outside of absolute identity. Moreover, the primacy of the affirmative *yes* is 'a demand that the response to the Other be demanded by the Other', and that this request is 'to be asked, to be addressed' (Gasché, 1994: 242–243). Going one step further, Gasché asserts that 'if the Other is to be respected as Other, even the *yes* of the address to it must be owed by, or owed to, the Other' (Gasché, 1994: 243). Thus the deconstructive *yes* involves both a response to the other as other and an address to the other as other. Consequently, all relations with the other must be preceded by this structural requirement if the other is to be irreducible to me by 'becoming *my* Other, the Other of myself' (Gasché, 1994: 242).

Gasché does not take issue with Derrida's view that the other appeals to no other structure or relation, nor that it is answerable to anything else but itself. The other negates, posits and addresses itself to itself without losing its own heterogeneity and irreducibility. Gasché has no serious problems with the asymmetrical relationship between the other (as that who demands to be addressed in its singularity) and the self (which presumably becomes subsumed under the demands of the other). The only problems he raises derive from the fact that the other, which must be 'addressed in an appeal to say *yes* to the address prior to all possible acts or engagements[,] can also lend itself to acts of negation or denegation of the Other' (Gasché, 1994: 243). He brushes away this problem by asserting that 'this possibility is not the symmetrical counterpart of the enabling fundamental structure in question. All negation or denegation of the Other presupposes it' (Gasché, 1994: 243). In other words, this risk is eliminated in the very structure of the *yes* as a double *yes* that refers to an event which, in order to be such, requires repetition, and affirms itself 'only by being confirmed by the Other, by an entirely other event' (Gasché, 1994: 244–245).

The two *yes*es, as Gasché analyses them apropos of Derrida's essay, 'Ulysses Grammophone', refer to the combined meaning of "saying yes" and "hear say" (or hear say yes), which involves an untranslatable double of doubling. Gasché explains that what the first *yes* refers to 'is the place of the Other, and it refers to it according to a relation of *implication*' rather than judgement and cognition (Gasché, 1994: 282, n.20). The second *yes*, according to Gasché, does not refer to an already constituted other, although this is the *yes* with which everything begins. I would argue, however, that Gasché underplays the problems relating to the treatment of the other, which is conceived in Derrida's later works as not merely affirmative but also injunctive. The other is not simply a category that embodies a responsible response through the double *yes* to the other; it has both constitutive and generative power. In becoming a transcendental category, the other not only refers to the place of the other according to a relation of implication, but the *yes* to the other becomes part of the structure of the other. Gasché's interpretation of the double affirmative *yes* and its relation to the other allows the other to become another quasi-transcendental infrastructure, but without exploring either the demands of the other or the effects of the other within the problematic of the self.

In attempting to give the problematic of identity a new turn by 'questioning', Derrida reifies the concept of the other, not simply into an affirmative *yes*, but also into a concept that overdetermines both the subject and the self. The result is a transcendental other, which in becoming a source of ethics and morality, announces if not the death of the subject then at least the subsumption of the question of the self within a transcendent other that is self-referential and self-generative. The thought of the other, however, side-steps rather than resolves questions of identity and the intersubjective recognition of identity, because it moves them to a level at which they cannot be resolved satisfactorily.

1.5 Critical responses from analytical philosophy

The most critical responses to Derrida have come from analytical philosophers such as Searle, literary critics such as John M. Ellis, and phenomenologically-oriented philosophers such as Claude J. Evans and Manfred Frank. These responses range from explicitly political and polemical attacks, such as those which occurred when Derrida was being considered for the award of an honorary doctorate by Cambridge University, to scholarly demolition of his one-sided reception of the phenomenological tradition.

Ellis' book *Against Deconstruction* represents the crude end of the anti-deconstructionist side of the debate, and is informed by the tradition of American analytical philosophy. Ellis aims to examine 'the logic of the central issues and arguments' in deconstruction and concludes that it has ignored, misinterpreted or simplified advances in the theory and practice of Anglo-American criticism and philosophy (Ellis, 1989: x). Concentrating primarily on the kind of literary criticism and textual interpretation that comes out of deconstruction, he dismisses all its claims to originality and radicality. For Ellis these are based on deliberate obscurity and the psychological appeal of a 'position that *feels* different', rather than on any intellectual challenge. Essential to the appeal and logic of deconstruction is 'the sense of belonging to an intellectual elite, of having left behind the naiveté of the crowd, of operating on a more sophisticated intellectual plane than that crowd' (Ellis, 1989: 151). Ellis finds that the logic of deconstruction is 'not well adapted to productive, original thinking, but rather to creating its illusion', and that it excludes the probing, analytical and testing style of genuinely new scholarship (Ellis, 1989: 144). Ellis seems more at ease when using adjectives such as 'crackpot' to describe deconstruction, rather than those more often used by adherents of deconstruction such as 'shocking', 'bold', 'provocative', 'innovative' and 'sophisticated'.

When Ellis is not engaged in crude sociological reductionism or simple abuse, he tries to interpret deconstruction as a method or a theory for literary criticism. In doing so, he fails to see how deconstruction undermines notions of method and theory. Moreover, he ignores the fate of the subject in Derrida's thought, as well as its specific emphasis on alterity and writing. Ellis' book is a study in reception and by concentrating on the appropriation of deconstruction by American thinkers (especially literary critics) it ignores the function that literature has in Derrida's work. As noted already, literature is for Derrida the 'non-site' from which to question the basic premises of Western metaphysics, rather than something from which to derive a method of interpretation.

A more philosophical and critical response comes from Claude J. Evans, whose book on *Strategies of Deconstruction: Derrida and the Myth of the Voice* (1991) is an important contribution to the debate about Derrida's relationship to phenomenology, as distinct from Gasché's attempt to read Derrida in the context of German idealism as a whole. Evans examines carefully 'the argumentative strategies' used by Derrida in early works such as *Speech and Phenomena* (1967) and *Of Grammatology* (1967), which he subjects 'to a logical critique' that invokes the idea of knowledge as 'the demand for infinite justification' (Evans, 1991: xvi). Because his work is situated (like Ellis') within that tradition of analytical philosophy which aspires to propositional correctness, Ellis' cannot take seriously Derrida's critique of the very idea of propositional statements.

His aim is to undermine Derrida's main thesis about phonocentrism, namely, that Western metaphysics privileges the voice and renders writing secondary in the constitution of meaning. After dealing with Derrida's theoretical assumptions concerning the phonocentrism in the thought of Husserl and Saussure, Evans concludes that it would be useful to emphasise 'the treatment of writing as the key to the introduction of *différance*' (Evans, 1991: 175). He argues, however, that this reading depends on the validity of a phonocentric thesis which breaks down when Husserl and Saussure are read properly. Evans claims that this is an immanent critique, in so far as Derrida's arguments about the phonocentrism of Western metaphysics 'fail to live up to their own standards', and that consequently 'on a careful reading Derrida's texts "nail" themselves' (Evans, 1991: 167–168).

Evans is preoccupied with the question whether or not Derrida's reading of various thinkers, especially Husserl and Rousseau, conforms to the norms of traditional scholarship. Questioning the philosophical rigour of Derrida's early works, he concludes that *Speech and Phenomena* can be regarded as an example of dual writing; that is, on one level it tries to adhere to the norms of philosophical scholarship, but on another level aims merely to give pleasure to its readers. Even on the former level, however, it 'turns into a cute and self-indulgent game – a *mere* game that has lost contact with its opponent, the metaphysics it was supposed to deconstruct'; and on the latter level it fails the test of close reading and careful examination (Evans, 1991: 174). Consequently, these early texts 'can at most . . . be considered a private pleasure, and even that status may well rest on a misunderstanding' (Evans, 1991: 180). Unlike Rorty, who appreciates the private pleasures of Derrida's later texts, Evans condemns the earlier texts on precisely those grounds. As a result, he is both dismissive and contemptuous of deconstruction's claim to be not only philosophy but also a radical project for deconstructing Western metaphysics.

1.6 Rorty: from the public philosopher to the private ironist

Richard Rorty is an important philosopher in his own right. Having worked his way out of analytical philosophy toward a version of American pragmatism that has strong affinities with continental philosophy, he is predisposed to offer a favourable, if tendentious, interpretation of Derrida. Rorty's earliest work is also concerned with the reflexion model, which he criticises from a standpoint that blends pragmatism with hermeneutics. This led him to construct a strongly anti-representationalist account of how language functions in relation to the world, and that brought him inevitably into the orbit of the Derridean conception of proto-writing (Rorty, 1979). The contingency of our conceptual structures makes Rorty more concerned with their pragmatic uses than with deconstructing their metaphysical grounding. He is therefore less bound to the philosophical tradition, and more open to science.

Unlike Evans, Rorty sees the early Derrida as a serious academic and public philosopher, whereas the later Derrida is 'eccentric, personal, and original' engaged in 'ironist theorising' and 'private fantasy' (Rorty, 1989: 123–125). This enables the pragmatist Rorty to reject Gasché's reading of Derrida for being transcendental. Transcendentalism is dismissed also by Derrida himself, since it is based on a distinction between the public and the private which Derrida thinks he has performatively problematised (Mouffe, 1996: 79). It is hard not to conclude that Rorty's positive reception of Derrida is attributable to his sense of a shared struggle against representationalism. This makes him insensitive to everything in deconstruction that goes beyond this narrow optic. It also leads him to such asinine statements as that 'Derrida is a sentimental, hopeful, romantically idealistic writer' – which Derrida himself was polite enough to receive graciously (Rorty, in Mouffe, 1996: 13, 77). To be fair, however, Rorty does indeed admit both the partiality of his reading and his complete non-comprehension of the Levinasian strains of Derrida's thought. But when these are taken into account the connections between a Darwinian-oriented pragmatism and the other-orientation of Derrida simply collapses.

1.7 Frank: reading phenomenology otherwise than Derrida

Manfred Frank is an important critic of post-structuralist thought and its claims to radicality and originality. Like Derrida, he wrestles with the German idealist tradition and Husserlian phenomenology. But unlike Derrida, he tries to expound its complexity, and to formulate a different conception of the subject and the self. He begins with the work of Schelling who provides him with a conception of the self which is more fruitful, in so far as it accommodates both identity and difference without falling into either the pitfalls of phenomenology in particular or the philosophy of reflection in general (see also Zizek, 1997).

Frank has also critically assessed both the sources of Derrida's thought and Derrida's claim with regard to the deconstruction of the Western metaphysics of presence. Most importantly, he aligns Derrida's critique of the metaphysics of presence with its historical antecedents, and explores the question of subjectivity in the German idealist tradition. In his metacritique of recent French critiques of metaphysics, Frank (1992) asks whether self-consciousness is a case of '*présence à soi*'. Analysing both Heidegger's and Derrida's critique of subjectivity, he questions their validity not only as interpretative paradigms of the Western philosophical tradition but even as serious and radically new alternatives to the theory of subjectivity. Frank argues that Derrida does not break away, but rather continues the Heideggerian tradition of working within a model of subjectivity that conceives of it in relation to self-presence. As a result, subjectivity is constructed by the logic of the reflection-model, that mirror model of representation which explains self-consciousness as produced by the turning back of consciousness on to itself. Self-consciousness therefore becomes connected to the idea of reflection or representation, which name the operation through which the self both posits itself and becomes conscious of itself.

Derrida's adoption of this model is simplistic, Frank argues, because it reduces the complexity of German idealism's construction of subjectivity. The immediate precursor of this model is Heidegger, whose central deficiency is that he 'does not know the difference between reflexive self-representation (*Selbstvorstellung*) and the feeling of self which does not rest on representation' (Frank, in Wood: 1992: 224). In short, Frank accuses this tradition of adhering to a cognitively truncated concept of subjectivity. Consequently, Heidegger's critique 'of the subject as the most extreme sharpening of metaphysical interpretation of Being (*Seinsauslegung*) as presence becomes strangely blunt' (Frank, in Wood: 1992: 224). The problem identified here by Frank is not solved by Derrida, who continues to operate within a model of self-presence which is based on the traditional formula of the reflection model as a mirroring back. Hence, instead 'of the play of reflection attesting or confirming the identity of what is reflecting with what is reflected, the detour through reflection is sufficient to deprive the self of its identity for ever' (Frank, in Wood: 1992: 229).

Frank concludes that 'Western metaphysics is not endangered by Derrida's deconstruction of the subject.' For although Derrida 'succeeds in demonstrating the absurdity of the reflection-model . . . it does not cross his mind for a moment that this model is simply wrong (inappropriate for the phenomenon) and should be replaced by another' (Frank, in Wood: 1992: 232). Derrida thus fails to provide a 'new' and 'better' model to enable us to move beyond the one bequeathed by Western metaphysics. Deconstruction works, in other words, only on out-dated models. Parasitically, it continues to pick on the bones of inherited concepts, because these models remain even if '*sous rature*'. Derrida 'just gives up "subjectivity" – which he, in Heidegger's footsteps, considers to be the most extreme intensification of the Western repression of Being, of *différance* – and with it gives up the gesture [*Gestus*] of traditional philosophising altogether' (Frank in Wood: 1992: 232). Whereas Gasché argues that

Derrida's thought deals with that tain in the mirror which makes possible the process of reflection, Frank seeks to side-step the problem of the tain and concentrate on the notion of what is reflected, as well as on the relationship between the reflection and what is reflected. The tain represents simply the neglected side of the reflection model, not a radical break with it.

Unlike Derrida, Frank seeks a non-relational conception of self consciousness. This leads him to argue that 'one can no longer believe it is possible to get closer to the phenomenon with descriptions like "*identité à soi*" or even "*présence à soi*"' (Frank in Wood, 1992: 232). He therefore discounts Derrida's claim to have deconstructed Western metaphysics and (more specifically) the concepts of identity, presence, and the subject. Even if Derrida has succeeded in deconstructing Western metaphysics that would not be a post-metaphysical act. A post-metaphysical theory of the subject therefore eludes Derrida, in so far as he remains the jester trapped in the distorting mirrors of the fun-house of Western metaphysics. Derrida's later work on the other hand by-passes, rather than escapes, this critique. That disembodied and congnitivist conception of the self to which Derrida wrongly reduces the Western conception of the subject in order to deliver it up to deconstruction disappears from the stage, and is replaced by an equally problematic conception of the other.

1.8 Counter-narratives of subjectivity

There are alternative ways of dealing with the conception of the subject in Western metaphysics and, more specifically, the question of the self. I have argued that some major critiques of Derrida's thought on questions of the subject, self and other fail to engage with its deeper implications. In order to explore such implications, we need to distance ourselves from Derrida and examine philosophical alternatives proposed by phenomenologically oriented thinkers such as Paul Ricœur and Charles Taylor. Unlike Derrida, Ricœur maintains a conception of the subject and the self that is still grounded in notions of action, agency, narrativity and autonomy, even as he tries to reformulate the entire problematic of self and other. Taylor, who also investigates the problematic of the self, does so in a manner which addresses the complexity and diversity of the conception of the self within both the Western tradition and contemporary thought. Each of these thinkers allows us to evaluate and criticise Derridean thought from other perspectives that might signal a way out of the overdetermination of the Derridean conception of the subject by the other. To engage in such work, however, involves going beyond questions of reception (see Chapter 4).

2. The Partial Exit from Phenomenology

Derrida's concept of writing is closely bound to the concept of the sign. His deconstruction of the sign informs his concept of writing, and it is through the notion of writing that Derrida re-defines subjectivity, self and otherness. Derrida's analysis of the sign in Husserl leads him to deconstruct what he sees as the determination of Being as presence in Western metaphysics. In the thought of Husserl, the notion of inner self-consciousness makes the sign 'live' and determines its proximity to being. Derrida's strategy is to mount a critique against such idealist notions of subjectivity in Western metaphysics, which reduce the sign to pure externality and affirm uncontaminated interiority as the precondition of a concept of identity that refuses alterity or the absolute other. According to Derrida, the transcendental subject of the phenomenological tradition either brackets out alterity or absorbs it within the same by constructing an analogical relationship with the 'I'. As Derrida puts it in *Of Grammatology,* the 'deconstruction of presence accomplishes itself through the deconstruction of consciousness' (*OG*: 70). The deconstruction of consciousness, however, accomplishes itself through the deconstruction of the sign.

There are several reasons why Derrida's deconstruction of the sign should be regarded as the pivotal work in his *oeuvre.* First, Derrida is a thinker who has been shaped profoundly by the phenomenological tradition. He does not belong, however, to the generation of Sartre and Merleau-Ponty, who first imported phenomenology into French philosophy, and whose work was rejected so decisively by French structuralism. Derrida accepts the structuralist critique of the 'humanist' version of phenomenology, and returns to Emmanuel Levinas, who at that stage was a forgotten and early exponent of French phenomenology. Second, Derrida is a thinker for whom the concept of writing and the idea of literature have assumed central importance. It should be remembered in this context that the early Derrida was associated with the avant-garde literary journal *Tel Quel*, and that the nature of the 'literary' has been the point around which his deconstruction of metaphysics has circled (Marx-

Scouras, 1996). Hence, Derrida's initial deconstruction is a coming to terms with the tradition out of which he emerges, and in relation to a concept that centrally concerns him, namely, the sign and the process of signification. The deconstruction of the sign, therefore, is a pivotal work that 'unifies' the Derridean *oeuvre* throughout its various phases. Derrida himself argues that his deconstruction of the sign is of crucial importance because 'the sign . . . is deferred presence' (*MP*: 9). And what he says about the notion of the signifier, he further asserts, 'holds for the notions of *representation* and *subject*' (*POS*: 83).

Derrida's argument is that Western metaphysics determines the formal essence of the sign in terms of presence, definable ontologically as the intersection of subjectivity and reason (*OG*: 18). Derrida aims to 'unsettle' self-presence as the determinant of being and the 'being-there' that is subjectivity. He replaces the notion of presence with that of writing or the trace and similar 'non-concepts', which allow for a 'non-originary' otherness to function as co-determinant of being. The idea of otherness informs almost all of Derrida's works. In his early writings he is concerned with the ontological implications of the idea, whereas later the ethico-political dimension comes to be of central importance. What I would like to emphasise here, however, is that the problematic of the other is continuous in Derrida's thought, and that it is connected initially to the problematic of writing. Derrida's critique of phenomenology sets out the parameters within which his thought moves.

It is my contention that Derrida's deconstruction of Husserl's concept of subjectivity results in a construction of subjectivity that is neither linguistically grounded nor intersubjectively mediated. Derrida's post-subjectivist thinking introduces the idea of the non-originary and non-oppositional concepts of writing, *différance* and otherness. These emerge as the Derridean equivalent of Heidegger's notion of ontological difference; that is, the question of being (*Sein*) as such (*die Seinsfrage*), as opposed to the being of beings or entities (*Seiendes*). It should go without saying, of course, that Derrida is as little concerned with the specific regions of being as Heidegger, which are left for the natural and historic-hermeneutical sciences to pursue. Derrida conceives of Being not as a gathering but as dispersal, as otherness, as *différance.* Consequently, *différance* can be conceptualised as something beyond Being itself (*epekeina tes ousias*). Otherness – that which is otherwise than Being – functions as that quasi-ontological 'ground' which replaces subjectivity as presence, or Being, or a gathering, or a 'ground'. The paradox is that this new 'ground' no longer conceives of its functioning as foundational. I further contend that this rejection of the foundational role of subjectivity is essentially correct. The resultant task, however, is to develop a post-metaphysical concept of the subject that is constructed linguistically, and mediated by narrative and the mnemonic processes of identity formation. The idea of a conscious, inter-subjective, and narratively-constituted subject in possession of agency and reflexivity is not recoverable from the ruins of Derrida's deconstruction of subjectivity.

2.1 The deconstruction of the concept of the sign in Western metaphysics

Derrida has emphasised consistently that a major part of his project is to re-examine the issue of the sign, and especially the preoccupation with language – 'the sign "language"' – in the modern age (*OG*: 6). Derrida's intellectual program consists in demonstrating how what has been 'gathered under the name of language is beginning to let itself be transferred to . . . the name of writing' (*OG*: 6). He thus aims to move away from language as such, and to construct a 'new sign' – writing – which will encompass and exceed 'language'. Derrida sees writing as the site on which to question and dislocate the conception of the sign, which is based on the philosophical principle of presence in Western philosophical thought. The concept of writing, therefore, is radicalised by Derrida, and becomes a 'non-concept' that both comprehends language and exceeds previous concepts of the sign. He locates writing at the root of the possibility for language to emerge as both writing and/or speech. A corollary of this manoeuvre is to conceptualise the subject who speaks.

Both the constitutive power of the subject and its narrative construction are made subject to writing which consequently becomes a precondition for their emergence. Although it lacks the structure of linear time, writing is anterior to language, and cannot be contained within the schematism of time and space. Writing is neither an historical nor an empirical category. It cannot be reduced to any notion of intentionality or pure self-consciousness, as it is in the work of Husserl. 'Writing' in this sense is not what is commonly understood by that word. It is ontologically significant, in so far as (according to Derrida) it has the structure of a trace, and is subject to the seminal structure of *différance*. Within such a post-idealist framework subjectivity has no seminal or foundational status. This 'dethronement' of the subject entails the concept of the other. For Husserl, pure self-consciousness is based on the exclusion of otherness. The other, therefore, is not constitutive of the subject: it has no ontological significance, except in so far as it is determined by the 'I'. Derrida tries to question this onto-theological conception of subjectivity by deconstructing both the transcendentalism of phenomenology and its theory of the sign. He sums up his project in *Of Grammatology*: ' It is . . . the idea of the sign that must be deconstructed through a meditation upon writing which would merge, as it must, with the undoing [*solicitation*] of onto-theology, faithfully repeating it in its *totality* and *making* it *insecure* in its most assured evidences' (*OG*: 73).

Derrida has consistently linked his deconstruction of logocentrism with that of the sign. In *Writing and Difference*, he asserts for example, that 'the metaphysics of presence is shaken with the help of the concept of *sign*' (*WD*: 281). In an interview, published in 1991, he reaffirms this point: 'of course the critique of logocentrism is also a critique of the sign: it provides a critique of the signifier/signified tradition'. According to Derrida, this results in the 'subjection of the signifier to the signified' and leads him 'to suspect the structure itself of the concept of the sign' (Derrida, in Mortley, 1991: 105). He goes on to say that

> one can recognise within the concept of sign the characteristic mark of logocentrism. So there's a critique of the idea of the sign. This is why I prefer to talk about 'mark' or 'trace' rather than 'sign': with the idea of trace, the distinction between signifier and signified is no longer at all possible, and the distinction of the authority of the word, the unity of the word, is called into question (Derrida, in Mortley, 1991: 105).

The critique of the concept of the sign, therefore, enables Derrida to unseat the unity and authority of the word, and thus of the *logos*. Consequently, he questions the oppositional hierarchy between the signifier and the signified, the subjugation of writing to the voice as incarnation of the *logos*, and the unity of the word as the transcendental signified.

The notion of the sign (as a part of its own construction) implies a distinction between signifier and signified, and is linked by Derrida with 'that logocentrism which is also a phonocentrism: absolute proximity to voice and being, of voice and meaning of being, of voice and the ideality of meaning' (*OG*: 11–12). The voice articulates, through its absolute proximity to being, both its meaning and the ideality of this meaning. The self as 'I' is constructed in terms of a phonocentric narrative of subjectivity. This narrative is based on the idea that consciousness is the privileged signified. Furthermore, it depends on the idea of a fixed subject which produces meaning and knowledge. Derrida's task is to dissolve such claims to subjective fixity, and shift the emphasis on to the movement from self-identity to the other. The truth of the subject is thus displaced from an inner subjective certitude (accorded to it through inner self consciousness) to the realm of *différance*. Derrida wants to deprive the subject of its reliance on phonocentric legitimation and the concomitant privileging of self-presence. As a result, the construction of subjectivity loses its claims to both transcendentality and empirical validity. In place of inner self-consciousness, Derrida institutes *différance*, which is both an 'irreparable loss of presence' and a 'relation to the absolute other' (*SP*: 150). The 'absolute other' or 'radical alterity' is 'removed from every possible mode of presence', and is characterised by 'irreducible after effects, by delayed effects' of what he calls the trace (*SP*: 152).

Derrida regards the sign as the hinge that articulates both the phonocentrism and the logocentrism of Western metaphysics. The sign as an onto-theological concept is thus deconstructed by Derrida, and its 'historical *closure* is . . . outlined' (*OG*: 14) by subjecting all linguistic signs to writing (see *OG*: 14–15). Language itself, therefore, becomes subordinate to writing. In this respect, the sign announces the 'closure' as well as the deconstruction of its own historical specificity. Derrida recognises, however, that the concept of the sign is so deeply embedded in Western metaphysics that the task of deconstruction cannot be to wrestle the sign from it. Instead, it should attempt to make the sign part of the deconstructive process by demonstrating its paradoxical function, namely, that 'the metaphysical reduction of the sign needed the opposition it was reducing' (*WD*: 281). In other words, metaphysics had to make the signifier dependent upon the signified in order to construct the concept of the sign. As a result of this constitutive opposition, however, the signifier remained external and subordinate to the signified.

Derrida's deconstruction of the concept of the sign not only marks the beginning of his project but also exemplifies his strategy for deconstructing other concepts within Western metaphysics. 'What we are saying about the sign', he writes, 'can be extended to all the concepts and all the sentences of metaphysics' (*WD*: 281). Consequently, both Derrida's treatment of the sign and his critique of the phenomenological tradition, which attempted to reinstate self-consciousness and intentionality, are prolegomena to his examination of the status of the subject and subjectivity. What came to be recognised within Western metaphysics as 'subjectivity' and 'the subject' undergo a radical dislocation and reformulation by Derrida. His deconstruction of the sign allows us to see how he deals with the issue of subjectivity, and more specifically with questions of the subject, the self and the other.

Having radicalised the sign by deconstructing the opposition between signifier and signified, Derrida deals with a number of other dualisms to which it gives rise. To treat the idea of the sign in general with suspicion, he contends, is not a

> question of doing so in terms of the instance of the present truth, anterior, exterior or superior to the sign, or in terms of the place of the effaced difference. Quite the contrary. We are disturbed by that which, in the concept of the sign – which has never existed or functioned outside the history of (the) philosophy (of presence) – remains systematically and genealogically determined by that history (*OG*: 14).

The sign, therefore, can not simply be replaced by a new concept, but must be thought of outside the constraints of logocentrism, which involves comprehending and then going beyond such constraints. The concept of the sign must also comprehend and exceed the sign 'language'. By extending this 'logic' to the construction of subjectivity, we can see that the subject can be neither constructed linguistically nor determined by discourse.

Although Derrida accepts the Saussurean argument that language is differential in structure, he attempts to free it from the constraints of that logocentrism which Saussure ends up adopting in conceptualising the sign. Derrida's assertion that 'there is no linguistic sign before writing' (*OG*: 14) signals the emergence of his radicalisation of the concept of writing. He thus seeks the 'closure', rather than the end, of the epoch of *logos*. Writing becomes the opening which logocentrism itself provides: the epoch of writing as *proto-writing*, as a non-totalising concept, as *différance*. Thus, subjectivity and the self become part of the engendering power of writing. Writing makes possible the emergence of subjectivity by affirming that the subject's own language is a 'species of writing'. Subjectivity itself becomes 'a species of writing' and notions associated with it (such as intentionality, consciousness, desire, etc.) become part of a deconstructive process that allows no such totalisation as a subjectivity which rests on self-identity.

Ultimately, Derrida's deconstruction of Husserl's subjective idealism targets his construction of the other. Otherness, in Husserl, appears in the guise of the signifier-writing. It therefore has a derivative status on account of the link that Husserl makes between the subject and voice. For Derrida, writing is associated with otherness in so far as they both generate or 'make possible' the emergence of identity and difference. It is a 'non-originary' concept, anterior to the dichotomy that locates the construction of subjectivity in such paired terms as same/other, conscious/unconscious, voice/writing.

2.2 Husserl's theory of the sign as expression and indication

Derrida's point of departure for the deconstruction of logocentrism is Husserl's phenomenology, especially his conception of that binary opposition between speech and writing in language which centres on a theory of the sign. Husserl embarked on a project to restore Western metaphysics. He did so by moving away from a psychological account of the origin of logic to a formal and more properly philosophical level. His aim was to design a 'first philosophy' free from empirical presuppositions. Derrida objects that Husserl's project remains within Western metaphysics, partly because it is grounded on the meaningful sign as full presence, and partly in its construction of intentionality. Derrida accuses Husserlian phenomenology of endeavouring to protect 'the spoken word, to affirm an essential tie between *logos* and *phonè*' (*SP*: 15) by privileging *phone* at the expense of writing. Writing has no essence in Husserl's philosophy. It possesses only a mediating function as the signifier of full speech, and its effects can be neutralised and derived from the transcendental signified. As conceived of by both Husserl and Saussure, this transcendental signified 'in and of itself, in its essence, would refer to no signifier, would exceed the chain of signs, and would no longer itself function as signifier' (*POS*: 19–20). Thus, the signified cannot be affected by either the signifier or by signification in general. Derrida attempts to overturn this conception of the signified by recognising that 'every signified is also in the position of the signifier' (*POS*: 20). Thus, the signified is no longer outside language, outside writing, and outside signification. It is contaminated irreducibly by what it excludes, by what opens up the differential opposition between signified and signifier; namely writing.

For Husserl, the sign is both indication and expression. This distinction is based on functions rather than essences; the two functions remain heterogeneous, although parallel, to one another. By asserting that the sign has two heterogeneous functions, Husserl questions its unity. At the same time, however, he restores unity to the sign through his conception of self-consciousness, which privileges the sign as expression, and eliminates or brackets out the sign as indication. His distinction between these two elements of the sign, then, serves to show where this distinction or difference is absent, and where its problematic is resolved. The unity of the sign is restored, therefore, in terms of the further distinction between voice and writing, where 'voice' is viewed as an expressive function of the sign and writing as its indicative function. This distinction between *phone* and writing informs Husserl's theory of the sign and directs Derrida's critique of the phonocentrism of Husserlian phenomenology. For Derrida, the unity of the sign is splintered by what is regarded as external to the voice: writing as the signifier of the signifier. Writing also 'destroys' the idea of the self as self-consciousness, as being-present to itself.

For Husserl, 'indication' is that element of the sign which takes place in Nature. Deprived of sense, it is only an empty signifier, unconnected to the signified. Signification is present, but only as a content devoid of meaning. Meaning is yet to come. 'Indication' lacks that meaning-intention which is always connected to a consciousness, and through which the voice which animates the sign comes into being. It is that body of language which needs the animating voice of a consciousness fully present to itself. Husserl conceives of indication as purely psychic: it lacks ideal objectivity because it refers to the object in empirical reality. Only ideal objectivity is equatable with truth in Husserl. For Husserl,

Derrida argues, 'the indicative sign falls outside the content of absolutely ideal objectivity, that is, outside truth' (*SP*: 30). Indication belongs therefore to the realm of non-ideality, that is, to those signs which are not related to an intentional act of consciousness.

Expression is the only form of signification that Husserl finds meaningful. It is the sign that means, that wants to say (*vouloir-dire*), and its meaning is based on the principle of intentionality. It is animated by the living voice – *phone* – of an intending consciousness which is connected not to an empirical consciousness but always to an ideal object. For Husserl, Derrida argues, 'there is no expression without the intention of a subject animating the sign, giving it a *Geistigkeit*' (*SP*: 33). Expression, as a purely linguistic sign is a logical sign, animated by the voice as self-consciousness – hearing oneself speak in absolute proximity to oneself. This auto-affection is based on pure self-presence; that is, consciousness must be fully self-present, and retain claims to universality while never leaving its own realm. Within this theoretical framework, there can be no expression or meaning without speech, voice and consciousness. Sign-as-expression is thus tied to *phone,* and on this basis the distinction between indication and expression is made.

Derrida argues that, for Husserl, expression is always 'voluntary exteriorisation; it is meant, conscious through and through, and intentional' (*SP*: 33). Speech and oral discourse make this possible. Behind every sign that 'wants to say', to mean, there is the subject as consciousness, and consciousness as intentionality. For Husserl, Derrida argues, 'pure expression will be the pure active intention (spirit, *psyche*, life, will) or an act of meaning . . . that animates a speech whose content . . . is present . . . in consciousness' (*SP*: 40). The voice in Husserl's phenomenology is thus '*being produced in the word as pure auto-affection*', and 'this auto-affection is no doubt the possibility for what is called *subjectivity*, or the *for-itself*' (*SP*: 79). The voice therefore has a privileged status as a result of being *the* vehicle for consciousness and subjectivity: 'the voice is the being which is present to itself in the form of universality, as consciousness; the voice *is* consciousness' (*SP*: 79–80). The subject and the self are embedded in consciousness as the centre point of that closed circle which links consciousness as intentionality or expression back to that consciousness which apprehends or 'hears itself speak'. Noemata, or the intentional and cognitive correlates of consciousness, never encounter what they continually promise to come into contact with: '*die Sache Selbst*'. They exist as pure *idealiter* of consciousness.

Since the voice is that which animates the sign, and pure expression is pure self-consciousness hearing itself speak, pure expression eliminates indication. Husserl thinks that consciousness is constituted as pure auto-affection, pure self-presence. It is based on the conception of time as the '*now*' – a moment which allows for no difference within that moment. Since consciousness is always a consciousness of something, the object to which it must refer is conceived of as ideal. It can be reiterated indefinitely, therefore, while remaining the same. Repetition in signification and in language is thus repetition of the same without alterity. Pure expression is pure self-consciousness and pure objectivity. In Derrida's reading of Husserl's theory of the sign, 'the ideality of the object, which is only its being-for a nonempirical consciousness, can only be expressed in an element whose phenomenality does not have worldly form. *The name of this element is the voice. The voice is heard.*' (*SP*: 76). Indication, then, is external to expression because it lacks voice, which thus becomes the pure medium for consciousness to express itself in, uncontaminated by either the marks of writing or the materiality of inscription. The idea of the 'voice', therefore, is integral to the spiritualism of Western metaphysics.

Consciousness as pure expression is present to itself in inner life and is not connected to empirical reality. It achieves pure objectivity by eliminating the sign as indication. The signifier is in absolute proximity to and identity with the signified. Infinitely repeated as the same, the sign therefore escapes both difference and temporality. For Husserl, 'the *sameness* of the word is ideal; it is the ideal possibility of repetition, and it loses nothing by the reduction of *any* empirical event marked by its appearance' (*SP*: 41). Husserl therefore deals with the problem of repetition in signification by idealising it, and by moving pure expression – where intentionality, meaning, the subject and its ideal object all take place without the mediation of signs – into inner life, into a pure consciousness that transcends empirical reality. In doing so, Derrida argues, Husserl remains within that framework of interiority which, in the Western intellectual tradition has constrained the self from Augustine onwards. Indication has no place in such a schema, because it is connected to empirical reality: 'whenever the immediate and full presence of the signified is concealed, the signifier will be of an indicative nature' (*SP*:

40). Pure expression is achieved by eliminating the threat of both the sign as indication and the signifier *tout court*, as that which cannot be contained within the signified, the *phone*, the *logos*. Indication therefore becomes external to expression, for it is excluded from inner mental life, where 'a word is thus only represented' (*SP*: 43). Language as expression is conceived of purely through speech, and by the intentional consciousness which achieves full presence thereby.

In Western metaphysics the sign is derivative, subsumed under the ideality of presence and the infinite repetition of the same. According to Husserl, Derrida argues, 'self-presence must be produced in the undivided unity of a temporal present so as to have nothing to reveal to itself by the agency of signs . . . it is the experience of the absence and uselessness of signs' (*SP*: 60). For Husserl, 'the present of self-presence would be as indivisible as the *blink of an eye* (*im selben Augenblick*)' (*SP*: 59). The sign is therefore irrelevant, since meaning can be fully appropriated without needing to detour through the sign. Consciousness is conceived of as auto-affection, pure self-presence; and it is based on the conception of time as the now, or as a moment that allows for no difference or alterity. The self as pure self-consciousness remains uncontaminated by otherness. This privileging of the present, Derrida argues, 'defines the very element of philosophical thought, it is *evidence* itself, conscious thought itself, it governs every possible truth and sense' (*SP*: 62). There is no room for alterity or spatio-temporalization in such a conception of the sign. The origin has its beginning in self-consciousness, where difference and non-identity are effaced. Derrida argues that for Husserl 'the relation with the other as non-presence is . . . impure expression. To reduce indication in language and reach pure expression at last, the relation with the other must perforce be suspended' (*SP*: 40). Logical language cannot admit the other, since it rejects anything which would conceal the self-identity of the signified. Expression thus means the elimination of indication from the field of ideality, where both subject and object are freed from both empirical reality and spatio-temporal determination. Husserlian phenomenology can conceive of the subject and the self within self-identity and self-presence.

Derrida argues, however, that Husserl introjects time into self-presence by conceding the continuity of the now and the not-now. By thus admitting

> the other into the self-identity of the *Augenblick*, nonpresence and nonevidence are admitted into the *blink of the instant*. There is a duration to the blink and it closes the eye. This alterity is in fact the condition for presence, presentation . . . precedes all the dissociations that could be produced in presence (*SP*: 65).

For Derrida, therefore, in every act of consciousness there is a now and a not now that produce an irreducible alterity which strikes at the core of the principle of being as self-presence. Husserl's conception of the uselessness and absence of signs in full self-presence, as outlined in the *Logical Investigations* (cf. my later discussion of Husserl's *Phenomenology of Internal-Time Consciousness*), is therefore seriously undermined. With respect to Husserl's conception of presence, Derrida argues that 'the fact that nonpresence and otherness are internal to presence strikes at the very root of the argument for the uselessness of signs in the self-relation' (*SP*: 66). In Derrida's understanding: signs are no longer dependent on acts of a transcendental consciousness, nor can they be excluded as useless from inner mental life. Pure self-consciousness cannot escape this irreducible alterity and spatio-temporalization.

Contrary to Husserl's schema repetition is for Derrida the 'constitution of a trace' which inhabits the phenomenological 'pure actuality of the now'. The possibility of repetition is constituted 'through the very movement of *différance* it introduces' (*SP*: 67). Derrida's concept of *différance* thus enables the possibility of repetition without self-identity, and of the sign as indication. Against Husserl's systematic curtailment of the indicative function of the sign, and the dependence of the function of the sign on acts of subjective consciousness, Derrida wants to

> restore the original and non-derivative character of signs . . . [and] . . . at the same time to eliminate a concept of signs whose whole history and meaning belong to the adventure of the metaphysics of presence. This also holds for the concepts of representation, repetition, difference, etc., as well as for the system they form (*SP*: 51).

The notion of trace or *différance* radicalises, therefore, the concept of presence and temporality, since it 'is always older than presence and procures for it its openness, [and] prevents us from speaking about a simple self-identity '*im selben Augenblick*'' (*SP*: 68). *Différance* is a precondition for both presence and non-presence, for repetition and signification, whether we are considering signs as indication or signs as expression.

The Derridean subject is produced by the movement of *différance*, which is independent of transcendental notions of subjectivity. The movement of *différance* 'is not something that happens to a transcendental subject; it produces a subject. Auto-affection . . . produces sameness as self-relation within self-difference; it produces sameness as the non-identical' (*SP*: 82). Self-identity – as sameness of the transcendental subject – is conceived of in terms of 'self-relation within difference'. Pure self-present identity is impossible, because the subject has a non-identical relation to itself. Alterity is not simply *within* the subject, but is that which produces it. For Husserl, however, the sovereignty of the self-conscious subject ('I') is assured through the exclusion of the other. The voiceless other can be voiced only by a self-present conscious subject. The other can affirm itself through only me as 'I'.

2.3 Towards a philosophy of writing

Derrida questions 'the phenomenological value of the voice, its transcendent dignity with regard to every other signifying substance' (*SP*: 77). In other words, he queries the privileging of the *phoneme* over the *grapheme*, and the assumption that the *phoneme* is the most ideal of signs. He argues that 'the apparent transcendence' of the voice in phenomenology 'results from the fact that the signified, which is always ideal by essence, . . . is immediately present in the act of expression' (*SP*: 77). This is the case because 'the phenomenological "body" of the signifier seems to fade away at the very moment it is produced; it seems already to belong to the element of ideality' (*SP*: 77). Derrida claims that 'this effacement of the sensible body and its exteriority is *for consciousness* the very form of the immediate presence of the signified' (*SP*: 77). The materiality of the signifier is thus subsumed and effaced without remainder by that voice which functions as the transcendental signified. The absolute proximity of the signifier to the signified is again achieved by the voice which renders redundant the signifying function proper. Difference is linked to the exteriority of the signifier, which pure expression bypasses.

Both the written sign and writing in general comes in existence only when the materiality of the signifier is eliminated, and its effacement is interiorised as expression through its idealisation by a transcendental consciousness. Writing can then re-emerge as a derivative fixation of consciousness. Husserl conceives of writing as phonetic writing because

> it proceeds to fix, inscribe, record, and incarnate an already prepared utterance. To reactivate writing is always to reawaken an expression in an indication, a word in the body of the letter, which, as a symbol that may always remain empty, bears the threat of crisis in itself (*SP*: 81).

It is through the voice that writing receives its idealisation, meaning, and life. A crisis, therefore, is always a crisis of signs that cannot be elevated, that cannot be turned into pure expression. A crisis of signifiers cut off from the *logos* therefore results in empty signs with neither meaning nor truth. Writing-as-signifier is a detour in the process of reactivation. By its very attribution as indication, it cannot alter the signified, and thus remains external to what is represented. Writing-as-representation is a repetition of the origin (sense), but without the possibility of difference or non-identity. It is external to an originary self-identity, where both consciousness and its ideal object are fully present in and for themselves.

Expression is achieved by the death of the body of language. The origin or source of expression is the voice of a consciousness which, in unity with itself, hears itself speak in the blink of an eye. The intending voice of a subject stands always behind the *grapheme*, and turns a phoneme-*phone* into expression, into a sign that wants to say, to mean. Writing announces its own death as an empirical sign in its affirmation as expression. For Husserl, there is an intentional consciousness – as the voice of a subject (author) – which gives it expression. This is not an empirical and psychological subject, however, but a transcendental subject within a field of ideal objectivity. Husserl attributes absolute objectivity to writing on the basis 'of an intentional analysis which retains from writing nothing but writing's pure relation to a consciousness which grounds it as such, and not its factuality which, left to itself, is totally without signification' (*ORG*: 88). Writing in order to mean – to want to say – depends therefore on the intentionality of a subjective consciousness. By contrast, Derrida conceives of writing as constituting a transcendental field which is subjectless. This he takes to be 'one of the "conditions" of transcendental subjectivity' (*ORG*: 88). Thus, from the very beginning, Derrida writes the subject out of transcendental subjectivity.

Truth in writing is consequently a transcendental concept, contained not in the signs themselves, but in their connection to full presence. In Husserl, Derrida argues, by means of a written inscription 'one can always repeat the original sense, that is, the act of *pure thought* which created the ideality of sense' (*SP*: 81). By definition, writing therefore cannot recapture the act of pure thought. Derrida argues with respect to Husserl's conception of writing, that

> the originality of the field of writing is its ability to dispense with, *due to its sense*, every present reading in general. But if the text does not announce its own pure dependence on a writer or reader in general (ie, if it is not haunted by a virtual intentionality), and if there is no purely juridical possibility of it being intelligible for a transcendental subject in general, then there is no more in the vacuity of its soul than a chaotic literalness or the sensible opacity of a defunct designation, a designation deprived of its transcendental function (*ORG*: 88).

For Husserl, on the one hand, intentionality is what makes a text legible and saves it from a 'chaotic literalness'. But Derrida wants to argue on the other hand that the sign is independent of acts of subjective consciousness, and that the *grapheme*-as-trace is present already in the voice, which is itself subject to temporality and therefore to difference and delay. Pure intentionalities are always breached by otherness, the not-now, repetition without identity. The *grapheme* (writing) cannot be totally appropriated by the voice, full presence or pure consciousness, because it is structured by that trace – *différance* – which is Derrida's central concern, and to which self and subjectivity are consequently subject.

Within Husserl's theoretical framework, both the text and its interpretation are connected to its intentionality, the unveiling of which acts as a transcendental signified that eliminates the text's 'literalness'. The unity, origin, and truth of the text are connected to the intentional act of a present self-consciousness, which transcends the non-ideal side of signification (that is, the empirical, non-ideal side of the written signifier). The text becomes expression when the univocity of the signifier is affirmed. Its multiplicity narrowed and defined, the written signifier is subsumed under the transcendental signified. Since it exists in the world, it becomes idealised, although it is not itself ideal. The task of interpreting literary texts, then, is to efface the materiality, literality, and non-ideality of writing (the signifier), and to subjugate it to an ultimate referent: the transcendental signified. The meaning of the text is produced by reference to that transcendental signified; that is, by restoring the original sense, hearing the voice of the text, and conceiving of it as a signified fully present to itself. The text achieves a unitary meaning by turning its indicative signifiers (writing) into expressions (logical, unitary signifieds) which are representations of an intending transcendental consciousness that can function in the absence of the empirical subject and the object world.

The historicity of the text is not connected to worldly empiricism, but idealised. For Husserl, Derrida argues, 'truth depends on the pure possibility of speaking and writing, but is independent of what is spoken or written, in so far as they are in the world' (*ORG*: 92). Thus, since writing remains external to speech – to voice – as idealised expression, it has no constitutive meaning. It cannot constitute its own truth independent of the spoken signifier as an idealised signified. Embedded in the origin of pure consciousness and full presence, truth is beyond the empiricism of both writing and speech. It is the property of the *logos,* and meaning is a property of the text which expresses it. Derrida argues, that Husserl treats writing in an ambivalent and paradoxical manner. While recognising it as the medium for attaining ideal objectivity, Husserl excludes from the field of ideality the empirical reality of writing. Thus,

> writing is a body that expresses something only if we actually pronounce the verbal expression that animates it, if its space is temporalized. The word in a body that means something only if an actual intention animates it and makes it pass from the state of inert sonority . . . to that of an animating body . . . This body proper to words expresses something only if it is animated . . . by an act of meaning . . . which transforms it into a spiritual flesh . . . As such, it needs no signifier to be present to itself. Indeed, it is as much in spite of its signifiers as thanks to them that it is awakened or maintained in life (*SP*: 81).

For Husserl, therefore, writing is a body whose empirical flesh has to be converted to spiritual flesh by losing all its corporeality and literariness. The proper body of writing is a dead body, whose signifiers can be eliminated. Writing and reading become passive activities which record, represent, and idealise what is already ideal – the hearing of the voice speak without experiencing a gap between thought and speech. That voice escapes difference and non-identity in the unity of absolute self-presence. Derrida concludes that the

> *history of metaphysics therefore can be expressed in the unfolding of the structure or scheme of an absolute will-to-hear-oneself-speak.* This history is closed when this infinite absolute appears to itself as its own death. *A voice without différance, a voice without writing, is at once absolutely alive and absolutely dead* (*SP*: 102).

This phonocentric and phenomenological way of thinking gives rise to a kind of literary criticism – or textual interpretation – which assumes the self-identity of the text by conceiving of it as a book which encapsulates a voice, and an intention. The book thus becomes an ontological concept, which implies intentionality, completion, and truth coming to itself. By moving toward idealisation, interpretation suppresses *différance* as inscribed both in speech and writing. Inhabiting the Husserlian sign as both indication and as expression, *différance* functions as a 'non-originary' origin or 'infra-structure', to use Gasché's term (Gasché, 1986). Writing thus comes to be added to speech as the other, because speech as self-presence and auto-affection had 'already from the start fallen short of itself' (*SP*: 87). As that which makes possible both speech and writing, *différance* becomes a condition of signification.

2.4 Différance, Writing and Subjectivity

Whereas Husserl's conception of the sign depends upon full presence, Derridean *différance* is non-derivative. It cannot be reduced to either speech or writing, since it is a pre-condition of their appearance without being an origin. *Différance* is thus a kind of writing that 'writes' both writing and speech. As Derrida puts it, *différance* is 'writing in speech' (*OG*: 139). Self-presence as auto-affection – hearing oneself speak – does not admit the other or non-presence within speech. Deconstruction seeks to unmask, therefore, the metaphysical residue in texts which the structure of *différance* makes both possible and erasable. *Différance* constitutes the 'structure' of the sign by avoiding problems in its phenomenological construction. *Différance* contains otherness as an *a priori* of signification. It allows for the articulation of both the 'fictional' and the 'non-fictional', by not reducing signification to expression.

For Husserl, communication in inner life – in self-consciousness – excludes the emergence of indication. As Derrida remarks, 'when the second person does emerge in inner language, it is a fiction: and, after all, fiction is only fiction . . . a false communication, a feigned communication' (*SP*: 70). In other words, the 'you' that the 'I' calls forth possesses a purely fictive otherness. Derrida argues on the contrary that because 'every sign whatever is of an originally repetitive structure, the general distinction between the fictitious and effective usages [expressing intentionality] of the sign is threatened. *The sign is originally wrought by fiction*' (*SP*: 56). Hence, signification both works *by* otherness (through the differential nature of the signifier) and reproduces itself *as* otherness (in the signifying chain). This formulation overcomes such metaphysical dualities as original and copy, animating intention and defective realisation, dialogue of the soul and intersubjectivity.

Transferred to the field of literary criticism, Husserl's self-identity of consciousness becomes the self-identity of the text. To thematize the text as a book is to treat it as a chain of signifiers reducible to the *cogitationes* of a transcendental subject. The written signifier becomes merely a means of re-appropriating the full presence and original meaning of the transcendental subject which produces it. Derrida's critique of the phenomenological conception of the sign makes it possible to relativise fact and fiction, and to devise a theory of the general text. This is why Derrida questions Husserl's assertion that a book can be described 'in its unity as a chain of significations', and that such 'unity can be more or less ideal and necessary, and therefore universal, according to the book's sense-content' (*ORG*: 90).

In opposition to this ontological conception of the 'closed' book, Derrida develops his theory of the 'open' text, which is both incomplete and dispersed. Husserl's metaphor of the 'stratum of *logos*', Derrida argues, needs to be replaced by a 'properly *textual* metaphor, for *fabric* or *textile* means *text*' (*SP*: 112), and 'the texture of the text is irreducible' (*SP*: 113). Yet he does not want to anchor his thinking to a theory of metaphor which is always contained in the signified it refers back to. For the metaphysics of phonocentrism Derrida substitutes the problematic of the *graphe* and the notion of the 'trace'. As the otherness of speech, writing has to be admitted into it: writing in speech is made possible through *différance*. The notion of language as a differential structure goes beyond that of self-presence and consequent phonocentrism, which informs both Husserlian phenomenology and structuralism. What phenomenology treats as self-identity, Derrida argues, 'is always already a trace' (*SP*: 85). He can thus deconstruct the phenomenological idea of 'a simple present whose life would be within itself' by substituting the non-concept of the trace for the concept of the sign. 'The self of the living present', he asserts, 'is primordially a trace' (*SP*: 85): its structure is based on 'proto-writing' (*SP*: 85), which inscribes *différance* in full presence (*SP*: 85).

The signified is not self-referential, according to Derrida, for by entering into play with the other, with the signifiers of the other it risks loss of meaning. The signifier can be neither totalised by the self-presence of the signified as expression nor effaced. Since writing, as Husserl conceives of it, has to announce its own death as an intentional act of consciousness in order to appear, then truth is the death of the signifier. By questioning the very basis upon which phenomenology rests, Derrida rejects intentionality as that all-encompassing signified which is the truth because it contains all possible meaning. Derrida questions Husserl's conceptualisation of the graphic sign and writing as something that 'defines and completes the ambiguity of all language' (*ORG*: 92); and guarantees objectivity as something that permits 'the ultimate freeing of ideality' (*ORG*: 90).

For Husserl, Derrida argues, 'all factual writings, in which truth could be sedimented, will never be anything in themselves but sensible "exemplars", individual events in space and time . . . Since truth does *not* essentially depend on *any of them*, they, could *all* be destroyed without overtaking *the very sense of* absolute ideality' (*ORG*: 94). Since, for Husserl, truth is not language's captive, while it 'depends on the pure possibility of speaking and writing' it is 'independent of what is spoken or written, in so far as they are in the world' (*ORG*: 92). Truth is not encapsulated in language but transcends it, and thus truth remains a transcendental concept in its sense-of-being. Even though Husserl treats writing as the most ideal of signs, it can neither contaminate nor constitute the transcendental nature of truth. It can only represent or record it.

Husserl regards truth as conceived through that intentional act of consciousness which can be 'reactivated and captured in its origin'. Yet in order to achieve ideality as an originary presence, it must transcend both the empirical subject and the empirical consciousness. Origin is thus conceived of as repetition of the same, where copies, doubles, and fictions are effaced, where truth as identity is fully present to itself, and where the object and the subject can exist in ideality as absolutes. For Husserl, however,

> words and language in general are not and can never be absolute *objects*. They do not possess any resistant and permanent identity that is absolutely their own. They have their linguistic being from an intention which traverses them as mediations. The 'same' word is always 'other' according to the always different intentional acts which thereby make a word significative (*ORG*: 104).

Signification can never be divorced from either subjectivity or intentionality, in which the truth of the sign is embodied. There is no truth in the sign *per se*.

Against this devaluation of writing and its treatment as the signifier of a signifier, Derrida announces that science of writing which he terms 'grammatology' (*OG*: 4–7). It '*comprehends* language' and at the same time exceeds it (*OG*: 7). It deconstructs 'all the significations that have their source in that of the *logos*. Particularly, the signification of *truth*' is questioned (*OG*: 10). *Logos* is taken by Derrida to mean the re-appropriation in thought of full presence whose 'essential link to the *phonè*' as the transcendental signified 'has never been broken' (*OG*: 11). Furthermore, he equates logocentrism with the metaphysics of phonetic writing, which is conceived of as essentially ethnocentric (*OG*: 3). According to Western metaphysics, 'writing *should* erase itself before the plenitude of living speech, perfectly represented in the transparence of its notation, immediately present for the subject who speaks it, and for the subject who receives its meaning, content, value' (*POS*: 25). In this schema, truth is directly linked and assigned to *logos*; and results in the 'debasement of writing, and its repression outside "full" speech' (*OG*: 3).

Derrida's project, then, is to treat writing as inscribed in speech, and to assign a non-mediating function to the signifier. The transcendental signified becomes a signifier of *différance*, although *différance* itself does not become a transcendental signified. The first task is to deconstruct the exteriority of writing to speech. Exteriority is connected to the idea that 'the formal essence of the signified is *presence*, and the privilege of its proximity to the logos as *phonè* is the privilege of presence' (*OG*: 18). Writing, considered as the 'translator of a full speech that was fully *present* (present to itself, to its signified, to the other, the very condition of the theme of presence in general), technics in the service of language, *spokesman*, interpreter of an originary speech itself shielded from interpretation' (*OG*: 8) could never be accorded the status of *phonè*.

In that new 'science' of writing which Derrida tries to establish the '*gram*' or '*différance*' is based on the play of differences that results in an interweaving of these differences into syntheses and referrals while forbidding the presence of any of its elements, in and of itself 'referring only to itself' (*POS*: 26). There are no simple presences or absences in this interweaving which encompasses the field of writing and linguistics; 'there are only everywhere differences and traces of traces' (*POS*: 26). For Derrida,

> *différance* is the systematic play of differences, of the traces of differences, of the *spacing* by means of which elements are related to each other. This spacing is the simultaneously active and passive . . . production of the intervals . . . it is also the becoming-space of the spoken chain– . . . a becoming-space which makes possible both writing and every correspondence between speech and writing, every passage from one to another (*POS*: 27).

Différance, then, is that irreducible spacing between binary oppositions which makes writing possible. *Différance* ensures that no element dominates the interminable chain of differences.

While the systematic play of differences is not random, it cannot form a structure whose centre determines the relationship between one element and another, or any element and the centre. Transformations within this space depend on a 'generative movement', rather than on a static organisation and re-organisation of different combinations of various elements within the structure. For as Derrida argues, 'differences are the effects of transformations, and from this vantage the theme of *différance* is incompatible with the static, synchronic, taxonomic, ahistoric motifs in the concept of *structure*' (*POS*: 27). Although *différance* is the 'generative movement in the play of differences', it is not astructural (*POS*: 27–28). Language is not outside that generative movement of *différance* which makes it intelligible (*POS*: 28), but part of it, in so far as difference makes possible the emergence of language. Since language is structured by difference and delay, its effects are those of *différance,* which can be neither totalised nor fully contained by connections with the full presence of *logos*. The main characteristic of *différance* is that 'nothing –

no present and in-*different* being . . . precedes *différance* and spacing. There is no subject who is agent, author and master of *différance*. Subjectivity – like objectivity – is an effect of *différance*, an effect inscribed in a system of *différance*' (*POS*: 28).

2.5 Différance and time

The strategy of deconstruction, as previously mentioned, involves reading the texts of Western philosophy in a way that convicts them of logocentrism while at the same time following the internal breakdown of that attempt at logocentric closure which they seek to effect. This strategy often uses texts that are seemingly irrelevant or peripheral to the main corpus. For example, Derrida will fasten onto a footnote, a marginal note, an unpublished text, etc.. In the case of *Speech and Phenomena,* the main text under discussion is Husserl's sixth *Logical Investigation,* which is concerned with the theory of signification. The critique of Husserl by Derrida in *Speech and Phenomena* is essentially a critique of this text. Hence, the notion of *différance* emerges as a way of thinking through those iterative differences that make meaning possible, as opposed to any theory that privileges pure auto-affection. Indication, therefore, is not secondary, but in a certain sense primary. What is remarkable here, however, is that the argumentative warrant which Derrida uses to make this argument against Husserl comes itself from Husserl – not the Husserl of *Logical Investigations* (1977), however, but the Husserl of the *Philosophy of Internal Time-Consciousness* (1964) or, to give its re-translated title, the *Phenomenology of the Consciousness of Internal Time (1893–1917)* (1991). Derrida, therefore, has recourse not to a text conceived and published solely by Husserl, but to a text of lectures and notes put together by his assistant and finalised by Heidegger (see Husserl, 1991: xi–xviii for this history).

Although, like Derrida, we are not 'able, here, to follow the rigorous development of this text' (*SP:* 64; see Bernet, Kern and Marbach, 1993: 101–114 and Wood, 1989: 39–133 for extended accounts), Derrida's reconstruction of this text is of relevance to this book. Derrida seeks to retrieve from Husserl's work on time, as an 'irreducible spreading-out', the idea that 'no now can be isolated as a pure instant, a pure punctuality'. At the same time, however, he criticises Husserl for conceiving of this 'spread' on the 'basis of the self-identity of the now as point, as a "source-point"' (*SP*: 61). The task, therefore, is to think Husserl *against* Husserl. In this context, Derrida makes three points. The first we have just identified. What must be added, though, is that Derrida links the idea of the privileging of the 'present-now' (from Greek metaphysics onwards) to the modern metaphysics of presence as self-consciousness. Furthermore, against the 'idea as representation' Derrida invokes the 'unconscious', or more precisely a 'theory of nonpresence *qua* unconsciousness; that is, being as original presentification, as opposed to representation, is never simply now, never simply present to itself in a simple act of consciousness (*SP:* 63). This leads to Derrida's second point, which asserts that 'the presence of the perceived present can appear as such only inasmuch as it is *continuously compounded* with a nonpresence and nonperception, whether of retention or protention' (*SP*: 64). With respect to retention, which particularly concerns Derrida, this means that the past is present in a 'presentative way' and not in a 'representative way'; that is, it is not a modality of the 'present-now', but instead the admission of the 'not-now' into the 'now' (*SP*: 64–65). This admission paves the way for the idea of 'the constituting flux' in Husserl's theory of time. Derrida's third point is that the Husserlian distinction between retention and representation is less primordial than his insight into the 'trace-like' character of retention as presentification. Consequently, Derrida reconceptualises 'transcendental temporalization' as the *différance* or *trace* out of which presence emerges, rather than as a presence from which temporal modifications depart. Through a discussion of time, which thinks Husserl *against* Husserl, Derrida mounts his decisive arguments against Husserl's theory of the expressive sign and the secondary character of indication. Like retention, indication injects non-presence into original presentification; and without this non-presence, meaning itself would not be possible.

The work of Rudolf Bernet is of central importance both to the question of Husserl's theory of time and to the question of the relationship between retention and the unconscious. Bernet's reading of Husserl provides further confirmation of the Derridean analysis of Husserl's theory of time. For Bernet, Husserl's concept of retention can refer either to a 'derivative modification of the consciousness of the now' or 'a differential repetition [*Wiederholung*] of the primordial impression' (Bernet, 1982: 86). The former preserves Husserl's position, in so far as the intentional consciousness has its intended object, which it perceives at the 'now-point' as the 'source-point' for consciousness. The latter, however, entails the presupposition that the 'not-now' is as decisive for conscious perception as the 'now', and that what makes perception possible is retentional consciousness *qua* consciousness of 'a momentary consciousness of the elapsed phase' (Husserl, as quoted in Bernet, 1982: 102). Husserl tries to save his primary insight by conceiving of retentional consciousness as the tail of the comet, whose head is intentional consciousness *qua* the primordial-impressional consciousness of the now. For Bernet, this solution is unworkable. Taking up a concept invoked but rejected by Husserl, Bernet argues for the notion of '*post-factuality*'. 'Retentional self-appearance', he writes,

> alters with every new 'phase' of the flow and does so in such manner that every new 'phase' recapitulates the whole 'elapsed' flow in an ever new way. The flow thus appears exclusively as past and this mode of appearance is itself constantly altering. We called this mode of appearance '*post-factuality*' and distinguished it from all primordial, immediately-now present, perceptual givens (Bernet, 1982: 108–109).

Husserl's primordialism, his attachment to the metaphysics of presence, prevents him from arriving at this solution, which approximates Derrida's solution with its emphasis on the past, the 'not-now' and iteration. Bernet turns to Derrida at this point, however, not for confirmation of his own interpretation of the 'post-factual', but for an explanation of Husserl's fascination with presence. 'How would the desire for presence ever permit of being destroyed?', Derrida asks. 'It is desire itself' (Derrida, quoted in Bernet, 1982: 111).

In a later article, Bernet evokes the psychoanalytical idea of transference (as invoking 'a third person', a 'passage' and 'metaphor') to suggest that when Derrida reads Husserl on time he does so in terms of the Freudian concept of the unconscious (Bernet, 1994: 141). In the same way that the unconscious thought is not only 'never present in itself', but also 'never fully present in its representation', retention is

> not a process that keeps a former original present present despite its fading in to the past. It is rather the first givenness of a present now which can only appear with delay. A pure now, instead of being the 'original source-point' of the present (as Hus-

> serl claims), is something impossible: it would lack all temporal qualification and distinctness. Retention is therefore indeed a 'trace' or an 'originary supplement' that produces with delay that to which it is said to be added. The trace is thus a form of original alterity . . . (Bernet, 1994: 145).

This parallelism leads Bernet to suggest that Derrida is offering 'a new understanding of transcendental consciousness rather its destruction' (Bernet, 1994: 148). He does this by deconstructing the Husserlian understanding. First, he reverses the priority of presentation over representation by invoking the Freudian insight that representations are not secondary but fundamental to presentation. Second, he displaces the distinction between presence and re-presentation by arguing that re-presentation takes place through indicative signification and not through self-presence (Bernet, 1994: 148–149). Bernet concludes, therefore, that it is the difference between Husserl and Derrida over the status of the concept of retention that is fundamental to the question of the critique of the self-present subject, although it is not its sole determinant (Bernet, 1994: 149).

2.6 Implications for the concept of the subject

Independent of considerations of agency, authorial intention or writing, *différance* both constitutes subjectivity and opens up the possibility of its emergence. Since neither the self nor self-consciousness is constitutive of *différance,* they cannot affect its movement and effects. There is no *a priori* subjectivity or self-referential subject to be grasped in terms of consciousness, agency or will. Derrida is not concerned to establish the conditions of possibility in which differing forms of subjectivity could be constituted. What he affirms here is the elimination of the subject (as a self-conscious agent) from the act of constructing itself *as* a subject. Both the writing of the 'I' and its relation to the object-world become an effect of *différance*. As such, they cannot be thought of as embodying intentionality, agency and self-identity. What we recognise in writing is not the subject but the trace of a presence which is not a presence. Effects become central to writing, because they are independent of both the totalising signified and that kind of signified which relies on the voice to give it life and connect it to Being as presence.

As a result of *différance*, 'the relationship to the present, the reference to a present reality, to a *being* – are always *deferred*' (*POS*: 29). Oppositions constituted on the principle of presence are thus dismantled or, rather, enter the play of *différance*. Their interweaving is made possible by endless substitutions, which are not metonymic but interchangeable. Another effect is that 'the subject is not present, nor above all present to itself before *différance*' but is 'constituted only in being divided from itself, in becoming space, in temporizing, in deferral' (*POS*: 29). The subject cannot be constitutive of *différance* because its own subjectivity is an effect of the generative movement of *différance*. Generative in both the passive and active senses, it simultaneously eliminates the possibility that oppressive or dominating effects will result from the process of its constitution. *Différance* thus makes it possible to admit the other without being dominated by it. As a result we can formulate the logic of logic, the negativity of negativity, and so forth.

Furthermore, since *différance* is not only independent but constitutive of both ideal and empirical subjectivity, no system of meaning can be anterior to it. Meaning, then, cannot refer to an originary essence, to an originary truth, since its constitution is an effect of *différance*. Seeing that speech and writing are part of the generative movement of *différance*, oppositional distinctions between them are merely a futile attempt to control and suppress its effects. Transcendental self-consciousness is no longer the site where both transcendental subjectivity and objectivity are produced. In Derrida's schema, the subject has no language, and language is not constituted by the subject: subject(s) must enter language(s), recognise language(s), interpret language(s), write in language(s), and recognise themselves or other subject(s) in language(s). Once the subject and the self become part of textual deconstruction, they can neither reinscribe themselves in discourse nor be part of it. The only subject that can be part of discourse is a dead subject: its materiality – like the materiality of the sign in Husserlian phenomenology – has to be bracketed out.

Also eliminated is the idea that the self can be present to itself. Self-consciousness, however conceptualised, cannot be established. I would like to argue, however, that although we have to take account of Derrida's attempts to introduce into the well-worn binarisms of Western metaphysics the irreducibility of the other, we cannot dispense with the 'fiction' of subjectivity anchored in identity (if not self-presence), even if that is partial and with many qualifications. To dispense entirely with the idea of identity is to leave the self vulnerable to an indeterminate drift from which it can be retrieved only as a 'dead self'. The fate of the signifier in Husserlian phenomenology anticipates the fate of the self in Derridean *différance*.

2.7 Concluding remarks

For Derrida, then, writing fissures the tautological relationship between the signifier and the signified at the level of its production, and subjectivity and the self become part of this process. Nevertheless, this becomes problematic in my opinion when *différance* is taken to be constitutive of subjectivity as such. Even if intentionality is questioned, the problem of responsibility still remains. As we shall see Derrida deals with the question of responsibility in his later work. However, this is informed by his early deconstruction of Husserlian phenomenology and his anti-subjectivism. Moreover, the problem of power relations cannot be resolved through a vague appeal to difference. At a more theoretical level, the notion of textuality simply avoids questions of agency and praxis. The fact is that writing takes place within the world, and therefore it cannot be made into a transcendental category, free from all considerations of addresser, addressee, intention, etc. The Derridean project becomes less radical than it appears because of avoiding these issues.

Husserl can neither think the question of the other nor take account of questions of intersubjectivity, spacing and temporalization outside of a framework of thought that does not reduce them ultimately to a philosophy of constituting subjectivity, despite the intimations of alternative approaches within Husserl's reflections on time. By instituting the idea of the trace Derrida tries to deal with the question of the other. But he does not address the problem of intersubjectivity. Whereas the phenomenological concept of consciousness is limiting, and places the subject outside the empirical world, Derrida's concept of the trace makes the subject contingent while endeavouring to avoid both empiricism and idealism. By divorcing the subject from any notion of identity, Derrida institutes the impossibility of writing the self *as* identity, and the concomitant idea that the self writes itself *for* itself and *to* itself. Moreover, the notion of the self that emerges out of the play of difference is curiously disembodied and 'other-worldly', since it is the product of a 'quasi-transcendental' field or infrastructure rather than a lived relationship. In his later work, as I will show, Derrida attempts to resolve this problem by appealing to the other as a category which subsumes the relationship between self and other.

It then becomes a question of whether Derrida has resolved the problem of the subject and the self by appealing initially to *différance,* and later to the other, or whether it may return via the very concept that he abandons. Can the concept of identity-signified be eliminated completely, or does it need to be reconceptualised, albeit in a more complex way than it is in Derrida's model of subjectivity. Manfred Frank (Frank, 1989) has criticised Derrida's model of subjectivity for relying heavily on the mirror-reflection model, which conceives of the subject in terms of a tautological analogy. In other words, the subject in Derrida is closed in on itself, since the distinction between the subject as 'I' and as 'you' is eliminated. Although Frank's critique is valid, he provides no model for a new concept of identity that takes into account deconstruction's concerns. Moreover, Frank ignores the fact that Derrida's model of reflection has a labyrinthine and abyssal structure. Derrida's answer to the problematic of reflection is that no reflection can be representational; instead, it is endless and refractory. This early idea is replaced in Derrida's later work by the idea of a mirror without an image. In other words, Derrida's answer is that reflection does not embody identity. Furthermore, Frank does not take up the question of the other as developed in the later work, and whose deconstructive relation to the subject I will address in subsequent chapters.

Husserl's conception of the subject remains within the framework of idealist philosophy because his phenomenology is idealistic. Transcendental idealism enabled him to escape psychologism, which is a form of empiricism. The paradox of phenomenology, however, is that its orientation to the object could avoid the pitfall of empiricism only by lapsing back into idealism. Derrida's deconstruction of idealism, on the other hand, leads back to a non-originary origin, that is, an origin which is not anterior and does not effect closure. Whether it is called *différance* or *proto-writing*, this non-originary origin' is beyond being, in so far as it generates both being and beings, including being-there or subjectivity. What arises in the wake of the death of the metaphysical subject is therefore a rather desiccated and derived subject. Furthermore, it is debatable whether the concept of *différance* accounts completely for the true complexity of the subject, reflexivity and intersubjectivity. Finally, whether it is possible or desirable to 'write off' the narrative and self-reflexive dimension of embodied subjects is equally debatable. In short, although Derrida's theory of the subject is a product of his deconstruction of phenomenology, it appears to me to remain trapped within its phenomenological starting-point.

3. Beyond the Subject – 1: Deconstruction and the *Gay Science* of Indeterminacy

Two questions arise in relation to writing and, more specifically, in relation to the writing of the self: is it possible to 'write' the self as self-identity, and how it is that the other becomes constitutive of self-identity? The concept of writing enables Derrida, through his readings of Plato, Rousseau, Condillac, Freud and Lévi-Strauss, to initiate a 'new science' that opens up the space for the other. It is thus impossible to understand Derrida's construction of the concept of the other without examining its relationship to writing within these constraints. These deconstructions inform and set the agenda for the later ethical, political and cultural concerns of Derrida. There the other is used to deconstruct and radicalise not only the expressivist and rationalist conception of subjectivity and its associated politics, but also the conceptions of an ethnocentric anthropology.

Derrida is concerned once again how ideas of origin, presence, and representation ultimately refer to *logos*, and with the resultant effacement of writing as a constitutive and radical force that deconstructs the subject. Derrida embarks on a project to rehabilitate writing by introducing the concept of the other into its problematic. This project involves deconstructing ideas of need and desire, writing and memory, origin and representation, centre and play in order to free the idea of writing from the well-worn binarisms of Western metaphysics.

In this chapter I will argue that 'supplementarity', 'play', '*pharmakon*' and other 'non-concepts' introduced by Derrida have implications for the idea of the subject and the self. These early deconstructions have consequences also for Derrida's conception of politics and his emphasis on the other as the basis of the 'new' thinking. Within Western metaphysics, Derrida argues, the development of 'science or knowledge [is] oriented toward the appropriation of truth in presence and self-presence, toward knowledge in consciousness-of-self' (*WD*: 29). It is this connection between the subject and truth that Derrida deconstructs. For Derrida, the self is always already written: subject to supplementarity, *différance* and trace, it is therefore never fully present to itself. Derrida opens up a space for 'writing the other' in a way that avoids that fundamental binarism of the 'same/other', and the categories of identarian philosophy which reduce the latter to the former. He thus escapes the metaphysics of full self-presence by problematising identity, self and subjectivity in general.

In order to open up the space of writing, Derrida has to disassociate need from desire, origin from self-identity, representation from self-presence, and centre from fixed origin. He must also make writing internal rather than external to memory. This results in a conception of the self quite different from that authentic and natural self which is present to itself, and endowed with both a centre which governs, directs and arrests play, and a living memory which contains both *hypomnesia* and *anamnesis*. The disassociation of writing from the knowledge of truth and, more precisely, 'of truth in the knowledge of the self' (*D*: 69) becomes central to his various deconstructions, and leads to a repudiation of narrative and reflexive constructions of the self. Self-knowledge is not equated with truth, and truth becomes independent of the category of subjectivity.

This chapter will look, more specifically, at the series of deconstructions that Derrida undertakes of the empirical, romantic, Platonic, structuralist and psychological notions of subjectivity in order to open up the space for the other. Derrida examines the ways in which thinkers associated with these various traditions have conceived writing, and how their texts betray the effects of what they try to suppress, render external or absorb within their operational categories. Notions of the sign in these intellectual traditions are once again central to both his deconstruction of Western subjectivity and the self, and those concepts of supplement and play which he introduces into the larger framework of writing and textuality. The result is that 'gay science' called grammatology, which ultimately will cede way to a more sober ethic of responsibility.

3.1 The age of Rousseau

Derrida's early work centres on what he terms the age of Rousseau or Rousseauism. It includes both Condillac and Rousseau as well as those who write in their wake, such as the structural linguist Saussure, and the structural anthropologist Lévi-Strauss. The age of Rousseau acquires such emblematic importance for Derrida because he sees in it an attempt to come to terms with the crisis in the problematic of writing and the sign. The eighteenth century, Derrida argues, displaces idealisation and restores 'the rights of sensibility, the imagination and the sign' (*OG*: 98). After deconstructing the twentieth-century idealism of phenomenological rationalism, Derrida seizes the opportunity to deconstruct also eighteenth-century attempts at grounding language and the sign empirically.

Dethroning both the empirical and linguistic conception of the subject, Derrida makes memory, imagination, need and desire independent of the categories of empirical subjectivity. Writing's relationship to the self no longer depends on the principle of full self-presence. 'Writing' deconstructs the analogical relationship between writing and imagination, and the subordinate relationship of writing to memory. Neither the subject nor the self can act as the origin of an empirical subjectivity which affirms and safeguards its own identity. What deconstructs the unitary, unfissured subject of the philosophy of identity is the concept of writing as the necessary supplement.

Derrida draws his argument from eighteenth century thinkers 'in order to isolate Rousseau, and, in Rousseauism, the theory of writing' (*OG*: 99). It is also the century whose writings invite approaches which show both the power and the limits of logocentrism. By demonstrating the failure of these thinkers to overcome the limits of a phonocentric logocentrism, Derrida describes what logocentrism cannot account for, and therefore opens the way to its deconstruction in the very texts that defend it. These thinkers fail, according to Derrida, by resorting to the principle of full self-presence. Thus, while they problematise a number of dualisms, they attribute a secondary function to anything that threatens full self-presence. The self-consciously knowing subject becomes the privileged paradigm upon which such thinkers base their treatment of writing and alterity in general.

Although eighteenth-century thinkers open up the problematic of non-presence – and, in Rousseau's case, the disappearance of the origin – they resolve it within the interpretative categories of Western metaphysics. Hence, the scope and impact of their insights are limited. Nevertheless, these texts contain the possibility of their own deconstruction, which is achieved by drawing attention to what is irreducible to any type of binarism, namely, what does not conform to the 'logic of identity and to the principle of classical ontology' (*OG*: 215). Reading, then, is a process of making explicit what these writers 'say without saying, see without seeing' (*OG*: 215). Language exceeds the intentions of author(s) by being placed above and beyond the intending, conscious, thinking and narrating subject. Both Rousseau and Lévi-Strauss, Derrida argues, adhere to the principle of full-presence: they presume the existence of a centre, the transgression of which represents an external broaching of the origin in a way that merely reaffirms its unity and identity. Anything which introduces difference into the origin – into Nature conceived of as a unity and identity is treated by both thinkers as secondary, and condemned as something inauthentic, dangerous, and alienating. Representation, for instance, becomes secondary and external to self-presence, and is therefore seen as particularly dangerous. The presumed unity and identity of the origin, centre, self, and Nature function as the transcendental signified.

Derrida is interested in the relationship between the transcendental signified and textuality. By means of these concepts he transforms the classic philosophical opposition between transcendent criticism (such as Kant's attempt to clarify our categories of understanding in order to discern what we can know) and immanent criticism (as in Hegel's attempt to know by first engaging in the act of knowing). By arguing that no transcendental signified or referent governs the text from the outside, Derrida reduces it to a meaningful signifier that reproduces the self-identity of the signified. He then links writing and reading – both of which are ordered around their own blind spots – to the production of texts. 'We know this a priori,' he writes 'but only now and with a knowledge that is not a knowledge at all' (*OG*: 164). They are both subject to what Derrida calls textuality.

Yet although the text's blind spots order our reading and writing, they can never be fully illuminated, reduced to a signifier, elevated to the status of the signified, or result in a concept of knowledge based on the certainty of the knowing subject. Thus while blind spots can orient our reading, they can neither preempt it nor bring about that unity of the signifier with the signified which leaves no remainder, graft, supplementarity. The production of each reading and writing has its own blind spots, around which other readings and writings can be organised indefinitely without ever achieving plenitude. Each dislocates the centered self, since the writing and reading of the self becomes embedded in this process. Self-presence, expressed through the elimination of such blind spots, remains a utopia of Western metaphysics. The 'I' cannot affirm itself in either the writing or the reading of texts. It becomes instead an effect of the textuality of the text.

In his reading of Rousseau, Derrida sees 'the concept of the supplement' as 'a sort of blind spot in Rousseau's text, the not-seen that opens and limits visibility' (*OG*: 163). These blind spots, which are called 'undecidables' in *Positions* and 'levers of disorganisation' in the *Archeology of the Frivolous,* simultaneously open and limit the horizon of interpretation. Such a reading is never free of the disseminating power of *différance*, supplement, etc., because it moves within the logic of identity while always exceeding it and remaining irreducible to it. This strategy contains the structure of what Derrida also calls a '*double mark*'. Although it is always entangled in the structure of a binary opposition, the '*double mark*' is irreducible to either of its component terms: it works the entire field of textuality, preventing the suppression or externalisation of *différance*. According to the logic of the '*double mark*', every concept 'necessarily receives two similar marks – a repetition without identity – one mark inside and the other outside the deconstructed system', which in turn gives 'rise to the double reading and a double writing' (*D*: 4). Instead of assuming the existence of an external referent which governs the text and reduces it to the concept of the book, Derrida institutes textuality as the double mark and the play of the trace.

The function of the trace is to resist the reduction of a text to effects such as meaning, content, theses, theme, intention, author, etc., and ultimately to self-referential presence. The 'economic movement of the trace . . . implies both its mark and its erasure – the margin of its impossibility – according to a relation that no speculative dialectic of the same and the other can master, for the simple reason that such a dialectic remains an operation of mastery' (*D*: 5). What interests Derrida is the question of the semantic after-effects – their non-totalisation, and what he calls 'dissemination' which 'interrupts the circulation that transforms into an origin what is actually an after-effect of meaning' (*D*: 21). Thus, dissemination disrupts any attempt of arriving or forming an origin which denies the idea of the endless after-effects of meaning. 'Dissemination' becomes a third term that goes beyond the dualisms of Western metaphysics without leading to an Hegelian *Aufhebung*. Dissemination denotes the effect 'of a strategic re-mark, a mark which, by phase and by simulacrum, refers the name of one of the two terms [in a binary pair] to the absolute outside of the opposition, to . . . absolute otherness' (*D*: 25). It is this otherness that philosophy has failed to conceptualise. The consequence of exiling the absolute other, or what Derrida refers to in other contexts as the 'parasite' ('Plato's Pharmacy'), is the hyper-subjectivism of Western metaphysics. From Plato to Husserl, subjectivity as self-referential presence is anchored in a notion of identity that excludes the absolute other.

Derrida's deconstruction of Plato, Rousseau, Condillac and Lévi-Strauss rehabilitates writing within Western philosophy. Self-referential presence is targeted by the 'counter-concepts' of the trace, supplement, *pharmakon* and play, through which Derrida raises the question of the other. His concept of writing – of writing the self as non-identity – displaces notions of subject, self and identity. It forms part of his attempt to radically conceive of the other outside the binarisms of Western metaphysics. I want to argue that the question of autobiography, confession and similar genres which claim some kind of privileged access to subjectivity within writing cannot be conceived of within deconstruction, whose object is an '*autobiography*' of 'pure loss and without a signature' (*D*: 41).

What the signature and the writing of the self (*autos*) reveal is pure loss of presence, and the absence of both author and subject. *Logos*, as the father of writing, *cannot* be constituted in its radical absence and effacement. *Thoth,* the god of writing, becomes for Derrida

> the father's other, the father, and the subversive movement of replacement. The god of writing is thus at once his father, his son, and himself. He cannot be assigned a fixed spot in the play of differences. Sly, slippery, and masked, an intriguer and a card, like Hermes, he is neither king nor jack, but rather a sort of *joker*, a floating signifier, a wild card, one who puts play into play (*D*: 93).

The subversive movement of replacement is what puts play into play in an endless and therefore non-fixable play of differences. Derrida's 'gay science' plays off the indeterminacy of the 'undecidables'. Replacement, substitution and repetition, whose movements structure the supplement and writing, become constitutive also of the subject. Derrida argues that *Thoth*

> repeats everything in the addition of the supplement: in adding to and doubling as the sun, he is other than the sun and the same as it; other than the good and the same, etc. Always taking a place not his own, a place one could call that of the dead or the dummy, he has neither a proper place nor a proper name. His propriety or property is impropriety or inappropriateness, the floating indetermination that allows for substitution and play (*D*: 93).

3.2 Frivolity and the deconstruction of Condillac's empiricism

Derrida's deconstruction of Condillac is related to the problematic of writing, especially imagination, need and desire. Derrida aims at a non-analogical relationship between self-identity and imagination, and a concept of desire that is not based on need. His further aim is to avoid the instrumentalisation of both writing and empirical conceptions of language and subjectivity. He sees the problems inherent in the concepts of metaphysics, imagination and desire as providing the 'disorganising lever' in Condillac's texts. His objective, however, is not to establish an internal formal contradiction, but to answer an unanswered question about the production of the new metaphysics, based on the idea of analogy, which gives prominence to the quantity of connection (*AF*: 72). Moreover, it is clear that both Condillac's texts and Biran's interpretation of them raise for Derrida the question of a reading which constitutes 'a formal contradiction, hesitation, or systematic incoherence what', in Biran 'is claimed or assumed to be duplicity' (*AF*: 59). Derrida wants to examine why 'the couple activity/passivity give[s] rise to a contradiction in Condillac, but to the analysis of duplicity in Biran?' (*AF*: 59).

In other words, a reading that finds or constitutes a formal contradiction, hesitation, or systematic incoherence in the text does not amount to discovering the meaning of the text, since the same contradiction can provoke different readings, interpretations or theoretical constructions. It is erroneous to argue that the dualism 'passivity/activity' establishes both their relationship and meaning. Textuality, an interminable movement of signification, breaches all dualistic constructions, and defers their interpretative closure. Thus, to reduce a text to dualisms does not amount to determining either its meaning or the deconstruction of those dualisms. Because the possibility of repetition – iterability – is inscribed in each term of a dualism, alterity and alteration are embedded within the dualisms themselves. A deconstructive reading of Condillac cannot, therefore, claim to correct other 'misreadings'. It differs also from that evolutionary and empiricist model of reading which purports to demonstrate that Condillac's system has achieved its end through a central deficiency.

On a more philosophical level, Derrida's reading focuses on Condillac's attempts to establish a new metaphysics which, because it is based on the empirical methodology of analogy, aims at correcting bad metaphysics. Moving away from a metaphysics of causes and principles, Condillac constructs a metaphysics of phenomena and relations (connections). Yet although his concern with phenomena leads to a preoccupation with language and signs, it remains nevertheless within the framework of a metaphysics of presence, retraced through imagination and repeating the origin. Although Condillac does not begin at the origin, he returns to it through the analogical method in order to analyse its production and generation. Unlike Husserl, he regards the construction of a new metaphysics as a matter of replacing 'the first philosophy while inheriting its name. Or better still: supply[ing] it' (*AF*: 36). The correction of metaphysics remains for Condillac a task of philosophy, but he conceives of it as a question of method and order. Above all, 'by elaborating another theory of signs and words by using another language', he wants to avoid the employment of 'undeterminate [sic] signs' (*AF*: 36).

Philosophy must therefore produce a new language that will 'reconstitute metaphysics' prelinguistic and natural base' (*AF*: 38). For Condillac, Derrida argues, 'good metaphysics *will have been* natural and mute' (*AF*: 38) before the advent of language and its ambiguities. The category of good metaphysics thus contains two distinct notions: one is prelinguistic and pertains to origin, instinct and feeling; the other is the highest elaboration in language, which cures the ills of bad metaphysics by correcting them. For Condillac, then, 'metaphysics as such must *develop* and not degrade the metaphysics of natural instinct; metaphysics as such must even reproduce *within* language the relation it has, as language, to what precedes all language' (*AF*: 38). This means that language is reproducing in language its own origin which, nevertheless, is prelinguistic. Language and signification in general embody a knowledge that was already there: all we need do is retrace its genesis as a prelinguistic and non-signifying origin. For Condillac, both the correction of what has preceded and the production of a new language are a matter of making 'amends through language for language's misdeeds, [so as] to push artifice to that limit which leads back to nature' (*AF*: 37).

This going back to the origin or to nature is achieved by means of analogy, which is based on the principle of identical propositions. The origin is in itself unmodifiable. Thus Condillac explains the productive function of analogy by 'the principle of a difference of degree' (*AF*: 44), without abandoning 'the rule of the "identical proposition"' (*AF*: 45). This implies that

> the genealogical return to the simple – and that progressive development can only be done by combining or modifying a material unmodifiable in itself. Here sensation. That is the first material: informed, transformed, combined, associated, it engenders all knowledge (*AF*: 45).

Language and the sign are simply external to this first material, their function being to impose logical order on otherwise confused sense-material. This means in turn that for Condillac

> there would exist a mute first material, an irreducible core of immediate presence to which some secondary modifications supervene, modifications which would enter into combinations, relations, connections, and so on. And yet this metaphysics . . . this sensationalist metaphysics . . . would also be throughout a metaphysics of the sign and a philosophy of language (*AF*: 46).

Sensation, being the simple element, is conceived of by Condillac as a 'germ' (*AF*: 46). It leads us not to theoretical but to practical knowledge, which 'does not need signs or language' (*AF*: 95). Only theoretical knowledge and distinct ideas need language or signs whose function is to classify and define distinct ideas. In Derrida's view, the importance accorded to signs by Condillac means that

> from the most natural articulation up to the greatest formality of the language of calculus, the sign's function is to 'account for', is to give the *ratio* to itself according to its calculative essence. But this calculus remarks, its force repeats a force older than itself, on the side of action, passion, need. The theoretical is only a supplying remark . . . of the practical (*AF*: 99).

Thus, the sign becomes an element of remarking through repetition. It is a force that supplements a need inscribed in that practical knowledge from which Condillac excludes language and the sign.

Imagination is the faculty which, by means of signs, produces combinations between the prelinguistic stratum and ideas (objects). In Condillac's theory, the sign comes into existence '*the moment* the present object comes to be missing from perception, the moment perception is absent from itself [:] at that moment the space of signs, with the function of imagination, is opened' (*AF*: 95). The sign as detour thus becomes necessary when the object is absent from the origin. When the sign takes the place of the object perception (retracing) begins through imagination. The sign is never there at the beginning, because it is excluded from the origin, experience and 'the operation of the soul' (*AF*: 95). It is unnecessary for practical knowledge of those first 'knowns', which make all other knowledge possible through analogy. The production of knowledge is but a difference of degree. The imagination is accorded a productive function in fashioning the new only when, 'by analogical connection and repetition, [it] bring[s] to light what, without being there, *will have been* there' (*AF*: 71).

On the one hand, therefore, imagination is conceived as that which retraces and produces 'as reproduction the lost object of perception' and does so at the moment when 'attention (of which imagination is nevertheless only the first modification) no longer suffices to make the object of perception *subsist*, the moment the first modification of attention breaks with perception and regulates passing from weak presence to absence' (*AF*: 71). On the other hand, Condillac conceives of imagination as a force which, by connecting the present to the absent, liberates the production of the new, although it is unable to create anything new that deviates from the principle of the identical proposition of analogy. In other words, it invents or reproduces only what was there already. Imagination can thus link one signified of the already-there to another, but without alteration – i.e. alterity – entering into the signifieds connected by the signifier. Repetition comes to be part of the signified only as repetition of the same.

Although imagination-as-reproduction 'traces the perceived', it 'invents or innovates nothing; it only combines in relation to each other the given's finite presences' (*AF*: 76). 'In order to supply' language, the productive imagination 'adds something more' (*AF*: 76). Its freedom, however, consists of transferring and mastering the strongest possible connections between the present and the absent, between ideas and perceptions. For Condillac, 'to supply a language's defects is a *theoretical* and *methodical* operation of *remarkin*' after the fact. Thus

> to supply is, after having remarked and 'retraced' the origin of the lack, to add what *is necessary*, what *is missing* . . . But what *is necessary* – what is lacking – also presents itself as a surplus, an overabundance of value, a frivolous futility that would have to be subtracted, although it makes all commerce possible (as sign and value) (*AF*: 100–101).

The sign in Condillac thus embodies a knowledge already known to practical knowledge, and its function and meaning are determined by notions of need and utility. Any overabundance of value produced 'by what supplies the lack gives rise to commerce, both economic and linguistic, as well as to trade and the frivolity of chitchat' (*AF*: 103). The genesis of the sign is linked to commerce when it institutes the arbitrary sign which frees the operations of the soul. Although the operations of the soul are the property of natural signs, the natural sign is not a proper sign. For Condillac, then, 'the *proper*, the *property* of the sign is the system of the arbitrary' (*AF*: 112).

Articulated language as a system of arbitrary signs, becomes the exemplar which contains the whole; that is, it contains the natural sign while remaining external to it. In his *Truth in Painting*, Derrida critiques this idea of an exemplar based on the principle of analogy, by turning analogy against itself. In Condillac, however, the sign does not refer either to the idea or the referent, or to any useful connection. Having no value, it becomes useless, and gives rise to frivolity. In so far as it does not refer to the absent object, the sign falls far from the idea, from sense itself, and from the origin. In Derrida's view, Condillac's

> frivolity consists in being satisfied with tokens. It originates with the sign, or rather with the signifier which, no longer signifying, is no longer a signifier. The empty, void, friable, useless signifier (*AF*: 118).

For Condillac the sign cannot be present to itself without referring to an object, without repeating it through the principle of identity. The semantic identity of the sign is contained in the idea, in its link to the principle of identical propositions. Any sign that falls outside this schema is 'unnecessary' and 'hollow' (*AF*: 119). What organises the usefulness or frivolity of the sign is need.

By resorting to the 'values of the same, of analogy, of analysis, of the identical proposition', Condillac had to guard against frivolity 'as if from its infinitely unlike double' (*AF*: 119). In order to avoid frivolity in discourse, Condillac uses analogy to saturate indefinitely semiotics with 'semantic representation, by including all rhetoric in a metaphorics, by *connecting the signifier*' (*AF*: 119). Consequently, all language relates metaphorically to the origin, and the signifier must always connect with the signified (object, idea). The sign must mean, and its meaning derives from the origin as identity. Unconnected signifiers – meaningless, futile and thus disposable – introduce frivolity into the sign. Condillac accepts the process of correcting deficiencies in language, and of creating a new language by supplying it. Supplementation and lack are thus quite central issues in Condillac's thought. What he condemns is frivolity in language, that is, the sign which repeats itself merely in order to repeat itself, and lacks both an object and semantic value which originates in a need.

Writing becomes 'evil' whenever it is unintelligible, lacks semantic content, or falls away from the origin – that is, when the signifier-as-detour remains a detour without return. The written signifier poses the greatest threat of deviating from the origin. For Condillac, Derrida argues, 'the root of evil is writing. The frivolous style is the style – that is written' (*AF*: 126). Because the written signifier has no object, no interlocutor, it repeats itself without reference to any signified. Any signifier that leads to an indeterminate detour from the origin is simply frivolous. Thus, for Condillac

> [f]rivolity begins its work, or rather threatens the work of its work in repetition in general, ie., in the fissure which, separating two repetitions, rends repetition in two. The repetition of the idea, the identity of ideas is not frivolous. Identity in words is frivolous (*AF*: 127).

Because writing has the greatest potential for frivolity, the frivolous style must be eliminated.

So too must repetition as non-identity in writing. For Condillac, the difference between these two forces of repetition – identity in ideas, and non-identity in writing – produces the gap between the serious and the frivolous. Condillac, Derrida argues, 'tied the two forces of repetition to one another', and as a result 'the limit between the two repetitions within repetition itself cannot be reproduced, stated, or come to signification without engendering that very thing the limit excludes' (*AF*: 127–128). Frivolity in writing thus appears inevitable, because the written signifier – instead of bridging the gap between the two repetitions – introduces a fissure which condemns it to frivolity. Thus, 'frivolity originates from the deviation or the gap of the signifier, but also from its folding back on itself in its closed and nonrepresentative identity' (*AF*: 128). Although Condillac recognises nonidentity in language, he views it as metaphor and makes it 'the primordial structure of language only in order to begin its analogical and teleological reappropriation' (*AF*: 128).

In other words, language is a secondary modification of this primordial, prelinguistic structure. Metaphor and analogy can be conceived of only in terms of a reappropriation of the origin, and the nonidentical only as the nonidentity of an identity. As the representation of the absent object, the sign must refer always to that object and be identical with it if it is to mean. The force which determines the need for the presence of the object is the desire rooted in empirical subjectivity. Since the values of use and need orient Condillac's theory of the sign, frivolity becomes also 'the seeming repetition of desire without any object or of a floating desire': it is 'need left to itself, need without object, without desire's direction' (*AF*: 130). In Condillac, therefore, desire derives from need in the same way as imagination does from sense. Although imagination, need, desire and repetition produce the sign, they must not suspend its relation to an object that ties it to the origin. In one respect desire 'opens the direction of the object, [and] produces the supplying [*suppléante*] sign which can always work to no effect . . . by means of vacancy, disposability, extension' (*AF*: 134). But in other respects, 'need is itself frivolous. Need without desire is blind. It has no object, is identical to itself, tautological and autistic' (*AF*: 134). Condillac thinks that desire must relate need to an object in order to avoid frivolity.

In the place of a derivative desire and imagination, Derrida develops a radicalised concept of desire which is not derived from need. It is *a need to desire* which, having no object, it becomes the object itself. For Derrida,

> no longer is desire the relation with an object, but the object of need. No longer is desire a direction, but an end. An end without end bending need into a kind of

flight. This escape sweeps away the origin, system, destiny, and time of *need* (an exempt . . . word and a concept without identity) (*AF*: 135).

The written sign that is no longer connected to an object becomes a need to desire. For Condillac, the need to desire in writing is what threatens the principle of analogy, whereas for Derrida it frees writing from the dichotomy between use and frivolity.

By conceiving of writing as a need to desire, Derrida liberates it from instrumentalization, derivativeness, and the need to refer back without loss to an origin *qua* identity which entails a particular destiny or interpretative framework. Freeing writing from all of that, desire directs it into a kind of interminable 'flight' from such fundamental concepts of Western metaphysics as origin, system, destiny and identity. The subject has no origin, need or desire connected to either an object or a self as identity. The writing of the self thus enters into an interminable 'flight' that eliminates the self, its identity, and origin. The subject, therefore, cannot write its desire, because writing contains desire without depending on human agency and subjectivity. Desire is disassociated from that notion of subjectivity which rests on self-referential presence and need as origin. In Derrida, desire is freed from its locus in the subject even as something unconscious. In his later work Derrida becomes more emphatic when he argues that even in relation to desire of God 'we do not determine *ourselves before* this desire, as no relation to self can be sure of preceding a relation to the other' (Derrida, 1995a: 37).

Derrida's deconstruction of Condillac shows the limits of an empirical conception of the sign and subjectivity that appears to have the same shortcomings as Husserl's idealist conception of the sign. For whereas Husserl brackets out the signifier, because it does not lead to full presence and transcendental subjectivity, Condillac condemns it for not being connected to an object and therefore unable to reappropriate the origin. Neither the frivolous sign in Condillac nor indicative sign in Husserl is connected to semantic value. Both meaningless, they thus pose a threat to the origin *qua* identity. Both Husserl and Condillac think that the written sign as representation is necessary for communication and understanding. But it also threatens the principle of identity, whether it is conceived in terms of sense, or as an intended consciousness of an ideal subject and object.

Condillac excludes the written sign from both prelinguistic sense and the faculties of the soul, and derives its meaning through an analogical relationship to the origin. Its status is to supplying corrections through secondary modifications, although these modifications remain external to the origin. Writing is what establishes the strongest connection between ideas, threading one signified to another by detours through the signifier. Writing, however, also poses the greatest threat – through frivolity – of falling away from the origin. In Husserl, writing is external and secondary to the signified, even though it is the most ideal of signs. Its meaning is derived though its connection to an intended consciousness. The sign itself being unconnected to intentionality, is both empty and meaningless. In his critique of Husserl, Derrida frees writing from both intentionality and subjugation to a transcendental signified; and by his critiquing Condillac he frees it also from being instrumentalized in relation to origin and need. Writing is no longer dependent upon and directed by a conception of desire connected to an empirical subjectivity. Need, desire and imagination are divorced from their dependence on notions of subjectivity as self-identity.

Derrida's thought becomes problematic, however, once we examine his deconstruction of the sign, which leads him to *différance* and other concepts. Especially problematic in his analysis of Condillac is Derrida's treatment of the subject and the writing of the self. Two questions arise: how one can write or read the self – especially in autobiographical and/or confessional writing in the absence of the subject, subjectivity, the 'I' or indeed any notion of the self which rests on a principle of identity? How, if one elevates writing to a transcendental concept that is beyond not only speech and writing but also the transcendental or empirical subject, can the project of writing the transcendental or empirical self be possible?

In deconstructing Condillac, Derrida argues for a conception of subjectivity divorced from empirical subjectivity and not conceived of – in the manner of both Lacan and Freud – in terms of desire (which in the early Lacan's case (1977) means desire and recognition of the other). Derrida thinks of desire as embedded in an indeterminable flight, in which the relationship between desire and its ends cannot be grounded in subjectivity. No longer integral to subjective self-consciousness, desire has neither an *arche* nor a *telos*. While desire is turned back ceaselessly upon itself, need becomes the need to desire.

In Hegel, desire is connected to need, whereas Levinas separates desire from enjoyment. Both are reluctant, however, to disassociate desire from subjectivity. For Derrida, however, desire 'permits itself to be appealed to by the absolutely irreducible exteriority of the other to which it must remain infinitely inadequate. Desire is equal only to excess. No totality will ever encompass it' (*WD*: 93). Desire is outside the metaphysics of the same and consequently outside the categories of subjectivity conceived in terms of identity. The subject is not the locus or the destination of desire. Desire itself becomes an 'opening and freedom' without return (*WD*: 93). Desire is the frivolity of the sign, the excess of need and Nietzsche's 'eternal return'. The 'other' again breaks the circle of desire by opening it to an asymmetrical relationship with the other. As an irreducible exteriority, desire is beyond any relationship of adequation to or analogy with the self.

Derrida's deconstruction of the empirical concept of the sign proposes a conception of the self which by transgressing the basic tenets of the empirical tradition, frees the self and subjectivity from psychological categories. He postulates a redefinition of selfhood which negates the concepts of need, desire and imagination, partly by abolishing the distinction between frivolity and usefulness, and partly by questioning the relation between sign and object. Subjectivity – as a self-contained entity, anchored to an origin – disappears in order to make room for a new conception of selfhood, which will become more evident in Derrida's deconstruction of structuralism and Rousseau.

3.3 Structure and the deconstruction of empiricism's antipode

Derrida's other major point of departure in deconstructing logocentrism is his critique of structuralism and its concept of structure. Some elements of structuralist thought, he argues had began already the process of the displacement of logocentrism: these include the idea of bricolage and also of myth as discourse which questions notions of authorship and unique subjectivity. On the other hand, he targets structuralist conceptions of both centre and structure, because they retain vestiges of a subjectivism rooted in ideas of identity and presence. Derrida also attacks structuralism's anthropological concept of man which derives its assuredness from basing its knowledge and claim to truth on the organising principle of the centre. Derrida argues that although the concepts of centre and structure both claim to denote transubjective categories, they still rely on the notion of origin as presence. The subject and the self are still part of this mode of thinking, in so far as the configurations of difference they allow for are nevertheless fixed by appealing to a centre that permits no alterity. This results in a kind of ethnocentrism – the byproduct of a subjectivist anthropology that constructs difference within a model of assuredness.

Although Derrida continues to maintain the importance of the concept of the sign, its deconstruction now encompasses ethnocentric discourses as well as associated constructions of subjectivity and otherness. Situating structuralism within Western metaphysics, Derrida states in his interpretation of Lévi-Strauss that 'the absence of a center is here the absence of a subject and the absence of an author' (*WD*: 287). The fate of the centre is also the fate of the subject and the self. Because the structure no longer retains the centre, neither the linguistic nor any other structure can be instituted in order to rescue the subject. Derrida makes this clear when arguing that the concept of structure, especially in Lévi-Strauss' work, is 'like the concept of the sign' in so far as it 'can simultaneously confirm and shake logocentric and ethnocentric assuredness' (*POS*: 24). Once again we are confronted with the concept of the sign as that which guides methodology and grounds validity. This connects structuralist scientificity to the *logos* determined as method.

Derrida argues that in Lévi-Straussian structuralism the sign is used in order to overcome the opposition between the sensible and the intelligible. It fails because 'the concept of the sign cannot in itself surpass this opposition' (*WD*: 281) if it is conceived of within a system which reduces the signifier to the signified by submitting the sign to thought. This problematic of the sign extends also to that 'discourse on structure' which is based on the concept of the centre. Structuralism, Derrida argues, is a '*phonologism*' which 'is undoubtedly the exclusion or abasement of writing' (*OG*: 102). It is based on a hierarchy which places speech (on account of its phonematic character) above writing and consequently nature above culture. Derrida argues that because structuralism elevates nature into the transcendental signified, speech and oral language are accorded a certain 'naturality'.

Like Rousseau, Lévi-Strauss conceives of writing as something external to nature and artificial. Language is separated from writing, which is placed 'below and outside' (*OG*: 120). For Lévi-Strauss, writing's 'essential function . . . is to favour the enslaving power rather than the "disinterested" science' (*OG*: 128). Writing becomes the tool of oppression, that element in language which destroys the authenticity of nature, and which lacks the scientificity accorded to it by Husserl. Writing, for Lévi-Strauss, then becomes 'inauthentic' (*OG*: 136–137), associated with a violence and hierarchization which result in exploitation. Once again, writing is the disruption of presence. Structuralism's basic principle – 'structure' – functions as the transcendental signified: it is a totalising concept that aims to arrest or suppress the signifier (written inscription) by relegating it to social inauthenticity, to a violence. 'From then on', Derrida argues 'the anthropologist's mission carries an ethical significance: to find and fix . . . the "levels of authenticity"' (*OG*: 137). The anthropological division of peoples into those with writing and those without it betrays the preoccupation with authenticity as the transcendental referent of a natural full presence and true origin, uncontaminated by what is inauthentic.

The concept of structure in Western metaphysics is thus perceived as having a centre which refers 'to a point of presence, a fixed origin' (*WD*: 278). The function of the centre is to orient, balance and organise, and limit 'the *play* of the structure' (*WD*: 278). Play is restricted to the elements *within* the structure. There is no possibility of either the transgression or the substitution of the elements; nor can the uniqueness of the centre be destroyed. The centre is thus outside the play, whose rules it sets and governs by. Being simultaneously both within and outside the structure it therefore escapes structurality. At the center, Derrida argues 'the permutation or the transformation of elements (which may of course be structures enclosed within a structure) is forbidden. At least this permutation has always remained *interdicted*' (*WD*: 279). Transgression reorganises the elements and dislocates the centre, whose function is to provide a locus where 'play is constituted on the basis of a fundamental immobility and reassuring certitude', and where 'anxiety can be mastered' (*WD*: 279).

This schema does not allow for a mode of being which is caught in the game of differences. It allows a mode of being based on a desire for certitude, and for a centre that always determines the elements and configurations of the structure. Because it figures structure as closure, this conception of the centre can be called the origin or end, *arche* or *telos* of 'repetitions, substitutions, transformations, and permutations [which] are always *taken* from a history of meaning [*sens*] – that is in a word, a history – whose origin may always be reawakened or whose end may always be anticipated in the form of presence' (*WD*: 279). Structure, then, is determinable and predictable, a 'full presence which is beyond play' whose centre is always assured (*WD*: 279).

Derrida argues that in Western metaphysics the names given to the centre were always 'designated an invariable presence – *eidos, arche, telos, energeia, ousia* (essence, existence, substance, subject) *aletheia*, transcendentality, consciousness, God, man, and so forth' (*WD*: 279–280). The function of the structure is to reappropriate the origin, the organising principle; it is truth present to itself without alterity, without difference. The problem of the transition from one structure to another is overcome by bracketing out history and spacing. Difference, rupture, etc., are contained at the moment when the structure is created, rather than being essential elements of or prerequisites for that formation. Consequently, the idea of an ongoing dislocation or absent centre is denied. Derrida's project, however, is to decentre the centre as the totalising principle of logocentric structuration and as the transcendental signified. He wants to totally radicalise the concept of structure by conceiving of it as without a centre. By submitting the centre, to the structurality of the structure, he aims to open up a process of decentering and of non-totalisation.

Derrida attempts to effect this dislocation by introducing the concepts of rupture (or disruption) and redoubling, which open up the possibility of play and substitution. Rupture or disruption comes into existence when the structurality of the structure is thought of as repetition (*WD*: 280). Repetition is not bound to the identity principle, however, but to the admission of alterity. Instead of substituting one centre for another, it disrupts and dislocates infinitely the formation of any structure governed by the centre. Derrida thinks of the centre as something devoid of anteriority. It is a structure with no centre in 'the form of a present-being'; having 'no natural site', it is 'not a fixed locus but a function, a sort of nonlocus in which an infinite number of sign-substitutions [comes] into play' (*WD*: 280). The structure and the place vacated by a centered language is decentred by the 'joyful science' which is a 'science' of the play of differences:

> a system in which the central signified, the original or transcendental signified, is never absolutely present outside a system of differences. The absence of the transcendental signified extends the domain and the play of signification infinitely (*WD*: 280).

Totalisation, conceived of as the arrest of play within a structure, cannot be achieved. Play disrupts and dislocates any attempts either to totalise or to saturate the field with empirical instances. It therefore attempts to escape reductive empiricism in both language and structuralism. Moreover, in the absence of a transcendental signified which is beyond play, both the division between signifier and signified and their parallel relationship are cancelled. The new field which is opened up, and which is not determined by either empiricism or idealism, 'is in effect that of *play*' which is conceived of as 'a field of infinite substitutions only because it is finite' and 'instead of being an inexhaustible field, . . . instead of being too large, there is something missing from it: a center which arrests and grounds the play of substitutions' (*WD*: 289). Meaning, truth and origin thus enter the play of infinite substitutions. They do so, however, not (as is often argued) on account of their inexhaustibility, but because of a lack which is inherent in signification and language. The movement of play supplements this lack through substitution, without the possibility of achieving either plenitude or that kind of centered formation which would arrest play by locking the movement of signification into binary oppositions.

The movement of play, Derrida asserts

> permitted by the lack or absence of a center or origin, is the movement of *supplementarity* . . . [and] occurs as a surplus, as a *supplement*. The movement of signification adds something, which results in the fact that there is always more, but this addition is a floating one because it comes to perform a vicarious function, to supplement a lack on the part of the signified (*WD*: 289).

As when critiquing Husserl's conception of the sign, Derrida introduces a non-originary origin in order to designate a lack on the part of the signified. No signifier is ever completely contained, without remainder by the signified. With regard to structure, play becomes the 'disruption of presence' (*WD*: 292), the stand-point from which nontotalization can be perceived. For Derrida,

> play is always play of absence and presence, but if it is to be thought radically, play must be conceived of before the alternative of presence and absence. Being must be conceived as presence or absence on the basis of the possibility of play and not the other way around (*WD*: 292).

As both absence and presence, play therefore inscribes the very possibility of the binary opposition, presence/absence.

Play is not the loss or absence of a presence (as centre, origin, truth, etc.) that needs to be reappropriated. It is outside the structuralist thematic of the 'lost or impossible presence of the absent origin . . . of broken immediacy' (*WD*: 292). It has more in common with the Nietzschean affirmation than with either the structuralist quest for the authentic or Rousseau's search for an originary Nature. As conceived of by Derrida, play is a

> joyous affirmation of the play of the world and the innocence of becoming, the affirmation of a world of signs without fault, without truth, and without origin which is offered to an active interpretation. *This affirmation then determines the noncenter otherwise than as loss of the center* (*WD*: 292).

By affirming play as the play of the world, and by attributing to the world of signs no fault, truth or origin, Derrida's 'aesthetics of existence' does away with teleological and ontological concerns. In the world of signs, non-purposive play and the innocence of becoming are linked to an active mode of interpretation unencumbered by metaphysical concerns.

Freed from the domination of teleocracy, interpretation is given up to joyously affirming the play of the world. This idea has important implications for the theory of subjectivity. For if subjectivity cannot attain the status of an origin, then both the subject and the self are also set adrift in the play of the world. In particular, the writing of the self enters a world of signs which are without fault, truth, or origin. The self is consequently without either responsibility or meaning, for 'meaning is a *function* of play, [and] is inscribed in a certain place in the configuration of a meaningless play' (*WD*: 260). The subject can be seen as either trapped in the sureness of the structure or given over to the play of chance. As Derrida argues, 'the trace is the erasure of selfhood, of one's own presence, and is constituted by the threat or anguish of its irremediable disappearance, of the disappearance of its disappearance' (WD: 230).

Derrida also contends that 'there is a *sure* play', in the sense of 'that which is limited to the *substitution* of *given* and *existing, present*, pieces'.

This is because 'in absolute chance, affirmation surrenders itself to *genetic* indetermination, to the *seminal* adventure of the trace' (*WD*: 292). It is therefore the indeterminacy of the trace that guides the act of interpretation as the affirmation of a form of play that does not have as its *telos* both the return to the origin and the end of play. The substitution of given and existing pieces is left to absolute chance, that is, to the non-systematisation of their formations. Writing as trace is constituted by its own erasure, its own disappearance. For Derrida, 'an unerasable trace is not a trace' but 'full presence, an immobile and uncorruptible substance, a son of God, a sign of parousia and not a seed, that is, a mortal germ' (*WD*: 230). The trace then carries within itself the seeds of its own death, its own erasure. As the play and work of *différance,* the trace can be neither hypostasised nor made part of any empirical or structural concept that arrests the play and work of *différance*.

The trace is never fully absent and never fully present. Because the sign itself 'represents the present of its absence' (*MP*: 9), the trace is thus the other of signification. Interpretation cannot be connected, therefore, to an act of subjectivity. Writing, as trace, carries within it not only its own erasure but also the erasure of selfhood. This becomes clearer in Derrida's reply to Searle about the deconstruction of speech acts. There the notion of iterability in language announces the death of the author as well as of the intentionality which supposedly is embedded in all speech acts. Nor is it possible to subject the trace to a psychoanalytic approach, in which the text and its reading become tools with which to psychoanalyse its author. Writing cannot be 'limited to the interpretation of the *lapsus calami*' that will lead back to the interiority of the subject itself (*WD*: 230). The very idea of the subject as a desire for self-presence, for a fixing of a centre, becomes part of the deconstructive process. The subject's self-presence is deferred indefinitely. So too are the *lapsus calami* and the absolute unveiling of the unconscious through their subjugation to the language of *logos*.

For Derrida, the text cannot become an expression, production or representation of the self at either a conscious or unconscious level. The text cannot be fully present to itself in terms of either meaning or truth. Selfhood is subject to the seminal adventure of the trace. Because the self writes its own erasure, it cannot be the locus of its own self-contained truth, in full speech, and through some uninterrupted connection to the *logos*. Writing as trace or *proto*-writing will always interrupt full presence, and dislocate both its centre and its certitude. The Derridean self is playful but uncertain, because its desire for immediate self-presence and self-proximity is always disrupted and interrupted by its other. Anchored to the notion of full presence, both the authentic subject and the authentic self are subject to the kind of play which Derrida defines as 'the disruption of presence' (*WD*: 292). To conceive of structure as a totality with a fixed centre (which forbids play, substitution or transgression) implies a conception of both the subject and the self as self-enclosed entities with assured centres. But in Derrida's understanding, neither the subject nor the self can become centres for either asserting the authenticity, truth and meaning of the self or for reappropriating it as an origin at the level of identity, consciousness or presence. Play is subject-less transgression.

3.4 Rousseau: authenticity, representation and the threat of writing

Derrida aims to deconstruct Rousseau's model of self-presence which is based on the idea of the sensible cogito. He does so in order to deconstruct the political agenda of a philosophy of presence which constructs subjectivity by excluding supplementarity. He uses Rousseau's *Confessions* to deconstruct the presence-and-absence problematic within self-presence. Rousseau's *Social Contract* enables him to problematise the relationship between presence, presenter, representation, re-presentation, representer and the represented. And with reference to Rousseau's *Origin of Languages* he can critique the philosophical premise which conceives of the origin as full appropriation. In each case he mobilises the supplement and play in order to dethrone presence. In place of presence Derrida institutes the supplement, and redefines the origin as the supplement of a supplement.

The self likewise becomes the supplement of a supplement, which can never appropriate its origin either as presence, authenticity or identity devoid of alterity. For Derrida, the truth of the self and the authentic self are no less a mirage than presence itself. The origin, which always eludes us in both writing and speech, 'is possible and conceivable only in disguise'

(*WD*: 8). That is, as concealment rather than as a Heideggerian unconcealment. Various questions then arise. How can we think of a subject of representation which does not rely on an originary presence that can be evoked and instituted? How can one think of a politics of the self and a politics of representation that does not rely on the principle of presence? Can we have politics, justice and morality without co-present subjects?

For Derrida, the answer is contained in his notions of supplement and play, his critique of the idea of representation, and ultimately in a construction of the other which undermines the notion that subjectivity is based on identity. The supplement and play radicalise the notion that the origin is natural and authentic. In addition to introducing Derrida's conception of the other, they also deconstruct ideas of representation which rely on origin for their authentication. This early critique of the political problematic of representation confutes the argument that only in his later work does Derrida become political. I argue that these early deconstructions inform those later works by Derrida which address directly the political, social, ethico-moral, and cultural issues that characterise his thought. In effect, the deconstruction of Rousseau's conception of presence instantiates his political, social and ethico-moral concerns.

Derrida argues that Rousseau starts from a new model of presence: 'the subject's self-presence within *consciousness* or *feeling*' (*OG*: 98). This radical departure is still embedded, however, in a concept of writing that presents a danger to self-presence. As a result, Rousseau tries to exclude writing from the construction of subjectivity because of its problematic relationship to self-presence, which (he argues) constitutes the authentic, inner self. Although he uses the privileged discourse of confession to assert the empirical unity of both the self and the subject in general, he fails, according to Derrida, to step out of Western metaphysics. This failure is significant because it not only heralds a new concept of the authentic self, but also problematises that politics of presence which seeks to exclude re-presentation and supplementarity.

Focusing once more on writing, Derrida deconstructs Rousseau's dichotomy between a 'representative' and a natural, divine, or 'living' writing. The first represents the Common writing, the dead letter, exemplifies the former; while the latter is represented by that living, divine voice which 'one hears upon retreating into oneself' (*OG*: 17). The inner self, which unites with the voice, excludes the disruption and aphoristic energy of writing (See *OG*: 18). In order to reach the truth about ourselves, each one of us needs to retreat into our inner self, which is expressed as the writing in the soul and as the voice of conscience. It is by deconstructing this inner, authentic and original self that Derrida problematises expressivist conceptions of the modern self (see Taylor, 1989). The inner and true self constitutes an origin that excludes writing and representation. The voice becomes the signified-origin, while writing is merely the signifier.

Derrida's deconstruction of Rousseau uncovers the logocentric foundations of both representation and imitation. In this theoretical schema, *logos* is the governing principle which, being 'infinite and self-present', can be '*produced as auto-affection*' through the voice (*OG*: 98). The unity and consciousness of the subject and the self are assured through the voice, which reaffirms self-presence by excluding writing. Writing is merely a signifier, external to and representative of the subject's self-presence within consciousness or feeling. Derrida thus argues that Rousseau presupposes a first presence that representation must either restore or reappropriate, if thought is not to become alienated. Subjectivity and the self are anchored on the idea of a first or authentic self-presence that representation cannot affect.

In Rousseau, however, the relationship between voice and signifier is complex. The voice is that which denotes the disappearance of the object, and it interiorises this disappearance violently by transforming it into *akoumene*. Derrida objects that Rousseau assumes that the 'disappearance of presence in the form of the object, the being-before-the-eyes or being-at-hand, installs a sort of fiction, if not a lie, at the very origin of speech' (*OG*: 240). Consequently, the disappearance of the object is a precondition for its appearance or substitution in speech. Paradoxically, speech obliterates the empirical nature of the object in the very act of articulating and interiorising it as voice. Speech as full presence – as the only route to the heart – is thus based on a fiction which, Derrida argues, is inscribed in the origin itself. For speech never 'gives the thing itself, but a simulacrum that touches us more profoundly than the truth, "strikes" us more effectively' (*OG*: 240). As the interiorization of the object *qua* simulacrum, speech expresses a fiction that guarantees authenticity via the paradox of expression. This paradox was also explored by Rousseau's sometime friend and rival theorist Diderot. In his 'Paradox of the Actor', Diderot argues that actors need reason rather than sensibility, since what enables a great actor to give 'authentic' performances is not real feeling but an ability to create the simulacrum of real feeling (Diderot, 1994).

3.5 Rousseau: the new logic of the supplement

The concept of representation that Rousseau adopts is based on a process of returning, recovering, and remembering an immutable origin whose integrity is appropriated retrospectively, but which is nevertheless guaranteed in advance. What Rousseau wants to exclude is supplementarity and any representation that does not enable the origin to be reappropriated as identity. This results in the conception of an authentic and natural self, as opposed to that which is inauthentic and artificial. It is this representation that Derrida deconstructs in an attempt to dislocate the absolute nature of the origin, and to substitute for it the notion of the non-originary supplement, trace and play. Thus, for Derrida, subjective self-consciousness has no absolute origin: the subject cannot constitute the foundational principle or the origin of either writing or speech. He aims also to develop a strategy for deconstructing both the primacy of the origin and the emergence of what he calls 'primary writing' (*OG*: 7), which replaces the writing of the self as a self-assured 'I'. In 'primary writing', the self is written out of erasure through the 'new logic of the "supplement"' (*OG*: 7). This new concept of writing, and its paradoxical function as supplement within Rousseau's thought, was used subsequently by Derrida to deconstruct a number of widely accepted notions and dichotomies.

As we have seen already, Derrida's concept of writing goes 'beyond the extension of language. In all senses of the word, writing thus *comprehends* language' (*OG*: 7). This historical closure of the sign and of language, and the opening of the 'science' of writing, is for Derrida a slow movement – spanning twenty centuries of Western thought – which 'finally succeeded in being gathered under the name language', and is now 'beginning to let itself be transferred to, or at least summarised under, the name of writing' (*OG*: 6). What interests Derrida is the movement of a language which has no origin other than a structure which 'can be expressed as "signifier of the signifier"', and which 'conceals and erases itself in its own production' (*OG*: 7). The field of language, therefore, can no longer be constituted, contained or arranged through the binary opposition of signifier and signified. This new conception of writing as something which comprehends language again entails destroying 'the concept of "sign" and its entire logic' (*OG*: 7). The sign becomes unmotivated, and is liberated from the dualisms of logocentrism.

Writing – as the signifier of a signifier – is added by Derrida to the origin of language, but without itself constituting an origin. Language therefore, can be subsumed under the name of the writing which engenders its production, since, as the signifier of a signifier, it comprehends and exceeds the signified-language. While overturning the hierarchy which privileges speech above writing, it does not allow writing to become the 'new' governing principle. Language becomes subject to proto-writing and supplementarity while simultaneously entering a kind of free play. Since the self is embedded in language, inevitably it becomes part of this supplementarity and free play, although without having resort to full presence. Its corresponding uncertainty is not the result of a lost origin that must be reappropriated. On the contrary, Derrida sees it as a liberation from logocentrism's conception of the self and subjectivity in terms of full presence as a fixed centre or an origin. The narrating and narrated subject can be no more grounded in language than self can be in its own narration. For Derrida, then, the self cannot be constructed within either a structural linguistic framework or a humanistic paradigm.

Rousseau, however, conceives of writing as a supplement to the origin, to memory and to all forms of representation. As such, writing is external to full presence and plenitude: it adds without adding. Writing indicates an absence which leads to the full presence of what is represented or presented. It does so by uniting the presenter with the represented. Consequently, Rousseau develops a critique of representation, especially within social and political relations, which does not lead to the origin as presence. He presupposes the existence of an originary self-presence that representation, if it is not to be alienating, must restore in full. The co-present subject is the model for political and social relations that do not allow the evil of representation to take the place of presence as origin. Thus, for Rousseau, the evil of writing befalls the origin (speech) when it allows the representer (writing) to represent what is represented. Therefore, any form of representation (political, social, etc.) that replaces what is to be represented is condemned, because it does not lead to the origin as voice. Writing is condemned only when it appears 'to suspend the voice' (*OG*:

99). Rousseau, like other thinkers, links the voice to full presence, free speech, origin, nature – indeed to anything which effects the return (as the full reappropriation) of the origin as identity.

Rousseau's texts also raise the problematic of the absence of the origin, or of articulation and writing within speech. This can be demonstrated best in Rousseau's treatment of both the supplement and supplementarity in general. His condemnation of writing as a supplement to full voice – as that which threatens the return to the origin, and to nature as a transcendental signified – stands in a paradoxical relationship to his recognition of the importance and necessity of the supplement. For although he recognises and describes the problematic function of supplementarity, he avoids its *aporias* by rendering it external to the origin. Thus, in Rousseau, as in Western metaphysics, writing is thought of as sensible, finite and on the side of 'culture, technique, and artifice; a human procedure, the ruse of a being accidentally incarnated' (*OG*: 15). On the one hand, Rousseau condemns writing for being opposed to Nature: it is the 'dead letter' and 'carrier of death' because it 'exhausts life' (*OG*: 17). In this sense, writing is the falling away from the origin. When speech allows itself to be represented by the presenter (writing), enslavement begins. On the other hand, Rousseau conceives of writing in its 'metaphoric sense' as 'natural', 'divine', 'living', and 'venerated' because 'it is equal in dignity to the origin of value, to the voice of conscience as divine law to the heart, to sentiment, and so forth' (*OG*: 17). For Rousseau, 'metaphoric' writing is natural writing, 'immediately united to the voice and to breath' (*OG*: 17). No longer mere representation, it incarnates that full presence associated with consciousness and feeling. It is the Husserlian hearing-oneself-speak in the true and undivided presence of a conscious inner life. It presupposes the superiority of the sign as expression (voice) to that exteriorisation of the signifier which is writing.

Derrida points out that both Plato and Rousseau distinguish good from bad writing: 'the good and natural is the divine inscription in the heart and the soul; the perverse and artful is technique, exiled in the exteriority of the body' (*OG*: 17). For Rousseau, 'natural writing is immediately united to the voice and to breath. Its nature is not grammatological but pneumatological' (*OG*: 17). Natural writing thus denies its own body and grammatological structure in becoming *Geist*, spirit, or *pneuma*. It is the mark of self-presence as identity, and its exclusion of otherness in speech and language is safeguarded by the nexus between 'voice' and 'full presence'. If writing is to achieve its ultimate goal of ideal objectivity, then it must be a transcription of the natural, divine inscription or breath. The written text must imitate, in an eidetic form, that divine Book of Nature which contains neither artifice nor dissimulation. The meaning and truth of writing derive from, and are fully comprehended by, the Book of Nature conceived of as a totality.

Consequently, it became necessary to externalise the disruptive power and effects of writing rendering them secondary to the 'natural' writing of the soul and the heart. In this sense, writing is merely a mnemotechnic tool, a detour *en route* to that unification of voice and thought which expresses the primary signified. Meaning and voice tautologically relate to one another. Writing loses its own corporeality, and becomes exterior to speech rather than its other. It is prohibited from entering into the play of signification and differences. The relation between memory and writing corresponds to that between writing and the origin. For Rousseau (as for Saussure), writing is but 'a mnemotechnic means' which, 'supplanting good memory, spontaneous memory, signifies forgetfulness' (*OG*: 37). Writing is a menace to living memory, for if forgetfulness could be eliminated, writing would have no use. Writing, then, performs an auxiliary function which, by signifying forgetfulness, paradoxically reasserts and recaptures the immediacy of speech without rupture. That entire system of signification which is grounded on the voice implies that writing – as a representation of voice – contains no discontinuities, ruptures, deferrals or differences that cannot be elevated to the voice and thus resolved. Writing is therefore independent of language as a phonetic system, in as far as it cannot affect either its production or self-identity. For Rousseau, language within speech escapes the violence – the ruses and threat – of writing. The speaking subject can write its own unity without the menace of representation.

As Derrida shows, however, an opening in Rousseau's texts paves the way for writing to emerge as a supplement to speech within a chain of substitutions. Derrida argues that the theme of supplementarity in Rousseau is not simply part of a chain of supplements. Instead, it

> *describes the chain itself, the being-chain of a textual chain, the structure of substitution, the articulation of desire and of language, the logic of all conceptual oppositions taken over by Rousseau*, and particularly the role and the function, in his system, of the concept of Nature. It tells us in a text what a text is, it tells us in writing what writing is (*OG*: 163).

What Rousseau's texts try to efface and suppress therefore escapes total reduction. This concept of the supplement – and especially of writing as supplement – is irreducible on account of the textuality of Rousseau's texts, that is, the very thing he is trying to render external to their meaning. For Derrida, however, those indefinite substitutions which supplementarity implies have 'always already *infiltrated* presence, always already inscribed there the space of repetition and the splitting of the self' (*OG*: 163). That splitting of the self (which is an effect of supplementarity) prevents the self from achieving a self-enclosed identity. Repetition as non-identity becomes internal to the self, making impossible its constitution as the same within presence. Supplementarity, as an endless chain of substitutions, splits the self and its identity by both inhabiting it and making possible its very emergence.

For Rousseau, however, the supplement adds itself from outside to a plenitude which lacks nothing. Obliged to remain external to presence, the supplement thus adds without adding, in so far as it is not permitted to threaten the unity of the subject and of the self in particular. The supplement therefore breaks in only as something dangerous, as 'a *substitute* that *enfeebles, enslaves, effaces, separates*, and *falsifies*' (*OG*: 215). Although Rousseau recognises supplementarity, he denies its effects because his writings and thought are grounded on the principles of Western metaphysics. The true self, according to Rousseau, would experience immediate presence, and would not require the mediation of a supplement which results inevitably in enslavement, separation and falsification. The true self is the self which does not allow the presenter (writing) to take the place of the presented. The supplement is a broaching of the origin which nevertheless can be rendered external to it. The self can be written without the threat of supplementarity. As an external supplement, writing adds nothing to the unity of the subject and the self. Thus although Rousseau conceives of writing as a post-originary malady to language his texts show that 'the space of writing operates at the origin of language' (*OG*: 229).

What Rousseau makes external to the origin, Derrida argues, is already present there:

> man allows himself to be announced to himself after the fact of supplementarity, which is thus not an attribute – accidental or essential – of man. For on the one hand, supplementarity, which *is nothing*, neither a presence nor an absence, is neither a substance nor an opening of this play that no metaphysical or ontological concept can comprehend. Therefore this property [*propre*] of man is not a property

> of man: it is the very dislocation of the proper in general: it is the dislocation of the characteristic, the proper in general, the impossibility – and therefore the desire – of self-proximity; the impossibility and therefore the desire of pure presence (*OG*: 244).

This impossibility, which appears to be the precondition of a desire for self presence, is nevertheless unattainable. Man cannot announce himself to himself without being constituted through a supplementarity, which simultaneously prevents him from announcing himself to himself within the ontological and metaphysical categories of identity and the proper. Any form of writing which claims to present the self – to reveal it in its unmediated and unbroached identity – is as impossible as that which claims the self to be present to itself. For Derrida, the writing of the self is possible only within a structure of supplementarity which simultaneously denies its emergence as identity, as a proper name, and as a writing of truth. Embedded in both language and in writing, the subject becomes part of the structure of *différance* and supplementarity. The self becomes textualised in conditions where beyond and behind the text 'there have never been anything but supplements' (*OG*: 159). Consequently, no univocal authorial voice betokens the existence of either a unitary subject or the self as a hearing-oneself-speak.

There is no proper name, and no presence, but always interval, discontinuity, deferral, and alterity. The self becomes part of that endless chain of nonsynonymous substitutions implied by the structure of supplementarity. In addition, Derrida argues, it is the

> strange essence of the supplement not to have essentiality: it may always not have taken place. Moreover, literally, it has never taken place: it is never present, here and now. If it were, it would not be what it is, a supplement, taking and keeping the place of the other (*OG*: 314).

The supplement escapes temporalization and spatialization conceived of in terms of Being as presence, and the other becomes constitutive of Being. The supplement cannot become an essentialist category, nor can it be hypostasised, since its essence is to have no essence. By escaping empirical historicity and temporal periodisation it thus opens up the possibility of an unlimited freedom. For if the supplement is beyond the usual constraints of metaphysical categories, and is subject to an unlimited play of substitutions, it becomes free of power relations and responsibility as well as of value-oriented or teleological discourses. The idea of the self as a thinking subject ('I') – as an essentialist or even non-essentialist category – cannot be accommodated into this schema. 'Man', himself anchored on a humanistic conception, can no longer announce himself in terms of presence. Instead, he can announce himself only in writing, and only by writing his own erasure. This liberates the self from humanistic-centred conceptions of agency, as well as from the illusion that self can be fully revealed in writing, speech or language in general.

The writing of the self, therefore, cannot be anchored on the principle of identity. Language is always falling short of itself, which is why it needs the supplement at the level of its production-genesis, and thus escape the process of rationalisation. This is the crux of Derrida's critique of the project of Enlightenment. What Derrida also wants to emphasise is the inability of reason to comprehend the logic of the supplement. For him, the supplement 'can only respond to the nonlogical logic of a game. That game is the play of the world' (*OG*: 259). Play is what prevents any closure of the game and the seminal *différance* of meaning. Whereas Nietzsche's notion of play escapes the aetiological question of 'why?', Derrida's is closely connected to his conception of writing as supplement and its connection to presence. He thus critiques Rousseau's inability to conceive of play, arguing that although 'supplementarity is possible' in Rousseau, 'nothing has yet come into play' (*OG*: 263): Rousseau's notion of the festival, for instance, 'excludes play' (*OG*: 263). Meaning is thus situated outside play. For Rousseau, representation and supplement take place 'within the horizon of an infinite restitution of presence' (*OG*: 298). Representation becomes external to the origin, a mere addition, a contingency which avoids the trace of the supplement.

The supplement and supplementarity are constituted by that 'play of presence and absence' whose 'opening . . . no metaphysical or ontological concept can comprehend' (*OG*: 244). Dissociated from any ontological grounding, the 'limitlessness of play' marks that 'absence of the transcendental signified' which entails 'the destruction of ontotheology and the metaphysics of presence' (*OG*: 50). Play informs not only Derrida's concept of the supplement but also his concept of writing and trace. Supplementarity becomes the very condition for the opening of play and meaning; as such, it negates both meaning (as full presence) and the closure (of the game). 'All meaning and therefore all discourse is caught' in what Derrida terms the 'graphic of supplementarity' (*OG*: 246). Furthermore,

> all concepts determining a non-supplementarity (nature, animality, primitivism, childhood, madness, divinity, etc.) have evidently no truth-value. They belong – moreover, with the idea of truth itself- to an epoch of supplementarity. They have meaning only within a closure of the game (*OG*: 245).

Thus, such concepts are relegated to a process of meaning-production that relies upon the closure of the game through the exclusion of supplementarity. As writing comes to be perceived 'more and more as another name for this structure of supplementarity' (*OG*: 245), supplementarity and play consequently become constitutive of writing. No signified can escape 'the play of signifying references that constitute language' because 'the advent of writing is the advent of this play' (*OG*: 7). Since writing is present at the origin of this play – although without constituting its origin – writing is inevitably part of the play.

Derrida also uses his concept of play to attack reason. 'The graphic of supplementarity is irreducible to logic', he argues, 'primarily because it comprehends logic as one of its *cases* and may alone produce its origin'. Furthermore, because the '*supplementary possibility is inconceivable to reason* . . . the supplement can only respond to the nonlogical logic of a game' (*OG*: 259). Play is therefore constitutive of language, reason, and truth because it is there at the origin. In Derrida's radical view of it, the origin, whose structure can be expressed in writing, is what 'conceals and erases itself in its own production' (*OG*: 7). That origin which can be written under erasure makes full reappropriation of the origin an impossibility. For the origin cannot institute itself as such, nor can it be a governing principle whose authority and authenticity are unchallengeable. Consequently, the voice cannot be the origin and governing principle of writing. Writing thus becomes 'the name of two absences' (*OG*: 41), the signatory and the referent. In other words, writing involves the loss or absence not only of that self-identical subject who authenticates the text by signing, but also of the externality of the referent that writing would merely bring to representation.

This absence, however, does not result in a loss of force, because the trace is an 'opaque energy' which '*no concept of metaphysics can describe*' (*OG*: 65). Although the trace is anterior to all concepts of Western metaphysics, the past which it contains is no longer signified by the present past. This is because Derrida introduces the notion of spacing into the concepts of present, past and future. 'Spacing' articulates both space and time: it is 'the becoming-space of time and the becoming-time of space' which, in turn, is 'always the unperceived, the nonpresent, and the nonconscious' (*OG*: 68). Presence thus contains what it cannot articulate and present. It is always contaminated by what cannot be perceived, presented or become conscious, and by what cannot be subsumed under the logic of the reappropriation of an authentic self-presence. Conceived of in terms of writing, spacing is 'the becoming-absent and the becoming-unconscious of the subject' (*OG*: 69). Writing negates the construction of the subject as both self-consciousness and self-presence. Derrida's project is thus to dislocate what he calls the 'metaphysics of presence or conscious subjectivity' (*OG*: 68).

As an active movement and demotivation of the sign, the trace is also a starting-point for Derrida's conception of the Other. For Derrida, the trace is

> where the relationship with the other is marked, [and] articulates its possibility in the entire field of the entity . . . which metaphysics has defined as the being-present starting from the occulted movement of the trace. The trace must be thought before the entity. But the movement of the trace is necessarily occulted, it produces itself as self-occultation. When the other announces itself as such, it presents itself in the dissimulation of itself (*OG*: 47).

The possibility and emergence of the other cannot be conceived without the movement of the trace and its anteriority to any entity. The movement of the trace marks and opens the relationship to the other. Yet the trace, by an account of its self-occultation, cannot be defined, nor can it give us the wholly other. The other presents itself as dissimulation of itself, and never allows itself to be constructed in terms of identity. Both the self and its relationship to the other are marked by the structure of the trace, which prevents a definitive conception or contextualization of the self and/or other. Derrida argues that

> the field of the entity, before being determined as the field of presence, is structured according to the diverse possibilities – genetic and structural – of the trace. The presentation of the other as such, that is to say the dissimulation of the 'as such,' has always already begun and no structure of the entity escapes it (*OG*: 47).

Rousseau wants to attribute to writing an origin which is not only empirical-historical but also pure and constant. He does not admit that empirical or historical conditions can change the essence of the origin as full presence. Writing connects itself to an origin which is a mute sign, a sign which does not need writing in order to constitute its truth and meaning. By deconstructing Rousseau's texts, Derrida arrives at the idea that the supplement is constitutive of the origin. Rousseau maintains the idea of the origin as presence by designating imitation, representation, repetition, and writing as mere addition which adding nothing – which cannot be substituted for the origin, or be auxiliaries for its reappropriation. By making all these features internal to the origin, Derrida arrives at the idea of the origin as the supplement of a supplement. He thus does away with the origin (in Rousseau's sense) by anchoring the supplement to a non-originary origin. Representation, imitation, repetition, supplementarity are already present at the origin. It becomes impossible to write the self without grounding it in an origin that admits all that the structure of supplementarity implies. The written work, and writing in general, become part of the process of disguising the origin. But for Derrida, I have argued, the origin 'is possible and conceivable only in disguise' (*WD*: 8). Whereas Rousseau expels the supplement from the origin, for Derrida the supplement becomes the non-origin of the origin. Like *différance*, it simultaneously constitutes and erases the origin, and thus renders any return to the origin as yet another failed attempt by Western metaphysics to adopt the logic of supplementarity.

Because it is structured by supplementarity, writing denies the nostalgic return to an origin and to a plenitude of meaning from which its lacunae are eliminated. No interpretation or meaning attributed to the text can be anything more than a supplement in the chain of supplements which can be substituted by other supplements, without ever reaching a plenitude that requires no further supplement. Nothing – not even the silence of a prayer – escapes that supplementarity. The mute sign, language, subject and self are always already subject to the trace, supplement and play. Returning to the origin is impossible, since the origin itself is but a supplement. In his analyses of Husserl in the *Origin of Geometry*, Derrida argues that 'the problematic of writing was already in place as such, bound to the irreducible structure of "deferral" in its relationships to consciousness, presence, science, history and the history of science, the disappearance or delay of the origin, etc.' (*POS*: 5). Here again the problematic of writing serves to deconstruct both consciousness (by admitting otherness) and also presence (by admitting repetition and representation within presence). In short, Derrida deconstructs the idea of the origin by admitting substitution within the origin. Consequently, he cannot deal with that conception of the subject which has been conceived of and constructed in terms he himself has already deconstructed. For supplement and play are concepts that free not only writing and language but also the self from the notion of origin as a full presence devoid of representation, dissimulation, doubling, forgetfulness, imitation and disguise. Being itself beyond 'good and evil', writing is thus liberated from those evaluative and ethico-moral considerations which seriously challenge the later Derrida's more fully-rounded considerations of both the other and responsibility.

Derrida's deconstruction of writings by Condillac, Rousseau and Lévi-Strauss demonstrate the alterity in the origin to which concepts such as supplementarity, play and the trace refer incessantly. The alterity that Derrida develops is one that puts the accent on the aesthetico-political aspects of indeterminacy and is, therefore, oriented to the deconstruction of the aesthetico-political construction of authenticity and the critique of representation associated with romanticism. Difference, as a non-originary origin, is a playful difference. It is 'the joker' as the indeterminate card that holds the key to the play. The concept of 'nature' – whether internal or external – cannot function as the final determinant of the authentic. The subject can no longer be conceptualised as either authentic or inauthentic because it is a product of the 'joker', that is, of the play of difference and the trace. It is this orientation that is mainly responsible for the partly justifiable critique that the early Derridean notion of the other lacked an ethico-political dimension or, more accurately, gave rise to an ethics and politics grounded in a Nietzschean concept of aesthetic transgression. This critique, for which Derrida has partly held himself responsible, is made amends for in his later work, where the ever present reference to Levinas becomes even more insistent.

3.6 Concluding remarks

In Derrida, desire is freed from its locus in the subject even as something unconscious. There is little room for a narrative construction of the self that can reclaim even a differentiated or multiple identity. The gendered construction of desire that Freud, Lacan and Irigaray, among others have developed, is not part of Derridean deconstruction. Derrida's concept of desire is very radical in its construction not only because it is subjectless and disembodied, but also because it cannot be contained within language and/or writing or any other teleology or ontology. Of course feminists already have criticized Derrida for ignoring the category of the woman or refusing to consider the feminine (Irigaray, 1985). These are all subjectivist categories and since Derrida's anti-subjectivism underpins his thought these are not concerns that can be accommodated within his thought in the terms that much of the feminist debates wish to pursue (see Irwin, 2010; Grosz, 2005; Birmingham, 1997; Holland, 1997; Feder et al, 1997).

The attempt by Peg Birmingham to inject the feminine into Derrida's thought relies on the idea of fiction. She argues that Derrida has moved towards 'an understanding of "fiction" as the engendering activity of sexual difference' (Birmingham, 1997:145). She avoids the charge of the embodied, self-present subject by making the feminine not only a fiction, but a shadow and an erotic excess without abandoning sexual difference which 'occasions the singular and the unique' (Birmingham, 1997: 145). So for her 'the imperative of desire is not the call of the Other still positioned at the margin, but rather the imperative to respond to the *upsurge* of the singular' (Birmingham, 1997: 145). However, in Derrida the concept of the Other, and its relation to sexual difference, is far more complex than this statement would suggest, especially when considering the last phase of his work (see chapter 7 and 8). The other is certainly not positioned in the margin but is a central element of his thought. Moreover, Derrida's concept of desire comes out of his deconstruction of Condillac. It is through a careful analysis of his concept of desire and its connection to identity and subjectivity that we can arrive at a more germane critique of Derrida.

The political and ethical dimensions of Derrida's deconstructions present numerous challenges, with some scholars even doubting the existence of deconstruction, exemplified by Wolfreys' often repeated refrain 'deconstruction (if such a thing exists)' (Wolfreys, 1998: 185). Howells in her book *Derrida: Deconstruction from Phenomenology to Ethics* maintains that 'Derrida's first major discussion of ethical issues' can be located in his first encounter with Levinas in his 1964 essay 'Violence and Metaphysics' (Howells, 1999: 123). She rightly points out that the concept of the subject is vital for understanding the ethics and politics of deconstruction (Howells, 1999: 130). However, she links the deconstruction of the subject to the question of ethics more than politics, while maintaining that Derrida's conception of the subject 'appears closer to the *non*-subject of structuralist discourse than to a radically deconstructed subject' (Howells, 1999: 135). This reading again underemphasizes Derrida's thinking on the subject and the question of the other and their connection to politics and ethics.

Other scholars adopt a non-critical approach to Derrida's thought. To take an example, among many, Thomas Keenan argues that '[e]thics and politics – as well as literature – are evaded when we fall back on the conceptual priority of the subject, agency or identity as the grounds of our action' (Keenan, 1997: 3). He asserts that '[t]he experience of literature, ethics, and politics, such as it is (and it cannot be the experience of a subject), emerges only in the withdrawal of these foundations' (Keenan, 1997: 3). Eliminating the subject from politics and ethics is often associated with Derrida's thought, but one needs to retrace Derrida's own development on these issues. Although it would be correct to state that Derrida 'eliminates' the subject, he does so within a theoretical and philosophical framework that tries to maintain questions of ethics and politics at the core of his thought. This he achieves through his pre-ontological concept of the other which becomes an integral part of any radical reformulation of politics and ethics and any deconstruction of the subject. I would like to argue that from the very beginning Derrida's deconstructions of what he saw as subjectivistic categories of Western Metaphysics, had implications for his notions of politics and ethics, especially those connected to identity.

To conclude, Derrida's encounters with Rousseau and Rousseaunism are important for understanding his political and ethical concerns as well as his reluctance to anchor the subject on notions of self-identity, authenticity and presence. Memory becomes a non-subjectivist category, which is incessantly inscribed by both *Lethe* and *Mneme*. It is this play of memory and forgetfulness that escapes writing and contaminates the authentic. The politics and the ethics of authenticity cannot be instituted within the deconstructive paradigm. The appeal to an immutable principle or origin that underpins political institutions and representative democracies is a negative, empty gesture. The authority of the individualist and the collective subject is disconnected from the politics of representation. Likewise the unity of the self cannot be achieved by eliminating the supplement. There is no return to an origin, authenticity or inner self.

The politics of deconstruction are not those of representation, and are disconnected from the idea of the co-present subjects. This de-subjectivization of politics radically alters our ideas of Western politics, which are a politics of representation. The Athenian model of co-present, self-present subjects who participate in the politics of the polis is based on an ethics and a politics of representation. Engaging in the political process is a horizontal rather than a vertical exchange and interchange. Mutuality and reciprocity are integral to this process and the irreducible alterity of the other does not need the desubjectivization of politics. The body politic becomes the origin and the source of authority and represents a kind of political power that can be always re-appropriated through the conscious, intentional acts of political actors. Contrary to this model, Derrida's politics are the politics of a democracy *to come* and his ethics is based on the other which is unconnected to notions of identity.

Derrida in his deconstruction of Rousseau radically questions the politics of presence and representation, which rely on primary, unmodifiable presence. Mimesis, representation and re-presentation as referring back to an origin that can be fully reappropriated are simply ways of dealing with the threat of supplement and its uncontainable effects. Within Derrida's schema any subjectivist conception of politics that claims to overcome re-presentation and refers to some kind of an authentic, autonomous polity is but a mirage of the logocentric paradigms of Western metaphysics. Within Derrida's thought we can have the politics and ethics of the supplement (simulation), or in his later works specter, which move away from naïve representationalism and authentic subjectivity or polity. These 'new' politics present us with a hint of Derrida's later preoccupation with spirit, spectre, memory, time and vision that splinter all attempts of representation resting on notions of self-presence. The politics of alterity and difference are the Derridean alternative to the politics of presence.

However, one has to seriously question the nebulous concepts of the supplement, other, specter and spirit as alternatives to co-present subjects engaged as political actors within a defined body politic. Its radicality might be the double-edged sword of empty, simulated politics where ethics comes from the external power of the other rather than the endless *askesis* that autonomy requires. In an age of doubtful political agendas and global imperatives Derrida's gesture is grand and one can anchor on it the immanence of anything. This may or may not be as radical as its claims suggest.

4. Beyond the Subject – 2: 'Passages and Departures Towards the Other'

Derrida's conception of the subject, I have argued, is closely bound up with his deconstruction of Western metaphysics' conception of the other. His radicalisation of the concept of Being results in such concepts as trace, receptacle, elusion, dissimulation, letting be, and the subject's staging of its own disappearance. Being is no longer conceived of as sameness; instead, otherness becomes constitutive of and immanent in Being. The differential structure of Being makes thinking possible. Being is conceived of not as the opposite of non-Being, but in terms of a pre-originary and non-oppositional structure of Being and non-Being. By abandoning the philosophy of origins and its search for first principles, Derrida's concept of Being opens up the problematic of the other, and thus goes beyond previous philosophies of Being.

Within this philosophical and theoretical schema, opened up initially by Heidegger, the problematic of the subject is raised. Heidegger's critique of the voluntarism of the Western concept of the subject is reformulated by Derrida in terms of a critique of self-referential presence. As the absolute and certain foundation of knowledge, the modern subject is modelled on the notion of the voice that hears itself speak. This is why Derrida began by deconstructing phenomenology, the last great philosophical attempt to make the subject the bearer of meaning. Derrida moves away from notions of the subject constructed in terms of consciousness, because it cannot think either other consciousnesses (*autrui*) or alterity (*autre*). Because of its differential structure, writing is used as a critical paradigm for rethinking the other and otherness. Speech, with its seemingly spontaneous unification of intention and utterance, is rejected: only writing 'erases the presence of the self-same [*propre*] within speech' (*OG*: 270). For Derrida, subjectivity is not so much constructed as taken to be part of the effects of *différance*. *Différance* makes it impossible to formulate a notion of the 'subject' in terms of an essential self-sameness that excludes difference and deferral. In Derrida's interpretation of Western metaphysics, the self-as-'I' can be neither conceived of nor written outside the matrix of identity and identitarian philosophy. Deconstruction shows what remains out of this account by demonstrating where Western philosophy lapses into performative contradictions on account of its inability to effect systemic closure on the basis of a principle of subjectivity. What is left out is irreducible alterity, which Derrida wants to conceive of in both epistemological and ethical terms.

Fundamental to Derrida's deconstruction of the subject is his conviction that the other is outside those categories traditionally associated with it, such as identity, self, agency and consciousness. The subject is not so much reconceptualised as both textualised and decontextualised. It is textualised in so far as writing serves as the frame within which the 'subject' is thought. But because the iterative structure of difference is determined quasi-transcendentally rather than historically located, it is also decontextualised. Derrida's attempted explanation of deconstruction illuminates his insistence that agency and subjectivity are inadequate concepts. Deconstruction, he explains, is not reducible to

> a set of rules and transposable procedures . . . It must be made clear that deconstruction is not even an *act* or an *operation*. Not only because there would be something 'patient' or 'passive' about it . . . Not only because it does not return to an individual or collective *subject* who would take the initiative and apply it to an object, a text, a theme, etc. Deconstruction takes place, it is an event that does not await the deliberation, consciousness, or organisation of a subject, or even of modernity. *It deconstructs it-self. It can be deconstructed* (*DR*: 273–274).

Because deconstruction appears to be an impersonal and reflexive mode, the use of a third-person impersonal reflexive clearly suggests that the connection between the subject and reflexivity (and in particular between the 'I' and the reflexive form of the pronoun) is lost. The subject has staged its own disappearance, and the possibility of individual or collective subjectivity is denied. Although the hypostatising of both individual or collective subjects is something to be avoided, Derrida's quasi-transcendental theory of deconstruction as an event side-steps important philosophical, political and ethical dilemmas. If Husserl's concept of consciousness was thinkable without a body, Derridean deconstruction is thinkable without a (conscious) subject. The subject as source of an operation or action cannot initiate the event of deconstruction. The deconstruction of the subject is part of the 'event' of deconstruction.

Several important questions arise from such a philosophical position. How is the problematic of the subject posited? What then replaces the subject? Is the subject as identity deconstructed or 'dismantled'? Can the subject be written or inscribed within deconstruction, and if so how? Can the subject be conceived of outside the category of self-consciousness as self-referential presence? If consciousness is an inadequate paradigm for grasping the 'subject', must we remain within this tradition even as we deconstruct it? Or rather, is it not possible to think the 'subject' and 'identity' in different terms? In order to establish a critical counterpoint to Derrida's deconstruction, I want to discuss three different conceptualisations of the problematic: a psycho-analytically derived concept of identity as autonomy; a narrative conception of identity that stems from the hermeneutical tradition; and finally, an inter-subjectively located concept of identity that stems from a re-working of the Hegelian concept of recognition.

4.1 Outside the subject

A concept of the subject based on a revised notion of identity cannot be thematised in Derrida's thought. What can be thematised is the other, which by inscribing the subject within a matrix of non-oppositional differences, prevents both the subject and the self from emerging as identity or absolute self-sameness. The other becomes that which traverses, mediates and constitutes any notion of subjectivity – the *a priori* of the notion of the subject in all its modalities. Subjectivity is linked inextricably with the notions of trace, *différance* and writing, all of which are anterior to its constitution and a precondition of its emergence. The subject *qua* identity disappears. The metaphysics of subjectivity become the source of almost all ills of any thought based on the notion of Being as presence. What one needs, Derrida argues, is a new type of radical and liberating thinking, which does not rely on the metaphysics of subjectivity and its well-worn dichotomies of Same/Other, Life/Death, Conscious/Unconscious, Animal/Human etc. This thought is based on a notion of the other which is charged with overcoming that repressive and problematic metaphysics of subjectivity which treats the subject (in all its modalities) as the undisputed locus of identity, and does so at the expense of alterity. The question of the ethical dimension of the other will be taken up in the next two chapters. Here I shall focus on the epistemological dimension of the other in relation to that one-sided conceptualisation of the subject with which deconstruction operates.

Derrida seeks a post-subjectivist mode of thinking, based on the deconstruction of identity and the idea of self, which he sees as dominated by such terms as the Same and the One. In his reading of Levinas, he sympathises with the construction of a kind of thought variously described as 'an *exhalation* . . . a prophetic speech' (*WD*: 82) and a 'messianic eschatology' (*WD*: 83). Instead of merely relating the thought of the other to an explicitly theological framework, Derrida draws attention to an 'empirical' turn in Levinas's philosophy. The type of thought toward which Levinas moves, he argues,

> seeks to be understood from within a *recourse to experience itself.* Experience itself and that which is most irreducible within experience: the passage and departure toward the other; the other itself as what is most irreducibly other within it: Others' (*WD*: 83).

At this stage of his intellectual development, Derrida is reluctant to follow Levinas towards an 'exceeded philosophy' (*WD*: 83), which he defines as 'the opening of opening, that which can be enclosed within no category or totality, that is, everything within experience which can no longer be described by traditional concepts, and which resists every philosopheme' (*WD*: 83). Derrida is prepared only to point towards such an opening 'faintly and from afar' (*WD*: 84).

Because deconstruction prevails over meta-philosophy in his early work, Derrida has often been charged with nihilism. But seeing that the gestural or figurational component of his philosophy becomes more insistent in his later work, charges of nihilism become, as a consequence, increasingly redundant. For Derrida, as for Nietzsche, what renders modern thought nihilistic is precisely its subjectivism. Subjectivism also makes any easy recourse to theology impossible without conceptual regression. For Levinas, the solution is a quasi-empirical philosophy of the other, into which theological baggage can be smuggled. For Wittgenstein, the solution was silence, because although the remaining logico-mathematical problems could be solved the essential ones could never be. Derrida's solution is different again. Deconstruction recognises that there is no simple way of escaping from occidental thought, even as it recognises the totalising and contradictory project of this thought. By tracking these points at which Western thought reaches its limits and becomes 'unbuttoned', Derrida speculates (if only negatively) on how thought might exist outside the subject (*hors sujet*).

The consequences of such an idea are many. But for the purposes of this study I would like to emphasise that the more Derrida gestures towards what is 'outside the subject', the more one-sided his understanding of the Western conceptions of the subject becomes. The work of Charles Taylor on the multi-dimensional character of the Western concept of identity shows clearly the limitations of Derrida's perspective. For Taylor modernity suffers from a loss of frameworks. The culprits here are subjectivism and naturalism. Without such frameworks, modern identity lacks a broader context within which to construct itself, and thus loses both sense and moral sense *tout court*. What are these frameworks? According to Taylor, they go far beyond any minimalist list of basic values, although it is equally clear that they must include respect for life, and integrity. Such values are not rich enough, however, to shape a coherent sense of self. Frameworks proper contain those 'strong evaluations' which shape our sense of selfhood and identity. 'My identity', writes Taylor,

> is defined by the commitments and identifications which provide the frame or horizon within which I can try to determine from case to case what is good, or valuable, or what ought to be done, or what I endorse or oppose. In other words, it is the horizon within which I am capable of taking a stand (Taylor, 1989: 27).

This leads Taylor to the somewhat controversial conclusion that the affirmation of difference in terms of choice of sexual orientation is trivial, and typical of that relativism which modern subjectivism brought into being. A non-trivial (or, to use the term that Taylor risks, 'authentic') self is characterised by 'demands that emanate from beyond the self' (Taylor, 1991: 41) – a phrase with clearly theological resonances.

This phrase also signals partial agreement with Derrida's Levinas-inspired remarks about a 'passage and departure toward the other'. Both phrases clearly reject the subjectivism of the Western tradition, and (as I shall argue later) equally clearly have a recourse to theology. What separates them is the lynch-pin of Taylor's argument: Taylor uses historical contextualisation to identify the multiple sources of those 'demands'.

This contrasts with Derrida's corresponding reliance on the Judaic tradition. For Taylor, the modern Western conception of identity has three sources, that is, three inescapable horizons or frameworks that constitute the moral languages from which those 'demands' that fashion the self can emerge. One source is the Platonic conception of the good, and the attendant notion of rational self-mastery, which develops into the Augustinian concept of interiority in Western Christianity before becoming 'epistemologised' by Descartes at the onset of modernity. The second source originates in the seventeenth century with the Protestant affirmation of ordinary life, and the third in that expressivist revolt against Enlightenment which became known in the nineteenth century as Romanticism. Indeed, Taylor sees that conflict between Romanticism and Enlightenment as 'the great intramural debate of the last two centuries' (Taylor, 1989: 101). All three sources provide that reservoir of moral languages with which the modern self can shape itself in accordance with 'demands that emanate from beyond the self'.

It is clear that Derrida regards rationalist language (and the attendant rationalist concept of the subject) as the sole source of modern reason and the modern self. In this respect, his reading of Western philosophy is completely in line with Heidegger's unilateral account of the history of Being as the history of its subjectivisation. Missing from both accounts, however, is precisely the richness and complexity of the Western tradition. As Taylor rightly remarks, both fall into the Romantic expressivist current of contemporary Western thought. Taylor errs, however, in seeing Derrida as doing 'nothing but deconstruction', and in 'occluding what is spiritually arresting in this whole movement of contemporary culture', namely Romanticism (Taylor, 1989: 490). It may be suggested that Taylor errs here because he himself is blind to the non-Western sources of both modern culture and the modern self which he subsumes habitually under the label of 'Romantic expressivism'. Taylor's strongly theist theological preferences thus fail to register the Judaic resonances in Derrida's appropriation of Levinas. As a result, although both point towards what is beyond the self, Taylor emphasises 'interiorisation' and 'the things that matter', and not the Derridean problematic of 'otherness'.

4.2 The questioning of the 'proper'

In conceiving of writing as both inside and outside language, Derrida is able to open the space of the other, and thus treat the self as always written, spoken and re-presented as other. This emphasis on a particular inflection of the 'linguistic turn', however, cannot result in the notion of the subject (and more specifically of the self) being abandoned. Derrida poses the question of the other as an inability to write the self as self-enclosed identity. But he does not thematise related questions, such as autonomy of the self (Kant, 1956; Castoriadis, 1991), 'oneself as another' (Ricœur, 1992), and recognition (Hegel, 1979; Taylor, 1992; Honneth, 1995). In attempting to rehabilitate writing within Western metaphysics, Derrida valorises the other over the same, and collapses the self into the other. As irreducible difference, the other becomes the source of both ethico-moral interdiction and the 'alteration of identity and of identification with the other' (*OG*: 206). 'Identity' becomes the recognition of, and the identification with, the other. The writing of the self is achieved by dislocating identity and erasing selfhood. Consequently, the writing of the self as an autobiographical subject becomes part of the problematic of proto-writing, and can be achieved only in the name of the other and in the place of the other.

Writing becomes the concept which safeguards alterity and enables the other to emerge in all its modalities. 'To recognise writing in speech, is to begin to think the lure', Derrida argues. 'There is no ethics without the presence *of the other* but, also, and consequently, without absence, dissimulation, detour, differance, writing' (*OG*: 139–140). As I will show in the next two chapters, the other has an ethico-moral dimension which is connected to the deconstruction of the concept of spirit as well as to notions of promise and avowal. The construction and emergence of the other becomes independent of such categories in the philosophy of consciousness as the 'I' and the self. It is thus possible to radicalise the subject as conceived of in traditional categories such as reflexivity and agency. The categories Derrida employs to deal with the question of subjectivity 'breach' the Cartesian, Empirical, Structuralist, Romantic and Heideggerian constructions of the subject. Derrida intends to institute in their place a number of non-concepts, which operate outside or against any conception of the subject as identity. In short, he proposes concepts which are irreducible to the categories of the subject as constructed within Western metaphysics. By inscribing us 'before' language, the notion of promise escapes the demand for presence, and thus avoids that problematic relationship with the other which is the legacy of a philosophy based on self-referential presence. Derrida's concepts of avowal and 'spirit' as 'flame' are similarly irreducible to the categories of Western metaphysics.

Not only linguistic and psychological constructions of the subject but also interpretative paradigms prevalent within such fields as literature, culture and the law need to be deconstructed. Within this philosophical framework, the subject cannot act as an *arche* or *telos* of either speech or writing, nor can it engineer the closure or suppression of what Derrida calls the effects of *différance*. Questions of origin, authorship, addressor, addressee, destination, destiny, inheritance, truth, meaning, memory, imagination, desire, need, authenticity, centre, relationship of cause and effect, linear chronology, representation, and presentation are all linked by Derrida to the conception of the subject as self-referential presence. As constructed within Western metaphysics, they all rely on an affirmation of the subject as identity. The subject as 'I' is based on the idea of the same and is constructed by the binary opposition same/other, where 'other' signifies the neutral, submissive, weak, and dependent part of the hierarchical dualism. In this sense, the other can be constructed only in terms of the subject conceived of as identity: thus externalised and subordinated, the other has no constitutive power independent of the subject. Derrida aims to institute a structure of alterity which is 'even more irreducible than the alterity attributed to opposition' (*CP*: 283).

He argues that both the written and the speaking subject stage their own disappearance and absence. Any notion that the author is either the proprietor of speech or writing or the origin of the work becomes untenable. So too does the idea that the addressor and the addressee are respectively the origin and destination in a trajectory of speech or writing which leads from one subject to the other. It cannot be sustained because it is based on ideas of origin and destination which cannot accommodate the possibility of loss and theft. For Derrida, as soon as the 'I' speaks, it cannot hear itself do so without what he terms 'elusion':

> elusion is produced as the original *enigma*, that is to say, as the speech or history (*aimos*) which hides its origin and meaning: it never says where it is going, nor

> where it is coming from, primarily because it does not know where it is coming from or going to, because this not knowing, to wit, the absence of its own subject, is not subsequent to this enigma but, rather, constitutes it. Elusion is the initial unity of that which afterward is diffracted into theft and dissimulation (*WD*: 178).

Because knowledge is grounded on the principles of *arche* and *telos*, cause and effect, origin and destination – as well as on the production of meaning from these notions – they cannot be instituted within deconstruction. Both origin and meaning are hidden, and in their constitution as such they are diffracted endlessly into theft and dissimulation. Instead of uncovering or hinging on to the notion of subject, meaning becomes a quest for the original enigma of its constitution. The subject is dispersed and simulated by processes which endlessly defer its impossible construction as identity. For Derrida,

> the speaking subject is no longer the person himself, or the person alone, who speaks. The speaking subject discovers his irreducible secondarity, his origin that is always eluded; for the origin is always already eluded on the basis of an organised field of speech in which the speaking subject vainly seeks a place that is always missing (*WD*: 178).

Derrida accords the speaking subject no origin – not because it cannot be appropriated, but because it is always missing. The subject therefore cannot return to or be grounded in an origin. The subject's irreducible secondarity is connected to speech, that is, to the very act which accords it presence in the Western philosophical tradition. Moreover, the speaking subject discovers that its own secondariness is irreducible, and that the subject-as-'I' cannot become the locus of a unitary identity. Because both the narrating subject and the narrating self are already textualised, they erase themselves as origin in the very act of narrating.

Furthermore, that organised field which Derrida also speaks about cannot be understood in terms of linguistics or psychology, since neither the subject nor language can be anchored on the idea of the psyche as an originary structure or principle. Language itself, for Derrida, also has the structure of theft, and as such 'already lodges (itself in) the relation of speech to language' (*WD*: 178). 'Speech is stolen', he writes:

> since it is stolen from language it is, thus, stolen from itself, that is, from the thief who has always already lost speech as property and initiative. Because its fore-

> thought cannot be predicted, the act of reading perforates the act of speaking or writing. And through this perforation, this hole, I escape myself (*WD*: 178).

Seeing that the acts of speaking, reading and writing effect the disappearance of the subject, it cannot be reappropriated or reconstituted through those acts. As Derrida concludes, the fact

> that speech and writing are always unavoidably taken from a reading is the form of the original theft, the most archaic elusion, which simultaneously hides me and *purloins* my powers of inauguration. The mind *purloins*. The *letter*, inscribed or propounded speech, is always stolen. Always stolen because it is always *open*. It never belongs to its author or to its addressee, and by nature, it never follows the trajectory that leads from subject to subject (*WD*: 178).

Derrida therefore acknowledges that the signifier, being autonomous, is independent of both the subject and intersubjectivity. Consequently, the notion of the author – as a proper name, and as an exclusive proprietor of speech or writing – is rejected. Speaking, writing and interpretation are all perforated by the very act of reading, that is, by repetitions which admit alterity. Structured like theft, language both conceals and prevents the subject from repeating its inaugural act as sameness and without alterity. By making language itself subject to the 'most archaic elusion', Derrida attempts to free subjectivity from linguistic constructions of it.

Husserlian phenomenology, Condillac's analogical relation to the other, Rousseau's origin, Plato's *mneme* and structuralism's authenticity all conceive of subjectivity and the self as mediated linguistically. The living voice, *phone,* comes to reassert the identity of the subject and safeguard it against the ruses of writing, albeit in different ways: there is always an immutable core that repeats itself without alterity. For Derrida, by contrast, the narrated self is embedded in the differential structure of repetition – that is, proto-writing – and as such cannot constitute itself as identity through narrative. Not even a discourse on invention can establish a structure for an event which secures its present or future singularity within what Derrida calls the economy of the same. Instead, such a discourse 'would be stating the inventive beginning by speaking of itself, in a reflexive structure that not only does not produce coincidence with or presence to itself, but which instead projects the advent of the self, of the "speaking" or "writing" of itself as other, that is to say, *in the manner of the trace*' (Derrida in Attridge, 1991: 317–318). In this schema, no discourse of the self can establish itself within the modality of identity. The self writes and speaks of itself as other, and the concept of trace dissolves the division between writer and speaker.

This is even more evident in *The Post Card* where by making Plato dictate to Socrates, Derrida questions traditional conceptions of Plato as the one who writes and Socrates as the one who does not. He also critiques Heidegger's conception of being as a gift, and questions writing's various connections – with destination and arrival, voice and return, message and authenticity, relay and sender, addressor and addressee, addressee and destination, receiver and inheritance – which he sees as depending on *subjectivist* thinking. Derrida attempts to break down the nexus between writing and subjectivity by supplanting the transitive question ('who writes?') with the intransitive question ('to whom does one write?'), which for him 'amounts to the same, to the other finally' (*CP*: 17). 'To whom one writes' is encapsulated in the concept of the other: because one always writes to the other and the place of the other, this informs what is written.

Derrida poses the question 'of a relation to oneself as a relation to the other' in a form that frees writing from its dependence on the categories of subjectivity and authorship (*CP*: 403). The notion of authorial responsibility is connected to the other and not to the subject-author as an individual 'I' or self. Consequently, the question of the relationship between writing and self yields to that between self and other. Disconnected from the writer as subject and self-identity, writing ceases to be his or her property. 'When I write, right here, on these innumerable post cards,' Derrida asserts, 'I annihilate not only what I am saying but also the unique addressee that I constitute, and therefore every possible addressee, and every destination' (*CP*: 33). Because the text refers to itself, it cannot act as a referent for either the author or the addressee. It does not '*destin*' itself; instead, its structure is one of '*adestination*'. In his critique of Lacan's interpretation of Poe's *The Purloined Letter,* Derrida replaces the notions of narrator and author with those of inscriber and inscribing, which he views as 'original functions that are not to be confused with either the author or his actions, or with the narrator and his narration, and even less with the particular object, the narrated content' (*CP*: 431). By excluding the subject-author and decontextualising the narrated content, Derrida wants to take account of the remainder (as that 'which can fall'), and to 'do so not only in the narrated content of the writing (the signifier, the written, the letter), but in the operation of writing' (*CP*: 436). He is interested in problems of framing, bordering, signature, parergon and the delimitation of narrative, all of which are 'invisible but structurally irreducible' (*CP*: 431) to logocentric categories. These not only prevent the construction of truth as adequation, re-adequation and revelation, but also 'problematise' the concept of the proper and restitution.

Derrida also uses the concepts of the post card, *envoi* and *facteur* to overturn and invert traditional relations, and to allegorise 'the catastrophic unknown of the order' (*CP*: 21). Once the sequential model of chronological order (which depends on the idea of *arche* and *telos*) is overturned, then so too by implication is the importance attached to what is before and what is after. Various concepts which rely on a sequential, chronological, philosophical, communication and linguistic model – the subject as 'I', lineage, writer, speaker, reader, sender, receiver, addresser, addressee, of destination, etc. – become part of what Derrida calls 'posts', which are moments or effects of '*restance*'. In other words, no point functions as a marker of fixity and certainty in any textual operation: there is always a differential relay. Derrida rejects most strongly the connection between addresser-addressee and destination. Having no addressee, writing and speech never arrive at that ultimate destination which is the *telos* and fulfilment of their own destiny. The points of emission, destination and arrival of any communication are relativised and deconstructed. Writing remains like a post card, part of the 'post', the mode of an endless relay with no fixed topology, chronology or sequence, and no self-present subject. The 'condition for it to arrive is that it ends up and even that it begins by not arriving. This is how it is to be read, and written, the *carte* of adestination' (*CP*: 29). There is always the possibility of non-arrival, delay, jams, interception – what Derrida calls the 'fatal necessity of going astray' (*CP*: 66).

Derrida uses the concept of 'envoi' to criticise Heidegger's conception of both destiny and Being as gift. He argues that because: 'the gift itself is given *on the basis of* "something", which is nothing, which is not something', it is therefore 'like an "*envoi*" . . . which sends nothing that is, nothing that is a "being", a "present". Not to whoever, to any addressee as an identifiable and self-present subject' (*CP*: 63). Nothing is sent or received by a self-present subject. The classical notion of 'envoi' is connected to both the gift and the self-present subject through what Derrida calls 'absolute forgetting'. By absolving you of the gift and its associated debt, it results in a 'forgetting of what you give, to whom, why and how, of what you remember about it or hope. A gift, if there is one, does not destine itself' (*CP*: 167). In other words, while Derrida aims at a concept of Being that has the structure of a gift, he dissociates it from notions of debt, destiny and the subject. Language itself becomes separate from any notion of subjectivity. There is always '*restance*' or postal *différance*, which does not await 'language, especially human language, and the language of Being'. What characterises both is 'the mark and the divisible trait' (*CP*: 66), which negates the positioning of the subject either as an origin or destination of a narrative. The structure and the force of the 'envoi' is such that the possibility of its non-arrival is inscribed before it is written. Derrida argues that 'even in arriving (always to some "subject"), the letter takes itself away *from the arrival at arrival*' (*CP*: 123). The letter is thus lost for the addressee 'at the very second when it is inscribed'. Because 'its destination is immediately multiple, anonymous . . . the sender, as they say, and the addressee, yourself' (*CP*: 79) cannot act as a point of origin or destination.

Derrida rejects the distinction between single, unique, identifiable addressors and addressees. That simple opposition 'between the original "in person" and its mark, its simulacrum, its double', he argues, 'tends to allay uneasiness' (*CP*: 270), because its objective is to acquit itself of the double. By instituting instead the logic of the double – and what he calls the epistolary simulacrum, which upsets the order of representation – Derrida eliminates the idea of authenticity and the self-present subject (that is, the writer, etc., 'in person'). Because this duplicity is uncontrolled, it disrupts 'every verification of an identity' (*CP*: 460). Divisibility, fragmentation and partition always prevent the subject from announcing, writing, speaking or constituting itself as a unity, as the unique author. Derrida states explicitly that if any of his concepts are to refer to a "unity", it is neither that 'of the subject nor that of consciousness, the unconscious, the person, the soul and/or the body' (*CP*: 402).

The idea of the person is haunted by the totally other, that is, by the double which does not double upon itself, and has no possibility of either coming back or representing itself without leaving itself. In this construction, the double does not appease by reducing its effects, but instead multiplies them 'by expanding them, by expanding the effects of duplicity without an original' (*CP*: 270).

Whereas traditional metaphysics constructively assimilates the effects of the double in its conception of the self-present subject, Derrida sees there only 'deconstructive dissimulation' (*CP*: 268) and 'differential heterogeneity' (*CP*: 280). For Derrida, there is no indivisible self which articulates and inscribes itself within the matrix of originality, authenticity, destiny, origin and identity. Consequently, he problematises that classical division between the narrator, the narrated and the narrating which relies on the concept of repetition, and is based on an empirical or idealist conception of the subject. He achieves this by showing that the 'constitutive duplicity of all repetition' is the 'incalculable double bind (*double bande*)' which enables an illegible to become illegible (*CP*: 352). The 'constitutive duplicity of all repetition' allows for no programmatic reading, writing and interpretation.

Derrida also problematises the subjectivist categories of the proper, the signature and the proper name:

> the proper name does not come to erase itself, it comes by erasing itself, to erase itself, it comes only in its erasure, or according to the other syntax, *it amounts to, comes back to* [*revient à*] *erasing itself. It arrives only to erase itself.* In its very inscription, *fort:da*. It guards itself from and by itself, and this gives the 'movement.' It sends [*envoie*] (*CP*: 360).

No subject can act as the agent or the origin of a narrative, or as the proprietor of writing or speech, because the subject is possible only under erasure. Derrida uses a similar argument about the signature. He rejects Austin's idea that the signature '*tethers*' a written text to its origin, because it assumes that the absence of an immediately present subject gives rise to the possibility of a written text going astray. The signature, for Derrida, possesses the structure of 'a repeatable, iterable, imitable form', and as such it is 'detached from the present and singular intention of its production' (*LI*: 20). By emphasising iteration, he criticises the idea that meaning is bestowed originally by the unique status of the constituting act or event.

He also argues in *Of Grammatology* that writing, which simultaneously constitutes and dislocates the metaphysics of presence,

> is other than the subject, in whatever sense the latter is understood. Writing can never be thought under the category of the subject; however it is modified, however it is endowed with consciousness or unconsciousness, it will refer, by the entire thread of its history to the substantiality of a presence unperturbed by accidents or

> to the identity of the selfsame [*le propre*] in the presence of self-relationship. And the thread of that history clearly does not run within the borders of metaphysics. To determine an X as a subject is never an operation of a pure convention, it is never an indifferent gesture in relation to writing. Spacing as writing is the becoming-absent and the becoming-unconscious of the subject . . . As the subject's relationship with its own death, this becoming is the constitution of subjectivity. On all levels of life's organisation, that is to say, of *the economy of death.* All graphemes are of a testamentary essence. And the original absence of the subject of writing is also the absence of the thing or the referent (*OG*: 69).

Derrida makes writing a post-subjectivist concept that announces the death of the conscious and unconscious subject. By arguing that all writing is testamentary in nature, he implies that it presupposes the death of its author as subject. If Nietzsche proclaims the death of God, Barthes and Foucault the death of the author, Derrida proclaims the death of the subject as both presence and absence. Blanchot's reflections on 'Literature and the Right to Death' (1981) are clearly influential here. The subject's relationship to itself is a relationship with its own death. Derrida affirms thanatography as opposed to logography which depends on both the co-present subject and the opposition life/death. Signalling both the absence and the death of the subject, writing dissolves the dichotomy between life and death: being beyond the life and death of the subject – beyond the dichotomy of body and soul – it cannot refer to the life of a subjectivity. In his essay on 'Edmond Jabès and the Question of the Book', Derrida argues more radically that 'in its representation of itself the subject is shattered and opened. Writing is itself written, but also ruined, made into an abyss, in its own representation' (*WD*: 65). Even inscriptions, which are taken to represent the subject itself, are thus splintered and defracted representations, given over to the destructive and abyssal operation of writing.

Derrida also aims to free the concept of writing from collective subjectivity and from its association with enslavement and repression. He discards any notion that writing corrupts an innocent society or collective subjectivity. That state of innocence and authenticity which is associated with the absence of writing is the impossible dream of an ethnocentric, and more particularly Eurocentric, anthropology. For Derrida, no state of nature or culture is outside the matrix of proto-writing, which, by effacing the proper name and all proprietorship, frees subjectivity from these categories. For Lévi-Strauss, for instance, writing is a 'violence' linked to exploitation and oppression, because it is monopolised either by the privileged few or by other cultures which possess writing. But for Derrida, access to writing

> is the constitution of a free subject in the violent movement of its own effacement and of its own bondage. A movement unthinkable within the classical concepts of ethics, psychology, political philosophy, and metaphysics (*OG*: 132).

In other words, writing is linked to a freedom which is neither established nor asserted by the subject's identity. Instead, it comes from both its own subjection and disappearance of the subject. By respecting the other and erasing selfhood, the subject realises its own freedom.

4.3 Deconstruction and the philosophies of the cogito

Descartes initiated a tradition of reflexive philosophy grounded on the primacy of representation. Derrida critiques philosophies of subjectivity based on the Cartesian cogito, and uses Foucault – supposedly a critic of subjectivity – to reject the Cartesian tradition. In 'Cogito and the History of Madness' Derrida critiques the conception of the subject in Foucault, which he situates within that philosophy of presence which defines logocentrism (and more specifically, within its Cartesian version). Derrida argues that Descartes' famous formulation – *cogito ergo sum* – links the 'I' with thought. The Cartesian subject is secure in its consciously thinking subjectivity, which is the basis of all representational or objective knowledge. The 'I' is linked to thought and existence through a neutralisation of the factual world.

Descartes' cogito, as read by Foucault, excludes madness from reason by exiling it (in the first phase of natural doubt) from the interiority of thought. Foucault, however, wants to answer the question of the history of madness by allowing madness to speak of its own 'experience and under its own authority' (*WD*: 34). This procedure is designed to avoid the repressive language of classical reason. Foucault links madness to silence, to a voiceless subject, and to an absence of the work or non-meaning.

Derrida, on the other hand, wants to re-examine how the cogito is related to the division between reason and madness. In posing the question of whether a history or an archaeology of silence is possible, he again seeks to institute a writing that 'exceeds, by questioning them, the values "origin", "reason", and "history"'(*WD*: 36). He accuses Foucault of locating the division between madness and reason within a structure 'subsequent to the unity of an original presence', and thus confirming metaphysics 'in its fundamental operation' (*WD*: 40). Derrida rejects the idea of a division between language and silence, and also the possibility of a voiceless subject. For Derrida, 'silence plays the irreducible role of that which bears and haunts language, outside and *against* which alone language can emerge – "against" here simultaneously designating the content from which form takes off by force, and the adversary against whom I assure and reassure myself by force' (*WD*: 54). Silence not only inhabits language and the work but also 'speaks' the subject. There can be no voiceless subject, because the subject is written before silence. Like non-meaning, silence 'is the work's meaning and profound resource' (*WD*: 54). Thus, by questioning the possibility of a voiceless subject, Derrida problematises the relationship between silence, language and subjectivity. The subject can neither be contained in the saying nor rendered silent. The differential structure which precedes language escapes both language and silence.

Because the Cartesian cogito is inscribed within the structure of repetition, it cannot posit itself outside a relationship with the other, even if this other is oneself. 'It is through this relationship to the other as an other self', Derrida argues, 'that meaning reassures itself against madness and nonmeaning' (*WD*: 59). In other words, the subject cannot posit itself as 'self' without thereby positing that self as other than itself. Its meaning and security are produced by its relation to self as other. The Cartesian cogito, on the one hand, falls under the spell of its own demonic and hyperbolic doubt, which produces an excess that cannot be contained or totalised either in language or thought. To be Cartesian, Derrida argues, is

> to attempt-to-say-the-demonic-hyperbole from whose heights thought is announced to itself, *frightens* itself, and *reassures* itself against being annihilated or wrecked in madness or in death. *At its height* hyperbole, the absolute opening, the uneconomic expenditure, is always reembraced by an *economy* and is overcome by economy (*WD*: 61–62).

The relationship between madness, reason, and death has the 'structure of [a] deferral whose irreducible originality must be respected' (*WD*: 62). Any attempt to say the 'demonic-hyperbole', Derrida argues, cannot be completed by 'the saying of it, or by its object, the direct object of a wilful subjectivity' (*WD*: 62). This is because the attempt to say is a condition of silence and

> a first passion. It keeps within itself the trace of a violence. It is more written than said, it is *economised.* The economy of this writing is a regulated relationship between that which exceeds and the exceeded totality: the *différance* of the absolute excess (*WD*: 62).

No subject can exhaust or know its object by saying the object. Both saying and silence constitute an excess which regulates, without the intervention of a wilful subjectivity, the relationship between reason, madness and death. Again the subject is the result of *différance*, but this time as an absolute excess conceived as writing.

When the idea of the co-present subject is rejected, the subject absents itself in the very act of positing the question of I. The 'I am' and the 'I think' are haunted by an economy of absolute excess, which cannot be inscribed either within the relationship of subject to object, or within the subject's knowing relationship to itself. The subject cannot preserve its self-positing and self-reflection as an original, fundamental and founding act. Removed from its place behind the Cartesian cogito, the Derridean subject is disconnected from notions of reflexivity, agency and the question of positionality.

4.4 Derrida and Heidegger on the question of the subject

The relationship between Heidegger and Derrida is so complex that it cannot be explored fully in this study. As the principal philosophers of difference, however, they both criticise subjectivism. Heidegger's project is to go beyond that modern conception of the subject which constructs Being in terms of what can be known by the conscious subject. Apropos of medieval Scholasticism, he had earlier questioned the 'thereness' of the subject (*Dasein*) through the analysis of being (*Sein*). *Dasein,* therefore, is 'there-Being' (Heidegger, 1978). The later work, through an appropriation of the pre-Socratics, raises the question of being (*das Seinsfrage*) in relation to language and outside the thematic of the subject. His critique of Nietzsche's conception of the subject occurs in this later phase and indicates his preoccupation with Being rather than the subject. According to Heidegger, even in the work of Nietzsche 'being as a whole [is] . . . interpreted in man's image and thus made subjective' (Heidegger, 1987: 228). Heidegger's project seeks to articulate a post-subjectivist conception of Being which would enable him to complete Nietzsche's attempt to go beyond Western metaphysics. But because Heidegger treats Being as an appropriating event (*das Ereignis*), it is tied to the concept of origin, gathering together, and presence.

For Derrida, on the other hand, Being is never an originary gathering or presence, since 'presence' is still a term implicated in the metaphysics of subjectivity. This is why he posits the question of subjectivity in terms of the other. Even Heidegger's radical formulation of Being as spirit (*pneuma)* is still embedded in subjectivity (*OS*: 37–40). For whereas Heidegger emphasises the 'unifying' essence of spirit as that 'originally unifying unity' which is 'pneuma' (*OS*: 77), for Derrida:

> *Geist* is always haunted by its *Geist*: a spirit, or in other words, in French [and English] as in German, a phantom, always surprises by returning to be the other's ventriloquist. Metaphysics always returns, I mean in the sense of a *revenant* [ghost], and *Geist* is the most fatal figure of this *revenance* [returning, haunting]. Of the double which can never be separated from the single (*OS*: 40).

The spirit's double, the ghost, haunts Heidegger's thought, and enables it to break away from the metaphysics of subjectivity.

Derrida takes up this theme again in *Specters of Marx*. Derrida argues that Heidegger conceives of *Geist* as having an irreducible meaning in the German language – a meaning which implies a historical and linguistic foreclosure. Derrida compares the German *Geist* with the Latin *Spiritus,* the Greek *pneuma* and the Hebrew *ruah.* By introducing the other into Heidegger's thought, Derrida intends to deconstruct his notion of spirit. Derrida sees *Geist* as linked not only to the metaphysics of subjectivity but also to Nazism and similar kinds of rhetoric and discourse. Such political and intellectual practices are humanistic residues of the metaphysics of subjectivity. Instead of seeking the originary event of appropriation, Derrida describes what he calls here the *origin-heterogeneous* as an 'archi-originary and yet-to-come event' (*OS*: 111). The *origin-heterogeneous* is irreducible because it is simultaneously originary and heterogeneous to the origin, and it is 'heterogeneous *because* it is and *although* it is at the origin' (*OS*: 108). The Heideggerian notion of spirit as a gathering together is replaced by the Derridean '*trait*', which is 'flame and fire-writing in the promise' (*OS*: 111).

Derrida emphasises both the 'not yet thinkable' and that which 'remains to come' (*OS*: 111–112). By conceiving of truth as memory, and memory as a promise, he appeals to the 'entirely other in the memory of a promise or the promise of a memory' (*OS*: 113). For Derrida, the future is yet to come and inscribed in this coming is that notion of promise which connects and dissolves the notion of time as a modification of presence. No individual subject or self is endowed with the knowledge of this event. The self is adrift, and gives itself up to this promise of memory. Derrida conceives of the spirit as that which 'keeps watch in returning [*en revenant,* as a ghost] [and] will always do the rest. Through flame or ash, but as the entirely other, inevitably' (*OS*: 113). Ghost, promise, and memory-as-promise escape the demand for presence, because they are inscribed in the present by the fact of their future immanence. The demand for presence is replaced by the promise that introduces the absolute alterity of the other, which cannot and will not be assimilated into the metaphysics of subjectivity. The subject has not been colonised by the other. Instead, it has been inscribed as the future promise in a kind of messianic thought which prevents the emergence of any subject-as-identity. The subject-less promise excludes the certainty of the Cartesian cogito, that clearing wherein Heideggerian Being appears, and intersubjective recognition. All Western metaphysical concepts are traduced by the construction of the other both as a promise and an event which is yet to come. As Derrida puts it in *Specters of Marx*, what must be thought is the other, and others beyond '*the living present in general*' (*SM*: xx), and the future-to-come which makes itself manifest 'on the basis of the movement of some disjoining, disjunction, or disproportion: in the inadequation to self' (*SM*: xix). 'Inadequation' characterises the relation of the self to all forms of promise. The self never comes back to itself as 'adequation', but only in the form of a ghost which escapes the demand for self-presence and identity. Adequation and reciprocity must be abandoned if the demands of absolute alterity are to be met, and if absolute alterity is to be liberated from the categories associated with subjectivity.

4.5 The positing of the subject in terms of 'Who?'

In an important interview with Jean-Luc Nancy entitled 'Eating Well, or the Calculation of the Subject', Derrida deals explicitly with the fate of classical conceptions of the subject. He also posits the question of subjectivity in a manner that encompasses the 'who' and what answers when it is addressed. Derrida wants to retain both the interrogative function of the 'who' and its association with the call; and what he wants to discard is its association with subjectivity. The point of positing the question in this way is to deconstruct *doxa* about the subject; and to institute a new way of formulating the problematic of subjectivity. The point of re-interpreting, displacing, decentering, and re-inscribing the problematic of the subject is to avoid reasserting the politics of identity in Western metaphysics. For Derrida, the subject has deconstructed itself. It is therefore impossible to reconstitute or reconstruct the subject in terms 'of stance or stability, of permanent presence, of sustained relation to self, everything that links the "subject" to conscience, to humanity, to history [. . .] and above all to the law, as subject subjected to the law, subject to the law in its very autonomy to ethical or juridical law, to political law or power, to order (symbolic or not)' (*EW*: 99). All these questions need to be thought anew and outside the conception of the subject as self-referential presence.

How the subject relates to these issues becomes part of a new problematic, namely, what is anterior to the positing of the subject as 'I'? Derrida tries to think about the subject in a way which defines it 'as the indefinite experience of nonidentity to self, as the underivable interpellation inasmuch as it comes from the other, from the trace of the other' (*EW*: 103). Because the other delimits the concept of the subject, the self's relationship to itself is better defined as 'ex-appropriation' than re-appropriation. For Derrida, ex-appropriation implies 'the irreducibility of the relation to the other. The other resists all subjectivation, even to the point of the interiorization-idealization of what one calls the work of mourning' (*EW*: 107). What the other dislocates is self-identification. The subject cannot ground itself on the concept of self-presence. Nor can the other ground itself on any notions associated with subjectivity, whose discourse is one of mastery and hierarchisation.

Derrida replaces the question of the subject with the question of 'who?', which is susceptible to both the adventure of the trace and the disseminatory power of *différance*. Unlike the overdetermined subject produced in the discourses of Western metaphysics, the 'who' is indeterminate. Located in 'the text or in writing', its topology is a 'locatable non-place, at once necessary and undiscoverable'. As such, the 'who' is what Derrida calls 'an instance (without stance, a "without" without negativity)' (*EW*: 99–100). The subject absents itself whenever one tries to attribute to it a position either within the text or within writing in general. The 'who' is 'besieged by the problematic of the trace and of *différance*, of affirmation, of the signature and of the so-called "proper" name, of the *jes[c]t* (above all subject, object, project), as *destinerring* of missive' (*EW*: 100). The 'who' is thus anterior, something given which has an affirmative structure and enables one to ask questions about itself. The affirmative 'yes' is possible even before the asking of the question and the formation of the subject as an 'I'. Its emergence into responsibility is not dependent on the notion of an autonomous subject. In this philosophical schema, the 'relation to self . . . can only be *différance*, that is to say alterity or trace' (*EW*: 100). The self relates to itself by means of *différance,* and has no connection with the notion of Being as '*ousia*, presence, essence/existence, substance or subject' (*WD*: 203). Moreover, Derrida argues, 'life must be thought of as trace before Being may be determined as presence' (*WD*: 203). The life of a subject loses both its historical specificity and its certainty of presence. Responsibility becomes embedded in this notion of affirmation, rather than in action and the concept of agency. The notion of responsibility arises from respect for the other and answering its call. The subject as a moral, ethical, social and historical entity is thus unthinkable except in relation to the other, which prevents it from emerging as an autonomous subject. Responsibility is disassociated also from the notion of duty as debt. Its structure of supplementarity prevents totalisation and closure. Derrida's notion of responsibility does not involve subjective and intersubjective reciprocity. Responsibility, he writes,

> is always exercised in my name *as* the name of the other, and that in no way affects its singularity. This singularity is posited and must quake in the exemplary equivocality and insecurity of this 'as' (Derrida in Wood, 1992: 10–11).

The responsibility of the 'I' is anchored in pure exteriority. Self-relation *per se* is lost.

By positing the question of the subject in terms of 'who', Derrida deconstructs the classical conception of it. There is a singularity in the 'who' which 'dislocates or divides itself in gathering itself together to answer to the other, whose call somehow precedes its own identification with itself, for to this call I can *only* answer, have already answered, even if I think I am answering "no"' (*EW*: 100–101). To answer the call of the other is to go beyond the conception of the subject as identical to itself, conscious of an identity which it seeks to establish (in relation to the other) as a secondary effect of the relation to self-as-identity. The answer to the call of the other is determined no longer by the egological form of subjectivity or intersubjectivity, but by an interrogative and imperative form of calling which precedes the subject's formation as identity. The 'who' as the call 'provokes or convokes "conscience" and therefore opens up responsibility, precedes every subjectal determination' (*EW*: 110). Because the call of the other originates neither in divine nor human subjectivity, it must 'remain nonreappropriable, nonsubjectivable, and in a certain way nonidentifiable, a sheer supposition, so as to remain *other,* a *singular* call to response or to responsibility' (*EW*: 110–111). This strand of thought also informs his later work. An obligation to safeguard and protect the other's otherness motivates Derrida to deconstruct the concepts of subject, self and other in order to free them from subjectivism. This raises the question of why Derrida valorises the other as non-subjectivist and non-transcendental, and what are the implications of this manoeuvre.

4.6 Autobiography, signature and subjectivity

Derrida has always been preoccupied with the question of autobiography and confession. A constant theme in his thought is the autobiographical writing of the self and other. Especially since the 1980s, his deconstruction of both the writing of the self and the confessional mode of writing has become more prevalent. His emphasis on the question of how autobiography, confession and the other interrelate constitutes a more elaborate critique of subjectivism and the narrative construction of identity. By criticising, parodying and attempting to write 'autobiography' in a new manner, Derrida aims to unseat its privileged position in the narrative construction of the self. His key concept in this endeavour is the other, which makes it impossible for the self to write, present and represent itself as identity within the category of the Same. According to Derrida, the narrative construction of the self is achieved *through* the other and *by* the other. We can confess the other and others only within a structure of absolute heteronomy. Consequently, neither the self nor narrative identity can be sustained in any modality of identity based on subjectivist categories.

In Western metaphysics, the privileged discourse of the self as 'I' – beginning with St Augustine and culminating in Rousseau – has been autobiographical. The signature has been treated as an undivided mark of the self-identity of the subject-author. The signature is assumed to authenticate, stabilise and certify the truth of the identity of the subject, and the author is taken to be a unique and identifiable signatory. Since Derrida uses writing in order to dislodge the conceptions of subjectivity-as-'I' and the self as self-referential presence, he questions the idea that autobiography can affirm the truth and identity of an 'I' and express the life of a given subjectivity. By deconstructing both the proper name and the signature, he attempts to break the nexus between subjectivity, self-identity and writing, and thereby show the impossibility of autobiography. The target of his attack on subjectivity, however, is not only autobiographical writing but also pictorial media, especially self-portraiture in painting. In both cases, the subject as author, creator and signatory of the work is absent. What is emphasised is the notion of the other, which underpins the deconstructive and non-subjectivist function of writing, self-presentation and representation in all its modalities (see *MB, CAS*). By refusing to turn the other into a subject capable of being known through its writing, and by denying the subject its status as identity, Derrida deconstructs the notion of autobiography.

Derrida's attack on the notion of the authorship is part of his ongoing critique and deconstruction of the subject. Instead of treating the author in a traditional manner as the creator, proprietor, locus and origin of the work, he makes writing and text the central issues. Death and the absence of either the conscious or unconscious subject precondition both the autobiographical and confessional mode of writing. This is evident in his earliest works, when he asserts that 'the "subject" of writing does not exist if we mean by that some sovereign solitude of the author' (*WD*: 226). The 'original' author (or message or text), the 'first' reader (or interpreter or presenter), become mere oxymorons. In the scene of writing there are only traces, each representing that double force of repetition and erasure which institutes a multiplicity of agencies and origins. The erasure of selfhood and self-presence constitute one operation of the trace, which is itself erasable.

These ideas are encapsulated in Derrida's early remarks on text, textuality and play. The function of these non-concepts is to delimit those interpretative paradigms which, by anchoring the meaning of the work to notions of origin, effect a kind of closure. For Derrida, the work is a 'text', a fabric of traces which mark

> the disappearance of an exceeded God or of an erased man. The question of writing could be opened only if the book was closed. The joyous wandering of the *graphein* then became wandering without return. The opening into the text was adventure, expenditure without reserve (*WD*: 294).

Writing is a feature of the text rather than the book. It institutes an economy based on notions of adventure, loss and no return either to self-presence or origin.

In this construction, the text has no determined content which might constitute its subject, and no author who originates the writing. The text reduces the relation of writing to the self, and the notion of selfhood, to the effects of textuality and the seminal adventure of *différance*. Both within the text and outside it, the self exhibits a non-relation to writing. Autobiography becomes an 'autography' of pure loss and without signature (*D*: 41). For Derrida, there is no opposition between the text and what exceeds it, because there is always more to it than is containable within subjectivist categories such as author, truth, intention, revelation and conversion. What interests Derrida is the remainder, which cannot be elevated through the Hegelian *Aufhebung*. Since, in this sense, nothing within or outside the text can function as absolute referent, there is nothing 'outside the text'. 'Masterful' authors, interpreters, 'authoritative' meanings and 'final' truths merely signify an unrealisable desire for mastery, self-presence and self-proximity. To saturate any work with its context is a forlorn attempt to repress its left-overness. In this way, Derrida deconstructs inherited notions of the 'proper' meanings, 'determinable' contexts, and 'original' authors and works that have dominated occidental theories of the text.

Context and iterability, as Derrida understands them, not only deconstruct the concept of an authentic author and text but also elucidate those ideas of textuality and the other by which he articulates and develops his critique of the subject and the self. Derrida claims that semantic saturation is impossible, whether as context or content. By delimiting the notions of context and signature, he disassociates writing from both intentionality and authorship. Neither the singularity of the author nor the idea of auto-representation is acceptable to him. His notion of the iterability of the graphic mark deconstructs the idea of an authentic author as well as of an original and originary text. The signature is one such graphic mark, and its iteration and transformation are always authorial possibilities. Derrida signed his essay on 'Jabes' (in *Writing and Difference*) 'Reb Riba', and the famous (or infamous) 'SEC' was also signed – more precisely, the signature of a previous communication was quoted or (as he put it) counterfeited. The rejection of the notion that identity is lodged in the mere repetition of a graphic mark is meant to discredit the idea that 'identity' entails 'sameness', where 'sameness' means 'emanation from the same spirit or authorial origin'. Derrida was caught out in his own game, however, when he insisted on keeping proprietary rights to texts that appear over his own signature. His mocking reference to Searle as SARL ('Société à Responsibilité Limitée') came home to haunt him when he refused permission for one of his texts to appear in an anthology on the politics of the Heidegger Affair, despite the fact that in this case he may have already yielded his proprietary rights to the original French publisher. Derrida's insistence on his 'property rights' is a *de facto* admission of the importance of the institution of law in the social stabilisation of the graphic mark (Wolin, 1993).

The notion of absence as elaborated by Derrida in an essay on 'Signature Event Context' (reprinted in *Margins of Philosophy*) pertains to the structure of writing. 'Absence' here signifies a break in presence rather than a modification of it. By making iterability internal to the structure of writing, Derrida can introduce the other as both repetition and as absence of 'every empirically determinable "subject"' (*MP*: 315). 'In order to be what it is', Derrida argues, 'every writing must be able to function in the radical absence of every empirically determined addressee in general' (*MP*: 315–316). The structure of iterability allows writing to break away from those internal and external contexts which frame it, including those which produce, send and receive it. Iterability also enables writing to be cited, extracted and grafted on to an interminable number of linguistic and non-linguistic chains.

In the absence of an intending consciousness, the saturation of a context becomes impossible. This does not mean, however, that 'the mark is valid outside its context'; on the contrary, what it means is 'that there are only contexts without any center of absolute anchoring' (*MP*: 320, n.6). Derrida ignores the demand for a conscious, intending, and present subject constructed (in Austin's terms) by the 'I' who signs the work. While Austin and Searle treat the signature as a link between presence and origin, Derrida sees in it nothing but reproducibility and iterability in general. The signature detaches itself from 'the present and singular intention of its production'; by 'altering its identity and singularity', its sameness 'divides the seal' (*MP*: 328–329). There is thus no self-present and conscious subject who, by signing the work, can denote its undivided identity, intention and origin. The iterability of the signature dislocates the idea of a singular author and an individual self.

The subject is thus dislodged from practically every relation and connection to those categories associated with writing, interpretation and communication. Iterability fissures the concept of the subject by introducing distance, delay and division into writing. What is taken to be the expression of an undisputed source or origin – the signature – demarcates neither the limits nor the author of a work. Instead, it opens up the work to a multiplicity of traversing, competing, intervening and generally delimiting textual operations. In the place of the signature as seal, Derrida institutes in his later work on *The Ear of the Other*: *Otobiography, Transference, Translation* the notion of 'crypt'. 'Autobiography' is replaced by such concepts as 'heterography', 'allobiography' (in Derrida's 'Introduction' to Lacoue-Labarthe: Fynsk, 1989), and 'thanatography'. Heterography and allobiography denote the deconstruction of narrative identity, and thanatography the 'death' of the author as an identifiable and empirical subject within writing. Thanatography also relativises the question of biography. Derrida aims to restructure the autobiographical *récit* 'on the basis of a project that is also biographical or thanatographical' (*EOa*: 45). This involves writing out of the death of the subject, whose 'I'-ness cannot be instituted within identity as the narrative of a life. For Derrida, all writing – and specifically autobiography – is of a testamentary nature. As Derrida points out, in his autobiography Nietzsche 'died as always *before* his name and therefore it is not a question of knowing what he would have thought, wanted, or done' (*EOb*: 28–29). Thanatography is a precondition of autobiography.

Derrida concludes by eliminating the *autos* from writing. He argues that in Nietzsche's autobiography

> it is the ear of the other that signs. The ear of the other says to me and constitutes the *autos* of my autobiography. When, much later, the other will have perceived with a keen-enough ear what I will have addressed or destined to him or her, then my signature will have taken place (*EOa*: 51).

The other, perceived here as an ear (because that organ perceives difference), seals otherness by writing autobiography as allography. Thus, the autobiographical 'I' can be constituted only through and by the other. The function of the 'I' is placed in the future-past, and its narration is prescribed by the testamentary, differential and determining structure of the other. In so far as the 'I' receives its autobiography from the other, all narratives of the 'I' are received narrations. The signature, as a mark of identity and a claimant to that narration, is always deferred. It belongs to the 'I' only in the sense of something received from and destined to the other.

Derrida also conceives of the other as a woman who, by being multiple, can write in the place of the 'I' and prevent it from becoming a site of either identity or return. The detour through the other always prevents the 'I' from narrating itself as a conscious and reflexive subject capable of bracketing out the differential structure of the other. Moreover, Derrida argues, when the 'I' is in a relation of distance from the other, it cannot be identified or constitute itself as an 'I'. Consequently, whenever Nietzsche or any other author

> writes himself to himself, he *writes himself to the other* who is infinitely far away and who is supposed to send his signature back to him. He has no relation to himself that is not forced to defer itself by passing through the other in the form, precisely, of the eternal return . . . When he writes himself to himself, he has no immediate presence of himself to himself. There is the necessity of this detour through

> the other in the form of the eternal return of that which is affirmed, of the wedding and the wedding ring, of the alliance (*EOa*: 88).

The concept of affirmation as a positive 'Yes' is connected to the eternal return as that which annuls itself in its own return. There is no self-presence that is not given and mediated by the other.

Of particular interest in this respect is *Circumfession,* the text in which Derrida attempts to write in an autobiographical and confessional manner. A complex text, it defies any programmatic narration or interpretation by breaking down the boundaries between confession, autobiography, literature, philosophy, personal memoirs, chance events and marginalia. Instead of privileging the confessional 'I' as that which allows access to the self and the subject, Derrida instantiates the impossibility of confession as a mode of knowing and revealing the truth of the subject and the self. Derrida interlaces his narrative with various texts – including St. Augustine's *Confessions* – and what are supposedly his own notes, photographs, paintings, drawings, etc. – in order to question the confessional and autobiographical 'I' in terms of his new concept of 'circumfession', a portmanteau word incorporating both 'circumcision' and 'confession'. The former signifies a somatic writing in the form of a marking of a singular event without return; the latter refers to what Derrida calls 'a form of theology as autobiography' (*CIR*: 87).

Derrida connects circumfession to the event of 'nothingness', namely that which comes back without ever having taken place, and which is disassociated from the truth and knowledge of the self. In the absence of a narrating and narrated subject, circumfession articulates avowal which does not 'close itself on its own possibility', but instead leaves 'the circle open' (*CIR*: 14). No complete confession, revelation, conversion, atonement of sins, expiation, or payment of debts can be made through writing, by exposing and revealing one's inner, authentic and true self. Confession is replaced by circumfession, which is 'always simulated' (*CIR*: 125). The spectre of the simulacrum haunts writing, and Derrida sees his own writing as a 'simulacrum of avowal' (*CIR*: 46), a remark which reminds us that the promise inscribed in language is 'always a denouncing of self' (*CIR*: 69). This signals Derrida's abandonment of the narrative identity of the subject. What one confesses, he argues, is not the self but the other, which in this text takes the names of the mother, God, friend, Bennington, etc. Death is the only relation possible between the other and the narrating subject as identity.

In the following extract, Derrida's inversion of the Augustinian/Cartesian *cogito* indicates how he treats the subjective 'I':

> she smiled at me the other day, at least she smiled at someone, replying, when I said, 'You see I'm here,' 'Ah, you're here,' it remains to be known who will be there, if she will still be alive if I arrive, before the end of this year if I survive it, at the end of my 59 periods, 59 respiration, 59 commotions, 59 four-stroke compulsions, each an Augustinian *cogito* which says *I am* on the basis of a *manduco bido, already I am dead*, that's the origin of tears, I weep for myself (*CIR*: 127–128).

Both the Augustinian self-confessor and the Cartesian subject – present to its own representation – cease to exist: the 'I am' is replaced by the *I am dead* and marked by the past anterior of the *already*.

The entire circumfession takes place, therefore, within the spectre of the death of the mother, that emblematic other who is '*symbolic and inaccessible*' (*CIR*: 255). She holds the ring of that alliance which binds him to the event of circumcision, whose foreskin is '*the lost part of myself, which has moreover the form of the Ring*' and '*return[s] upon oneself in the alliance*' (*CIR*: 255), and thus to belonging-without-identity. Derrida therefore views his writing as witnessing his radical absence. He aims in this circumfession to disinterest himself from himself, and to withdraw from death 'by making the I, to whom death is supposed to happen, gradually go away, no, be destroyed before death come to it' (*CIR*: 190). Just how far Derrida has distanced himself from the reflexive pronoun of autobiography is indicated by his reference in that '*interrupted autobiothanatoheterographical opus*' entitled *Circumfession* to '*the "my" circumcision*' (*CIR*: 213).

4.7 Beyond Heidegger and Levinas

Several criticisms can be made of Derrida's deconstruction of the subject. For Derrida, the answer to the call of the other is an unconditional response based on affirmation – of saying yes to the call of the other before the advent of subjectivism. Imperative and immediate, the call of the other awaits no subject to be established. In fact, the other, like the subject, is more written than spoken, and disappears as presence in the very act of constituting itself as other. One needs a notion of subjectivity, however, if one is to raise the question of who answers the call of the other. Derrida's position is that the 'I' writes in place of the other, to the other and for the other; similarly, the self as 'I' answers the call of the other in the place of the other, and in an affirmative, imperative and immediate manner. Because the call of the other is injunctive, it relates to the self-as-'I' in terms of inadequation and ex-appropriation. The call of the other is thus beyond subjectivism, and our responsibility to answer it is anterior to the formation of our subjectivity and all categories that depend on self-referential presence. If, however, a subject does not answer the call of the other, and if no subject-as-other makes the call, then how can the modalities of the call and the answer to it be formulated?

Derrida's 'other' is beyond both the Heideggerian ontological difference and Levinas's 'other', each of which remains within the metaphysics of presence and thus falls prey to the dogmatism of subjectivist thought. In order to transcend the Heideggerian notion of ontological difference and develop the notion of absolute alterity, Derrida institutes the non-concept of *différance.* Gasché argues that because Derrida's *différance* remains 'indebted' to ontological difference it therefore deals with the same problematic. Nevertheless, he thinks that *différance* possesses a kind of radicality lacking in the Heideggerian notion, and goes beyond the horizon of Being by allowing all ontic differences to 'lose their specificity' (Gasché, 1994: 100). In addition, *différance*

> recognises an irreducible difference between differences, a difference finally antithetical to the notion of a ground, even if that ground were, impossibly difference *as such. Différance* is a cluster of a number of concepts of difference (Gasché, 1994: 104).

Gasché argues that because *différance* is anterior to the Heideggerian notion of ontic difference, the latter does not constitute any kind of ground. Consequently, 'thought encounters the very limits of its limitlessness' in the non-concept of *différance* (Gasché, 1994: 106). If we accept Gasché's interpretation of *différance* as a cluster of non-groundable concepts of difference, then it follows that Derrida's concept of the other is lodged in a 'metaphysical' preference for the principle of multiplicity rather than of unity.

Levinas, on the other hand, prefers to construct his notion of the other as a higher transcendental value independent of human subjectivity. As a result, he ends up with a theology unwilling to abandon subjectivism, even though it is reserved for a quasi-material entity. This is achieved by making the human face the material form in which the other appears and interpellates the subject. The 'face' of the other immediately instantiates in the subject an ethical requirement that is neither an internal call of morality nor an intersubjectively motivated norm. The question is, what is the source of the demand made by the 'face' of the other? Here theology intrudes because what stands behind this concept of the 'face' of the other (as absolute alterity and immediate ethical injunction) is the Judaic notion of God as the absolutely other, rather than the mediated notion of the Christian trinity. Furthermore, traditional substantive morality fashions the content of the 'face's' injunctions. Without such theological concepts as mercy (*misericordia*) and that notion of the divine which legitimates them, there would be no substantive moral norms for a blank human face to project – and such norms, of course, are beyond any possible rational foundation (Levinas: 1969). Derrida is clearly opposed both to the traditional morality that Levinas smuggles into his theory of the 'face' and to the latent subjectivism of Levinas' reliance on the other as primarily a 'face'. Derrida's critique of Levinas' concept of the face and his subjectivist ethics continues in his later work (see *TAT*: 106). All that Derrida retains from Levinas is the generic notion of the other as absolute otherness, and a seemingly empty notion of a 'call' stripped of its traditional moral baggage. It must be asked whether the content of such a pared-down notion of the other-as-call can be anything more than negative, and how adequately it might resist the need for a proceduralist approach to ethics. In order to answer the call of the other in the 'correct' way, the notion of the subject has to be abandoned, as does the idea of any modality of identity which is based on self-referential presence. The push here for a post-subjectivism not only in ethics but in all thinking is underpinned by the deconstructive power of the other. If the subject shackles us to the repressive metaphysics of presence, the other promises us a kind of liberation that is always **imminent** and beyond the problematics of subjectivism.

4.8 Critical responses

In recent times the notion of the other has been popularised by being simplified. According to Luce Irigaray, for instance, there has been only one model of human *being*: 'one, singular, solitary, historically masculine, the paradigmatic Western adult male, rational, capable' (Irigaray, 1995: 7). Furthermore, in asserting the crucial role of Platonism in fashioning this subject, she places herself inevitably in the camp of the Nietzscheans, whose pre-eminent philosophical task remains the 'reversal' of Platonism. Irigaray aims at extricating the other from the same, but proposes to do this not by abandoning the notion of the subject, but 'by inventing [her]self as an autonomous and different subject' (Irigaray, 1995: 12). She simply wants to substitute a feminine subjectivity for the ideal masculine kind by showing that 'the subject is not *one*, nor is it singular' (Irigaray, 1995: 12). At the same time she asserts the independence of, and respect for, the other as another subject. Like Derrida, she connects the question of the other to ethics, democracy and liberation. Woman, after becoming an autonomous subject, can situate herself in relation to the other by recognising that man is other. Irigaray conceives the relation between self and other in intersubjective terms, but wants to emphasise the gendered aspect of the subject. As a result, she is reluctant to abandon the concept of the subject, for to do so would eliminate the problematic of the subject as *gendered* (see also Irigaray, 1993; 2008: 2, 65).

Despite many attempts at reducing the complexity of the Western philosophical tradition, various ways of thinking the other have survived: the other as the other of the self, the other as multiplicity, and the other as the absolute otherness of God. Furthermore, the historicisation of knowledge in the nineteenth century gave rise to the famous Hegelian dialectic of master and slave, whereby the slave, as the master's other, fashions himself into a subject (Hegel, 1979). Finally, of course, the scientisation of knowledge in the nineteenth century also gave rise to a notion of the otherness – in terms of reflexes, the unconscious, etc. – of the mental functioning of the subject itself. It is clear, moreover, that Derrida's deconstruction of the subject and concomitant turn to the other are resourced by the historical conception of God in the Judaeo-Christian tradition. In the case of feminists like Irigaray, on the other hand, the concern with otherness is principally gender-specific: women as 'other' by contrast with 'male' processes of liberation and self-fashioning which pretend to universality. What interests Irigaray is not the death of the subject but a 'subjective becoming' for women which parallels by different processes and with different effects a 'masculine' subjectivity.

My argument is that a notion of the self is inescapable, although it need not be that historical concept of the self 'as a rational subject' which deconstruction urges us to avoid because of its logocentrism and masculinism. The question of the subject must be raised not simply in terms of the 'I' which responds to the 'Who?', but in the context of a concept of a reflexive, narratively constituted and recognition-seeking self. To point out the limitations of Derrida's theory, I will sketch a minimal theory of the self, which is meant as a contribution to both cultural studies and social theory. Departing from the quasi-transcendental field of deconstruction, it seeks to articulate the formal presuppositions of a more context-dependent theory of the self as something reflexive, narratively bound, and open to the other also through 'struggles for recognition'.

Drawing on psychoanalysis, hermeneutics and critical theory, it develops a theory of the self as something embodied, as opposed to the intellectualist and textualist cast of deconstructive accounts of the subject which write off the subject to create an opening for the utterly other. The embodied self is embedded or context-saturated, in the sense used in those contemporary critiques of the epistemological objectivism which underlie accounts of the self and of ethics. I have in mind here the distinctive ways in which 'context' is elucidated in the work of Taylor (1989), MacIntyre (1985), Sandel (1982), Nagel (1986) and Walzer (1987). Here the self is theorised as possessing a collective as well as a personal identity, thus opening up the possibility that identity is forged in identity-conflicts or 'struggles for recognition'. These three levels correspond, therefore, to a pre-history of the self, a hermeneutics of the self, and a critical theory of identity conflicts. None of these three levels can be dealt with adequately in terms of a strictly philosophical analysis, and certainly not by means of either deconstructive or analytical philosophy. The most productive approach come from what will be called, for want of a better name, the human sciences.

To be more precise, I propose three different levels of analysis:

(a) the splitting of the subject: a self is fashioned only through a process of differentiation that sunders the original unity of mother and child, of the unconscious and the ego. Nevertheless, the notion of reflexivity must be retained as a possible mode of the subject.

(b) the narrative construction of identity: a self is fashioned through the continuous narrative fashioning of life-events by human beings. Because identity is thus a narrative construct, it can use elements resourced by history, including the history of philosophy.

(c) recognition by others: a self can constitute itself only when it is recognised by others. Whenever recognition is unjustly refused, struggles for recognition occur, and hence the moral patterns of historically significant movements of liberation can be reconstructed.

In what follows I will comment further on each of these three points.

(a) Derrida's most provocative statement is that 'there is nothing outside of the text'. Disregarding simplistic misunderstandings of this statement, it clearly refers to an ontological position that fundamentally determines how Derrida approaches the problem of the self. In his critique of contemporary French theories of the subject, Castoriadis delineates the two main models (Castoriadis, 1989). The one common to Lévi-Strauss, Althusser and Foucault denies the reality of the human subject in order to reconstruct 'processes without subjects'. My only reservation with this analysis is that it ignores the late Foucault's theory of subjectivation. Castoriadis' other model is common to Lacan, Barthes and Derrida, and re-absorbs the subject into language which functions as a kind of 'subject of the unconscious'. In the case of Derrida, however, it would be more accurate to say that the 'general text' functions as a quasi-transcendental framework or 'subject of the unconscious'. As a result of this orientation, the human subject *per se* goes unthought in favour of an ontological position that locates difference at the level of a philosophical theory of the general text. Derrida can focus, therefore, on deconstructing those theories whose attempts to give ontological primacy to the subject founder on that irreducible difference which he treats as a quasi-transcendental given.

In this respect, the subject is merely the name that is given to the epistemological centre of certain (mainly modern) philosophical discourses. By replacing Derrida's theory of the general text with a more pluralistic ontological position, it becomes possible to re-open the question of the subject. I would like to do so mainly by way of psychoanalytical theory from Freud to Lacan, Zizek and Castoriadis. The psychoanalytical conception of the subject, as interpreted within Lacanian thought, centres on Freud's decentring of it in his now famous remark that psychoanalytical theory shows 'the "I" is no longer to be the master of its own house' (Freud, 1973). What we see in Lacan is a radicalisation of this thesis. In Zizek's interpretation of the Lacanian position, the '*objet petit a*' defines that 'ontological void' which is called the subject. In other words, the subject's secret treasure or '*agalma*' (as Zizek puts it, quoting Plato) resides in a piece of the real which takes the shape of a 'stain' (Zizek, 1993: 48). Such reference to the real blocks those immanentist and textualist approaches to the subject which are to be found in deconstruction.

The theory of self-consciousness in Zizek's Lacanian account of the subject remains problematic. After defining self-consciousness as the 'object qua *objet petit a*, qua the gaze able to perceive the true meaning of the stain' (Zizek, 1993: 67), Zizek introduces the Lacanian distinction between '*sinthome*' and '*symptom*'. The '*sinthome*' is the stain within which the ontological void of the subject resides. Hence, self-consciousness is 'object-like' in character and not produced by a reflexive act of the subject. The stain also functions as a '*symptom*' or message to be interpreted by the analyst. Either way the truth of the subject is outside it. Derrida gives up the notion of the object in favour of a linguistic or textualist reading of the subject. Even though he criticises strongly the analyst's presumption that the subject can be brought to 'full speech', Derrida does so from the position of someone who thinks that the possibility of crediting the subject with reflexivity is equally remote. In fact, there is no account of reflexivity in Derrida.

The concept has been developed recently, however, as 'societal reflexivity' by Beck, Giddens and Lash (1994), for whom it indicates the capacity of society to thematise explicitly the process of its own transformation within 'second modernity'. But a more psychoanalytically aware concept of reflexivity can be found also in the work of Cornelius Castoriadis, for whom reflexivity is 'the possibility that the characteristic activity of the "subject" becomes "object"' by means of the imagination. As he puts it, 'it is only because the human being is imagination (non-functional imagination) that it can posit as an "entity" something which is not: its own process of thought' (Castoriadis, 1989: 27). This imaginative capacity of the subject is also at work in the construction of those narratives which shape and re-shape the biographical identity of a subject.

(b) Because Ricœur has developed the most complete account to date of narrative identity, I turn now to his work for some critical reflections on the missing pieces of Derrida's theory of the subject. Ricœur's is a *tertium datur* approach: 'the hermeneutics of the self is placed at an equal distance from the apology of the cogito and its overthrow' (*OA*: 4). This argumentative strategy quite rightly accepts the 'gains' achieved by deconstructing the philosophies of the *cogito,* but also seeks (unlike Derrida) to preserve what was valuable in them. Ricœur's hermeneutics of the self is comparable in intent with the approach of Castoriadis. Ricœur not only distinguishes reflective meditation from that immediate positing of the subject which is indicated in the grammatical distinction between 'self' and 'I', but accords the 'self' primacy over the 'I' (*OA*: 1). Ricœur proceeds to distinguish two senses in the term 'identity' by means of the Latin terms '*idem*' and '*ipse*'. Conceived of as '*idem*', identity implies 'permanence in time', and from a deconstructive standpoint quite clearly pertains to the metaphysics of presence. Applied to the subject, identity-as-*idem* refers to an 'unchanging core'. Like deconstructive critics, Ricœur wants to distance himself from this conception of the self. Hence he develops the notion of identity as the 'same', as it appears when the French use *même* to invoke a comparison referred to as '*idem*-identity'. Ricœur then evokes the equivocation in the French language – namely the appearance of *même* in the reflexive form '*moi-même*' – to introduce his concept of selfhood or '*ipseity*' as '*ipse*-identity'. This notion of identity presupposes reflection rather than timelessness (*OA*: 2–3). Ricœur's final manoeuvre is to show that if sameness is thought of merely as identity, then otherness offers nothing original. What Ricœur wants instead is an otherness that is constitutive of the self. This can be achieved only through a reflexive notion of identity as selfhood (*OA*: 4). 'Oneself' is that entity which can conceive of itself reflexively as 'another'. The result is a philosophy neither of the 'I' nor of that which responds to the 'who?', which are both criticised effectively by deconstruction. Instead, it is a philosophy of the self *qua* reflexive possibility or (to use Ricœur's precise term) 'imaginative variations'.

This term may cause confusion, however, in so far as Ricœur wants above all to figure the connectedness of life in terms of 'narrative identity'. The confusion disappears, however, if we think of narrative identity not as a totalising project but rather as a 'configuration' whose open-endedness allows for re-figurations to come into existence as a result of experiments with 'imaginative variations' or (to use another of Ricœur's terms) 'fictions'. Whereas Derrida uses *différance* in order to deconstruct notions of the '*propre*' or 'own-ness' and 'ownership', for Ricœur it is once again a question of *tertium datur*: 'I am applying the term "configuration" to this art of composition which mediates between concordance and discordance' (*OA*: 141). Although the implications of this are immense, I will limit myself here to Ricœur's analysis of the modern novel by way of illustrating what is at stake between Derrida and Ricœur. In his account of the 'confrontation' between the classical and modernist form of the novel, Ricœur identifies a 'conflict between a narrativist version and a nonnarrativist version of personal identity' (*OA*: 149). The classic novel is of course the novel of character, and in Ricœur's terms sameness or identity (*idem*) and selfhood (*ipse*) fuse in character. What makes the classical novel an impossible project, therefore, is the impossibility of maintaining this self-identical 'character'. The great Russian novelists, in Ricœur's interpretation, exemplify this impossibly complete coherence of character. The typically modernist novel for Ricœur is Musil's *The Man without Qualities*. As Ricœur points out, '*ohne Eigenschaften*' could be translated as 'without properties'; that is, the novel portrays the deconstruction of the '*propre*' or that sense of own-ness which the self experiences as ownership of its self. Because narrative form undergoes the same dissolution as the self, narrative closure therefore becomes impossible. The non-ending of Derrida's *Glas* illustrates, perhaps even parodies, this impossibility of closure (see Ferry and Renaut, 1990). Moreover, Derrida's favourite authors do not write novels, but '*récits*' or 'narratives' that are in effect works in which the impossibility of narrative is the '*récit*' itself.

For Ricœur, however, the modernist novel is a limit case of narrative, where selfhood is exposed by removing the support of sameness (*OA*: 149). Moreover, Ricœur sees a parallel here – significant for my interpretation of Derrida – between the modernist novel and the work of Levinas and others, who regard the dispossession of the subject as an ontological prerequisite for the irruption of the other. Ricœur once again navigates between the limit cases of full self-presence and the primacy of the other. 'It is still necessary', he writes, 'that the irruption of the other, breaking through the enclosure of the same, meet with the complicity of this movement of effacement by which the self makes itself available to others' (*OA*: 168). A glance at ethics and ethico-political topics – or, more accurately, their ontological foundations – demonstrates the issues at stake here in the different approaches of Ricœur, Levinas and (by extension) Derrida. According to Ricœur, Levinas constructs the subject as a separate and monadologically enclosed ego at the same time as he constructs the absolute exteriority of the other as a 'face' that breaks in and imposes itself upon the subject. Moreover, this other, according to Ricœur, is 'the paradigmatic figure of the type of a master of justice' (*OA*: 337). Everything hinges, therefore, on our response to the call of the other, rather than on a 'complicit' movement by the subject.

Within the domain of politics, it is its voluntarist character that is in question. In his recent work on 'the politics of friendship', Derrida takes up this issue only to side-step it. The deconstruction of the concept of friendship is an attempt to use Aristotle against the Aristotelian construction of politics along ethical lines. It is hardly surprising, therefore, that Derrida sees the notion of friendship as belonging to 'a *familial*, *fraternalist* and therefore *androcentric* political configuration' (*PF*: *12*). The challenge is to show that this configuration still lies behind contemporary political philosophy, and here Derrida has in mind the perhaps exceptional case of Carl Schmitt. The aim of the argument is to establish a concept of community different from one comprising co-present male equals or friends, and which is represented by that French tradition of thought that leads from Bataille to Blanchot and beyond Derrida to Luc-Nancy (Hart, 1995, reviews this tradition). The kind of community which is pointed to by these notions which Blanchot calls 'unavowable' and Jean-Luc Nancy 'inoperative' is a virtual one unstained by murderous communitarianism (Blanchot, 1988; Nancy, 1991). Such a concept of community, by allowing for difference, distances itself from the self-closure of a community of co-present subjects. While this is undoubtedly a 'progressive conclusion', it is far too minimalist to constitute the ontological foundation for a political condition that one could call democratic.

(c) The recent re-emergence of the concept of recognition has deepened our understanding of both the other and community. The notion of recognition derives from the Hegelian problematic of the master-slave dialectic. Especially interesting is the remobilisation of this dialectic in

Anglo-American thought, most famously in the work of Francis Fukuyama (Fukuyama, 1992), whose analysis is criticised savagely by Derrida in his *Specters*. More important however, is the reception of the concept of recognition within communitarianism, given the ways in which the critique of the 'unencumbered self' (Sandel, 1982) parallels the Derridean critique of the subject. Moreover, I shall argue, in the next chapter, that the outcome of this critique is also the same in both cases: a turn to the concept of community, even though what is meant by community varies radically.

In Anglo-American philosophy the commanding figure is John Rawls, who is quite rightly credited with re-inventing political philosophy by returning to its classical roots in contractarian thought. Rawls conceives of the subject as completely devoid of attributes, but operating like a kind of rational and utilitarian calculating machine. This subject chooses, behind a 'veil of ignorance', those principles which will shape the contract that brings society into existence, and guide it thereafter. The dominant image here is of a collection of isolated, rational and co-equal subjects who, not knowing what fate has in store for them, cannot make a merely self-interested choice of fundamental principles (Rawls, 1972). Although Derrida himself has not, to my knowledge, 'deconstructed' Rawls, the justly famous critique of Rawls by Michael J. Sandel is unintentionally Derridean in emphasis. Mirroring Derrida's deconstruction of the '*propre*' – the own-ness or proprietorship of the subject in the Western philosophical tradition – Sandel describes the Rawlsean subject as the 'subject of possession' (Sandel, 1982: 54–59). Two things characterise this subject: its identity exists independently of (and is distanced from) the ends that it chooses, and each self relates to another self with mutual disinterest. As Sandel points out; 'Rawls' account rules out the possibility of what we might call "intersubjective" or "intrasubjective" forms of self-understanding, ways of conceiving the subject that do not assume its bounds to be given in advance' (Sandel, 1982: 62).

A theory of the self in terms of 'intersubjective forms of understanding' is to be found in Taylor rather than Sandel. However, before discussing this topic more extensively in the next chapter, I wish to make a few preliminary points on Taylor's theory of the self. For Taylor, the self is no subject, because it is not construed as that primarily epistemological entity which Derrida deconstructs. Instead, the subject is – *qua* self – an entity whose identity is shaped fundamentally by its interaction with others. At this point, Taylor uses the famous Meadean concept of 'significant others' to analyse the way in which this shaping-by-interaction is present in the earliest days of the self. This more sociologically aware account of the subject *qua* self clearly dispenses with that 'subject of possession' which is dear to Rawls and to the Western philosophical tradition in general. Taylor's account of the self, however, is not merely sociological but also historical. His three *Sources of the Self* are the traditions of inwardness, ordinary life, and romantic 'inner nature', all of which shape indelibly the contemporary culture of the self (Taylor, 1989). Derrida's account falls short of Taylor's because it fails to recognise the full diversity of Western thought on the subject. Finally, Taylor's account is political. For if our identity is shaped partly by others, then what they think and do becomes vitally important. Modern social conflict is no longer centred on the social question, defined in terms of the striving of the working class to be included in the 'difference-blind' universe of liberalism. Instead, modern social conflict focuses on identity politics, defined as the striving of various groups to have their specific identity recognised in a 'difference-ordered' social universe. Identity, at both the individual and collective levels, is fundamental to modern social and cultural order (Gutman, 1994).

4.9 Concluding remarks

Derrida establishes a disengaged, disembodied and de-collectivised quasi-subject by denying the subject a self-identity. He does so because he assumes that self-identity necessarily implies sameness. The only engagement which the self is allowed is with the other, and effacement is the only process permitted. The 'I' which expresses selfhood is always in the place of the other, and speaks and writes of itself as other. Because the self dissimulates and erases itself in the very act of its own constitution, it never enters a process of differentiation, identification or recognition *vis-à-vis* other selves or collectivities. In this way the self is disengaged from all collective process(es) or struggle(s), and becomes embedded in an interminable drift. Its relationship with the other is one of future promise, and entails continual dislocation and decentering. The subject-as-self is disempowered by the process of its effacement, but empowered by its relationship with the other, which is based on an asymmetrical demand for a response to the call of the other. By interchanging its position as the other, and by bestowing on the other the power of its own constitution, the subject-as-'I' allows itself to step outside the very process that enables it to emerge as a 'writing' or 'speaking' subject. In other words, the self is never in control, and unable either to present or represent itself. All modalities of presentation or representation are disconnected from any notion of an original or inaugural subject, action, constitution, process of differentiation or recognition.

The Derridean subject is allowed no individual or collective project(s) through which it might act as an engaged agent and point of reference. The engagement of the subject-as-self in Derrida's thinking does not extend beyond that notion of affirmation which is nevertheless prior to the emergence of subjectivity. Because this affirmation is the answer to the call of the other, it becomes disconnected from notions of agency and individual responsibility. What results is the dislocated, uncommitted, diffracted, decentered and disengaged 'quasi-self'. Derrida sees this as a condition of freedom, since it dispenses with those ideas of the self and subjectivity which are based on self-referential presence. By stepping outside the categories that determined its constitution as identity, and by instituting a new relationship with absolute alterity, the subject delimits its own boundaries by allowing for a non-relational engagement with the absolute other. This other, in its pure exteriority and absolute immediacy, calls forth a radically redefined subject.

The relationship of the subject with either other subjects or the world becomes unthinkable, therefore, from within Derrida's thought. By effacing the subject and making the other the determinant category of deconstruction, Derrida attempts to sidestep the entire problematic of the subject-as-identity. However radical this position may appear, it falls short of dealing comprehensively with the problematic of the subject, no matter how successfully it deconstructs those philosophies which construe the subject as sameness. So although Derrida emphasises discontinuity, rupture and irreducible alterity, he cannot deal satisfactorily in my opinion with the problem of modalities in self-formation and self-fashioning. In other words, he cannot account for the ethics of self-creation or the aesthetics of self-fashioning. The self which enters into an asymmetrical relationship with the other has no power to constitute either that other or itself. The process of 'other-ing' is side-stepped by Derrida, because he removes both the self and the other from the problematic of Being and the world. By making the self and the other anterior to these, he thus avoids solving the question of both the historical and power-laden relationship between self and other. For a thinker who has aimed to delimit the concepts of subject, self and other, he has constantly conceptualised the self and the other in a way that leaves little space for the problematic of recognition and misrecognition.

Derrida also denies the self any power to transform and change. This is because he thinks of it as so totally effaced that what remains is entrusted to the other as absolute alterity. The other's ability (or inability) to transform itself or any other structures is never thematised, for Derrida treats the other as a quasi-transcendental category whose powers are interrogative and injunctive rather than transformative. These powers result in the embedding of a hidden and unelucidated ethico-moral dimension in all forms of delimited subjectivity. Subjectivity and the self are overdetermined by the other, and the other underpins not only the radical project of delimiting the freedom of the self, but also the transcending of the metaphysics of Being-as-presence. The other is able to do what it is entrusted to do, however, only because it both consumes and subjugates the subject. Neither the call of the other nor the pre-subjectivist responsibility of answering it can be instituted without thematising the question who answers this call, how, and within what philosophical, historical, and socio-cultural parameters it takes place. One cannot ignore both the modalities of the call and the answer, and the positions of the caller and the answerer. Even if one wanted to remove both the other and the self from the repressive and limiting aspects of subjectivist thinking, the problematic of subjectivity and the issue of intersubjectivity would still remain. In displacing these problematics by not making them subject to the demands of the co-present subject(s), one still needs to resolve satisfactorily the issue of how subjects – textual or empirical – relate to one another in the world. The call of the other must be answered, according to Derrida, prior to the formation of subjectivity as a self, and also before the other is constituted as other. What is not made clear is how this vertically constructed call emerges, and whether it ought to occupy the place of a more horizontally conceived ethics of intersubjectivity based on reciprocity.

5. The Other – 1: The Deconstruction of the 'Fraternal Other' and the 'Original Valley of the Other'

Derrida's preoccupation with the other is evident from his early writings and has remained a constant theme of his thought, which aims to break radically with the concept of subjectivity based on identity and to institute a new kind of thinking based on the other. Because Western logocentrism constructs otherness and the other as derivative of self-identity and sameness, the relation of the self to the other is based on the reduction of the other to the same. In other words, the other is absorbed into identitarian ontology through either negation, elevation or reconciliation. This is a result of transcendentalism's claim that the cogito has primacy, and constructs being in terms of presence. In contrast, Derrida – seeking a concept of the other which escapes Western metaphysics' demand for presence – deconstructs the categories of subjectivity, self and 'I' based on identity. His notion of the other aims to articulate a new and post-subjectivist thinking embedded in his concept of writing.

As early as *Writing and Difference,* Derrida articulated a program that has been executed only in the works of the eighties and the nineties. The 'double inscription' of the other is present here in the deconstructive gesture which aims at an immanent critique of the 'fraternal other' and the transcendent descent into the 'original valley of the other'. As Derrida himself puts it in 'Force and Signification',

> writing is the outlet as the descent of meaning outside itself within itself: Metaphor-for-others-aimed-at-other-here-and-now, metaphor as the possibility of others here-and-now, metaphor as metaphysics in which Being must hide itself if the other is to appear. Excavation within the other toward the other in which the same seeks its vein and the true gold of its phenomenon. Submission in which the same can always lose (itself) . . . But the same is nothing, is not (it)self before taking the risk of losing (itself). For the fraternal other is not the first in the peace of what is called intersubjectivity, but in the work and the peril of inter-rogation; the other is not certain within the peace of the *response* in which two affirmations *espouse each other*, but is called up in the night by the excavating work of interrogation. Writing is the

moment of this original Valley of the other within Being. The moment of depth as decay. Incidence and insistence of inscription (*WD*: 29–30).

The 'double inscription' of the other occurs, therefore, when writing becomes the adventure of interrogation rather than the peace of reconciliation. Writing is the 'outlet' that opens the space for the possibility of reaching the other in an interminable search whose *telos* is not a return to the same and the affirmation of self-identity. The other is not the 'fraternal' other, constituted through intersubjectivity, but the other as interrogation, as injunction, as questioning. Thus, the relationship between self and other is asymmetrical and outside the category of response.

In Derrida's later work, notions such as the 'cinder', 'gift' and 'spectre' denote a shift in his construction of the other. The other becomes that generative force which both produces and effaces; that is, the function of writing is transferred to the category of the other. The other becomes one of those non-synonymous substitutions that represent a radical break with the metaphysics of subjectivity. In the process, I have already argued, Derrida 'writes off' the subject in favour of a more radical concept of the other, which is supposedly free of the problems associated with the metaphysical subject. Such a project raises four questions that will guide my discussion of Derrida's 'concept' of the other. First, does the other represent a radical and desirable abandonment and overcoming of the metaphysical subject? Second, is the thought of the other as radical as Derrida claims? Third, can the question of the subject and the self be subsumed under the category of the other, and what are the implications of such a determination of the subject and the self? Fourth, does Derrida's thought sidestep the problematic of the subject in its search for a radically new thinking based on the thought of the other?

Derrida's thinking of the other has been shaped decisively by his encounter with Levinas, which ultimately led him to reject Levinas's subjectivism. The work of Ricœur, Taylor and other thinkers again provides an alternative problematisation of the question of the other and its relationship to the subject. My argument is that Derrida's attempt to outbid Levinas on the other, and to further 'de-subjectivise' the subject is untenable. I contend that the subsumption of the question of the subject and the self within the category of the other poses serious problems, because it abandons, above all else, even modest claims concerning the 'relative autonomy' of the subject. Consequently the subject becomes a *subjectum* to the other. In the process of instituting a thought based on the other, Derrida 'writes off' not only the traditional metaphysical concept of the subject (as I argued in the previous chapter), but even the possibility of constructing a post-metaphysical subject. The Derridean other becomes a non-relational concept that is constructed in terms of a calling, a promise, etc. It runs the risk of gesturing only to itself, and being unable to enter into any interactive, generative relation with either self or other. Moreover, if the other is constructed in terms of a call, one is left with the questions: To whom is the call made, if not to a subject? Who answers the call of the other if not a subject, even if we have to construct this subject anew? Can the other be beyond considerations of context, and beyond questions of recognition, misrecognition and the demands of a non-phenomenological concept of intersubjectivity?

I would further argue that the concept of the other in Derrida is quasi-messianic and becomes more messianic in the last phase of his work. It depends on a vertical construction of the other in relation to the subject and the self. Even though the concept of the other claims to be post-metaphysical, therefore, it is not post-metaphysical enough. It is post-metaphysical only in relation to the deconstruction of the subject. What comes out of the ruins of the subject, however, is a concept of the other that cannot disentangle itself from these ruins, except in a gesture of the prophetic '*logos*'; and that points to a future promise which, because it is always *à venir*, never arrives. Although such thinking delimits the scope of the metaphysics of subjectivity, and frees the self from the stifling confines of the same, it fails to give the subject and the self a new validity. I argue that we need also a 'horizontal' rather than 'vertical' conception of the other and its relationship to the subject. A horizontal concept of the other would not subsume the subject and the self, but instead reinscribes the self within a relatively transparent, interactive and communicative concept of both self and other. The other needs to be contextualised, and engage not only with itself as a generative force *sui generis*, but also become part of a concept closely linked with the issue of reflexivity and recognition. An unreflexive answer to the call of the other could be as solipsistic as the Husserlian voice without a soul.

5.1 The problematic of the other and the thought of Levinas

The linchpin of Derrida's concept of the other is the notion of an irreducible alterity that needs to be thought beyond the thought of Being as presence. Derrida's analysis of Being as presence, however, depends on a double reduction. First, Derrida takes from Heidegger's history of Western metaphysics the concept that the subject is what determines Being, and that this is axiomatic. Second, Derrida's construction of the other depends on a reading of alterity within Western metaphysics that is determined through the concept of identity as the same. This leads Derrida to ignore the question of reflexivity. Whenever reflexivity becomes a concern, it is constructed as an 'abyssal' structure that denies identity through endless refraction. Thus, by showing how irreducible alterity has been ontologised within identity, Derrida is able to rethink the other.

He does so through readings of Plato, Descartes, Condillac, Rousseau, Kant, Freud, Hegel, Nietzsche, Husserl and Heidegger. These involve rethinking the other beyond the binary opposition of the same versus the other, wherein the other is inevitably the derived concept. The attempt to conceptualise the other beyond the Cartesian cogito, the Hegelian negation, the phenomenological philosophy of consciousness and Heideggerian ontology involves returning to a something that is both within and beyond the west, namely Hebraic thought as re-interpreted most notably by Levinas.

Levinas was raised intellectually in that phenomenological tradition which he was the first to make known in the vastly different French intellectual culture of the mid-twentieth century. Although Levinas moved quickly from Husserl to Heidegger, he was from the very beginning a critical Heideggerian. For Levinas, the bracketing of everything leads back to that which is neither inwardness nor exteriority, to the 'impersonal, anonymous, yet inextinguishable "consummation" of being': the '*there is*' or '*il y a*' (Levinas, 1978: 57). In a specification of the '*there is*' – obviously picked up on by Derrida in *Specters of Marx* – Levinas suggests that 'spectres, ghosts, sorceresses are not only a tribute Shakespeare pays to his time . . . they allow him to move constantly towards this limit between being and nothingness where being insinuates itself even in nothingness' (Levinas, 1978: 62). More pertinently, Levinas refers to 'a presence of absence, the *there is* beyond contradiction'

(Levinas, 1978: 64). Before existents there is existence itself. Before beings there is the question of Being itself (die *Seinsfrage*), and being is the impersonal and anonymous *it* or *es* that something *gives* or *gibt*; this being is indeterminate because it is yet to be determined 'being'. This way of positing the question of being is also Derrida's.

Levinas then asks how *hypostasis* is possible? How can this anonymous being be suspended, so that something – a substantive – emerges? How, in brief, do beings or existents emerge from Being? The answer to this question in Western philosophy begins usually with a reference either to the first substance or the most primordial being, namely, the subject or the relationship that exists between an 'I' and itself. But because Levinas does not believe that the 'I' perdures unchanged through those instants called time, he thus breaks out of the Western idea of the 'I' as an unchanging self-identity immune to time. Levinas rejects the idea that the other of the 'I' is merely an *alter ego*. Consequently, he argues that Heidegger's concept of *Miteinandersein* really depends on the self-sufficient ego rather than on actual contact with otherness. For Levinas, the key relationship is the unmediated one between an 'I' and a 'you'; and here Levinas relies on the work of the Jewish philosopher Martin Buber (Buber, 1970). The basis of this relation is not symmetry but asymmetry which Levinas sees as constituted by Eros. 'Intersubjectivity', Levinas writes,

> is not simply the application of the category of multiplicity to the domain of the mind. It is brought about by Eros, where in the proximity of another the distance is wholly maintained, a distance whose pathos is made up of this proximity and this duality of Beings (Levinas, 1978: 95).

Symmetry and reciprocity are the domains of a fraternalism that denies the father. If this theme is certainly Derridean, the notion of intersubjectivity is self-evidently not. Nevertheless, Levinas sees asymmetry along the lines of a father-and-son relationship, which provides the model with which to criticise both exchange and the fungibility of things. As he puts it, 'asymmetrical intersubjectivity is the locus of the transcendence in which the subject, while preserving its subject, has the possibility of not inevitably returning to itself, the possibility of being fecund and (to anticipate what we shall examine later) having a son' (Levinas, 1978:96). The patriarchal nature of the Jewish inheritance is as clear here – returning to oneself as non-identical return is given through the son –

as it will be in his later and more famous *Totality and Infinity*, where woman is 'lovingly' depicted in her kitchen (Levinas, 1969). Derrida's relationship both to Levinas and the Jewish tradition as a whole is one of critical appropriation, in which the 'phallocratic' dimension is rejected. The task for a post-phallocratic agenda, therefore, is to appropriate the philosophical core while throwing away the patriarchal shell. In other words, Derrida wants to radicalise Levinas's thinking by leaving subjectivism behind and rethinking anew the absolute other. Derrida's encounter with the thought of Levinas demonstrates both the breaks within Derrida's thought and his departure from Levinas.

5.2 The development of Derrida's thought on the other

Derrida claims that within Western metaphysics the movement of the cogito towards the other is constructed either as the externalisation of the other or its absorption into and reduction to the same. The injunctive and constitutive power of the other is thus lost or ontologised. Derrida seeks to restore it and use it against such foundationalist concepts of Western metaphysics as subject, same, identity, and Being. The Derridean other is closely bound with what Heidegger calls the forgetting of Being, which Derrida counterpoises with his notions of trace, promise, avowal, repetition and with what he terms the '*origin-heterogeneous*'. Although Derrida's preoccupation with the other and his radicalisation of its problematic are still interlinked with his earlier concept of writing and the idea of erasure or effacement, the later work gives this perspective an ethico-political dimension that was previously missing or under-played. If the early work is under the spell of Nietzsche, the later work is under the spell of Levinas.

Derrida's thought on the other can be divided broadly into two periods. The first period includes his writings up to *Truth in Painting*. These works are dominated by the question of whether it is possible to open a relationship with the other through the deconstruction of the metaphysical concept of the subject. This early period is characterised by an emphasis on the concept of writing, supplement and the trace. The second period is marked by an attempt to articulate the construction of the other in philosophical, political, cultural, ethical and socio-economic terms. It includes two important texts that one can term 'autobiographical', *The Post Card* and *Circumfession*. They can be seen as instantiating a new form of writing that encapsulates Derrida's concerns with writing and its relationship to the self and the other. These works all emphasise that writing comes from the other, is for the other, and belongs to the other; as such it does not privilege the autobiographical 'I'. If the characteristic concern of the first period is to show the fate of irreducible alterity within the thought of Western metaphysics, Derrida's principal aim in the second period is to establish a new kind of thinking based on the other as a radical alternative to the metaphysics of presence. This Derridean other, takes the structure of the gift, such that the relationship of the other to both the subject and the self is based on non-mutuality and non-reciprocity. Asymmetry becomes the determining factor of the relationship of self and other. The other becomes a transcendental other which is constructed in terms of an *a priori* in relation to the concrete and generalised other and the subject.

Early texts which deal most directly with the question of the other are *Speech and Phenomena, Of Grammatology,* 'Violence and Metaphysics: An Essay on the Thought of Western Metaphysics', and *Limited Inc.* Among the later works, the most important are: *Of Spirit, Given Time: The Time of the King, Psyche: Invention of the Other,* 'Who Comes after the Subject', *The Other Heading: Reflections on Today's Europe, Specters of Marx, The Gift of Death, The Ear of the Other, Memoirs of the Blind, Aporias, On the Name,* various essays in *Points, Faith and Knowledge*, *On Cosmopolitanism and Forgiveness, On Touching – Jean-Luc Nancy, The Animal that Therefore I Am,* and *Copy, Archive, Signature*. Although these texts are by no means the only ones that deal with the concept of the other, they reveal a progressive deepening of Derrida's conception of the other and his shift from a deconstructive to a more direct treatment of it. This development is signalled by an insistence on the question of responsibility, which seems to situate the concept partly outside the idea of a 'general text'. It is signalled also by Derrida's attempt to subsume the question of the subject and the self under the category of the other, while at the same time attempting to free them from their construction through the category of the same.

5.3 From the deconstruction of identity to the concept of the other

In Derrida's early texts the question of the other is raised through the linguistically grounded deconstruction of the dichotomy same/other, whereas in the later texts it involves a more 'ethical' critique of the question of identity and the concept of Being. In *Writing and Difference,* Derrida argues that the relationship of other to the same cannot be 'absolutely exterior to the same without ceasing to be other', and that the 'same' is a 'totality closed in upon itself, an identity playing with itself, having only the appearance of alterity' (*WD*: 126). This early formulation signals Derrida's position that because the other is constitutive of both identity and difference, it can be neither reduced to the same nor the totally other. The other, therefore, is a non-relational concept, since it exists outside any reciprocal relationship either of identity or difference. It generates both without any moment of identity or *restance*. This formulation also signals the abandonment of any 'relationalist' ethics, such as virtue ethics, interactive ethics or communicative ethics.

Speech and Phenomena argues that both Husserlian phenomenology and Heideggerian ontology fail to think the absolute other without reducing absolute alterity to the Same. Derrida appropriates some of their philosophical radicalism even while aiming ultimately at a radical departure from both. According to Derrida, phenomenology takes *noemata* to be the objective correlate of the intentional acts – *noesis* – of the subject. In Husserl, the other can be neither absolutely other nor radically foreign to my world. As the objective correlate of my intention, alterity is reduced to 'egoity', in so far as it is my conscious production. Husserlian phenomenology contains a subjective *a priori* in which meaning is bestowed by an ego. Phenomenology avoids the neutral or absolute logic of Hegelianism only through a more radical bracketing of alterity. The other, according to Derrida, can be neither a totality nor a category within Husserlian egoity. Subjectivity, totality and infinity are categories which do not belong to the thinking of the other.

Almost all of Derrida's concepts in his early work, I have argued, are connected with effacement, erasure and disappearance and are effects of proto-writing and textuality. This is what Derrida calls the 'general text'.

His reading in *Truth in Painting* of Kant's use of the term *parergon* establishes it as part of textuality, and what opens the space of the other. For Derrida,

> the *parergon* stands out [*se détache*] both from the *ergon* (the work) and from the milieu, it stands out first of all like a figure on a ground. But it does not stand out in the same way as the work. The latter also stands out against a ground. But the parergonal frame stands out against two grounds [*fonds*], but with respect to each of those two grounds, it merges . . . into the other. With respect to the work which can serve as a ground for it, it merges into the wall, and then, gradually, into the general text (*TP*: 61).

Derrida goes on to argue that the parergon 'disappears, buries itself, effaces itself, melts away at the moment it deploys its greatest energy' (*TP*: 61). The parergon, then, has no form, since its property is disappearance. But it has energy which it deploys. Its effects cannot be defined either topologically or causally, nor can they be pinned down to a source, milieu or ground in order to be explained or exhausted. The parergon is a deconstructive category that opens the space of the other. Such categories are part of the question of the other but do not constitute it. In other words, the other is a post-deconstructive category, beyond the deconstructive categories and beyond the specific deconstructions Derrida effects on texts.

Of Grammatology is preoccupied with the question of the other and its relationship to the concept of the trace, which is another term Derrida uses to denote certain properties and operations of writing. At this stage, the concept of writing and the other are linked inextricably, and the trace becomes the concept which associates writing with irreducible alterity. The trace marks the point of relationship with the other. It cannot be defined as being-present, because its movement is occulted: 'it produces itself as self-occultation' (*OG*: 47). The other announces and presents itself in the 'dissimulation of itself' which antecedes notions of being as presence; moreover, 'no structure of the entity can escape it' (*OG*: 47). Derrida becomes more specific when he argues that the 'general structure of the unmotivated trace connects . . . the structure of the relationship with the other, the movement of temporalization, and language as writing' (*OG*: 47). In other words, the connection between other and writing is such that language is subsumed under the general category of writing, and the trace is at once before and beyond language. Because the relationship between trace and other is dissimulatory, it cannot be incorporated within the problematic of presence. Finally, and most importantly, the notion of the other is derived from that of the trace, which in turn pertains to that of writing. At this stage, therefore, Derrida's construction of the other still depends on his deconstructive attitude to writing.

Derrida's conception of the trace and its dissimulatory relationship with itself strongly parallels the idea of the self's relationship to itself. Within the matrix of the Derridean trace, the self can relate to itself through the other without ever instituting itself as identity or negative alterity. The same can be said for the concept of the other, which has not only a constitutive function (with regard to the formation of any concept of the subject or the self) but also an injunctive power. In *Of Grammatology,* Derrida states that 'arche-speech is writing because it is a law. A natural law. The beginning word is understood, in the intimacy of self-presence, as the voice of the other and as commandment' (*OG*: 17). Self-presence, therefore, can be thought of only in terms of the voice of the other and as a commandment. Although Derrida eliminates the *phone* as a privileged category of consciousness, it re-emerges here as the voice of the other, and in his later texts will become the call of the other that is signalled already in *Writing and Difference* (*WD*: 29–30). Irene Harvey has argued in this connection that in Derrida's model the subject is 'necessarily a "victim"', because 'its actions are always inscribed by the "other"; indeed by otherness itself' (Harvey, 1986: 179). This is an interesting perspective that I will take up later. For the moment, I think that Harvey goes too far, and that the subject is not so much a victim as a casualty of the cross-fire that issues from Derrida's over-drawn and over-generalised critique of the fundamental categories of Western metaphysics.

In his attempt to escape idealist and empiricist dilemmas concerning subjectivity, Derrida denies the subject any 'hypostasis' (to use Levinas's term) while at the same time wanting to confer constitutive and injunctive powers on the other. By giving it such powers, and by denying self-referential presence to the self and the subject, Derrida sets both the self and the other in an interminable textual drift, which is conceived of initially in aesthetic rather than theological terms. The trace

> articulates its possibility in the entire field of the entity . . . which metaphysics has defined as the being-present starting from the occulted movement of the trace. The

> trace must be thought before the entity. But the movement of the trace is necessarily occulted, it produces itself as self-occultation. When the other announces itself as such, it presents itself in the dissimulation of itself. This formulation is not theological . . . The presentation of the other as such, that is to say the dissimulation of its 'as such,' has always already begun and no structure of the entity escapes it (*OG*: 47).

The subject, however, even if conceived of as incorporating the trace of the other, needs a relation to itself that is not totally dominated by the injunctive power of the other (which is, of course, never co-present). In his later work Derrida conceives of temporality without a fixed mark, a present moment, a *stigme*. The other is not simply part of temporalisation, but (as we shall see) radicalises the idea of temporality itself. The other becomes an instance of messianic time and this positions the subject accordingly.

5.4 Into the labyrinth: the other and the deconstruction of representation

In *Of Grammatology* and *Writing and Difference*, Derrida deals also with the construction of the other through its link with the concept of representation. Through various deconstructions he attempts to disassociate the other from the concept of representation. The result is a non-representational concept of the other, which establishes it as what he terms the 'unthinkable unity of light and night' (*WD*: 129). The other means 'phenomenality as disappearance' (*WD*: 129). The self's relationship to the other is one of respect for the other '*as what it is*: other' (*WD*: 138). Both the externality and independence of the other *vis-à-vis* the subject are firmly established. The other cannot be mastered, controlled, modified, presented, represented and altered by the subject. It cannot be made an object for either itself or a subject, and its phenomenality cannot be reduced to any form of egoity.

Derrida further develops his thought on the other in *Positions*, where he distinguishes alterity from spacing. He argues that these concepts '*do not signify exactly* the same thing', but are 'absolutely indissociable':

> *Spacing* designates *nothing*, nothing that is, no presence at a distance; it is the index of an irreducible exterior, and at the same time of a *movement*, a displacement that indicates an irreducible alterity (*POS*: 81).

This indicates how Derrida thinks of the other as irreducible exteriority rather than as the basis of an intersubjective relationship. In a letter to Jean-Louis he asserts that spacing is 'the impossibility for an identity to be closed on itself, on the inside of its proper interiority, or on its coincidence with itself. The irreducibility of spacing is the irreducibility of the other' (*POS*: 94). Because the link between spacing and alterity is irreducibility, identity becomes divorced from notions of interiority and self-identity. Derrida further argues that spacing 'designates not only interval, but a "productive", "genetic", "practical" movement, an "operation"' (*POS*: 94). This process is again marked by the other, and is ongoing.

When considering how Derrida posits the question of the other, it is important to emphasise his insistence that the '*Other* is not a *being* (a determined being, existence, essence, etc.)' (*POS*: 95). The question of the other, therefore, cannot be posited within the philosophy of Being, because (in the Heideggerian sense) it is a question of the *Being* of *beings*. Derrida argues:

> if the alterity of the other is *posed*, that is, *only* posed, does it not amount to *the same*, for example in the form of the 'constituted object' or of the 'informed product' invested with meaning, etc.? From this point of view, I would even say that the alterity of the other *inscribes* in this relationship that which in no case can be 'posed'. Inscription, as I would define it in this respect, is not a simple position: it is rather that by means of which every position is *of itself confounded (différance)*: inscription, mark, text and not only *thesis or theme*-inscription of the *thesis* (*POS*: 95–96).

Since the question of the positing of the other is outside positionality, it does not belong to the 'proper' character of beings. It is a question interlinked with textual operations such as dissemination and *différance*, and as such can be posited only by displacing the question of what constitutes irreducible alterity. This question is the *Seinsfrage*: What *is* Being? For Heidegger, Being is a 'gathering', whereas for Derrida it is a 'dispersal'. This is why Derrida insists on the textual in his treatment of alterity.

When lecturing in 1971 on the idea of 'source' in Valéry, Derrida tackled directly the issue of the other in relation to the self. He argues that one cannot hear oneself speak because the

> source is always other, and that whatever hears itself, not itself hearing itself, always comes from elsewhere, from outside and afar. The lure of the I, of consciousness as hearing-oneself-speak would consist in dreaming of an operation of ideal and idealising mastery, transforming hetero-affection into auto-affection, heteronomy into autonomy (*MP*: 297).

Derrida wants to emphasise the 'surplus heterogeneity of alterity' (*MP*: 298), and heteronomy instead of autonomy. Heteronomy encompasses all aspects of the self and subjectivity in general. It becomes evident that Derrida ascribes to the self very little if anything at all. He treats it as a kind of receptacle for operations, for those things which are external to it but nevertheless, and paradoxically, become internal without the possibility of closure. Derrida wants a philosophy of heteronomy that would take into account the surplus heterogeneity of the other. In other words, he aims to go beyond the Hegelian conception of alterity. The Derridean subject possesses nothing and gives nothing: 'When I speak (to myself) without moving my tongue and lips, I believe that I hear myself, although the source is other; or I believe we are two, although everything is happening "in me"'(*MP*: 297).

Here Derrida fails to pluralise the concept of the self so that it can accommodate heteronomy without losing all claims to autonomy and identity. If heteronomy becomes the only characteristic of the self, then there is a danger that the self will become simply the Platonic *Khora*, where all things go, in both the active and passive senses. The loss of the self is not simply a giving-up of mastery, and a desire to turn all hereronomy to auto-affection, which is of course a radical critique of the metaphysical subject. It entails also a giving-up of the self to an other which is both external and other than alterity. This position, which Derrida maintains and develops in his later work, is based on the reduction of the self within a philosophy of identity which constructs identity within the category of the same. In this context, Ricœur distinguishes between positing the self as identity and positing it as other (Ricœur, 1992). This radical formulation of alterity within the problematic of identity makes the other both internal and external to the construction of the self, but without subsuming the self under the category of the other.

In *Dissemination,* Derrida places the question of irreducible alterity within the problematic of writing, and opens up the question of morality and knowledge that is not discoverable 'in ourselves by ourselves' (*D*: 74). This signals Derrida's attempt to anchor the problematic of self-knowledge within a quasi-transcendental framework, but without grounding it within a metaphysics of subjectivity. The *pharmakon* (as a term which denotes the other) is seen here as that which

> keeps itself forever in reserve even though it has no fundamental profundity nor ultimate locality. We will watch it infinitely promise itself and endlessly vanish through concealed doorways that shine like mirrors and open onto a labyrinth (*D*: 127–128).

The metaphor of the labyrinth appears frequently in Derrida, including the end of *Speech and Phenomena*. It is significant here because it connects the other not only with promise and reflection but also with a critique of the mirror model of reflection. Reflection, for Derrida, never repeats or gives an image of identity, but rather withholds what cannot be presented or represented. The promise of the other is always held in reserve as the unrepresentable. The opening to the other opens on to the labyrinth or (in Derrida's other writings) on to the abyss of infinite displacements and substitutions (*TP*: 7, 129, 291). Within this schema, interpretation cannot restore the full and true meaning to a narrative, since there is always the endless carrying off into 'a labyrinth of doubles without originals, of *fac-similes* without an authentic and indivisible letter, of forgeries without something being forged' (*CP*: 492).

5.5 The concept of the other and its relation to repetition

Derrida's concept of the other is connected also to the structure of repetition. *Dissemination* distinguishes two types of repetition embedded in Derrida's concept of the double as a condition of both the possibility and impossibility of the appearance of being-present in its truth. He argues that

> the being-present (*on*) in its truth, in the presence of its identity and in the identity of its presence, *is doubled*, as soon as it appears, as soon as it presents itself. *It appears, in its essence, as* the possibility of its own most proper non-truth, of its pseudo-truth reflected in an icon, the phantasm, or the simulacrum. What is not what is, identical and identical to itself, unique, unless it *adds to itself* the possibility of be-

> ing *repeated* as such. And its identity is hollowed out by that addition, withdraws itself in the supplement that presents it (*D*: 168).

Repetition destroys presence and identity as such. It is grounded in what Derrida calls the graphics of supplementarity, which supplies 'another unit which comes to relieve it, being enough the same and enough other so that it can replace by addition' (*D*: 168). Otherness, it appears, is not completely divorced from considerations of identity. But identity is always inscribed within repetition as the moment of non-truth, of non-resolution. Withdrawal, addition and substitution – which splinter identity as plenitude, adequation and reflection – become the condition of the non-appearance of alterity. This non-appearance of the other is an attempt by Derrida to construct the other as a non-phenomenon that escapes mastery and knowledge.

Repetition, moreover, is constructed not as repetition of the same but as

> the very movement of non-truth: the presence of what is gets lost, disperses itself, multiplies itself through mimemes, icons, phantasms, simulacra, etc. . . . Here, tautology is life going out of itself beyond return. Death rehearsal (*D*: 168–169).

The other is constructed as unreserved spending, as irreducible excess. Instead of identity we have dispersal, multiplication, phantasms and simulacra that defy the repetition of the same. In this way, Derrida interjects the concept of death. Later in the same text he introduces the concept of *cendre* in order to conceive of the other outside the philosophies of life and within a philosophy of the trace of the other. The fact that the concept of *cendre* reappears in Derrida's later works substantiates my claim that continuities (albeit with inflexions) are discernible between his early and later writings. It is important to point out, however, that Derrida argues also that the two types of repetition – repetition as the same, and repetition as supplement – can neither be separated from one another nor conceived of as separate. Derrida, therefore, inadvertently recognises the impossibility of thinking repetition without any reference to identity, even though he is reluctant to give identity a constitutive function with regard to alterity. Derrida's reference to reflection as leading not to recognition but to an abyssal effect eliminates the possibility of knowing or controlling reflection as representation. There is always dispersal within the origin rather than unity.

The concept of repetition is also tackled in *The Post Card* in relation to Freud, and especially in regard to the '*Pleasure Principle*' and the play of disappearance and return. Derrida argues against that classical concept of repetition which constructs it as something secondary and therefore derivative in repeating a prior original. He argues on behalf of a new logic of repetition, which is 'other, and nonclassical'. 'Repetition is "original"', he writes: 'it induces, through an unlimited propagation of itself, a general deconstruction: not only of an entire classical ontology of repetition, along with all the distinctions . . . but also of the entire psychic construction of everything supporting the drives and their representatives' (*CP*: 351–352). Repetition brings about deconstruction, and dissolves any relational structure which depends on a calculable and recognised double that repeats the original. There is not only *difference* in repetition, but also an inability to master that aspect of it which Derrida calls the double bind (*CP*: 352). Conceptualised in this way repetition allows for no connection between a psychic drive, no representation that can repeat itself as a return to a previous state, and whose effects can be calculated or known.

Another important text concerning Derrida's thought on the other is *Limited Inc*. Here the other is defined as the impossibility of adequation between saying and meaning: it is grounded in the 'graphics of iterability', which 'inscribes alteration irreducibly in repetition (or in identification)' (*LI*: 62). Iterability, however, is not simply repetition. Iterability as repeatability also 'ensures that the full presence of a singularity thus repeated comports in itself the reference to something else, thus rending the full presence that it nevertheless announces' (*LI*: 129). Iterability puts into question that notion of intentionality as primordial self-presence which endows objects with a meaning which merely repeat their origin. Derrida writes:

> What does 'intention' properly mean as the *particular* or *original work* (*mise en oeuvre*) of iterability? I admit this enigma grows increasingly obscure for me . . . My frequenting of philosophies and phenomenologies of intentionality, beginning with that of Husserl, has only caused my uncertainty to increase, as well as my distrust of this word or this figure, I hardly dare to say 'concept' (*LI*: 130).

In *The Truth in Painting,* the other is the untranslatable or the unbroachability of meaning. It is what remains outside the structure of reproduction and restitution as adequation. In this work, Derrida moves away from textual analysis, and deconstructs pictorial media, institutions and their discourses in a more autobiographical style. He posits the question of otherness in terms of parergon and remark, which are closely related to his concept of supplement. The parergon is that which reason fails to satisfy, that is, a moral need which depends on grace, mystery and miracles (*TP*: 55–56). Being both within and outside the work, it provides its unity as well as its delimitation. His analysis of the colossus and Kant's sublime introduces the other as that which is between presentable and unpresentable, and which allows 'the passage from the one to the other as much as the irreducibility of the one to the other' (*TP*: 143).

Using his concept of *cartouche*, Derrida attempts to eliminate the question of property, topography, paradigm and genealogy from the question of otherness. The idea of the *cartouche* – implying '(No) more narrative, (no) more truth' (*TP*: 220) – can be inscribed either within or outside the work. Derrida emphasises the order of the 'phantasmatics of a *contingent remaining* (beyond hierarchy and beyond phantasy)' (*TP*: 221). This remainder is without example:

> however one multiplies [*il a montré* [. . .] *qu'on a beau, vraiment beau*] approaches, assaults, attacks, however much one multiplies movements of appropriation, seduces the thing, tames it, domesticates it, tires it with one's advances, it remains, as remainder (really beautiful [*vraiment beau*]), indifferent, *cut off* from the world, from production as from reproduction (*TP*: 202).

The concept of *cartouche*, therefore, resists classification, framing, typification or exhaustive description. The remainder, as another concept designating alterity, is cut off from the world. This is an important aspect of Derrida's notion of alterity: paradoxically, it is transcendental without being metaphysical.

What becomes important in Derrida is not the *hypokeimenon* (the being-underneath) either as *subjectum* or as the Heideggerian ground, but as the 'under' of the underneath which opens on to the abyss. The notions of the abyss, offering, gift and ghost are all connected to the Heideggerian *es gibt*. For Derrida: '*It gives* in the abyss, it gives-the abyss. There is, *es gibt*, the abyss. Now it seems to me that *The Origin* can also be read as an essay on the gift (*Schenkung*), on the offering' (*TP*: 291). It is at this point that Derrida determines the object through his concept of the crypt, which dissolves the relation between subject and object, and introduces the notion of the other as a phantom '(who is another) in himself as the ghost of an other, etc.' (*TP*: 373). The double of identity is here replaced by a chain of irreducible otherness which haunts both the subject and the object. The other is absolved from a relational structure within both subjectivism and objectivism, and its 'ground' becomes the groundless abyss, or the labyrinth without Ariadne and her thread. The Minotaur is neither eliminated nor mastered by Derrida's thought. It represents the risk of the labyrinth without return, restitution, or appropriation. Unlike the mirror, which sustains the logic of reflection, the labyrinth denotes a logic of resonance. Derrida wants to propose 'a supplementary thread' in order to introduce the problematic of the breakage of identification (Lacoue-Labarthe, 1989: 40).

A non-relational concept of the other is also advocated in *The Post Card*, where notions of lineage and sequential and chronological order are overturned in an attempt to invert relations in general (*CP*: 22). Whereas identity has been conceived of as a relational concept, Derrida's irreducible otherness negates all relations which can be reduced to binary oppositions that establish a hierarchy, an order, a chronology, a lineage, an example, an origin, a destination, an arrival, an authentication, an inheritance, a relay between sender, writer, receiver, addresser and addressee, and a connection between filiation and authority. Against the concept that writing encapsulated irreducible alterity, *The Post Card* argues that the post and envoi 'naively overturns everything' and 'allegorizes the catastrophic unknown of the order' (*CP*: 21). Thus history and writing, in their archival forms, are posts: their topology is that of passage and relay within a system of other posts; they are stoppages of circulation. Their chronotope is governed by the moment or the effect of what Derrida calls 'restance'. Once again the other is that interminably repeated supplementation which allows for no completion and framing (*CP*: 313).

In *The Post Card* Derrida also spells out more emphatically the relationship between subjectivity and the other. The question of the relation of the self to itself becomes for Derrida 'a question of a relation to oneself as a relation to the other, the auto-affection of a *fort:da* which gives, takes, sends and destines itself, distances and approaches itself by its own step, the other's' (*CP*: 403). Derrida signals here the connection between the other and psychoanalytic thought, which he sees as attempting to reduce or eliminate what he calls 'the anxiety of alterity', which cannot be resolved within its paradigm of mastery. The other cannot be incorporated into questions like 'who are we?', 'how are we to know ourselves?', 'how are we to act?' These domains belong not to the subject but the other. The other does not eliminate the anxiety of no knowledge, of no meaning, since it delimits the horizon within which such questions can be asked. It defines the task of interpretation as an uncovering of that irreducibility of alterity which aims at a freedom that comes from the other. The irreducible heterogeneity of the other involves subjecting the self to the demands of the other. Questions of otherness replace the conscious, unconscious, and certain subject. One encounters the other outside a relational framework based on appropriation. As something which apparently negates all relations except that which refers to itself, the other becomes, like writing, a self-referential concept. But it is also unlike writing in being an all-encompassing concept.

5.6 Appropriation and critique: Levinas and the early and late Derrida

Derrida's notion of the other has been critically shaped by his encounters with Levinas, the earliest of which dates from the sixties and forms the substance of his first long essay on Levinas's thought, called 'Violence and Metaphysics'. Derrida's later work further emphasises the non-subjectivist nature of the other. His second encounter with Levinas occurred in the eighties, and is documented in *At This Very Moment in This Work Here I Am*. This signals a more radical break with Levinas which Derrida continues till the end. An examination of these two early texts will not only clarify the relationship of Derrida to Levinas, but also serve as an introduction to the question of the status of the concept of the other in Derrida's thought, which is the subject of the next chapter.

The dialogue between Levinas's and Derrida's thought is both complex and ongoing, and marked by differences and similarities (see Bernasconi and Critchley, 1991; Critchley, 1997). The most important difference is that Levinas, especially in his early work, is reluctant to abandon completely either subjectivity or the idea of God. Derrida's most significant engagement with Levinas begins with the latter's attempt to construct a concept of the other that goes beyond the problematic of totality, and which represents a radical shift away from both Hegelianism and Western philosophy in general. Reducing the problematic of totality to the same, Levinas counterpoises it with the concept of infinity as exteriority, expressed in his concept of the other as 'face'. This is a representational concept, for it is constructed on the resemblance between man and God. It is this aspect that Derrida will convincingly reject by showing how Levinas's thought remains within subjectivism and, more generally, the Western metaphysics of presence.

Derrida wants to transcend the concept of infinity, and to institute a philosophy of alterity which, through borrowing theological motifs – such as those of messianism, prophesy and future promise – will transform them in the context of a seemingly more secularised problematic. Although Derrida's thought has been interpreted as negative theology, he wants to avoid the problems associated with what he calls onto-theology, and denies any close association with negative theology (Hart, 1989). In Levinas's theological thinking, on the other hand, the idea of God expresses the other as positive infinity. In other words, Levinas institutes a theology in place of, and by means of, ontology and phenomenology. In contrast, Derrida's thought is (as he puts it in a different context) 'messianism without religion . . . messianic without messianism' or in a latter formulation messianicity '*without messianism*' (*SM*: 59; *FK*: 17). As a thinker who breaks with the idea of Being and co-presence, he institutes a kind of thought that incorporates both the future present and the past present. Neither totality nor infinity circumscribes his thinking, for they both negate their opposites.

Derrida's thinking is tied to the idea of coming, of immanence, of that which is yet to come. The encounter with the other, therefore, is not within the problematic of ontology as traditionally conceived. Instead of connecting seeing to knowing, it gives itself over to anticipation, to the event, and to the blind gaze of the other. For Derrida, as with Levinas, the infinitely other is the invisible and the unforeseeable. All saying is addressed to that other which 'precedes all ontology; it is the ultimate relation in Being' (*WD*: 98). Derrida signals his intent to conceptualise what makes rationalism both possible and impossible when he argues that:

> by definition, if the other is the other, and all speech is for the other, no logos as absolute knowledge can *comprehend* dialogue and the trajectory toward the other. This incomprehensibility, this rupture of logos is not the beginning of irrationalism

but the wound or inspiration which opens speech and makes possible every logos or every rationalism (*WD*: 98).

For Derrida, the other is what makes logos possible, even as a logos of the rational, knowing subject. The other is neither known nor spoken. Any reference to a verb that designates a subject ends up with the verb overflowing 'in its movement toward the other, what is called the speaking subject' (*WD*: 98). If knowledge of the self comes through the other, then the speaking subject – the privileged entry-point of phenomenology – is not simply questioned but eliminated. There is thus an asymmetrical relationship between the self (whether conceived of as an Ego or as being-there) and the other. Since the other becomes the interlocutor and addressee of both speech and writing, the conscious, intending, and self-positing subject is either eliminated or subsumed under the other. It is then a question of deciding whether this asymmetry between subject and other is a radical departure from the problems of subjectivity, or rather an attempt to avoid and over-simplify the problem of identity.

This notion of asymmetry also leads to critique that idea of intersubjectivity which he sees as integral to the Western tradition. Even in its most radically Heideggerian formulation, the Western idea of Being conceives of the encounter with the other as occurring within the structure of *Mitsein* – that is, within a structure characterised by reciprocity, exchange of equivalents, the co-junction of co-present subjects, and so forth. Derrida replaces this conception with the idea of encountering the other within a structure that has no reciprocity, and no exchange of equivalents which a subject articulates or acts upon (whether consciously or otherwise) within a pre-given ethical framework. Although Derrida develops this framework out of a critical appropriation of Levinas' thought, important strands of the Judaic tradition are behind it. The encounter with the other in Derrida, therefore, has the structure of the gift, which contains the notion of debt without return; it is an unconditional response to the call of the other. In Habermas's theory of discourse ethics, the symmetrical structure of the relations between discursive partners – or, more simply, the absence of power in them – makes possible pure reciprocity, defined as the free exchangeability of speaking and listening positions (Habermas, 1979; 1990). Within political theory as a whole, justice is always intra-, rather than inter-generational, and is therefore a question of and for co-present subjects. The encounter with the other as an asymmetrical encounter, an encounter where credits and debits are not meant to balance, has no place in the Western tradition as anchored by a notion of justice that is intra-generational. Derrida's position within this debate is unique. For whereas Levinas remains more wedded to the Judaic tradition and Habermas to the Western one, Derrida asks: 'Are we Greeks? Are we Jews? But who, we?' (*WD:* 153). The ambivalence of the questions begs no final answers. In Levinas, however, the ethical relation to the other underpins his thought and subverts the ontology of presence of Greek philosophy as well as the 'idealising subjectivity of ontology, which reduces everything to itself' (Levinas and Kearney, 1986: 27. What Levinas is trying to open up is an 'ethical or biblical perspective that transcends the Greek language of intelligibility – as a theme of justice and concern for the other as other, as a theme of love and desire, which carries us beyond the infinite being of the world as presence' (Levinas and Kearney, 1986: 20).

5.7 What is beyond the metaphysics of violence?

In his 1964 essay on 'Violence and Metaphysics' Derrida examines Levinas' concept of the other (as encapsulated in the concept of the face) as well as his radical departure from Heideggerian notions of subjectivity (*Dasein)* and intersubjectivity *(Mitsein).* Derrida argues that in Heidegger the subject loses its specificity within a collective representation. The subject is no longer an I, but an us; the other is on his/her side, but not facing him/her. The relation between subject and other is designated as 'with' (*mit*). Levinas, contrary to Heidegger, aims at a face-to-face encounter with the other, and without an intermediary or communion; it is at once absolute distance and absolute communion. Levinas, Derrida argues, conceives of the encounter with the other not in terms of contact but in terms of a separation that interrupts all totalities. 'This being-together as separation precedes or exceeds society, collectivity, [and] community' Derrida writes. 'Levinas calls it religion. It opens ethics' (*WD*: 95–96). Asserting the radical function of the other, Levinas institutes the concept of ethical responsibility based on the notion of the Other. Derrida maintains these ideas, arguing that there can be no ethical transcendence without the other, and that an ethical relationship to the other is a precondition for the emergence of ethics. Both Levinas and Derrida, therefore, think of the other as that which opens up ethics. Each conceives the ethical relation to the other as taking the form of an interrogation characterised by exteriority and asymmetry.

Derrida argues, however, that Levinas remains within Husserlian thought, because by retaining the concept of intentionality he fails to radicalise the phenomenological instant. As a result, Levinas conceives of the other as the existent. In other words, Levinas's thought remains within the metaphysics of Being and consequently within the metaphysics of subjectivity. For Derrida, on the other hand, absolute alterity makes possible the conception of time beyond the phenomenological instant, and opens up a conception of history in which neither future nor past is reduced to the present instant. Derrida argues that the 'absolute alterity of each instant, without which there would be no time, cannot be produced – constituted – within the identity of the subject or the existent', because 'it comes into time through the Other' (*WD*: 91). Without the other, which exists in a framework outside reciprocity, neither the subject nor the existent could have a history or an identity. By placing the relationship with the other beyond history, Levinas introduces a theological dimension. Derrida, however, argues that history begins with a relationship to the other, which enables the conception of difference and alterity within identity: 'the ego cannot engender alterity within itself without encountering the Other' (*WD*: 94). In other words, the asymmetry between the ego and the other is grounded differently in Derrida's thought as compared to Levinas, and this difference is founded in part, as we shall see, on their different readings of Husserl. The other determines how the ego relates not only to the other but also to itself. There is no self-relation without the irruption of the totally-other.

Derrida deals also with the idea of the other in Heidegger and its relation to Levinas's thought. Because Heidegger affirms the priority of Being over the existent, 'the neutral thought of Being neutralizes the Other as being' (*WD*: 97). Levinas attempts to overcome the Heideggerian notion of totality which – through its notions of infinity and face – neutralises the other as being. However, in a paradoxical manner, Derrida argues that 'this thought of infinity (what is called the thought of God) . . . would permit one to affirm the priority of ontology over theology, and to affirm that the thought of Being is presupposed by the thought of God' (*WD*: 150). In Levinas, the other is infinity, and the face expresses a concept of infinity. Consequently, Levinas remains within both the metaphysics of presence and the Hegelian problematic of the other when he conceives of the infinitely other as positive infinity, which expels negativity from transcendence. Levinas's notion of the face, however, is also theological because it is conceived of 'in terms of the "resemblance" of man to God' (*WD*: 102). Levinas asserts that 'it is only in God that speech, as presence, as the origin and horizon of writing, is realized without defect' (*WD*: 102).

In other words, speech is both the origin and horizon of writing, and God – the perfect Being – is full speech. Writing is subjugated to speech as the privileged entry to presence and otherness, while negativity is expelled from the perfect speech of God. Both writing and speech thus relate to the other as face, behind which stands the certainty and perfection of God. The absolute Other is God as positive infinity. In Levinas, the subject gains access to the meaning of the other 'on the basis of its "face" . . . [and] on the basis of an intentional modification of my ego' (*WD*: 128). The other is conceivable as such to the extent that, as a subject, it is an ego like me, and as an object it is 'simultaneously less other (not absolutely other) and less "the same" than I' (*WD*: 127). Consequently, Levinas fails to dissociate the subject, speech, self and 'I' from language, thought and knowledge. Since the concept of face in Levinas 'is presence, *ousia*' (*WD*: 101), it is embedded within the thought of subjectivity, even if it tries either to articulate irreducible alterity outside the phenomenological problematic of the subject or to retain the glance of the other as commandment.

In contrast, Derrida regards the encounter with the other as being outside representation: bearing no conceptual relation to the same, it cannot be encompassed by such linguistic concepts as infinity, experience or living present. Unlike Levinas, Derrida interprets Plato's *ta epekeina tes ousias* as that which leads 'beyond Being itself', and 'beyond the totality of the existent or the existent-hood of the existent (the Being existent of the existent), or beyond ontic history' (*WD*: 141–142). For Derrida, the encounter with the other is connected to ethics, commandment, interrogation, and absolute, irreducible alterity, all of which are articulated through a critical dialogue with Levinas. But because it is based on asymmetry and nonreciprocity, this encounter is beyond both subjectivism and onto-theology. In other words, it occurs at the limits of the categories of Western metaphysics. According to Derrida, Levinas chooses to remain within metaphysics because he wants to attain 'via the royal road of ethics, the supreme existent . . . as other. And this existent is man, determined as face in his essence as man on the basis of his resemblance to God' (*WD*: 142; *TAT*: 119). Derrida's concept of the other is post humanist, post-theological and beyond the thought of Being.

5.8 Levinas, Husserl and the 'alter ego'

To categorise Derrida's concept of the other as post-humanist may be misleading, however, in so far as it suggests a categorical rejection of such purportedly humanist categories as the 'ego'. Yet this is far from being the case, as we shall see from a closer reading of those passages in '*Violence and Metaphysics*' which differentiate Derrida's from Levinas' approach to Husserl's theory of the other. Before proceeding with this analysis, however, a brief overview of Levinas' philosophy is necessary in order to locate the decisive shift in his thinking about subjectivity. Levinas' *oeuvre* can be divided into two phases, each corresponding to one of his two great works: *Totality and Infinity*, published in 1961, and *Otherwise than Being or Beyond Essence,* published in 1974.

Levinas identifies the notion of *totality* with both war and that Western metaphysical tradition which reduces the individual to the *totality*; *infinity*, on the other hand, is identified with an eschatological vision without images that requires ethics as its optics. Eschatology is also defined as exteriority, and our relationship with it is through the face of the other. In this early work, however, there is still room for 'a defence of subjectivity'. This is to be conducted 'not at the level of its purely egoist protestation against totality, nor in its anguish before death, but as founded in the idea of infinity' (Levinas, 1969: 26). Subjectivity is conceived of, therefore, 'as welcoming the Other, as hospitality; in it the idea of infinity is consummated' (Levinas, 1969: 27). Derrida's early critique of Levinas' work focuses not only (as we have seen) on this idea of the Other as face but also on this rejection of subjectivity as, in some senses, egoeity.

In *Otherwise than Being* even this limited defence of subjectivity is abandoned. What is otherwise or beyond essence is no longer infinity apprehended through the face. Rather, it is the 'saying' as opposed to the 'said', the '*illeity*' as opposed to the 'I-thou', or indeed any interpersonal or intersubjective relationship. Both the 'saying' (as an an-archical origin) and the '*illeity*' (as the 'always absent' or trace *of the other*) are suggestive of Derrida's concepts of '*différance*' and the trace. It should be remembered in this context that *Otherwise* was published originally in the same year as *Glas*, and postdates Derrida's early essay on Levinas by ten years. It might be suggested, therefore, that Derrida's early critique of Levinas' 'humanist subjectivism' had its effect. 'The responsibility for the other', writes Levinas, 'can not have begun in my commitment, in my decision . . . The responsibility for the other is the locus in which is situated the null-site of subjectivity' (Levinas, 1981:10). The subject becomes expiation, substitution, subjection, pure passivity, sensibility or the hostage that occupies the 'null-site' of the break-up of the identity of man. The subject becomes pure exposure to the other.

Derrida's early reading of Levinas, however, concentrates on *Totality and Infinity*. Derrida regards Levinas' reading of Husserl in this book as quite conventional, in so far as he suggests that by

> making the other, notably in the *Cartesian Meditations*, the ego's phenomenon, constituted by analogical appresentation on the basis of belonging to the ego's own sphere, Husserl allegedly missed the infinite alterity of the other, reducing it to the same. To make the other an alter ego, Levinas says frequently, is to neutralize its absolute alterity (*WD*: 123).

Derrida makes three observations on this interpretation. First, he argues that Husserl is seeking the alterity of the Other, and does not reduce it by analogy with the ego. As Husserl puts it, other egos 'are not simple representations or objects represented within me, synthetic unities of a process of verification taking place "within me", but precisely "others"' (Husserl, quoted in Derrida, *WD*: 123). For Derrida, therefore, 'it is this appearance of the other as that which I can never be, this originary non-phenomenality, which is examined as the ego's *intentional phenomenon*' (*WD*: 123).

The intentionality which, in Husserl's thought, is aimed at the other is always mediated according to Derrida, who firmly rejects the idea of immediate access to the other on the grounds that such access would reduce the other to the same. Rather than seeing analogical apresentation as a problem, therefore, Derrida argues that it 'confirms and respects separation, the unsurpassable necessity of (nonobjective) mediation' (*WD*: 124). In this context, Derrida speaks of a double alterity or a 'double power of indefiniteness': the alterity of bodies and the alterity of the transcendent thing.

'The stranger', as an example of this double power,

> is infinitely other because by his essence no enrichment of his profile can give me the subjective face of his experience *from his perspective,* such as he has lived it. Never will this experience be given to me originally, like everything which is *mir eigenes,* which is *proper* to me. This transcendence of the nonproper no longer is that of the entirety, always inaccessible on the basis of always partial attempts: transcendence of *Infinity*, not of *Totality* (*WD*: 124).

Here Levinas falls into a trap. By eschewing the egological bases of our understanding of otherness (Derrida's position is Husserlian here), and by refusing the detour of mediation (in this respect Derrida is Hegelian), Levinas is left with no means of founding his own position. Derrida even conceives of such a foundation as an original act of transcendental violence, inescapable since there is no shelter from 'totality' in 'infinity'.

Derrida's third argument is that, contrary to what Levinas suggests, Husserl never claims that the perception of the other can be given *originaliter*, and that this constitutes a *dissymmetry* between ego and alter that Levinas would find unacceptable. For Derrida, egoity and transcendence towards the other are mutually indispensable. 'In my ipseity I know myself to be other for the other' he writes. 'Without this, "I" (in general: egoity), unable to be the other's other, would never be the victim of violence' (*WD*: 126). Ego and other – or, more precisely, ego and the transcendence toward the other – are (to risk an Hegelianism) dialectically related. This is why two seemingly antithetical statements can be equally and simultaneously true: 'the other is absolutely other if he is an ego, that is, in a certain way, if he is the same as I'; furthermore, 'the other as *res* is simultaneously less other (not absolutely other) and less "the same" than I' (*WD*: 127). Derrida grounds this seeming contradiction in the thought that the other cannot be 'absolutely exterior' (to use Levinas' term) without losing its otherness. Instead of opposing 'infinity' to 'totality', we should treat the relationship between the ego and the other, between identity and difference, as an 'economy' or, more powerfully, as ‘the transcendental origin of an irreducible violence’. As Derrida argues that

> this transcendental origin, as the irreducible violence of the relation to the other, is at the same time nonviolence, since it opens the relation to the other. It is an *economy*. And it is this economy which, by this opening, will permit access to the other to be determined, in ethical freedom, as moral violence or nonviolence (*WD*: 128–129).

Furthermore, any attempt to suspend this economy (which grounds the finitude of the ego) via the kind of eschatology envisioned by Levinas would risk falling into the ‘worst violence’, which is ‘an infinitist dogmatism in pre-Kantian style’ that cannot conceive of responsibility except as ‘divine responsibility’ (*WD*: 130).

Derrida’s strategy in this text is therefore twofold: to use Husserl in order to critique Levinas’ interpretation of Husserl, and to re-read Husserl against Husserl. Derrida adopts Husserl’s positioning of the ego as ‘archi-factuality’ or *Urtatsache,* that is, the idea of ‘the irreducibly egoic essence of experience’ (*WD*: 131). While not wanting to fall into solipsism, Derrida sees both the *alter ego* and God as having meaning only in relation to an ego. Furthermore, while Derrida agrees with Husserl that ‘egological life has as its irreducible and absolutely universal form the living present’, he adds that ‘only the alterity of past and future presents permits the absolute identity of the living present as the self-identity of non-self identity’ (*WD*: 132). Derrida, however, can argue this seeming contradiction and putative violation of the Husserlian thematic of presence only by invoking once again (as we have seen already in his interpretation of Husserl on time) unpublished against published works, and in this case the *Cartesian Meditations.* In the same way that the ‘not-now’ is constitutive of the ‘now’, war and peace, ego and alter, totality and infinity form a transcendental ‘non-originary’ origin or ‘generalised economy’. It is not Husserl but Levinas who privileges the other; similarly the ego is privileged only as a result of Levinas’ misinterpretation of Husserl. For Derrida, Husserl himself never falls into this error, at least not in his unpublished works.

5.9 'The gift of the other'

The second significant encounter with Levinas did not take place until 1980, when the essay entitled 'At This Very Moment in This Work Here I Am' is written. It further elaborates Derrida's concept of the other while critiquing Levinas's subjectivism. The concept of the other is discussed here in relation to restitution, debt, gratitude and trace. The concept of the other is linked to the structure of the gift and divorced from notions of restitution and debt. One gestures to the other, and answers the injunctive call of the other, within a relation of asymmetry. In other words, the self engages with the other on the basis that the other owes nothing and gives nothing that could be inscribed in the structure of the gift as either debt or restitution. Our engagement with the other is based on a positive affirmation of what Derrida calls 'the gift of the other' which, in not being part of the chain of restitutions, is beyond all restitution (*DR*: 410), and thus escapes those relationships of exchange which are based on mutual, symmetrical reciprocity.

Furthermore, Derrida argues that although 'the wholly other' is 'incommensurably heterogeneous to the language of the present and the discourses of the same', it nevertheless always leaves a trace of it (*DR*: 412). In this way, Derrida avoids ontologising difference. He also avoids placing the differential structure of the other beyond any attempt to say or to mark its alterity within the economy of the same. Because the Saying of the other cannot be contained in the Said, there will always be in any text an excess of alterity or the unsaid. Language itself becomes open to the wholly other, and as a result every work and every writing dislocates both the subject and the signature. No operation belongs absolutely to a determined and determinable subjectivity that could be conceived of as an active agent in its production. The subject appears in the accusative case, and the link between the subject-as-he and the 'bearer of the name is other' (*DR*: 420). What Derrida calls the other is a 'he' which 'is not the subject-author-signer-proprietor of the work' but 'a "he" without authority' (*DR*: 424).

Before the name – and before any pronoun that would designate an identity – there is the other and its letting-be, which allows both the past anterior and future anterior of the other to be irreducible. Derrida wants to emphasise that because his notion of the wholly other incorporates the 'always already past', in this way 'it will have drawn us toward an eschatology without philosophical theology, beyond it in any case, otherwise than it' (*DR*: 425). By embedding his concept of the other in the past anterior, Derrida seeks to escape theology; and by embedding the other within the future anterior he wants to escape the problematic of both presence and ontology. His statement, 'Here I am, (I) come', constitutes a non-subjective response to the 'he' – to the other. The 'I' and the self occupy the space of the other by its very immanence. Presence is a property that both the self and the other lose in their constitution.

What replaces presence, therefore, is the trace of the other. Derrida argues that the other as 'he'

> will not have been (a) present but he will have made a gift by not disappearing without leaving a trace. But leaving the trace is also to *leave* it, to abandon it, not to insist upon it in a sign. It is to efface it. In the concept of trace is inscribed in advance the re-treat [*re-trait*] of effacement (*DR*: 426).

The other is inscribed in the concept of trace as effacement; that is, the property of the other is not presence but its delimitation. The other 'appears' by not appearing, and its gift is to leave a trace by not leaving it. In other words, Derrida wants a concept of the other which cannot be ontologised, historicised or act as a lever of mastery and authority. As such it relies on effects, rather than marking and locating difference as a specific ontological category. The relationship with the other is based on the idea of a pre-originary differential structure, articulated through the concept of trace.

5.10 Alterity and sexual difference

It is within this conception of alterity that the issue of sexual difference is raised. In both his second essay on Levinas and his interview with Christie McDonald ('Choreographies') Derrida makes it clear that his concept of difference can accommodate the issue of sexual difference, but only outside a subjectivist and ontological framework. He accuses Levinas of collapsing sexual difference into an economy of the same by making sexual difference as femininity secondary. For Derrida, difference is embedded in his concept of the other. His 'wholly other' is at once beyond and anterior to sexual difference as inscribed in the opposition 'feminine/masculine'. It must be emphasised here that Derrida seeks neither to neutralise nor supersede sexual difference, since that would align him with both the Hegelians and, to a certain extent, the Heideggerian sexual neutralisation of *Dasein.* Derrida wants to avoid both the reductionism and the somewhat prescriptive positionality entailed by such oppositions as femininity/masculinity and homosexuality/heterosexuality/bi-sexuality since what these represent remains undecidable, and concerns 'not only but also the line of cleavage between the two sexes' (*DR*: 453).

Once again Derrida uses the idea of the gift – as that which disturbs ontological categories – in order to conceptualise sexual difference outside of binary oppositions and beyond the dialectical categories of Western metaphysics. Both the structure and function of the gift make it difficult to define (say) femininity as part of the problematic of oppositional sexual difference. Furthermore, for Derrida, the ethical relationship to the other *as* other is independent of sexual difference but not a-sexual. In other words, since the wholly other is a concept neither marked nor determined by sexual difference, an ethical relationship with the other can take place in undetermined multiplicities of sexuality. Because Derrida, like Heidegger, wants the other to be sexually neutral but not devoid of sexuality, he avoids defining sexuality either biologically or anthropologically. Sexual difference is for him an effect rather than a determining factor. It is not anterior to the other as absolute alterity. On the contrary, the other makes possible both the polyvocity and irreducible multiplicity of sexual difference embedded in Derrida's concept of textuality.

Textuality, in so far as it relates to sexual difference, is that which delimits such questions as the proper, property, and ownness. It is another instance of that asymmetrical relationship with the other which is not based on those traditional categories which inscribe sexual difference. In other words, the other represents not only a double asymmetry of sexual difference but also a relationship that, according to Derrida, goes 'beyond the grammar and spelling, shall we say (metaphorically), of sexuality' (*DR*: 455). Derrida's earlier work on autobiography clarifies his position on sexual difference and its relation to the other. He argues there that

> the sex of the addresser awaits its determination by or from the other. It is the other who will perhaps decide who I am – man or woman. Nor is this decided once and for all (*EOa*: 52).

This idea that sexual identity is determined by the other has intimations of Sartre's theory of the determination of identity – in his example, Jewish identity – by the other. It has suffered understandably at the hands of critics for whom identity is also a personal and collective practice (Sartre, 1991; 1948).

This position, which is consistent with Derrida's anti-humanism and anti-subjectivism, represents his reluctance to locate his thought within any logic of difference not derived from the absolute other. The title of the essay – Choreographies – also indicates Derrida's attempt to make the other independent of sexual difference. Like Matisse's painting of the dance, 'his dancers' are a-sexual without being devoid of sexuality. Although they can be substituted and interchanged, they nevertheless joyously affirm the dance without ever escaping the circle of the absolute other. Just as Derrida seeks to break away from Levinas' theological notion of the other, which is based on an analogical relationship between man and God, so too he wants to conceive of the other outside the opposition feminine/masculine (*SN*). The relationship with the other is not determined by the sexual ascription of either the other or any determined subject (*SN*: 49). Irigaray's concern that women and men relate differently to the other, and that for the woman man is the other, is thus not addressed by Derrida. His 'other' being structured like the gift, is non-gendered and has no connection with the problematic of mastery and authority. The Derridean gift is outside the circle of return, restitution, debt, gratitude and reciprocity. Because the relation to the other is non-subjective, it escapes intersubjective ideas of reciprocity and exchange. What Derrida calls the 'wholly other' has no contractual relationship to us, and thus escapes the demands of obligation and negotiation. Both the call of the other and the affirmative response to it take place before subjectivity is constituted. The idea of responding to the other is thus inscribed already in the other, which is charged with all the modes and forms of irreducible alterity.

6. The Other – 2: The Gift, the Politics and Ethics of Responsibility, and the Other

The concept of the other as constructed by Derrida has implications for politics and associated ethical concepts. If alterity is the point from which to begin thinking politics, the idea that the polis and democracy embody the politics of presence and subjectivity needs to be deconstructed and thought anew from the perspective of the other. In the 1980's Derrida began to expound the implications of deconstruction for politics. These also came to the fore in his defence of Paul de Man in the late eighties (see bibliographical appendix). By linking deconstruction with anti-totalising and anti-totalitarian discourses of both the right and the left, Derrida attempts to associate deconstruction with ethico-political concerns. The politics that he argues for rests on a concept of responsibility which 'requires the experience of the undecidable as well as that irreducibility of the other'. This means that before one answers and responds for oneself, one needs to do so 'to the other, about the other, *for* the other, not in his place as if in the place of another "proper self," but *for* him' (*MPM*: 230). Derrida, therefore, places the other at the centre of his political thought, and makes the subject answerable to the other and for the other. In *Memoires* Derrida also clarifies his notion that respect for the other is the first rule of any textual engagement with it and the basis of any ethico-political relation. To have respect for the other is to recognise 'the right to difference, in his relation to others but also in his relation to himself' (*MPM*: 238). This is to privilege the politics of difference above the politics of co-present and co-equal subjects.

6.1 The politics of the other

In his essay entitled *The Politics of Friendship,* Derrida attacks the idea that reciprocity underpins the concept of friendship. He argues that it has given rise to a particular kind of politics and a specific concept of community and responsibility. Derrida has tackled the problematic of responsibility elsewhere, especially in his early text *Dissemination*, where he argues that the first effect of dissemination is to displace the dominance of the values of 'responsibility and individuality' (*D*: 6). At this stage, however, Derrida does not link this to a particular conception of politics. But in the early eighties he once again describes deconstruction as attempting to 're-evaluate the indispensable notion of "responsibility"' (Derrida in Kearney, 1984: 121), although he admits he has some difficulty in connecting deconstruction to 'existing political codes and programmes' (ibid: 119), because they remain fundamentally within Western metaphysics. Seeking to connect deconstruction to a radical form of politics, Derrida 'injects' the problematic of the other into the notions of responsibility, politics and autonomy in order to radicalise them. His project, in sum, is to remove the residues of Western metaphysics from both the field of politics and the concept of freedom.

His essay therefore constructs the other as the source of notions of response, responsibility, and freedom. Derrida argues that the other assigns us before the organised *socius* or any kind of natural or positive law arise, and engages us in that process of response which involves responsibility without freedom. In other words, the social and the political dimensions of selfhood are given over to the other, which nevertheless appears without seeming to do so. Consequently, such concepts as response, responsibility and freedom become divorced from notions of autonomy and reflexivity. Freedom does not belong to us, but instead is given to us by the other: 'it is assigned to us by the Other, from the Other, before any hope of reappropriation permits us to assume this responsibility in the space of what could be called *autonomy*' (*PF*: 634). This assignation of responsibility by the other is a kind of political *a priori*, which predetermines conventional political concepts such as autonomy.

Derrida also connects friendship to notions of promise, waiting and commitment. Deconstructing the idea that friendship is given in the present, he opens up the idea of responsibility to the future and the past. He removes the idea of being-together, of co-presence, from ontological categories (especially those of the subject), and attributes the opening of the ontological space itself to something anterior to friendship, which again he connects to the idea of the trace. Friendship, as conceived of in the Greco-Roman philosophical tradition, valorises reciprocity. By contrast, Derrida's idea of friendship is tied to his anti-subjectivism and his privileging of responsibility before the other. He therefore questions the association of response with responsibility. After examining the various modes of answering, he argues 'one *answers for*, or *before*, by answering first *to*. This last modality thus appears more original, more fundamental, and hence unconditional' (*PF*: 638).

In order to institute this modality, or political *a priori,* Derrida makes the business of answering to the other encompassing both answering-for-oneself and answering-before-the-other. One answers for oneself by answering *to* the other, and one answers *before* the other by answering *to* the other. In order to make this mode of answering fundamental, original and anterior to all other modes, Derrida subsumes the question of response and responsibility under the category of the other. As usual, Derrida makes the 'I' and the self variations of the Same. By doing so he is led to argue that

> the 'oneself' or 'myself' . . . supposes the unity, in other words the memory, of the one responding. This is often called the unity of the subject, but one can conceive such a synthesis of memory without necessarily having recourse to the concept of *subject.* Since this unity is never secured in itself as an empirical synthesis, the recognition of this identity is entrusted to the instance of the name (*PF*: 638).

Derrida here sidesteps the issues both of selfhood and recognition by arguing that they can be addressed only 'via the royal road' of the other, whose memory is non-subjective. Derrida thus preserves the idea of the unity of memory, which enables at least a linguistic construction of oneself to emerge. Nevertheless, he still separates the whole issue from the concept of the subject by making the subject part of the problematic of the proper name. His idea of an anonymous memory untied from any particular subject remains, however, implausible.

Derrida emphasises that the response or answer to the other is more original for two reasons: first, 'one does not answer for oneself and in one's own name, one is not responsible except before [*devant*] the question, request, challenge, "instance", or "insistance" of the Other'; secondly 'the proper name that structures the "answering for oneself" is in itself for the Other, whether the Other has chosen it . . . or whether because, in any case, it implies the Other in the very act of naming, its origin, its finality, its use' (*PF*: 639). In other words, 'responding' always presupposes the other in the relation to oneself, and this relationship is asymmetrical. Freedom is thus entrusted to the other, whose anteriority annuls the idea not only of autonomy but also of co-present and co-equal subjects. What we answer, to whom we answer, and in what modalities – all of these come from and are directed towards the other. As the source and destination of political, ethical, moral, and legal considerations, the other does not occupy any ontological space. In Derrida's schema, therefore, that ethical responsibility which we have to the other precedes our knowledge and recognition of it, and is independent of that notion of the self which grounds it in identity. The call of the other is both beyond recognition and intersubjective exchange. What requires us to answer to the other belongs to an ethics of injunction rather than an ethics of mutual recognition and respect.

I take issue with Derrida's understanding of reciprocity, freedom/autonomy and recognition. For if we accept Derrida's notion that responsibility and politics are based on the other rather that reciprocity, then the structure of the other becomes problematic, because it is as self-referential as Derrida's concept of writing. As a non-concept, the other is beyond the subject and beyond Being. The subject cannot act as a foundational principle of politics. If both the subject and the self are effects of the other, then the other becomes an all-powerful yet unknowable force, whose referent is nothing. The other begins to look as solipsistic as the Husserlian 'I' which is transposed on to it. To negate the subject as an 'I', is to restrict the scope of subjectivity and its politics. I think that Derrida goes too far when he announces that the 'new thinking' and the 'new politics' are to be thought through the other not as mediating force but as an absolute heteronomy.

The other thus allows us to take responsibility for responding to and answering the call. But these activities are impossible, because to respond to the other as subject is to eliminate the other's otherness and absolute externality. This leaves us with a self that responds and answers to the call of the other because it cannot fail to do otherwise. As Derrida puts it, 'all these "fors" . . . make responsibility *undeniable: there is some, one cannot deny it, one cannot/can only deny it* [on ne peut (que) la dénier] *precisely because it is impossible*' (*MPM*: 230). This double non-logic of the other leaves little scope for the self to reflect upon an impossible possibility. In the final analysis, that regulatory mechanism which is entrusted to the other will always call for responsibility, even if the subject – as a self-reflecting and engaging agent – is no longer possible. In a politics entrusted to the heteronomy of the other, however, the other will not merely guard but also determine ethico-political relations. By itself, the absent subject cannot solve either questions of power or processes of 'othering'. For the other – as a quasi-transcendental structure – imposes its injunctive and interrogative power prior to the erection of political structures, and does so with an almost prophetic gesture. One cannot underestimate either the radicality of this gesture or the effect on a political concept of subjectivity when subjectivity itself is reduced to a sameness that denies alterity.

6.2 The call and the asymmetrical relation between the self and the other

When interviewed by Richard Kearney in 1981, Derrida argued that

> the rapport of self-identity is itself always a rapport of violence with the other; so that the notions of property, appropriation and self-presence, so central to logocentric metaphysics, are essentially dependent on an oppositional relation with otherness. In this sense, identity *presupposes* alterity (Derrida in Kearney, 1984: 117).

Because Derrida, like Levinas, wants a non-violent, non-oppositional relation with the other he is led to an ethical position of seeing the other as a notion beyond self-identity. By making alterity the foundational principle of identity, Derrida reverses the relation between them. Although he argues that the self should be conceived of as identified with (rather than opposed to) the other, he articulates this identification within a non-relational structure. Consequently, the other is conceived of not in terms of another 'I' or a you, but in terms of a call. Answered in the affirmative, this call of the other determines the relation of the self to both itself and the other. This call of the other, and the affirmative answer to it, constitute the foundational principle of deconstruction. In associating deconstruction with affirmation, however, Derrida emphasises that he does

> not mean that the deconstructing *subject* or *self* affirms. I mean that deconstruction is, in itself, a positive response to an alterity which necessarily calls, summons or motivates it. Deconstruction is, therefore, vocation: a response to a call. The other,

> as the other than self, the other that opposes self-identity, is not something that can be detected and disclosed within a philosophical space and with the aid of a philosophical lamp. The other precedes philosophy and necessarily invokes and provokes the subject before any genuine questioning can begin. It is in this rapport with the other that affirmation expresses itself (Derrida in Kearney, 1984:118).

The other provokes and invokes the subject not so much to constitute itself, but in order to answer the call of the other. When the relation of the subject to itself is annulled, the relation of both the subject and the self to the other becomes a question that can be neither raised nor answered within conventional philosophical discourse. The issue of the lamp and light, as well as the sign, would subsequently preoccupy Derrida in the terrain of the theological.

Who answers the call of the other becomes a vexing and unresolved question. Derrida does not consider the possibility of a reflective (as against an unreflective) answer to the call of the other. Neither the subject and the self nor their interrelation with the other is linked to the question of reflexivity. To whom is the call made? How does one answer it, and why? By making the answer to the call of the other conditional upon and prior to the emergence of the question of the subject, Derrida displaces rather than answers the question of subjectivity, which correspondingly is subsumed within the problematic of the other. The 'Iness' of the 'I' does not relate to the other, for it effaces itself in the constitution of itself as 'I'. Derrida thus avoids both the problem of narcissism and the cannibalisation of the other simply by taking the subject out of the picture. When the self becomes subject to the demands of the other, what results can only be an ethics of submission. The absolute other increasingly resembles the absolute subject of Western metaphysics; and if so, then Derrida effects merely a transference of power rather than a radical break with the metaphysical residues of the logos. Both the self-transparency of the metaphysical subject and the transparency of the other are eliminated. But they are replaced only by a generalised other, which determines the subject's relation not only to itself but also to other subjects.

If the subject as such must enter a process of reflection in order to know itself, then it must become an object to itself. The self, however, is not an object in the usual sense of the word. Reason, language, freedom and imagination are proper to the subject, although Derrida would have us believe that all of them emanate from the other. The self can neither engage with nor answer the call of the other unless there is an instance of self-identity within non-identity. The self needs to be posited as other in order to emerge from its solipsism. The subject, in becoming an object to itself, divides itself, and by doing so becomes other. The question is whether this otherness is prior to and/or beyond the subject, or whether the subject is other and constitutes itself through the other. Derrida's position is that the other effects both the 'original' dividing and the subsequent effacement of the self as self-identity. If so, then the whole question of self-reflexivity is eliminated, since the other becomes the locus of all processes, and is prior to all questions pertaining to the subject. In this theoretical schema, the subject cannot be 'written' into Derrida's discourse except through the other. And only as an erased subject can it be written at all.

The positing of the other as asymmetrical is seen most clearly when Derrida argues that it is 'beyond language and . . . summons language' (Derrida in Kearney, 1984: 123). Derrida's point in placing the other beyond language is to try to escape the connection between language and Being. Instead of Heidegger's dictum that language is the house of being, Derrida institutes his own, namely, that because the other summons language, language speaks the other (Heidegger, 1982). This abstract, generalised, and non-linguistically constructed other aims at a non-violent relationship with both the subject and the self. This is because the other dominates their relationship with it, and allows their emergence. In Derrida's schema, the total submission and dependence of the self on the other eliminates the possibility of violence.

6.3 From narcissism to death

The possibility of self-reflection is dealt with in the context of the theory of narcissism. For Derrida, non-narcissism

> is in general but the economy of much welcoming hospitable narcissism, one that is much more open to the experience of the other as other. I believe that without a movement of narcissistic reappropriation, the relation to the other would be absolutely destroyed, it would be destroyed in advance. The relation to the other – even if it remains asymmetrical, open, without possible reappropriation – must trace a

> movement of reappropriation in the image of oneself for love to be possible, for example. Love is narcissistic (*PO*: 199).

Here Derrida admits that the problem of the relationship between self and other cannot be divorced from the question of self-relation and reappropriation. By conceiving of this only as the Narcissistic component of love, Derrida fails to explore the concept of reflection in general and the way it operates in the myth of Narcissus. He thus fails to distinguish love of self from love of the other and their respective modalities.

The story of Narcissus epitomises not only auto-affection but also the myth of the moment when the image of the self *qua* object disappears. That is the moment of recognition, not only of oneself as other than the image, but also of the impossibility of achieving unity of the self both with the other and within love of self. Since what Narcissus longs for is nowhere, the object of his love eludes him for ever. Being only a reflection, it has no substance, essence, or reality. Narcissus, falling in love with a double not recognised as such, sees that the image repeats him without repetition. The moment of discovery comes when Narcissus understands that he has fallen in love with himself. Recognising that he cannot control the double, Narcissus arrives at self-knowledge through realising the impossibility of uniting and possessing both himself and the other. What the myth of Narcissus expresses is this double impossibility, rather than the complete independence and asymmetry of the other in relation to the self.

At this moment of self-understanding, Narcissus sheds tears which disturb the surface of the reflection and make the image of himself disappear. He thus recognises the impossibility of fully possessing the object of desire or love except by a process of splitting of the self and self-identity. He cannot abandon a narcissistic love in which there is no other, distinct and separate from one's own self. Self and other merge in an impossible union of non-union. By becoming subjective, internalised and inward looking, the self is unable to give the other independent existence. Moreover, the self is incapable of either positing itself as other or taking the place of another. Recognising its own solitude, the self realises that union with the other is impossible. Solitude, however, cannot be escaped through desire or love. The story of Narcissus shows how self relates to self through the mediation of reflection. Self-created, that reflection is other, in so far as the self is capable of positing itself as other

– not simply *through* the other (and dominated by it), but as part of a reflective process inseparable from the modalities of self-reflection. Moreover, the myth of Narcissus shows the limitations of modelling reflection on the mirror and fixity.

In an interview with Didier Cahen, Derrida goes on to argue that 'there are little narcissisms, there are big narcissisms, and there is death in the end, which is the limit. Even in the experience – if there is one – of death, narcissism does not abdicate absolutely' (*PO*: 199). By pluralising narcissism, and speculating that death does not limit its possibilities, Derrida signals his willingness to accept a mode of self-relation that is not totally dominated or determined by the other. Having argued in the early eighties that 'deconstruction is not an enclosure in nothingness, but an openness towards the other' (Derrida in Kearney, 1984: 124), Derrida now perceives this openness to the other as being moderated by an admission that love is narcissistic in character, and by the persistence of narcissism in the 'experience' of death. This moderate position, however, is abandoned in his later work, especially in *The Gift of Death*, where 'theological' overtones eliminate an earlier concern with the narcissistic moment of self-appropriation.

6.4 The cinder as the remains of memory

In the mid-1980's, Derrida introduces 'cinder' as an image for articulating a more advanced conception of the other. This represents a shift in emphasis rather than an abandonment of earlier conceptual models such as 'trace' and 'writing'. As Derrida himself explains,

> ashes or cinders are obviously traces – in general, the first figure of the trace one thinks of is that of the step, along a path, the step that leaves a footprint, a trace, or a vestige; but 'cinder' renders better what I meant to say with the name of trace, namely, something that remains without remaining, which is neither present nor absent, which destroys itself, which is totally consumed, which is a remainder without remainder. That is, something that is not (*PO*: 208).

By denoting merely a relation of what remains, the cinder is therefore unconnected to the question of Being.

The problematic 'to be' is displaced by the question of 'to remain'. Derrida argues that

> the cinder is not: This means that it testifies without testifying. It testifies to the disappearance of the witness, if one can say that. It testifies to the disappearance of memory. When I keep a text for memory, what remains there is apparently not cinders. Cinders is the destruction of memory itself; it is an absolutely radical forgetting, not only forgetting in the sense of the philosophy of consciousness, or a psychology of consciousness; it is even forgetting in the economy of the unconscious by repression. Repression is not forgetting. Repression keeps the memory. Cinders, however, is an absolute non-memory, so to speak. Thus, it communicates with that which in the gift, for example, does not even seek to get recognised or kept, does not even seek to be saved. Well to say there are cinders . . . is to say that in every trace, in every writing, and consequently in every experience (for me every experience is, in a certain way, an experience of trace and writing), in every experience there is this incineration, this experience of incineration which is experience itself (*PO*: 208–209).

In being neither a recollection nor what is repressed, memory is neither a successful nor a failed act of subjective appropriation. It resides, rather, in the physical remains of an incineration.

Derrida pursues this critique of memory and interiority in *Of Spirit*, where he deconstructs Heidegger's notion of Spirit. In order to free it from subjectivist constraints, Derrida introduces the material concepts of 'fire', 'return' and 'promise'. He suggests, for example, that 'memory' is inscribed in a concept of spirit, which by keeping 'watch in returning [*en revenant*, as a ghost] will always do the rest. Through flame or ash, but as the entirely other, inevitably' (*OS*: 113). Memory as the other is again that which appears as the (physical) remains of a conflagration, rather than what results from an (interiorising) act of appropriation. The concept of the ghost will 'appear' again in *Specters of Marx*.

6.5 From the ghosts of politics to the politics of ghosts

Derrida's long postponed deconstruction of Marxism, which was announced in *Positions,* is finally delivered in *Specters of Marx.* Beginning with a consideration of time, it criticises teleological accounts of history, and develops a concern with the question of justice. By figuring democracy in terms of the 'promise', it ironically proposes a New (virtual) International, and examines the notion of the spectral in Marx's own writings on history and ideology. It begins by playing on the phrase, 'The time is out of joint', which Shakespeare's Hamlet utters after swearing to his father's ghost. Instead of offering a mundane political reading of this phrase, which would centre on the circumstances of the late King's death and his brother's role in it, Derrida aims to show how the disarticulation of time is a precondition of justice itself. Neither the present moment nor a succession of temporal 'nows', Derrida's non linear concept of time means that time is disarticulated or haunted, that is to say, burdened by debt and filled with promise. In this respect, justice is something we owe not only to the present generation (since this would generate merely a 'politics of friendship') but also to past generations, to whom we incur a debt, as does Hamlet to his father's ghost. Haunted by absences, time can therefore never be fully self-present. In Derrida's reading of Shakespeare's play, a problem which is peculiar to Hamlet is thus generalised as a quasi-ontological condition.

Derrida uses this understanding of time to critique the then fashionable theses of Fukuyama on the *End of History and the Last Man* (Fukuyama, 1992). What haunts the 1990s is the ghost of Marxism after the revolutionary year of 1989. The question is how to exorcise it. Fukuyama's method is teleologically oriented: it is an amalgam of Hegel's notion of post-history and the struggle for recognition, the 'end of ideology' as understood in the early sixties, and the idea that all ideologically significant conflict had come to an end. All that was left was the rather petty happiness of the 'last man'. Fukuyama was forced to modify his thesis when post-history became more conflictual than had been anticipated and new ideological differences emerged (Fukuyama, 1999; 2007). Derrida's deconstructive force is directed against that teleological notion of history which Fukuyama borrows from Hegel. Ironically, Derrida's argument echoes Marx's comments on the Holy Alliance's hostility to revolutionaries inspired by the French Revolution. Fukuyama's new Holy Alliance, Derrida argues, is designed to exorcise the ghosts of the Russian Revolution in the context of a thesis concerning the end of history that Derrida describes as Christian eschatology. No shred of empirical history is allowed to spoil the happy ending, in which all the ghosts are exorcised and a happy neo-liberalism reigns.

The larger and less polemical question is what remains of Marxism (or, in Derrida's playful formulation, 'Whither Marxism')? What needs to be salvaged from the 'end' of Marxism is an eschatological spirit which is not so much 'Christian' as 'messianic'. The notion of promise – 'a certain experience of the emancipatory promise' – is 'irreducible to any deconstruction' (*SM*: 59). This notion of 'promise' enables Derrida to conceive of justice as beyond the exchange of equivalents, and of democracy as something which is 'to come'. It lies at the heart of what Derrida calls repeatedly a 'messianism without the messianic'. Messianic promise inscribes otherness in the present: the otherness of a past and a future. This 'otherness' links Derrida's newly politicised notions of the promise and responsibility, justice and democracy to his previous work as well as to the legacy of Marxism. Deconstruction is faithful to a certain spirit of Marxism because it inscribes 'the possibility of the reference to the other, and thus of radical alterity and heterogeneity, of differ*a*nce, of technicity, and of ideality in the very event of presence, in the presence of the present that it dis-joins *a priori*' (*SM*: 75). Alterity thus disjoins time, and in a way that is first determined messianically rather than politically.

This does not prevent Derrida, however, from making a political recommendation in the form of his proposal for a New International, designed to replace that one-sided version of globalization which neo-liberalism proposes. Derrida calls it 'an alliance without institutions', because horizontal alliances of co-present citizens would violate that condition of disjuncture enacted by the deconstructive event. Such an alliance is directed also against the idea of co-present nationals, because Derrida aims to disjoin the state and the nation as they exist in modern Western politics. He proposes an extension of international law so that it can intervene in supra-national processes, in the same way as human-rights law has been extended within national processes in order to facilitate legal intervention (*SM*: pp. 84–85). It is hard not to see New International as a kind of leftist version of the idea of a global civil society (see Falk, 1995). If so then although the scheme may be utopian, it is less 'messianic' than the original idea of the promise appears to indicate. In fact, the project of a legalisation and democratisation of world society is a lively topic in contemporary jurisprudence and political science (Cassese, 1990; 1995; Held, 1995).

6.6 From the death of the subject to the subject through death as promise

In *Memoires for Paul de Man* Derrida deals with the death of a specific other, namely his friend and colleague. He argues that

> if death comes to the other, and comes to us through the other, then the friend no longer exists except *in* us, *between* us. In himself, by himself, of himself, he is no more, nothing more. He lives only in us. But *we* are never *ourselves*, and between us, identical to us, a 'self' is never in itself or identical to itself. This specular reflection never closes on itself; it does not appear *before* this *possibility* of mourning, before and outside this structure of allegory and prosopopoeia which constitutes in advance all 'being-in-us,' 'in-me,' between us, or between ourselves (*MPM*: 28).

This relation to the other, therefore, rests not on a concept of the self as self-identity, but on a kind of mourning or endless reflection that never closes on itself. Death is not something that happens to a subject, but comes to us through the other.

The death of the other as a concrete 'other subjectivity' is not a given in Derrida's thought. Neither to speak of the other, nor to speak in or of the memory of self and other, is possible, because all speaking and writing are testamentary in nature, and open to endless future possibilities or comings. 'My friendship with Paul de Man', Derrida declares 'would have allowed me to say all of this *before* his death . . . And everything that we inscribe in the living present of our relation to others already carries, always, the signature of *memoirs-from-beyond-the-grave*' (*MPM*: 29). The other speaks to us – in us, for us and of us – beyond the grave and the life of a given, determined subjectivity. The finitude of memory, like finitude in general, can merely take the form of

> the trace of the other in us, the other's irreducible precedence; in other words, simply the trace, which is always the trace of the other, the finitude of memory, and thus the approach or remembrance of the future. If there is a finitude of memory, it is because there is something of the other, and of memory as a memory of the other, which comes from the other and comes back to the other (*MPM*: 29).

Since this structure can never be totalised, the questions of memory and mourning are determined by the other. Consequently,

> there can be no *true mourning*, even if truth and lucidity always presuppose it, and, in truth, take place only as the truth of mourning. The truth of the mourning of the other, but of the other who always speaks in me before me, who signs in my place, the hypogram or epitaph being always of the other, and for the other. Which also means: in the place of the other (*MPM*: 29).

The notion that the subject is determined by the abyssal structure of the other leads Derrida to relinquish 'in advance' notions of its '*autonomy*' (*MPM*: 32). For if the subject is determined through either the other or its death, then autonomy gives way to the idea that the subject arises in response to the cinders that constitute the other. Furthermore, that the "me" or "us", of which we speak, both 'arise and are delimited' in this way: 'only through this experience of the other' – and of the other as an other-who-can-die – is this memory of the other deposited as "me" or "us" (*MPM*: 33). Consequently, '[t]his terrible solitude, which is "mine" or "ours" at the death of the other, constitutes that relationship to self which we call "me", "us", "between us," "subjectivity," "intersubjectivity" and "memory"' (*MPM*: 33). This means that '[t]he *possibility* of death "happens," so to speak, "before" these different instances, and makes them possible. Or, more precisely, the possibility of the death of the other *as* mine or ours in-forms any relation to the other and the finitude of memory' (*MPM*: 33).

Memory is designated through the concept of a trace which is unconnected to presence, but constituted as such by 'traces of a past that has never been present, traces which themselves never occupy the form of presence and always remain, as it were, to come-come from the future, from the *to come*' (*MPM*: 58). In order to engage with 'the to come', Derrida elaborates the idea of the ghost as that which, although future-oriented, cannot be cut off from a past which does not constitute a stage in the past as presently understood. Derrida argues that

> ghosts always pass quickly, with the infinite speed of a furtive apparition, in an instant without duration, presence without present of a present which, coming back, only *haunts*. The ghost, *le re-venant*, the survivor, appears only by means of figure or fiction, but its appearance is not nothing, nor is it a mere semblance (*MPM*: 64).

The ghost that haunts is a concept of the other which again escapes the demand for presence. Appearance is replaced by semblance, and the phenomenal world is inhabited by the furtive figures of those ghosts – the survivors – which cannot be exorcised. The other always survives, and returns to disrupt any attempt to substitute “to be” for the question of “to come”. Beyond ontology and beyond phenomenality, the ghost always haunts.

The connection between the other and promise encompasses language, because language is inscribed in the notion of promise (Derrida, 1998: 71). Memory and promise are likewise connected, in so far as memory is promise, and the ‘promise prohibits the gathering of Being in presence, being even its condition. The condition of the possibility and impossibility of eschatology, the ironic allegory of messianism’ (*MPM*: 145). Derrida here suggests replacing the certainty of *logos* with the ironic allegory of messianism. The point of associating irony and allegory with messianism is to give it that radical turn which eschatology denies. In the land of deconstruction, Derrida remarks, the prophets are not far away (see Derrida, in Kearney, 1984: 119). Why then does he valorise messianism? I think that Derrida, by connecting the other with the promise, attempts to oppose a presence-oriented *logos* with a prophetic messianism which is ‘future-oriented’. Unlike Heidegger, Derrida argues that Being gives what cannot be given in a present, because it has the structure of the gift, ‘which does not occur without the aporia of the promise’ (*MPM*: 147). Thus, for Derrida ‘there is no gift except on the aporetic condition that *nothing* is given that is *present* and that *presents* itself as such. The gift is only a promise and a promised memory, here the future of Mnemosyne’ (*MPM*: 147). ‘Promise’ is what ‘pledges beyond death, beyond what we call, without knowing of what or of whom we speak, death. It involves, in reverse, the other, dead *in us*, from the first moment, even if no one is *there* to respond to the promise or speak for the promise’ (*MPM*: 149). Consequently, because a promise ‘has meaning and gravity only with the death of the other’ (*MPM*: 150), it is made in the name of the other.

6.7 The politics of responsibility

In the late 1980s Derrida attempted to take into account the issue of responsibility, which raises questions about the political and ethical implications of his thought. In his 1988 defence of Paul de Man, ‘*Like the sound of the sea deep within a shell: Paul de Man's War*', Derrida raises the issue of the relationship between responsibility, memory and the other. The controversy surrounding Paul de Man and Derrida's reaction to it was fierce (see bibliographical appendix). In this essay he associates responsibility with responding to '*unforeseeable* appeals, that is to appeals *from/of the other* that are addressed to us even before we decide on them' (*MPM*: 164). The other summons us before we decide to engage with it. Once again, the question of the promise is at the centre of Derrida's thought. Memory of the past is marked as an experience of the promise. As a promise to and from the other, it is "excessive", "unconditional" and "impossible" (*MPM*: 166). In other words, it promises more than it can keep.

The irony here is that when Derrida (as a concrete subject) defends Paul de Man (as a concrete other) he takes up the call of the other, which he has to answer unconditionally within the impossibility of a promise. Derrida himself uses the affirmative *yes* when asked to respond to accusations levelled against Paul de Man. As a result, problems in his notion of the other are displayed. For in dealing with Paul de Man as concrete other, Derrida embarks on a contextual analysis of his wartime writings. By analysing the historical and political specificity of the period, it aims to situate Paul de Man historically, politically, linguistically, culturally and ideologically. Here Derrida's abstract and ontologised other fails to dispense with those worldly aspects which embed a given subjectivity in historical specificity. He tries to contextualise de Man within a wider family, professional, social and cultural milieu, in which literature is taken to be what represents that *double edge or double bind* which undoes de Man's discourse. Derrida uses this phrase to denote how 'each term of this division never . . . [comes] . . . to rest in a monadic identity' (*MPM*: 218).

Derrida's analysis of de Man's writings attributes intention to their author, and places their narrative in context. Nevertheless, he sees context as a dangerous limit when it remains vague and silent instead of demarcating and framing a discourse (see, *MPM*: especially 206–207). Derrida, however, takes up the challenge to answer for de Man. In doing so, he talks about de Man's writings as reflecting the life of an agonising and suffering intellectual. This is achieved, however, through indirection, since what makes the wartime articles part of de Man's *oeuvre* is the signature of de Man rather than the writings themselves. By certifying the authorship of those writings, the signature bears the seal of responsibility for them, even though Derrida concedes the possibility of editorial intervention. He attempts to dissociate the memory of Paul de Man from the concrete subject. In this way, the response he affects so radically does not fail to be one of responsibility, and this comes from the other rather than a subject.

In this spirit, Derrida places his own – and indeed all – interpretation within the structure of the other, as that 'which goes and returns only to the other, without any possible reappropriation, for anyone, of his own voice or his own face' (*MPM*: 229). This makes responsibility impossible, since

> responsibility, if there is any, requires the experience of the undecidable as well as that irreducibility of the other, some of whose names are transference, prosopopoeia, allegory. There are many others . . . Before answering, responding for oneself, and *for* that purpose, in order to do so, one must respond, answer to the other, about the other, *for* the other, not in his place as if in the place of another 'proper self,' but *for* him. My ellipsis here, my economical aphorism, is a thought for all these 'fors' that make responsibility *undeniable*: *there is some, one cannot deny it, one cannot/can only deny it* [on ne peut (que) la dénier] *precisely because it is impossible* (*MPM*: 230).

Derrida here denounces any connection between responsibility and the self by making the self answerable to the other, which remains free of any subjective willingness or unwillingness to respond.

In emphasising the ruptures and discontinuities in de Man's work, Derrida wants to avoid totalising it in a way that makes alterity part of any textual function. He tries to formulate some rules about the relationship with and treatment of the other. His first rule is 'respect for the other, that is, for his right to difference, in his relation to others but also in his relation to himself' (*MPM*: 238). This means not only 'respect for the right to error' but also

> respect for the right to a history, a transformation of oneself and one's thought that can never be totalised or reduced to something homogeneous (and those who practice this reduction give a very grave ethico-political example for the future); it is also respect of that which, in *any* text, remains heterogeneous and can even, as is the case here, explain itself on the subject of this open heterogeneity while helping us to understand it. We are also the heirs and guardians of this heterogeneous text even if, precisely for this reason, we ought to maintain a differentiated, vigilant, and sometimes critical relation to it (*MPM*: 239).

His second rule is what he calls the 'regulating ideal', which is to avoid producing or reproducing the logic of totalitarian discourses. Here again Derrida associates deconstruction with absolute difference, and with that respect for it which heralds the politics of difference as against the politics of accusation.

Derrida attacks totalitarian discourses because they involve accusation and anathema: by imputing homogeneity to those wartime texts, they accuse de Man peremptorily of crudely pro-fascist sympathies and anti-Semitic tendencies. Arguing on the contrary that 'de Man's discourse is constantly split, disjointed, engaged in incessant conflicts' (*MPM*: 180), Derrida represents de Man's texts as heterogenous. Consequently, they are determined not by an 'ideological figuration' that would totalise them, but by a concern for that 'independent domain' of literature where the denunciation of literary texts on political grounds is forbidden. Derrida thus turns back upon de Man's critics the very accusation which they themselves are levelling against him, namely, that they are the ones engaged in a kind of totalising political judgement that ignores both literary value and literary autonomy. If de Man can be shown to have resisted this option during the Second World War, then what light does this shed on those detractors of deconstruction who now link deconstruction with fascism and Nazism? Furthermore, as a Francophile from Flanders, de Man had literary preferences that made 'him as much a nationalist of French culture as a Flemish nationalist'. And Flemish nationalism was already fissured, in so far as it was both anti-French and anti-German (*MPM*: 199). Finally, Derrida shows how de Man reveals his support for the independence of literature by including in the canon certain figures which an explicitly political judgement had excluded. In arguing for their inclusion, de Man lifts the 'accused ones' of the avant-garde 'out of repression's way' and does so in an exemplary fashion, since "the list could be extended indefinitely" (*MPM*: 212). Derrida tries to defend de Man against the charge of anti-Semitism by showing that he protected the avant-gardists by canonising them.

6.8 The tear: beyond the visible and the invisible

In the 1990s, Derrida began to refine his concept of the other as something outside the categories of seeing and knowing, of memory and recognition, and of gift, debt and restitution. In *Memoirs for the Blind* he again raises the issue of the other, and sees it as connected not simply to the call but to a kind of imploration. Imploration is directed towards the other within a structure of asymmetry rather than adequation as a gesture of repaying a debt or atoning for a sin through punishment. The other is now inscribed within the new concept of the *unbeseen* which connects it again both to the trait and the not-yet-visible. In this way, Derrida attempts to construct the other beyond those concepts of representation and reflection which would entrap it in an object-subject relation. After beginning this work with a question of faith, Derrida ends by conceiving of sight through the concept of 'tears that see'. His answer to the question 'Do you believe?' is rather enigmatic: 'I don't know one has to believe' (*MB*: 129). Faith is here an imperative that denotes both belief and disbelief. Faith goes beyond certainty by being a precondition for questioning it. Like his earlier image of 'the tain in the mirror', the 'tear' both prohibits vision and makes it possible because the tear is more 'proper' to man than sight (Caputo, 1997).

Memoirs of the Blind, The Self-Portrait and Other Ruins merits extensive analysis because it deals with how notions of vision, representation, reflection and memory relate to the other. In this complex work, Derrida makes use of dreams, paintings, drawings, autobiographical, biblical, philosophical, poetic, mythical and other texts and narratives in order to question sight and blindness. By connecting blindness and writing – and what he later calls the *trait* – with the other, he ends up conceiving of the other as an invisibility which preconditions both blindness and sight. As he has done already in *The Truth in Painting*, and in the later works, Derrida questions the possibility of theorising representation and vision in a way that would not entail the kind of blindness that gives itself over to anticipation, promise, waiting, imploring, withdrawing and reserve, and which treats the other as a simulacrum of sensible visibility. He takes the drawing and painting of sight and blindness as emblematic of the way in which vision has been represented within Western thought. At the origin of drawing, he argues, we should place allegory and ruins rather than representation. To conceive of every drawing as given over to 'the speech and gaze of the other' is again to annul the origin as an *arche*, and to make representation impossible (*MB*: 3). The gaze of the other disrupts and disjoins the connection between knowing and seeing, between blindness and vision. The gaze of the other does not enter into a discernible relation with the subject. This is because we are unable to see the gaze of the other, since it remains part of the invisible, and as such cannot be given over to sight and representation.

Derrida also disconnects vision from memory as a representation and reappropriation of the other. In its place he institutes the notion of blindness within memory, and in doing so not only divorces recognition from seeing, but also seeing from the positing of a subject or an object. Derrida rejects the 'theological' order of the visible by arguing that because representation remains inaccessible it draws on a '*quasi-transcendental* resource' (*MB*: 44). Representation carries death within itself, and the relationship between subject and object is not one of appropriation but of disappearance. Since the object has an invisibility 'that it reserves' (*MB*: 36), it is something which one sees without seeing. Derrida outlines a logic of the invisible which is both transcendental and sacrificial. The first, as the invisible possibility of every representation, would be disconnected from representation in general. The second would be that sacrificial event which would 'represent this unrepresentable' (*MB*: 41). 'The *event* [which] can give rise to the speech of narrative, to myth, prophesy, or messianism' (*MB*: 41) takes place between these two.

Once again, therefore, Derrida connects the logic of the invisible with a 'future-oriented' prophesy and messianism, and emphasises his radical departure from notions of presence. The prophetic is conceived of as a way of avoiding entrapment in the philosophy of presence. His logic of the invisible is further enabled by his concept of the trait, which does not conform to what is 'presently visible, to what would be set in front of me as a theme' (*MB*: 45). 'The *trait* must proceed in the night' he asserts:

> It escapes the field of vision. Not only because it *is not yet* visible, but because it does not belong to the realm of the spectacle, of spectacular objectivity – and so that which it makes happen or come [*advenir*] cannot in itself be mimetic. The heterogeneity between the thing drawn and the drawing *trait* remains abyssal . . . [Furthermore,] the night of this abyss can be interpreted in two ways . . . as a reserve of visibility . . . or . . . as radically and definitely foreign to the phenomenality of the

> day. This heterogeneity of the invisible to the visible can haunt the visible as its very possibility (*MB*: 45).

The abyssal structure of object, subject and source is expressed in absolute heterogeneity as a haunting. Derrida further radicalises his concept of the other by developing his notion of the 'ghost' to explore this haunting of the visible by the invisible. According to Derrida,

> the draftsman always sees himself to be prey to that which is each time universal and singular and would thus have to be called the *unbeseen*, as one speaks of the unbeknownst. He calls it, is called, fascinated, or recalled by it. Memory or not, and forgetting as memory, in memory and without memory (*MB*: 45).

There is thus invisibility in both memory and the other as the invisible. It is constructed as a series of calls, which constitutes memory as inconceivable in terms of an equation between what one remembers and the remembered. Called and recalled – both from the one that calls, and the one to whom the call is made – this *unbeseen* appears to be outside the constraints of memory and recall. A kind of exchange goes on, however, between these two sites of calling, even though Derrida refuses to conceive of them as belonging to both the subject and the other, since to do so would be to hypostatise the subject. In order to avoid the fixity of the point of view, Derrida questions the whole problematic of vision by transferring it to the invisible expressed in a call.

Derrida continues to deconstruct the concept of vision in Western metaphysics by raising the question of sight (Jay, 1993), and by divorcing sight and insight from the model of seeing. Derrida treats both knowing and seeing as a kind of writing which writes without seeing. In his interpretation of a painting depicting a blind man Derrida raises the question of reflection. He distinguishes reflection from self-reflection by seeing it as

> a strange flexion of the arm or reflection of the fold. A silent auto-affection, a return to oneself, a sort of soul-searching of self-relation without sight or contact. It is as if the blind man referring to himself with his arm folded back, there where Narcissus, inventing a mirror without image, lets it be seen that he does not see. He shows himself, he shows up, but to the other. He shows himself with his finger *as* blind (*MB*: 12).

Such self-relation is narcissistic only to the extent that it invents a mirror without image, and thus cannot represent or reappropriate itself within reflection. The image of the self is a non-image, a non-self relation that anchors itself on self-reflection. Narcissus shows himself to the other as blind, as devoid of the power and certainty of his own reflection. A non-reflexive self is devoid of that reflexive self-relation which, inscribed in a kind of blindness, allows the other to determine self-relation outside the philosophy of reflection. This kind of blindness allows for the possibility of seeing within that labyrinthine and nocturnal structure which Derrida wants to foreground.

Blindness also constitutes language, in so far as it speaks of itself and is a condition of all relations of seeing and knowing. Complete revelation and conversion is a model used in Christian iconography, through which it tries to eliminate its own blindness, its own other. Derrida argues that this kind of iconography encapsulates that Western tradition of the Greek *logos* which relates seeing to knowing. Reinterpreting this iconographic model, Derrida emphasises the importance of the outstretched hand of the blind man, which prevents the accident of his fall. He takes this as a sign that 'one must always recall the other hand or the hand of the other', because all representation, seeing and knowing originate in otherness (*MB*: 9). For Derrida, seeing is connected to an interiority which cannot sever itself from the external other. It is not the Christian sort of interiority, which asserts the uniqueness and singularity of that individual self which brackets out the other(s), or relates to the other within a structure of symmetry and exchangeability. Questions of representation, gift and giving become part of this structure. Instead of defending representational fidelity, Derrida argues that 'there is debt or gift' at the origin of the *graphein* (*MB*: 30), and that in this gift there is 'a sort of *re-drawing*, a *with-drawing*, or *retreat* [*re-trait*], at once the interposition of a mirror, an impossible reappropriation or mourning, the intervention of a paradoxical Narcissus, sometimes lost *en abyme*, in short, a specular *folding* or *falling back* [*repli*] – and a supplementary *trait*' (*MB*: 3).

This reappropriation makes not only self-representation but also representation in general impossible. Derrida's concept of the trait does not follow and 'does not conform to what is presently visible, to what it would be set in front of me as a theme' (*MB*: 45). Accordingly, self-portraits, self-narrations, self-revelations, and self-relation all become impossible. For 'like Memoirs, the Self-Portrait always appears in the reverberations of several voices. And the voice of the other orders or commands, makes the portrait resound, calls it without symmetry or consonance' (*MB*: 64). Since the other cannot be made part of the phenomenal world, it becomes a pluri-vocal voice, which commands us within an asymmetrical relation. Furthermore, 'the other, over there, remains irreducible, because he resists all interiorisation, subjectification, idealisation in a work of mourning'; this is why 'the ruse of narcissism never comes to an end' (*MB*: 70). Devoid of an image, the mirror of Narcissus resembles the Platonic *khora*, which acts as a threshold of reception that enables a happening, an event to occur without actor or reflection being the determining factors. For Derrida, a law of 'impossible and blinding reflexivity' relativises and prohibits a clear cut separation between the subject, object and its reflection (*MB*: 62).

Although *Memoirs for the Blind* constructs the other within a transcendental framework, Derrida refuses to give it directly theological overtones by refusing to connect it to that absolute other, God. Instead, the theological motif is carried by the construction of otherness as a gift. The gift is not part of the return and repaying of a debt, because our debt to the other is not only 'bottomless' (*MB*: 63) but also remains outside symmetrical and representational relations. This asymmetry within self-relation signifies in part our 'failure to recapture the presence of the gaze outside the abyss into which it is sinking' (*MB*: 68). In other words, the gaze of the other is independent, external and beyond the field of vision. 'From the moment of the first gaze', writes Derrida, the image always originates in ruin:

> Ruin is the self-portrait, this face looked in the face as the memory of itself, what *remains* or *returns* as a spectre from the moment one first looks at oneself and a figuration is eclipsed. The figure, the face, then sees its visibility being eaten away; it loses its integrity without disintegrating. For the incompleteness of the visible monument comes from the eclipsing structure of the *trait*, from a structure that is only remarked, pointed out, impotent and incapable of being reflected in the shadow of the self-portrait (*MB*: 68).

Notions of reflection and recognition, inscribed within the structure of a ruin, reveal our inability to present and represent the image either as face or figure. According to Derrida, 'the naked face cannot look itself in the face, *it cannot look at itself in a looking glass*' (*MB*: 69). In the place of reflection and thus recognition, Derrida institutes the idea of the mirror without an image. He speaks of that 'transcendental ruin of the eye' which one tries to exorcise by mirrors, telescopes, glasses, binoculars, monocles, etc. (*MB*: 70). Vision is again entrusted to the other, as is the connection between seeing and knowing. Both the invisibility of the other and the abyssal structure of representation signal Derrida's attempt to move towards a transcendental concept of the other independent of notions of reflection. The simulacrum is inevitable, because

> the desire for self-presentation is never met, it never meets up with itself, and that is why the simulacrum takes place. Never does the eye of the Other recall this desire more sovereignly to the outside and to difference, to the law of disproportion, dis-symmetry, and expropriation. And this is memory itself (*MB*: 121).

Because imploration is characteristic of the eye, 'tears and not sight are [its] essence' (*MB*: 126; Caputo: 1997). Moreover, Derrida argues, that

> contrary to what one believes one knows, the best point of view (and the *point of* view will have been our theme) is a source-point and a watering hole, a water-point-which thus comes down to tears. The blindness that opens the eye is not the one that darkens vision. The revelatory or apocalyptic blindness, the blindness that reveals the truth of the eyes, would be the gaze veiled by tears. It neither sees nor does not see: it is indifferent to its blurred vision. It implores: first of all in order to know from where these tears stream down and from whose eyes they come to well up. From where and from whom this mourning or these tears of joy? This essence of eye, this eye of water? (*MB*: 126–127).

By losing his sight man does not lose his eyes; it is only then that 'man begins to *think* the eyes' (*MB*: 128). The field of vision is replaced by that film of tears which recalls the other as the nonvisible visibility. Both recognition and representation are thus part of the unbeseen of the other.

6.9 The other as gift

Since Derrida sees the other as structured like a gift, he problematises the incompatibility between gift and exchange in order to raise both the problematic of giving and to criticise the logic of relation and exchange which underpins logocentric thinking. By deconstructing the gift as traditionally conceived, he can formulate the other as gift-like in structure, and therefore as functioning without return, exchange, reciprocity, symmetry, debt, responsibility, equivalence, or restitution. The other can then be connected to blindness, which sacrifices sight in order to submit to a faith that commands and precedes fidelity. The gift becomes disconnected from that circle of credit, debt, calculability and exchange in which the gift is conceivable only in terms of a repayment of debt or a restitution of what is owned. In Derrida's formulation, the gift escapes these demands, and becomes associated with excess, expenditure, destruction, absolute loss, secrecy and sacrifice, all of which entail a rejection of restitution, correspondence, rational calculation, equivalence, and symmetry (cf. Derrida's early reading of Bataille 'From Restricted Economy: A Hegelianism without Reserve' in *WD*).

The construction of the other as gift serves at least seven purposes. First, it enables a positive and affirmative response to the other before any determinant process of differentiation. Second, it renders the other independent of all the categories of presence. Third, by submitting all thought to the radicality, irreducibility and heterogeneity of the other, it places the subject under the category of the other. Fourth, it entrusts all modes of alterity to the gift. Fifth, it makes the other the deconstructive category of all forms of identity. Sixth, it deconstructs those political, ethical, socio-economic and cultural forms of thinking which are based on a concept of exchange with its rationality of calculability, restitution and balance. Seventh, it radicalises the concept of Being and time. Whereas the self becomes subsumed under the other, the other relates to the self by means of asymmetry, dissymmetry and verticality.

As noted already, Derrida deconstructed Heidegger's idea of being as *es gibt* very early in his career, although it is a theme he returns to in the early 1990s. In *The Post Card,* for instance, he asserts that

> when Being is thought *on the basis of* the gift of the *es gibt* . . . the gift itself is given *on the basis of* 'something', which is nothing, which is not something; it would be . . . like an '*envoi*' which, of course, does not send this or that, which sends nothing that is, nothing that is a 'being', a 'present'. Not to whoever, to any addressee as an identifiable and self-present subject (*CP*: 63).

While retaining the anti-subjectivism of Heidegger, Derrida goes further by conceiving of the other as beyond the thought of Being (as an indivisible sending of being without relay, delay, irruption, etc.). Ontic-ontological difference is replaced by the thought of the other beyond Being. Derrida intends to separate the gift from those philosophies of phenomenality or knowledge which are based on a notion of the gift as that which sets into circulation an economic, political, judicial, ethical and cultural system, based on exchange as reciprocity and equivalence. In that conceptual system, the gift creates an obligation and a debt which has to be repaid, and as such it is kept in memory. For Derrida, this concept of debt and repayment permeates the structures of Western thinking, which is based on *logos*, both as practical and speculative reason. Derrida offers both a genealogy of the gift and a reorientation of it away from subjectivity, symmetry and equivalence.

6.10 The gift of time

In *Given Time*: *I. Counterfeit Money* Derrida signals his attempt to make these questions part of a general critique of morality, ethics, justice, politics and socio-economic thinking which will strike at the core of Western thought. The gift escapes the economy of exchange because it cannot 'take place between two subjects exchanging objects, things or symbols' (*GTK*: 180). Prior to any conscious or unconscious relation to the subject, the gift is thus prior also to 'the determinations of Being as substantial being, subject or object' (*GTK*: 180). Derrida even admits to being 'tempted to say that a subject as such never gives or receives a gift' (*GTK*: 180). A more radical departure from his early anti-subjectivism is signalled when Derrida speaks of the gift as 'preceding' Being. Subject and object thus become products of the gift. Before it can emerge, both must be absent, because 'the subject and the object are arrested effects of the gift: arrests of the gift. At the zero or infinite speed of the circle' (*GTK*: 180). The thinking of the gift remains once more at the limits of the impossible. It involves faith, promise and a rethinking of a kind of 'transcendental illusion of the gift', which gives by giving nothing that can be conceived of within the paradigm of presence.

Neither what it is or was, the gift exists in the condition 'of not being or appearing to be the gift of anything, of anything that is or that is present, [having] come from someone and [being] given to someone' (*GTC*:

35). The gift is merely a possibility at the limits of *logos*, marked *a priori* by excessiveness, measurelessness and exaggeration. Disconnected from time, it becomes inscribed in 'a time determined by a term, in other words, a rhythm, a cadence' that escapes the circle of give and take in equal measures (*GTC*: 41). As such it becomes associated with forgetful expenditure, dissemination without return, and ashes. To give, the giving, the given, the one who gives – all are disassociated from the exchange paradigm. In this way, Derrida critiques the socio-economic logic of an exchange paradigm which emphasises economic rationalism and calculability, and a capitalism which fetishises surplus value, production and consumption. At the same time, he criticises a system of justice which is based on the logic of equivalence between giving and taking, debt and duty. He argues instead for a system of justice, morality and ethics which 'affirms the excess of the gift" and "lets the gift overflow"' (*GTC*: 67), and does so without reinscribing the gift within the logic of relation and exchange. As a further consequence, morality is freed from calculability and associated with excess in the form of excessive generosity.

Since neither the gift nor the event can give evidence of themselves, they cannot become part of the logic of give and take, for they can only promise themselves (*GTC*: 74, n.3). A pre-originary giving is part of the problematic of the trace and dissemination: 'a gift can take place, along with the excessive forgetting or the forgetful excess that . . . is radically implicated in the gift' (*GTC*: 101–102). The gift 'must *remain* unforeseeable, but remain so without keeping itself', writes Derrida. 'It must let itself be structured by the aleatory', because this enables the gift to escape the programmed and conditioned movement of logocentric thought (*GTC*: 122). Because 'the gift and the event obey nothing, except perhaps principles of disorder, that is, principles without principles', they have the 'status of incalculable or unforeseeable *exception* (without general rule, without program, and even without concept)' (*GTC*: 123, 129). Every gift relation is characterised by luck, chance and the aleatory. Contingency structures the gift.

Whereas previously the other has been an abstraction, in this work Derrida analyses what could be called a concrete instance of it. Beggars asking for alms signify 'the absolute demand of the other, the inextinguishable appeal, the unquenchable thirst for the gift' (*GTC*: 137). The demand of the other cannot be inscribed within that distributive form of justice which Derrida sees as part of an economic and symbolic system, which transforms alms 'into an exchangist, even contractual' arrangement (*GTC*: 138). Such arrangements give rise to the belief that calculation enables one to acquit one's debts and obligations to the other. In contrast, the demand which comes from the other (as Derrida understands it) is limitless and measureless, and thus exceeds calculative and speculative reason (*GTC*: 142). Consequently,

> when one sees the other see, and thus the seeing eyes of the other, these seeing eyes are no longer simply seen. Inversely, if they are seen, visible, and not seeing, they become invisible as seeing eyes and secrete, in this regard, or encircle the spectator's blindness. Likewise, when one sees the eyes, when they become invisible as such, one no longer sees them see, one no longer sees them seeing. Whence the act of memory and, one again, the act of faith, of credit, of belief, even of credulity that is inscribed in the most immediate intuition of the crossed gaze (*GTC*: 163).

The encounter with the other thus involves faith, credit and a kind of blindness that allows for no recognition that would either see and appropriate the other or keep it in memory.

Since the subject determines all the categories of Western metaphysics, heteronomy rather than autonomy determines our relation to the other. Being outside fraternal politics, the other eludes attempts to absorb it into a logic of relation and exchange. Both the encounter with and giving to the other are placed within a structure of forgetting, which is embedded in the notion of

> the gift as remaining [*restance*] without memory, without permanence and consistency, without substance or subsistence; at stake is the rest that is, without being (it), beyond Being, *epekeina tes ousias*. The secret of that about which one cannot speak, but which one can no longer silence (*GTC*: 147).

Derrida uses this secret to connect the other with that which 'will remain *eternally* unreadable, *absolutely* indecipherable, even refusing itself to any promise of deciphering or hermeneutic' (*GTC*: 152). The other and the gift, moreover, do not belong to speculative or practical reason. The gift

> should remain a stranger to morality, to the will, perhaps to freedom, at least to that freedom that is associated with the will of a subject. It should remain a stranger to the law or to the 'il faut' (you must, you have to) of this practical reason. It *should* surpass *duty* itself: duty beyond duty (*GTC*: 156).

The other, in its relation to duty, is beyond duty as a prescriptive, proceduralist, generalised or Kantian ethics. Both the gift and the event share the condition of being outside-the-law, which is characterised by 'unforseeability', 'surprise', an 'absence of anticipation or horizon, the excess with regard to reason, either speculative or practical' (*GTC*: 156). This construction of the gift again introduces prophetic and transcendental motifs (cf. the notion of *misericordia*), but within a secular framework that becomes harder and harder to sustain. Although it would be difficult to build a social security system on the notion of the gift as Derrida describes it, it is an idea that certainly illuminates the kind of 'vengeful' thinking which says that our gift/bebt must be re-paid in full and immediately by work and austerity measures (e.g. Workfare systems and austerity measures being instituted; the demonization of the participants in the recent riots in Britain, Greece, Spain, Italy and France; the vengeful justice meted out to participants in the British riots; and the politics of resistance of the Indignatos of Spain, Portugal and Greece).

6.11 The gift of death

Derrida's turn toward messianic thinking is most evident in *The Gift of Death*, where he analyses his indebtedness to and his departure from what he calls Judeo-Christian and Islamic thought. Derrida takes Christianity's notion of the *mysterium tremendum* as an aspect of Western thought which retains the connections between secret and mystery, faith and responsibility as an experience of the sacrificial gift. It allows the other and the gift to emerge as concepts outside the categories of incorporation and repression, giving and taking. The other gives giving in a pre-originary sense that allows for no symmetry between the donor and the donee which is expressed through giving back and repayment of debt as part of an economy of duty. The ethics, morality, politics and culture of this giving are constituted asymmetrically. This asymmetry places the subject in a relation of obligation and responsibility to the other and for the other which demands no recognition.

This obligation and responsibility to the other involve a giving that is connected to sacrifice, to a gift of death that one gives to oneself. The self thus becomes a singular self through the other, by losing itself without hoping to return as a self-present subject. Obligation and responsibility to the other also involves responding to its call. It is not a matter of a subject deciding to respond to the other as something capable of being known, recognised and reflected upon. On the contrary, the call is heard outside knowledge and recognition, and is answered as a commandment that one cannot fail to answer even by not answering it. Responsibility and irresponsibility thus become meaningless categories, because the demand of the call of the other does not await a conscious subjectivity to decide to answer the call. This frees responsibility from its subordination to objective knowledge.

The gaze of the other (or 'the gaze of God', as it is termed in this work) becomes the notion that determines how the other relates to the subject as both an 'I' and a self. The other does not enter into that kind of relationship with them which makes responsibility part of subjectivist thinking. Derrida's idea of what a responsible person is, and what s/he must be, involves 'exposing of the soul to the gaze of another person, of a person as transcendent other, as an other who looks at me, but who looks without the-subject-who-says-I being able to reach that other, see her, hold her within the reach of my gaze' (*GOD*: 25). The rejection of subjectivity is accompanied by a repudiation of theory. For Derrida, 'the activating of responsibility (decision, act, *praxis*) will always take place before and beyond any theoretical or thematic determination' (*GOD*: 26). Our relationship to the other is marked by dissymmetry rather than symmetrical reciprocity. The other cannot be seen, nor is it a part of an unveiling and uncovering process. Our responsibility to the other is beyond these considerations. Because the other remains secret it is not subject to revelatory logic. It remains invisible, transcendent and part of the mystery of the gift of death, and of an economy of sacrifice that does not keep what it gives up.

Derrida thus argues for a more radical conception of responsibility

> that exposes me dissymmetrically to the gaze of the other; where my gaze, precisely as regards me [*ce qui me regarde*], is no longer the measure of all things . . . This paradoxical concept also has the structure of a type of secret – what is called, in the code of certain religious practices, mystery (*GOD*: 27).

Here again Derrida resorts to a religious frame of reference in order to prevent the 'I' from being constructed in terms of a symmetrical relationship with the other. Derrida explains 'the dissymmetry of the gaze' as a 'disproportion that relates me, and whatever concerns me, to a gaze that I don't see and that remains secret from me although it commands me' (*GOD*: 27). This is the gaze of the other, which cannot be understood intersubjectively or as a relation between subject and object. To be involved with the other in this way is an experience of terror, and fraught with 'absolute risk, beyond knowledge and certainty' (*GOD*: 5). The other commands and gives the gift of death, which

> made to me by God as he holds me in his gaze and in his hand while remaining inaccessible to me, the terribly dissymmetrical gift of the *mysterium tremendum* only allows me to respond and only rouses me to the responsibility it gives me by making a gift of death [*en me donnant la mort*], giving the secret of death, a new experience of death (*GOD*: 33).

The gift and the gift of death are related to sacrifice and to that '*dying for the other*' which aims at ultimately de-subjectivising death (*GOD*: 33). Derrida sees this 'dying for the other' both as a possibility and impossibility, and as something which radicalises our relation to the other. An abyssal dissymmetry always 'occurs when one is exposed to the gaze of the other' and this dissymmetry determines our relation to responsibility, death and gift (*GOD*: 28).

In seeking to examine the relationship between death and gift, Derrida begins with a question: 'How does one give *oneself* death?'. What troubles Derrida, of course, is the 'oneself' in relation to death, sacrifice and the economy of the gift. In order to radicalise this notion, he begins with Patocka, Platonic thought, Christianity, Judaism, Islam, Heidegger, and Kierkegaard. In short, Derrida raises the question of the death of the self (and the modalities of this death) as both suicide, or giving death to oneself, and as 'sacrificing oneself for another, *dying for the other*, thus perhaps giving one's life by giving oneself death' (*GOD*: 10). The question he posits is whether the other can be excluded from death, or whether death constitutes subjectivity, given that no one can die in one's place. His answer to this question relies on how such concepts as faith, responsibility and gift relate to the other as absolute other. The dissymmetry of the gaze of the other in relation to the self calls into question not only the notion of death but also its relation to giving and gift.

As regards the relationship between death and the other, Derrida argues, that death is that which is coming, but which one does not see coming. Furthermore, death cannot be given to oneself 'in a pure and simple way'. This is because 'each time the self anticipates death by giving to it or conferring upon it a different value, giving itself or reappropriating what in fact it cannot simply appropriate' (*GOD*: 40). Derrida aims for a different way of giving or granting oneself death, which involves the notion of gift:

> this other way of apprehending death, and of acceding to responsibility, comes from a gift received from the other, from the one who, in absolute transcendence, sees me without my seeing, holds me in his hands while remaining inaccessible (*GOD*: 40).

Because the source of this giving is inaccessible (and therefore cannot be held in the memory), the donee is in a relation of dissymmetry both to what is given and what is received from the other.

On the other hand, the irreplaceability of both the subject and the self is effected by death. If no one can die for me and in the place of me, then nobody can die for the other or in the place of the other. This is the Heideggerian logic that Derrida tries to radicalise. If death cannot be given or taken from me, it escapes that logic of giving and taking which it institutes. Apropos death, Derrida argues,

> one has to *give it to oneself by taking it upon oneself*, for it can only be mine alone, irreplaceably. That is so even if . . . *death can neither be taken nor given*. But the idea of being neither taken nor given relates *from* or *to* the other, and that is indeed why one can give it *to oneself* only by taking it *upon oneself* (*GOD*: *45*).

Death is thus the paradigm which confirms that both the irreplaceability and singularity of the subject are given by the other. For Derrida, therefore,

> the identity of the oneself is *given* by death, by the being-towards-death that *promises* me to it. It is only to the extent that this *identity* [*ce même*] of the oneself is possible as irreducibly different singularity that death for the other or the death of the other can make sense (*GOD*: 45).

The relation to death which Derrida wants to institute is more ancient, more embedded in sacrifice, and entails

> the possibility of dying *of* the other or *for* the other. Such a death is not given in the first instance as annihilation. It institutes responsibility as a *putting-oneself-to-death*

> or *offering-one's-death*, that is, *one's life*, in the ethical dimension of sacrifice (*GOD*: 48).

Derrida wants to bring to the foreground this ethical dimension of sacrifice which is inscribed in the notion of the other. As for responsibility, he writes, 'once I speak I am never and no longer myself, alone and unique. It is a very strange contract – both paradoxical and terrifying – that binds infinite responsibility to silence and secrecy' (*GOD*: 60). This destroys any notion of linking responsibility to the public and to the non-secret. Ethics is not tied to speaking, giving reasons, justifying, or answering for one's actions according to some universal. It is tied to sacrifice. For Derrida the case of Abraham teaches us 'that far from ensuring responsibility, the generality of ethics incites irresponsibility' (*GOD*: 61; see also Kierkegaard, 1968). Abraham's sacrifice of Isaac becomes the paradigmatic example of a gift to the other and of dying for the other. In the asymmetry of sacrifice, the other called God remains 'absent, hidden and silent, separate, secret, at the moment he has to be obeyed' (*GOD*: 57).

This calls for an ethics in which duty and responsibility binds me to the other as absolute other in a limitless way. 'I am responsible to the other as other' Derrida argues:

> I answer to him and I answer to what I do before him. But of course, what binds me thus in my singularity to the absolute singularity of the other, immediately propels me into the space or risk of absolute sacrifice (*GOD*: 68).

Furthermore, '*every other (one) is every (bit) other* [*tout autre est tout autre*], every one else is completely or wholly other' (*GOD*: 68). Because 'every other one' is wholly other, it enters into a relation of dissymmetry with the self-as-I. The singularity of the other is irreducible to the singularity of the subject, and consequently our responsibility to the other can be activated without the decision of a subject. The question of the self thus needs to be reformulated: the question 'who am I?', means '"who is this 'I' " that can say "who"? What is the "I", and what becomes of responsibility once the identity of the "I" trembles *in secret*?' (*GOD*: 92). What is in question is the identity of the 'I'. Both the response and the responsibility of the 'I' to the other are prior to the formation of either the subject or the other as identity. The other splinters the identity of the 'I' at the moment of identification. Derrida is quite explicit about this:

> I decide in the name of the other without this in the least lightening my responsibility; on the contrary the other is the origin of my responsibility without it being determinable in terms of an identity (Derrida in Mouffe, 1996: 85).

Why then does the 'I' tremble in secret, and what is the secret? For Derrida, the secret is what is irreducible either to the distinction between public and private or to political and ethical concerns. The secret thus remains 'inaccessible and heterogeneous to the public realm', and as such it is connected to the opening (and to the leaving open) of both the political and the ethical (Derrida in Mouffe, 1996: 81). Derrida argues for a kind of messianism, which is embedded in all language and inscribed in the notion of promise 'as an irreducible promise and of the relation to the other as essentially non-instrumental' (Derrida in Mouffe, 1996: 83). The problem is that he assimilates exchange to the symmetrical and intersubjectivity to the instrumental. Although his answer is to make the other the source and destination of all relations, these become vertical rather than horizontal as a consequence.

The political difficulties of this position are revealed when Derrida argues that the finitude of the subject does not entail a finite response and responsibility to the other. He argues, in effect, that our responsibility to the other is marked by undecidability and infinitude:

> it is because we act and live in infinitude that the responsibility with regard to the other (*autrui*) is irreducible. If responsibility were not infinite, if every time that I have to take an ethical or political decision with regard to the other (*autrui*) this were not infinite, then I would not be able to engage myself in an infinite debt with regard to each singularity. I owe myself infinitely to each and every singularity (Derrida in Mouffe, 1996: 86).

Our own mortality and finitude become categories irrelevant to ethics and politics. The 'here and now' is always inscribed by that infinitude of the other which gives us the possibility to be ethical and political. If Derrida's thoughts on responsibility do not issue in a politics, it is because they are predominantly 'theologico-political'. In attempting to go beyond ethics, he elevates both the other and sacrifice into a post-ethical and quasi- or meta-theological position.

The other in Derrida is neither a generalised nor a singular, but a quasi-transcendental other, whose otherness is encapsulated in the gaze of that absolute other, God. The self-as-an-'I' exists in a condition of non-relation with the other. Therein lies the problematic of the subject and the other.

For what determines this non-relation between self and other is submission to the gaze of the other. The self entrusts itself to the other, to the gaze of the other, by submitting to its demands and answering its call. The hierarchical nature of this relationship is concealed, however, because Derrida makes the other prior to the emergence of both the subject and the other-as-a-concrete-other. In other words, the other needs neither a subject nor a concrete other in order to emerge and determine both the inter- and intra-relations between the subject and its other(s). The incommensurability of the other makes it incommensurable with these intersubjective relations which lie at the heart of both ethics and politics.

6.12 Concluding remarks

Because the debt and responsibility to the other remain limitless and incalculable in Derrida's formulation, they escape the socio-economic paradigm of equivalence and calculability. We cannot see, recognise, remember or commemorate the other, nor can we bear witness or do justice to it. The other involves memory as forgetfulness, for memory would place the other within the circle of auto-affection. The abyss, the night, the spectre, the voice beyond the grave, the mirror without image, the Narcissus that fails to return to himself, the labyrinth, and the gift that escapes the logic of relation and exchange are all connected to the irreducible alterity with which Western metaphysics fails to come to terms. The non-relation of self to the other is characterised by asymmetry and dissymmetry. Quasi-transcendental, the other annuls both the concrete other and the self-present subject, whose modalities are inscribed partly in the call of the other, and partly in response to that call. Our responsibility and duty to the other are part of the gift, embedded in the act of giving which, pre-originary, is outside the economy of exchange. Both the concrete and the general other are part of a philosophy that situates the other beyond general, proceduralist and intersubjective ethics. The ethics and politics of the other in Western thought are a part of a restricted economy. Derrida aims to relocate the other in a general economy in which it becomes the source of morality, ethics, politics, culture and socio-economic relations.

In his most recent writings, Derrida has related his concept of the other to the notion of responsibility. This involves not only a responding to the other but also being responsible to it. In this respect the other has become transcendent, partly in relation to the subject-as-an-'I' and as a self, and partly in terms of its radical critique of the politics, ethics, religion, economic models and culture that derive from what Derrida terms Greco-Roman and Christian thought. Instead of disregarding religious thought altogether, Derrida reinscribes it in a conception of the infinite and the absolute other, whose overtones are increasingly 'theological' and messianic. He seeks a kind of philosophical and metaphysical thinking 'that "repeats" the possibility of religion without religion' (*GOD*: 49). In other words, he wants to retain the sacred, the mysterious, faith and sacrifice, but without those religious vestiges which reinscribe them in an economy of exchange and revelation. By disconnecting the event from revelation, he wants to retain its transcendence – that 'coming' which has not yet been thought, but which 'can come' (Derrida in Mouffe, 1996: 83). Inscribed in the promise, this coming keeps an opening to a future. Although messianic in structure, the promise is supposedly not theological or teleological. It 'belongs to all language', because in so far as it is performative in character, all language is promissory (Derrida in Mouffe, 1996: 83). By making messianism a linguistic and universal construct, Derrida tries to avoid the accusation of theology and negative theology while using theiological rather than theological thought. This turn towards explicitly messianic motifs, and his use of theological discourses, marks a new phase in Derrida's work which will be examined in the next chapter.

As a result of conferring a messianic structure on the performative dimension of language, Derrida moves into a rapprochement with pragmatism in general, but in particular with Habermas' universal pragmatics. The fact that to say 'I lie' implies 'believe me' suggests that truth-telling is an inherent possibility of language – so much so as to render lying (as Habermas would put it) a strategically-oriented counterfactual usage of language (Habermas, 1990). But whereas Habermas uses universal pragmatics to salvage a post-metaphysical concept of cognitive and ethical truth based on discourse, Derrida remains wedded to a metaphysical concept of truth-telling, which is structured as a promise rather than a process. Whereas Habermas posits a pragmatic universal or *a priori* of language, Derrida comes up with a messianic *a priori*. Whereas

Habermas regards understanding as the telos of language in the here and now, Derrida projects it into the 'future' as a messianic promise. The difficulty inherent in Derrida's approach is that the promissory character of the *a priori* conflicts with that pragmatic characterisation of language on which it relies. Furthermore, it projects into the 'future' an emancipation that appears as a deliverance rather than a discursively-oriented activity (Habermas, 1994).

To preface the phrase, 'the terms of the contract are fair and just', with the words 'I assure you' or 'believe me' is to use a performative with a promissory intent. But what happens if the assurance is pure deception or, to use Habermas' terminology, the validity claim is unredeemable? In Derrida's account, the promissory character of the utterance renders nugatory any attempt to redeem discursively the validity claim which underlies the utterance. To transform the promissory character of a performative into a messianic *a priori* leaves one without any grounds or procedure for testing the claim. The messianic may well transform the present into debris so that the angel of redemption can arise. But when that happens, the empirical realm surrenders the concept of justice to the messianic. In Habermas's account, however, the validity claim which underlies the utterance can be thematised explicitly and tested. In so far as the law embodies procedural rationality, it raises questions (to return to our example) of both the reasonableness and fairness of the contract. In other words, it establishes a procedure for testing the assurance. Both law and politics may institutionalise such procedures imperfectly, but these are precisely those normative deficiencies which communicative theory seeks to redress. Despite all its talk of having an institutional character, deconstruction is not even in a position to attempt such a move. Derrida's inability to deal with those issues of reflection, subjectivity, intersubjectivity, politics and ethics which do not derive from an asymmetrical relationship with the other oblige me to conclude by looking at different formulations of these problematics. However, before I move to this stage I will outline in the next two chapters the last phase of Derrida's work in order to demonstrate the continuation of this thought on the subject, self and other and its indebtedness to his earlier formulations, as well as demonstrate the shift towards a preoccupation with the modalities of 'violence to the other' and an emphasis on hospitality and forgiveness.

7. Violence to the Other: Religion, Hospitality and Forgiveness

In the next two chapters, I will deal with some of Derrida's later texts in order to map out the final trajectory of his thinking on the subject, self and other. During the last phase of his work, Derrida again makes the problematic of alterity central to his thought. However, the centre of gravity shifts from a preoccupation with the ontological dimensions of the problematic of alterity to the ethico-political question of 'violence to the other' within diverse spheres. Derrida aims to institute a pre-ontological, post-metaphysical, post-subjectivist and post-human philosophy of non-violence to the other; a more messianic conception of the other as ahuman and beyond being; a futural politics and ethics based on the concept of the wholly other; and a non-violent, non-oppositional and asymmetrical relation of the subject and the self to the other. In the process of articulating his new thinking of the other, Derrida makes the subject both hostage and host of the other.

During this period, Derrida goes over old ground. His thinking regarding the subject, self and other remains indebted to his earlier deconstructions. The relation of the subject with the other becomes a non-relation or, as he puts it following Blanchot and Levinas, a '"*rapport sans rapport*"', that is, the relation without relation (Derrida in Critchley, 1997: 14). In other words, Derrida repeats elements of his earlier deconstructions and follows the path he had opened up by his seminal deconstruction of the sign and Husserlian phenomenology. This is demonstrated by the maintenance of the link between the notion of the wholly other and trace, as well as other non-synonymous substitutions, such as *khora, différance* and *oto*biography. As with his previous work, Derrida aims to go beyond the ipso-centrism of Western metaphysics by making the wholly other the generative force of almost everything. All conceptions of ethics and politics, within this schema, are inscribed by the non-concept of the other, and beyond any subjectivist categories of Western metaphysics.

Derrida again applies his strategy of deconstruction on various thinkers, discourses, practices and systems of thought, in order to expose the thinking and conceptual basis that underpin the 'violence to the other'. As in his previous work, Derrida's anti-subjectivism and anti-humanism become the linchpin of these later deconstructions, which aim to expose, within diverse domains, any remnants of the subjectivism of Western metaphysics, while at the same time expunging it from his project of deconstruction. However, it is debatable if Derrida achieves his aims or remains too close to Hegel and Heidegger, or appropriates Nietzsche's anti-subjectivism and anti-humanism rather uncritically (see Noys, 2010).

Derrida's approach is to deal with more concrete situations regarding the modalities of 'violence to the other' as a way of radicalizing the philosophical, political, ethical, religious, legal, economic and socio-cultural domains. This more radical turn is exemplified by Derrida's work on religion, archive, copy, signature, cosmopolitanism, forgiveness, hospitality and The Animal. In the texts that deal with these problematics, Derrida introduces a number of new concepts, such as *cosmopolitics, animot, animort, limitrophy, globalatinisation*, *zootobiographical*, *zoo-auto-bio-biblio-graphy*, *zoosphere*, *auto-motricity*, *and divanimality*, and shifts the emphasis towards the idea of a new ethics of hospitality. These new concepts encapsulate the new thinking, which aims to eliminate 'violence to the other', and mark a movement towards a more radical application of deconstruction in the domains of philosophy, ethics, politics, economics, law, and socio-cultural practices.

Far from being a philosophy of reading and undoing the textual totalisation, in this later phase, deconstruction is applied as a strategy that aims to overturn and radicalize all fields of knowledge and all systems of thought and praxis. Derrida seeks to institute a new thinking based on his philosophy of alterity, and articulates his new thought by problematizing a number of fields. One of the first fields he problematizes is religion and its connections to faith and truth. It is to this work that I will now turn to outline Derrida's project.

7.1 Religion, faith, messianism and the other

In the previous chapters of this book, I have argued that Derrida's later work has taken a messianic and theological turn. This has also been argued by others with a number of scholars pointing to Derrida's links with negative theology, nihilism, and weak affirmation (see Noys, 2010; Van Zilfhout, 2002; Critchley, 1997). Gaché and Hägglund developed the ideas of 'structural infinity' and 'infinite finitude' respectively, to define Derrida as a radical atheist and thus save him from the accusations of simply being another thinker who operates within the discourses of negative theology (Hägglund, 2008; Gaché; 1986).

At the outset, it needs to be stated that the place of religion in Derrida's thought is rather complex and cannot be fully explored in this chapter. Although numerous scholars have dealt with various aspects of his thought, what has not been explored is the inter- and intra-relationship between religion, faith and Derrida's notion of the other (see O'Connor, 2010; McCance; 2009; Llewelyn, 2008; Mjaaland, 2008). His work '*Faith and Knowledge: The Two Sources of "Religion" at the Limits of Reason Alone*' merits extensive attention because it links with his previous deconstructions in relation to his treatment of writing, memory and the Platonic concept of *khora*, and points to his more messianic and theiological formulation of the other. This work is also emblematic of his turn towards more ethico-political concerns and adoption of increasingly theological and messianic discourses upon which he bases his idea of the futural opening to the infinite other.

Derrida opens the space for the other within theological, epistemological and philosophical discourses by deconstructing a number of dualities, including the labyrinthine complexities embedded within the duality of faith and knowledge. He conceives of religion, faith, belief, revelation, knowledge and reason to have the same source, which is based on the pre-ontological and beyond ontology notion of the other as beyond being (*epekeina tes ousias*). Drawing on his earlier deconstruction of the sign, he re-introduces his concepts of literality and writing within these discourses and argues that language as '*idiom, literality and writing*', '*forms the element of all revelation and of all* belief, *an element that ultimately is irreducible and untranslatable*' (*FK*: 4). By injecting literality and writing at the heart of revelation and belief, he radicalizes faith and knowledge by making them irreducible and untranslatable. However, he makes idiom, literality and writing

> *inseparable from the social nexus, from the political, familial, ethnic, communitarian nexus from the nation and from the people: from autochthony, blood and soil, and from the evermore problematic relation to citizenship and to the state. In these times, language and nation form the historical body of all religious passion* (*FK*: 4).

Derrida's attempts to link questions of religion, language and nation and embed them within historical, socio-economic, political, ethnic and communitarian problematics, signal a willingness to acknowledge that even his appeal to the wholly other cannot side-step these issues. However, Derrida re-inscribes them within his radical thinking of alterity and within a messianic discourse of the future. This approach enables him to move the debate about religion onto his own terrain of deconstruction.

Derrida employs his strategy of deconstruction to open a new discourse on religion based on his notion of the wholly other. Aiming to disengage religion from its totalizing and theocratic tendencies, he disconnects religion from truth, and makes a distinction between theology as a discourse on God and theiology as a discourse on divinity – being divine (*FK*: 14). He critiques the contemporary '*machine-like return of religion*' and exposes its ongoing negative consequences. He sees religion, faith, belief, knowledge and reason as victims of '*the machine-like return of religion*', to which he applies his strategy of deconstruction in order to deal with the question of alterity within faith itself (*FK*: 14). To this end he connects faith to his deconstructive concepts of iterability (as a site of repeatability), irreducibility, and untranslatability which are part of the structure of alterity. The other is again connected to the call of and appeal to the faith of the other. He links the call of the other to the

> *performativity of calling in prayer (which as Aristotle says, is neither true or false), of its bond to that which, in all performativity, as in all address and attestation, appeals to the faith of the other and deploys itself therefore in a pledge of faith* (*FK*: 6).

Derrida disconnects faith from the binarism of true/false, and makes all forms of address and attestation part of the structure of the appeal to the faith of the other. He again Derrida invokes the other outside the notion of performativity expressed by analytical philosophers, such as Searle. He places his type of performativity within the *apophatic logos* of a prayer that deploys itself as a pledge of faith. Thus, language itself becomes part of the structure of a pledge of faith and anterior to the subject's address. However, as we will see, Derrida's valorisation of secularism in his last interview is in contrast to the call and appeal of the other, conceived increasingly within theological and messianic discourses, which are, paradoxically, devoid of their eschatological and teleological elements.

Derrida attempts to side-step the problems associated with the teleological and futural structure of theological and messianic discourses, by introducing duplicity at the origin of faith and knowledge. This allows for the coming of and the opening to the other without a *telos* or *arche* being instituted. He asserts that the 'origin is duplicity itself, the one and the other', and names them, though provisionally, the first as messianic and the second as *khora*. Derrida clarifies that his notion of messianic or messianicity is '*without messianism*' (*FK*: 17). He goes on to argue that his idea of messianic is

> *the opening to the future or the coming of the other as the advent of justice, but without horizon of expectation and without prophetic preconfiguration. The coming of the other can only emerge as a singular event when no anticipation sees it coming, when the other and death – and the radical evil – can come as a surprise at any moment* (*FK*: 17).

The advent of the futural other is connected to the singular event that cannot be foretold, foreseen, anticipated or prophesied in a deterministic way. The advent of the other is connected to justice, death and non-expectancy. Derrida's concept of justice is again futural and inscribed within a messianic discourse without prophecy, and devoid of the religious discourses of salvation, damnation, atonement, and pre-formatted revelatory narratives. The other is disconnected from the hermeneutical notion of horizon and has the structure of a singular event. Radical evil and death are constitutive of the other which can arrive as a surprise within a perpetual future opening. In this way the other is marked by infinitude, but without recourse to the concept of God.

Within this schema, the opening to the other in its futural advent is problematic in relation to subjectivity. When considering the subject and the self in relation to the other, Derrida continues to emphasize that the subject cannot posit itself as 'I' or 'me'. The subject is inscribed by the other and answers the call of the other. The decision of the subject to answer the call of the other is not proper to the subject, but belongs to the other and comes from the other. Even when the other appears itself in the 'I' or the 'me', the decision to answer the call of the other emanates from the other without the subject been absolved of its responsibility. Derrida asserts that '*even there where it appears itself, in me, the decision is moreover always of the other, which does not exonerate me of responsibility*' (*FK*: 17). Derrida's position is untenable. On the one hand, Derrida denies the subject any constitutive power, and on the other hand, obligates the subject to bear the ethical responsibility for the answer to the call of the other. Derrida's other is independent of any constitution of the subject and intersubjective relations. The subject exists only in so far as it is given the responsibility to answer the call of the other, but paradoxically the subject's decision to answer the call is given to it by the other. Within this 'other directed' and 'other derived' notion of ethics, religion, knowledge, truth, faith, belief, revelation, reason etc. the subject is acted upon through the other, but is not the agent of its own actions. If the subject's modalities of responsibility of the answer to the call of the other are to be given to it by the other, the subject needs to be constituted, albeit without the ipso-centrism of Western metaphysics that Derrida decries.

The solution that Derrida offers to the problem regarding subjectivity, is to retreat, as in his previous work, to the elusive and radical Platonic concept of *khora*. The other, like *khora*, is constructed as a pre-ontological category. The Platonic *khora* is conceived of as the receptacle which escapes the need for presence, and appeals to the *epekeina tes ousias* (beyond being). It is not surprising then that Derrida turns towards Plato's concept of *khora* to reinscribe within it his radical philosophy of alterity, and to indicate both its affinities to and departures from it. Derrida's use of the Platonic concept of *khora* in his work is equally complex as his concept of the other. As I have already discussed in previous chapters, the notion of the Platonic *khora* has preoccupied Derrida in his earlier work because of its affinities to his own deconstructions. Here the concept of *khora* is again defined as '*the thought of that which is beyond being (epekeina tes ousias)*', as '*an utterly, faceless other*' and as '*nothing (nobeing, nothing present)*' (*FK*: 19–21). The Platonic *khora's* pre-ontological character parallels Derrida's construction of the other. Like the non-originary Platonic *khora*, Derrida argues that the other as utterly other 'is inaccessible in its absolute source. And there where every other is utterly other' (*FK*: 33). Derrida's other is faceless, beyond being and its source is occulted. Although this formulation echoes the construction of God within negative theology, Derrida refuses to connect his notion of the other to God as the unknown and irreducible infinity. He goes on to argue that *khora*

> *[t]his Greek noun says in our memory that which is not reappropriable, even by our memory, even by our 'Greek' memory; it says the immemoriality of a desert in the desert of which it is neither a threshold nor a mourning* (*FK*: 21).

While the Platonic *khora* acts as a threshold of reception that enables a happening, an event to occur without actor or reflection being the determining factors, Derrida's conceptualization of the *khora* in this work is determined by the utterly other which is nobeing and nothing. The evocation 'of the immemoriality of a desert in the desert' announces a prophetic and messianic coming, unconnected to memory, mourning and any point of origin. The often repeated phrase 'from the desert prophets come', is very apt here.

However, we need to raise the question: who are these prophets without prophecy? What are the discursive or other possibilities of this prophetic discourse being as radical as it claims to be that the whole edifice of Western thought, as it developed since Plato, will be replaced by Derridean deconstruction? Derrida's answers remain problematic. However, what we can be certain about is that the politics of the new 'messianism without messianism' centres on the Other, and is based on his concept of cosmopolitics and on a new International (already announced in the *Spectres of Marx*). Within this model of alterity the political and ethical questions come again to the fore. However, since within the prophetic tradition everything is future, it is questionable if the radicalism of this new type of prophecy can deal with the challenges of the present, within a model of politics and ethics based on action, and engaged political and ethical subjects. In order to examine how Derrida deals with contemporary issues in the last phase of his work, I will turn to his two essays titled *On Cosmopolitanism* and *On Forgiveness*, where he expounds a new politics and ethics by examining 'violations to the other'.

7.2 Hospitality, cosmopolitics and violence to the other

Derrida, in a 1981 interview with Richard Kearney, charged logocentric Western metaphysics of self presence with doing violence to the other. He asserted that 'the rapport of self-identity is itself always a rapport of violence with the other' (Derrida in Kearney, 1984: 117). This axiom will mark all his later work, and will influence his analyses of concrete situations of 'violence to the other'. Derrida in his two essays *On Cosmopolitanism* and *On Forgiveness* addresses the 'violations to the other' by tackling pressing, contemporary, political, legal, ethical, economic, cultural and social issues relating to refugee, minority, immigrant, asylum, and human rights. In addition, he deals with hospitality, cosmopolitanism and ethnic struggles, and the meaning of forgiveness within traumatic historical situations. His aim is to expose the 'violence to the other' within diverse historical and socio-political situations, and to further articulate the political and ethical project of the philosophy of deconstruction. As in his previous work, the concept of the other becomes central to the way Derrida approaches these contemporary political, legal and ethical dilemmas. In the place of a politics and ethics embedded within the subjectivist and humanist discourses of Western metaphysics that do violence to the other, Derrida advocates a new politics and ethics based on a non-originary concept of the other, defined by non-violence, asymmetry and the messianic 'to come'. However, it is important to emphasize that in these two essays, Derrida shifts the emphasis from the abstract other to the concrete other, and makes hospitality a central concern.

In his work *On Cosmopolitanism*, Derrida expounds various modalities of violence to the other within diverse domains in contemporary society, including the institutional, state, legal, political and cultural spheres. He identifies a progressive increase in the spread of violence to the other, globally and within Europe. He demonstrates its global institutional and legal dimensions by identifying the absence of asylum rights within important international legal documents, including the Charter of the League of Nations – the precursor of the United Nations. Derrida locates the increase of violence to the other in the rise of the modern nation-state, and in the transformations to the law of hospitality that have occurred over many centuries. More specifically, he implicates the rise of the modern nation state because hospitality becomes subject to its laws and to its socio-cultural, economic, demographic and political demands. To expose the increase in state violence to the other, he analyses the role of state enforcement agencies as well as the political, legal, economic and other discourses that advocate control of refugees, immigrants and asylum seekers.

Derrida draws upon Arendt's work *The Decline of the Nation-State and the End of the Rights of Man*, to show that within the modern world of nation-states there is a progressive erosion of the sacred right to asylum of those persecuted. Examining the current situation in France and Europe, Derrida contends that the ideas of asylum rights, as encapsulated by the Enlightenment and the French revolution, have become 'controlled, curbed, and monitored by implacable juridical restrictions' (*CF*:11). The increased hostility towards immigrants, refugees and asylum seekers within contemporary societies, is due to what Derrida calls the 'control of the demographico-economic interest' of nation states rather than the actual validity of the applicants' claims. Thus, the rights of asylum seekers, refugees and immigrants become subject to the economic and demographic interests and needs of the nation-state. This is manifested by the absurd situation where the host country demands that refugees, asylum seekers, and immigrants, and generally persons who are fleeing persecution, should expect no benefits or economic interest from the host country, even if their applications are successful (*CF*: 12). These hostile attitudes are expressed within the political arena by both the right and the left, who adopt the economic and demographic discourses that emphasise immigration, refugee and asylum controls. As a result of these negative developments, there is a steady decline in the number of successful applications for granting refugee and asylum status. The interests of the nation-state for 'immigration control' and the needs of refugees, asylum seekers, displaced persons, and immigrants of all kinds are conflicting. How does one deal with this implacable dilemma? The concept of the other again becomes central to the ways Derrida deals with these concrete economic, ethical, legal, political, historical and socio-cultural realities. He connects these issues, especially the issue of asylum, to the concept of the absolute other, unconditionality, universality, justice and hospitality.

As already stated, the concept of hospitality in the last phase of Derrida's work is integral to the new ethics and politics based on the wholly other. In the place of the current politics and policies of nation-states in relation to 'the other', such as refugees, asylum seekers, immigrants, stateless, homeless and displaced persons, Derrida advocates for a different notion of sovereignty, a new ethics and culture of hospitality. He puts forward the idea of open and free cities of refuge based on a new politics and ethics of cosmopolitics. In order to institute his new thinking of open cities, sovereignty, and hospitality that do not do violence to the other, Derrida, while drawing upon the European heritage, deconstructs and critiques a number of different traditions and practices of hospitality.

Derrida begins by analysing Kant's right to universal hospitality in order to locate the contradictions within two opposing positions in contemporary thinking and practices in relation to asylum and human rights. On the one hand, there is the professed desire to offer political and other types of asylum unconditionally. On the other hand, there are the pragmatic realities of the contemporary European situation which restrict and heavily prescribe such rights through a number of institutions and laws. In addition, the idea of un-conditionality is subject to political, economic, socio-cultural and demographic imperatives of nation states, which determine immigration, refugee and asylum policies, and enforce them through state apparatuses. The resulting situation is what Derrida calls 'violations of hospitality' which are also violations to the other. The numerous processes associated with these violations heavily implicate the multiple law enforcement agencies and teletechnologies (*CF*: 14). Against the prevailing situation, Derrida advocates a charter of hospitality based on the principle of new cities of refuge where 'it will be necessary to restrict the legal powers and scope of the police' (*CF*: 15). In these new cities the police should be given 'a purely administrative role', and be 'under the strict control and regulation of certain political authorities' who will ensure that 'human rights and a more broadly defined right to asylum are respected' (*CF*: 15).

Derrida embarks on the task of establishing the new ethics and culture of hospitality by examining different traditions of hospitality. He does this in order to locate the great transformations that have occurred in the duty, culture and the law of hospitality, and analyse their implications. His aim is to draw upon these diverse traditions, and outline his project in relation to the duty of and the right to hospitality. He counterpoises the state defined law of hospitality to his own universal and unconditional law of hospitality, and makes hospitality an integral part of the new ethics based on non-violence to the other. He links hospitality to culture rather than an ethic of hospitality, because '[h]ospitality is culture itself and not simply an ethic among others' (*CF*: 16). Ethics is seen 'as coextensive with the experience of hospitality', because it relates to the ethos of how we 'relate to ourselves and to others as our own or as foreigners' (*CF*: 17). Here Derrida allows the introduction of subjectivity without the usual reference to the other. The subject and the other are given a relational and reflective dimension, instead of his typical subjugation of the subject to the other. In addition, there is a reference to self-relation and this presupposes a partial re-thinking of the issue of self and other. However, Derrida in the same breath goes on to explain the relation of self and other in similar ways to his early deconstructions. He argues that because one is

> at home with oneself (*l'être-soi chez-soi – l'ipséité meme* – the other within yourself) supposes a reception or inclusion of the other one seeks to appropriate, control, and master according to different modalities of violence, there is a history of hospitality, an always possible perversion of *the* law of hospitality (which can appear unconditional), and of the laws which come to limit and condition it in its inscription as a law (*CF*: 17).

Derrida's answer to the problematic relation of appropriation of or violence to the other is to institute a notion of hospitality where the subject is but eliminated.

Within Derrida's de-subjectivised concept of hospitality, based on absolute alterity, the subject as self-relating, even when it admits the other, does violence to the other. Thus, a notion of self that is connected to a conscious subject, as well as any notion of alterity connected to subjectivist categories, is eliminated. The self positing subject is connected to the other through modalities of violence such as appropriation, mastery and control. The subject and the self become again notions that have a negative relation to the other. Even when the self can posit itself as other, it does violence to the other because it takes the place of the other. The Derridean quasi-transcendental other comes to fissure any relation of the self to the other, based on modalities of violence. Derrida's other is in a relation of non-reciprocity, non-recognition, non-relation to the subject. Similarly, his notion of hospitality is a modality of his non-relational concept of the other. Thus, hospitality has to be severed from the subject and its categories, and be constructed within the new thinking of the other. In the same way, hospitality is dissociated from any forms of politics and ethics based on subjectivist categories. Within Derrida's schema, hospitality is beyond the conditionality of current laws, politics and ethics, which are based on the subjectivist and humanist thought of Western metaphysics which he charges with violence to the other.

To further develop his new thinking regarding the duties of and rights to hospitality, Derrida embarks on an exploration of various theological, philosophical, intellectual, political, legal and ethical traditions, as well as conceptions and practices of hospitality. He demonstrates how these traditions deal with the laws of hospitality and the treatment of the other. Drawing on these different traditions and practices of hospitality, he aims to overcome and eliminate the 'violence to the other' by instituting a concept of the other that preserves the links to the wholly other as non-appropriable by the subject and as irreducible to the laws that 'come to limit and condition it' (*CF*: 17). Unconditionality and exceeding of limits become constitutive of his concept of the other, which will inform his new concept and ethics of hospitality and new cities.

The first tradition Derrida examines is the Hebraic tradition, where hospitality is connected to religion and is part of the sacred duty towards the persecuted and aliens. He points out that God ordered Moses to institute 'cities of refuge' or 'asylum' for the 'resident alien or temporary settler' (*CF*: 17). Derrida again appeals to the work of Levinas *The Cities of Refuge* and Daniel Payot's *Refuge Cities*, to demonstrate the contemporary treatment of this theological and sacred tradition, in order to stress the importance of offering asylum to those who are persecuted. The concept of the cities of refuge and unconditional asylum, taken from this theological tradition, will inform Derrida's idea of the open cities of refuge and his concepts of the other and hospitality.

The second tradition which Derrida draws upon is the Medieval. Within this tradition, in contrast with the modern nation state, 'the city itself could determine the laws of hospitality' (*CF*: 18). He points out that in relation to asylum and the treatment of those persecuted, two important concepts were developed: *sanctuary* and *autocritas*. These concepts link to theological ideas, but also to the idea of the sovereign being above the secular application of the law regarding the law and duty of hospitality. The concept of *autocritas* was linked to secular power but, at the same time, exceeded it, because it 'allowed kings or lords to shield their guests (*hôtes*) from all those in pursuit' (*CF*: 18). This meant that the laws of the secular institutions could not overrule the right of the sovereign to protect those prosecuted. Providing sanctuary became an integral part of the ethics of hospitality, and the church played an important role in its development and practice. Churches offered sanctuary 'to secure immunity or survival for refugees' (*CF*: 18). Another important element within the medieval tradition was the establishment of cities of refuge for those who became refugees of wars. When waring cities vanquished another city-state, it was customary to have one of the cities become a sanctuary for the refugees of the defeated side. In other words, what the medieval tradition offers Derrida are conceptions of the other, asylum, and hospitality that exceed the secular powers and laws when it came to 'violations to the other', but also retain the links to theological traditions. These theological and secular traditions preserved the sanctity and inviolability of the other, and prevented violence to the other. The medieval tradition informs Derrida's new law of hospitality as exceeding the limits of the secular and sovereign powers of the nation-state.

The third tradition Derrida draws upon is the cosmopolitan. He argues that this tradition is 'common to a certain Greek stoicism and a Pauline Christianity, of which the inheritors were the Enlightenment' (*CF*: 19). The stoic notion of cosmopolitanism included the ideas of *xenoi or hospites*, as both foreigners and guests, and 'metic' or migrant, as *paroikoi* and neighbours, and incorporated the notion of universality. However, Derrida argues, the tradition of cosmopolitanism that ensued from Pauline Christianity 'revived, radicalised and literally "politicised" the primary injunctions of all the Abrahamic religions' regarding unconditional hospitality (*CF*: 19). Saint Paul, Derrida contends, gives these injunctions 'theologicopolitical names, since they explicitly designate citizenship or world co-citizenship' within a religious community (*CF*: 19). Although Pauline Christianity maintained its links to its theological heritage, it incorporated secular and global elements from stoicism. This meant the idea of the 'cities of refuge' lost its injunctive and religious heritage, and its connections to unconditional hospitality. Increasingly, the notion of hospitality became more secular and prescriptive, while, at the same time, it laid claims to universality.

The ideas of these traditions, in both their secular and theological elements, were later most forcefully expressed in Kant's law of universal hospitality (*CF*: 19). The movement towards greater secularization of this heritage is articulated in Kant's work *Definitive Article in View of*

Perpetual Peace, where he sets out the law of cosmopolitanism which restricts it 'to the conditions of universal hospitality' (*CF*: 19–20). Derrida identifies two important features in Kant's cosmopolitan law. Firstly, it encompasses 'universal hospitality without limits' (*CF*: 20). Secondly, it is 'a natural law' and as such it is 'both imprescriptible and inalienable' (*CF*: 20). The emergence of the idea of imprescriptibility will inform Derrida's work on forgiveness and human rights, because it defines responsibility to the other as being infinite.

However, Derrida argues, Kant's model 'excluded hospitality as a right of residence (*Gastrecht*)' and limited it 'to the right of visitation (*Besuchsrecht*)' (*CF*: 21). The right to residence becomes further secularized when it is 'made the object of a particular treaty between states' (*CF*: 21). Derrida singles out this important juridical aspect in Kant's formulation of the law of cosmopolitanism, to emphasise that hospitality is no longer unconditional and becomes subject to state sovereignty and state power. Thus hospitality, whether private or public, 'is dependent on and controlled by the law and the police' (*CF*: 22). This has grave consequences for the idea of hospitality and the 'violations of hospitality' within modern democratic societies (*CF*: 22). From the cosmopolitan tradition Derrida retains the concepts of universality and unconditionality, but jettisons the concept of sovereignty based on the modern nation-state and the legal and political frameworks that safeguard its often repressive functions, institutions and practices.

However, Derrida recognises the difficulties of negotiating between unconditional hospitality and the law as it currently stands. His answer is to place both democracy and cosmopolitanism within his project of futural politics and ethics, where the cities of refuge, the law, asylum and hospitality can be reinscribed within the yet to come and the ethics of the wholly other. He concludes the work on cosmopolitanism and his vision of the new cities, by stating that '[b]eing on the threshold of these cities, of these new cities that would be something other than "*new* cities", a certain idea of cosmopolitanism, *an other*, has not arrived, *perhaps*' (*CF*:23). As in his previous work, the other, even if it has arrived, is not yet recognised. This places the other outside prescriptive prophetic narratives, while leaving a perpetual opening to respond to the other's demand for justice and asylum. In other words, Derrida's new charter of hospitality, gestures towards a futural politics whose messianic character is annulled by Derrida's paradoxical formulation of 'messianism without messianism' (Derrida and Vattimo, 1998: 17). The politics and ethics of hospitality, based on the new thinking of the other, place them within the messianic promise of arrival that never arrives. The problematic of violence to the other is situated beyond the secular politics and practices of the nation state and beyond any subjectivist categories. The announcement of the new concepts of *cosmopolitics* and hospitality, based on the other, links to Derrida's new approach regarding the concept of forgiveness. It is to Derrida's work on forgiveness that I will now turn to further elucidate his messianic turn inscribed as an infinite coming of the infinite other.

7.3 Forgiveness and the other

Derrida continues his analyses of cosmopolitanism, hospitality and 'violations to the other' by examining concrete historical situations in relation to forgiveness, its meanings, and uses. In his essay '*On Forgiveness*', he points out that asking for forgiveness and the associated narratives of amnesty and re-conciliation have become globalized. They are used uncritically around the world by diverse actors, institutions and bodies, ranging from communities to sovereign heads of state. This indiscriminate, global saturation, amounts to an abuse of the notion of forgiveness. In addition, within the various global discourses of forgiveness, Derrida identifies a number of common elements that are embedded in the Abrahamic religious heritage, which encompasses Judaism, the various forms of Christianity, and Islam. The global adoption and spread of the discourses rooted in this theological tradition represent an uncritical appropriation and application of it. This is a result of the global domination of processes connected to what Derrida calls *globalatinisation.* This *globalatinisation* manifests itself even in countries and parts of the world where the dominant religious and judicial traditions differ, such as Korea, Japan, Algeria and South Africa.

The question that arises for Derrida is, whether the discourse of asking for forgiveness and forgiveness itself have fallen victim to forms of global politics and ethics which do violence to the other. Derrida uses again his notion of the other and its connections to irreducibility and unconditionality, to deconstruct the discourses, narratives, language and practices of forgiveness. By linking forgiveness to irreducible atlerity, he deconstructs any mode of thinking, politics and ethics which inscribes forgiveness within utilitarian, teleological, humanist and subjectivist paradigms. His aim is threefold: to critique forms of global politics and ethics based on *globalatinisation*; to deconstruct the global forms and narratives of asking for forgiveness; and to institute a new thinking of forgiveness which is dissociated from 'violence to the other' and disconnected from any utilitarian, normative and subjectivist paradigms of politics, justice and ethics.

In order to institute a new thinking of forgiveness, Derrida examines the inter-connections between forgiveness, reconciliation, amnesty, Human Rights, sovereignty, and the notion of crimes against humanity. He uses the examples of South Africa's Truth and Reconciliation Committee, France's treatment of the Vichy regime, and the Korean, Japanese and Algerian cases, to critique the globalization of asking for forgiveness, because it is 'at the service of finalities' (*CF*: 31). He goes on to emphasize that

> each time forgiveness is at the service of finality, be it noble and spiritual (atonement or redemption, reconciliation, salvation), each time that it aims to re-establish a normality (social, national, political, psychological) by work of mourning, by some therapy or ecology of memory, then the 'forgiveness' is not pure – nor is its concept (*CF*: 31–32).

For Derrida a pure notion of forgiveness is outside any form of finitude, conditionality and processes of normalization.

Derrida places forgiveness outside the normative, proceduralist notions of justice, restitution, salvation, reconciliation and psychological therapeutics. Given Derrida's anti-subjectivist and anti-humanist philosophical stance and his vehement opposition to Western metaphysics of presence, any notion of closure and finality would be within the paradigm of logocentric thought, where the irreducibility of the other is absorbed within identity without remainder. Accepting any notion of forgiveness based on subjectivist categories and connected to the work of memory as appropriation and as a work of mourning would be antithetical to his notion of alterity. As we shall see, he maintains his anti-subjectivist and anti-humanist position from his early deconstruction of the sign until the end.

Derrida's next task is to critique the forms of forgiveness linked to the processes of *globalatinisation*. These processes embed forgiveness within Western metaphysics and a Roman Christian theological and cultural discourse which over-determine the language of law, politics and 'the return of the religious' (*CF*: 32). Within *globalatinisation* discourses, the demand for forgiveness becomes part of normative and normalizing processes. Moreover, by subsuming forgiveness to historical and socio-political imperatives the end result is doing 'violence to the other'. In contrast, for Derrida, '[f]orgiveness is not, it *should not be*, normal, normative, normalizing', but instead '*should* remain exceptional and extraordinary, in the face of the impossible: as if it interrupted the ordinary course of historical temporality' (*CF*: 32). By linking forgiveness to the exceptional and extraordinary, and by placing forgiveness outside historical time, Derrida valorises the rupture effected by its event within time itself. Forgiveness is conceived within a framework of impossibility, rather than a process of normalization. He asserts, true 'forgiveness only forgives the unforgivable' and is unconditional (*CF*: 32, 38). The idea of un-conditionality is central to both forgiveness and hospitality and is connected to the structure of the event and the coming of the future. Derrida goes on to explain that 'forgiveness can only announce itself as impossibility itself' (*CF*: 33). In other words, Derrida raises the problematic notion of forgiveness, as it is currently practiced, in order to make forgiveness a herald of itself as an impossibility. Forgiveness, like his notion of the other, announces itself within a pre-originary, quasi-transcendental and non subjectivist configuration. Pure forgiveness is severed from any connections to notions of subjectivity and the self. It remains outside any normative considerations and any subjectivist discourses and philosophical paradigms based on Western metaphysic's demand for presence.

Consequently, Derrida dissociates forgiveness from notions of punishment, restitution, atonement etc. which connect it to the idea that forgiveness rests 'on a human possibility' (*CF*: 32). He takes forgiveness out of the model of ethics and politics based on co-present subjects or, as he puts it, 'the anthropological feature that decides everything' (*CF*: 36). Derrida's notion of forgiveness is beyond subjectivist and humanist notions of ethics, because it advocates for unconditional forgiveness 'which would be granted even to the one who did not ask for it' (*CF*: 36). In addition, Derrida's notion of forgiveness is dissociated from the economy of exchange, where forgiveness is in symmetry with punishment and aims at redemption and re-conciliation. He asserts that forgiveness is beyond the 'horizon of a redemption or a reconciliation' (*CF*: 36). Thus, the history of forgiveness would begin with the unforgivable and outside any notions that depend on human agency, the subject and the self. Within this schema, the ideas of intersubjectivity, accountability, recognition, agency, horizontality, reflection, and reciprocity are inadmissible.

Harping back to his ideas of the supplement, sovereignty, gift, economy of excess, philosophy of the limits, the abyss and non-equivocation of meaning, Derrida is emphatic in his critique of the uses and abuses of forgiveness and the role of political, religious and State apparatuses. He argues that '[t]ere is always a strategical or political calculation in the generous gesture of one who offers reconciliation or amnesty', and it is imperative 'to interrogate this calculation in our analyses' (*CF*: 40). Taking forgiveness and amnesty out of an economy of exchange, strategic and political calculations, reconciliation narratives, and judgement, Derrida declares that '[f]orgiveness does not, it should never amount to a therapy of reconciliation' (*CF*: 41). Making forgiveness part of individual or collective therapeutics instrumentalizes it and annuls its authenticity. Citing the case of a South African woman, whose husband was killed during the murderous years of Apartheid, Derrida questions the role of public state institutions and the connections of forgiveness to judgement and to the political and public spheres. The South African woman, who spoke in her own language rather than the Anglican-English of the Truth and Reconciliation Commission, refused to forgive the killers of her husband on his behalf. Derrida uses her refusal and inability to forgive, to point out that '[t]he representative of the State can judge, but forgiveness has precisely nothing to do with judgement' (*CF*: 43). The question that arises is: who has the right to forgive and on whose behalf? Derrida's answer is that only the victim has the right and authority to forgive and not an institution. Moreover, no one has the right to forgive on behalf of a dead victim (*CF*: 44). In other words, no subject can forgive in the place of the other and for the other. The impossibility of forgiving on behalf of the dead victim (other) makes the possibility of forgiveness an impossibility. Since a dead person cannot forgive, the solution to this implacable dilemma can only be effected through the mediation of a third element such as a subject, God, etc. Derrida rejects such solutions used by the prevailing narratives of forgiveness, because they eliminate the irreducibility of the other and are not based on unconditionality.

Derrida in order to radicalize the notion of forgiveness dissociates it from any mediating, inter-subjective and prescriptive elements. He identifies within the discourses of forgiveness a tension between two poles. On the one hand, '[s]ometimes forgiveness (given by God or inspired by divine prescription) must be a gracious gift, without exchange and without condition' (*CF*: 44). On the other hand, 'sometimes [forgiveness] requires, as its minimal condition, the repentance and transformation of the sinner'(*CF*: 44). The resolution to this onto-theological tension that Derrida offers is that 'pure and unconditional forgiveness, in order to have its own meaning, must have no "meaning", no finality, even no intelligibility. It is a madness of the impossible' (*CF*: 45). Forgiveness, as unintelligible, undefinable, and as madness of the impossible, connects to Derrida's previous articulations of the notion of the utterly other. He argues that 'alterity, non-identification, even incomprehension, remain irreducible' (*CF*: 49). As a result forgiveness is 'mad', and 'must plunge, but lucidly, into the night of the unintelligible. Call this the unconscious or the non-conscious if you want' (*CF*: 49). Forgiveness is anterior to consciousness and not subject to power, sovereignty and prescriptive processes. The injection of madness within forgiveness itself is akin to Nietzsche's Dionysian madness in his Ecce Homo, or what Derrida calls the madness that must watch over thought. What Derrida advocates is for 'a forgiveness without power: *unconditional but without sovereignty*' (*CF*: 59). Alterity demands that forgiveness is connected to irreducibility, illegibility, incomprehension and madness, but not to any notions of sovereignty, subjectivity or agency. Placing forgiveness within a theiological discourse, which conceives of forgiveness as an unconditional gift that has no return, dissociates it from any connections to exchange based on reciprocity, recognition, *globalatinisation*, and power relations.

Derrida recognizes the difficulty and impossibility of dissociating forgiveness from conditionality and sovereignty. He ends the essay with the question, 'Will that be done one day?', only to conclude that 'since the hypothesis of this unpresentable task announces itself, be it as a dream for thought, this madness is perhaps not so mad [...]' (*CF*: 59–60). The 'dream for thought', that forgiveness will be unconditional and free of the imperatives and restrictions of sovereignty, places forgiveness in the realm of a future vision. Such a radical position entails that forgiveness is severed from the current political and ethical spheres, because within these spheres forgiveness is part of an economy of reconciliation, restitution, repentance, adequation and transformation. This general economy of exchange aims to achieve some kind of finality or closure (to use a contemporary and more popular term). Moreover, it often uses a discourse of conscious calculability and gives prescribed meanings to forgiveness. For Derrida, these processes annul forgiveness's irreducibility and consequently do 'violence to the other'.

The notion of forgiveness that Derrida announces is futural and beyond a hermeneutical horizon. Based on his concept of alterity, it severs all connections to conditionality, sovereignty and ultimately power. Within his schema, the conscious, self-reflecting subject and the narrating self are eliminated from the discourse of forgiveness as is any form of agency. The questions that arise are: who forgives and for whom? Who and what is forgiven? Who requests forgiveness, from whom, for what, and why? Can one request forgiveness from oneself and not simply from the other?

For forgiveness to be requested or given there has to be a fault or wrongdoing. A notion of fault is connected to a subject as being culpable of the fault, the subject has to be designated as the agent of the fault(s) that requires forgiveness, and admits that s/he is the agent of the fault. If forgiveness presupposes fault, then this fault has to be attributed to someone and be recognized as such by the person(s) who is the agent of the fault committed. All these processes involve notions of subjectivity, intersubjectivity, self, selfhood, self-reflection, and narrative constructions. Derrida's elimination of these categories as being subjectivist, leaves forgiveness unconnected to notions of reflection, memory and narrativity. Such a situation is untenable, because forgiveness is emptied from its human dimensions. Although Derrida's approach to forgiveness is problematic, we need to keep from Derrida's schema its radical elements, that is, 'pure' forgiveness is to forgive the unforgivable; it is unconditional and divorced from notions of utilitarianism, sovereignty and power. However, his anti-subjectivist and anti-humanist stand that leads to the elimination of the subject and the self, have to be questioned and rethought.

It is to the work of Ricœur *Memory, History, Forgetting*, that we need to turn to re-inscribe forgiveness within a mode of thinking that aims to avoid doing 'violence to the other', but also does not eliminate the subject, intersubjectivity, self, self-reflection, agency, reciprocity and recognition. The work of Ricœur on forgiveness provides us with a different and complex approach to the issue of forgiveness and its connections to alterity and the self.

7.4 Ricœur and Derrida: On Forgiveness

At the outset it is important to note that Ricœur concurs with Derrida that pure forgiveness is to forgive the unforgivable; it is unconditional, and outside utilitarian considerations. Like Derrida, he questions the possibility and existence of such notion of forgiveness and also critiques discourses of forgiveness that aim at finalities (*MHF*: 490). However, unlike Derrida, Ricœur, places forgiveness within the hermeneutic and phenomenological traditions, albeit reformulated. He asserts that '[f]orgiveness – if it has a sense, and if it exists – constitutes the horizon common to memory, history, and forgetting' (*MHF*: 457). The common horizon between memory, history and forgetting embeds forgiveness within notions of temporality and human relations, rather than within the infinite immanence of messianic discourses. However, Ricœur acknowledges that this horizon is '[a]lways in retreat' and 'slips away from any grasp' making 'forgiving difficult … but not impossible' (*MHF*: 457). He accepts that the constant retreat of this horizon 'places a seal of incompleteness on the entire enterprise', and admits that forgiveness is difficult to conceive of, to give and receive (*MHF*: 457).

Ricœur, unlike Derrida, implicates the subject, self, and other in all processes of forgiveness. His concepts of fault and imputability become constitutive of forgiveness, and signal a departure from Derrida's other directed and futural messianic articulations. Ricœur goes on to map out the trajectory of forgiveness, locating its origin 'in the disproportion that exists between the poles of fault and forgiveness' (*MHF*: 457). He clarifies this difference as being one of altitude and vertical disparity 'between the depth of fault and the height of forgiveness' (*MHF*: 457). At the height of this polarity he places 'the hymn to forgiveness' and at the bottom end the 'avowal of fault' (*MHF*: 457). Furthermore, this polarity entails two speech acts: the first is connected to imputability 'where agents bind themselves to their action and recognize themselves as accountable', and the second 'can be heard in the great sapiential poetry that in the same breath celebrates love and joy' (*MHF*: 458). Within this schema, Ricœur links forgiveness to human actors and raises some very important issues with regards to its connections to subjectivity, self, agency, responsibility, memory, reflection, fault, admission, reciprocity, recognition, binding, unbinding, love and care.

To begin with, Ricœur introduces his notion of imputability into the process of forgiveness and links it to subjectivity, agency, fault, guilt, reflection and the other. He argues that the experience of fault entails thought and reflection, within which the fundamental structure of the imputability of our action is inscribed. He goes on to clarify that

> there can, in fact, be forgiveness only where we can accuse someone of something, presume him to be or declare him guilty. And one can indict only those acts that are imputable to an agent who holds himself to be their genuine author (*MHF*: 460).

If at the heart of forgiveness there is the assumption or evidence of fault, there has to be imputability. Any experience of fault is inscribed with the structure of imputability, and cannot occur without reflective thinking which binds the act to its agent. This means that the fault is imputed to an agent who is guilty of the fault, but also holds himself/herself responsible and recognises him/herself as being the genuine agent responsible for the fault. Ricœur's notion of imputability means that the self and self-reflection are implicated in all processes of forgiveness, because they involve attribution of actions and acceptance of responsibility by the actor as well as an analysis of memory and of oneself. Thus the ideas of fault, guilt and repentance cannot be divorced from forgiveness. Moreover, for Ricœur the concept of imputability, and its connections to the self and self-reflection, is fundamental because it underpins his concept of selfhood which, as we have seen, is constructed outside the ipsocentrism of Western metaphysics. He asserts that '[t]he tie between fault and self, guilt and selfhood seems indissoluble' (*MHF*: 466). By making forgiveness part of a reflective process, he re-introduces notions of responsibility and accountability in relation to actual human actors. The Derridean mode of thinking, where responsibility is based on an a priori response to the call of the other without any involvement of human actors, side-steps the issue of imputability and selfhood and its reflective structure, which links them back to a notion of subjectivity that does not jettison consciousness and forms of recognition.

For Ricœur the concept of imputability and its links to the notion of 'the capable human being', form an integral part of the articulation of the experience of fault, and are constitutive of the discourse of forgiveness. He argues that

> I can speak, act, recount, hold myself accountable for my actions—they can be imputed to me. Imputability constitutes in this respect an integral dimension of what I am calling the capable human being. It is in the region of imputability that fault, guilt, is to be sought. This is the region of articulation between the act and the agent, between the 'what' of the actions and the 'who' of the power to act—of agency (*MHF*: 460).

Any process of imputability of acts to a 'capable human being' necessarily involves agency, action, speech, memory, narrativity and reflection. Memory and self are inextricably linked through reflexivity. As Ricœur puts it, 'an objective analysis of memories as objects', and 'a reflexive analysis of memory and oneself' are part of the constitution of the self (*MHF*: 460). For Ricœur this is a question of the '*nexus* between the "what" of memories and the "who" of memory' (*MHF*: 460). The 'who' and 'what' are integral to the notions of fault and guilt, because they connect to memory and recognition. Moreover, the complex interrelations between the 'who' and 'what' involve notions of actor(s), actions, context, and content, rather than a de-subjectivised, pre-ontological other. Another important aspect of imputability, when dealing with fault, is the 'self-ascription of fault' which involves the conditions of a common recognition of a fundamental guilt (*MHF*: 461). The specific form which the recognition of fault and attribution of the fault to the self takes is avowal. Avowal is that speech act by which a subject takes up, assumes the accusation, and has two functions. Firstly, it 'bridges the abyss between innocence and guilt', and secondly it 'bridges the abyss between the act and its agent' (*MHF*: 461).

Ricœur, unlike Derrida, allows for a distinction, or even separation, between the act and its agent. He argues that 'it is legitimate to draw a line between the action and its agent. This is what we do when we morally, legally, or politically condemn an action' (*MHF*: 461). The binding of the agent to the act is necessary in Ricœur's schema, because for him if forgiveness is to have any meaning it needs to lead to the unbinding of the agent from the act. However, like Derrida, Ricœur agrees that forgiveness is impossible within certain situations, when the nature of the fault results in loss and debt to the victims that can never be atoned. Thus, Ricœur recognises impresciptibility as a very important legal and moral development, because it does away with the statute of limitations and acknowledges that certain crimes should not be erased from the ledgers of history, memory, nations, peoples and humanity. In this way, like Derrida, Ricœur questions the possibility of forgiveness since there are cases where the unbinding of the actor from the act cannot or should not occur.

To arrive at the desired end of forgiveness, which is to unbind the actor from her/his act, Ricœur maps out the Odyssey of forgiveness. I will not go through all the complex elements of this journey, which traverses the philosophical, political, ethical, religious, and finally the moral land of forgiveness. I will only deal with Ricœur's ideas that have relevance to Derrida's approach to forgiveness, in order to tease out some important issues in relation to memory, recognition, subjectivity, self and other.

Ricœur begins the Odyssean journey by examining the relation of forgiveness to promise, gift and giving. Like Derrida, he identifies the connections between forgiveness, gift and exchange, and notes that in many languages asking for and receiving of forgiveness denotes a form of exchange. However, unlike Derrida who rejects any connections between forgiveness and exchange as being within a market economy, Ricœur takes this exchange out of market mechanisms. In relation to the gift, he distinguishes three obligations 'giving, receiving and giving back', and for him the enigma of the gift lies in the connections between the three (*MHF*: 480). Drawing upon archaic forms of exchange and the gift, he identifies the importance of the counter-gift, where a gift is returned by the receiver to the giver of the gift. He locates in the counter-gift the bilateral and reciprocal dimensions of the gift and forgiveness. By introducing the idea of counter-gift, or giving back, Ricœur problematizes a concept of gift where there is no return or counter-gift. The idea of gift unconnected to return represents an absence of reciprocity and places the one receiving the gift in a position of unequal exchange. This institutes a hierarchical rather than a horizontal relation between giver and receiver, where the donor is at the top of the hierarchy. Within this asymmetrical structure the receiver of the gift remains forever indebted to the donor.

Ricœur, unlike Derrida who rejects any notion of gift as return, reinscribes the gift and forgiveness within inter-subjective, reciprocal, horizontal and equal relations. By placing forgiveness within these relations, he recognizes that human actors and agency are important dimensions. Within this schema, the request for and giving of forgiveness balance one another and happen within horizontal rather than vertical relations. However, Ricœur identifies situations where these relations are difficult to institute. The Christian imperative that one loves, not simply forgives, one's enemies constitute for him 'the absolute measure of the gift' (*MHF*: 481). However, this Christian imperative breaks the rule of reciprocity and requires 'the extraordinary' (*MHF*: 482). It is in these situations that Ricœur concurs with Derrida, that forgiveness requires the extraordinary and not the proceduralist approach of establishing commissions and the involvement of State apparatuses. Unlike Derrida who conceives of forgiveness within a structure of absolute alterity dissociated from any human intervention or mediation, Ricœur, as we will see, will use the mediating power of love and care to arrive at forgiveness, which will unbind the actor from the act. If the act and the actor are bound through the concept of imputability, it follows that the self is implicated both in the fault and forgiving. The questions that arise are: who appeals for forgiveness and what does this forgiveness consist of? What are its aims? How does it happen and who makes it happen? Who are the actors in this theatre of forgiveness? Is there a curtain call at the end, or is it a case of the Greek Catharsis being staged with modern actors in a troubled world?

Since, as we have seen, Ricœur, unlike Derrida, implicates the self in all processes of asking for and receiving of forgiveness, he seeks to end the Odyssean journey of forgiveness by locating forgiveness at the centre of the self. In the chapter of his monumental work *Memory, History, Forgetting*, titled 'The Return to the Self', he declares that '[i]t is now to the heart of selfhood that our investigation must be directed' (*MHF*: 486). Distinguishing selfhood from a notion of the self enables Ricœur to raise a number of important questions. The first question pertains to the type of power and courage that one can appeal to 'in order simply to ask for forgiveness' (*MHF*: 486). He links our ability to ask for forgiveness to time, and argues that '[i]t is from our ability to master the course of time that the courage to ask for forgiveness seems able to be drawn' (*MHF*: 486). In other words, action, time, and memory are intricately connected to forgiveness and selfhood. Even though our actions are bound by temporality, we can subject past, present and future actions to reflection and evaluation. This means that one draws the courage and power to ask for forgiveness, because one recognizes the violence and harm done to another. Requesting forgiveness implies that there is someone/something we can appeal to, and has the right and power to forgive. The questions arise: Who forgives? Who has the authority and the power to forgive? Where does the strength to ask for forgiveness come from? To whom do we appeal for forgiveness? How and why is this appeal made and to what effect?

Ricœur deals with the answers to these questions by examining the relationship between forgiveness and promise, and by drawing on different philosophical, theological, moral and ethical traditions. Firstly, Ricœur, in order to problematize the link between promise and forgiveness, draws on Hannah Arendt's work *The Human Condition*. He argues that Arendt identifies two human faculties: 'the faculty of forgiving' and 'the faculty to keep and make promises' (*MHF*: 487). For Arendt the 'power to forgive is a human power' (*MHF*: 487). This position places forgiveness within secular frameworks of power, and recognizes the opposition between forgiveness and vengeance, forgiveness and punishment. Ricœur argues that in Arendt's work a symmetry is instituted between forgiving and promising. However, he wants to question the 'symmetry between forgiving and promising in terms of power' (*MHF*: 487). He identifies a fundamental difference between promising and forgiveness in relation to power. For Ricœur forgiveness has a 'religious aura that promising does not' (*MHF*: 487). Promising is a wish to master the future 'as if it were the present', and is connected to politics and political discourses (*MHF*: 488). Forgiveness, unlike promising, is connected to love, and thus politics cannot appropriate it for its own ends. To prove this important point, Ricœur cites the 'sometimes monstrous failure of all efforts to institutionalize forgiveness' and 'the caricature of forgiveness found in amnesty', which for him amounts to 'the institutional form of forgetting' (*MHF*: 488). He asserts '[t]here is no politics in forgiveness' (*MHF*: 488). Like Derrida, Ricœur removes forgiveness from politics and political discourses, and recognises the uses and abuses of asking for forgiveness. However, by making love the mediating power of forgiveness, Ricœur appeals to Platonic and theological discourses. The Platonic Eros of the *Symposium,* where love reconciles the irreconcilable and is elevated to a mediating cosmic force, is appropriated by Ricœur via its formulation as *agape* within Pauline Christian theology (Plato, 1991; 1989). Unlike Derrida's appeal to the wholly other, Ricœur appeals to the other only to the extent that the subject through imputability recognizes the fault that results in violence and harm to the other.

Ricœur, unlike Derrida, places forgiveness within a schema of horizontal, reciprocal and symmetrical modalities of exchange, and pursues 'the odyssey of forgiveness to the centre of selfhood' (*MHF*: 489). Hence, within Ricœur's schema the concepts of selfhood, agency and the other are integral to any discourse on forgiveness. For him the ultimate goal of forgiveness 'should release the agent from his act' by unbinding the agent from the act (*MHF*: 489). Like Derrida, he acknowledges the gap 'between the unforgivable fault and this impossible forgiveness' and the difficulties of bridging it (*MHF*: 490). Derrida's solution to this dilemma is a conception of forgiveness which is based on the irreducibility of the other which is dissociated from subjectivist categories. The request for and receiving of forgiveness comes from the other and are enacted through the appeal to the other. This results in the elimination of the self and makes the subject hostage and host to the other. Within Derrida's schema, forgiveness is inscribed within a structure of non-relation between the subject and the wholly other. Forgiveness is unconnected to selfhood, agency memory, reciprocity, recognition, forgetting and symmetry.

In contrast, as we have seen, Ricœur's solution to the dilemma of the unforgivable fault and the impossibility of forgiveness is to 'separate the agent from the action' by a process of unbinding (*MHF*: 490). He argues that '[t]his unbinding would mark the inscription, in the field of the horizontal disparity between power and act, of the vertical disparity between the great heights of forgiveness and the abyss of guilt' (*MHF*: 490). The end result of forgiveness through unbinding is that the guilty person is 'rendered capable of beginning again', and that 'this would be the figure of unbinding that commands all the others' (*MHF*: 490). Ricœur asks the obvious question: if forgiveness is 'itself possible' within this schema (*MHF*: 490). He agrees with Derrida that if one forgives the person and condemns the act, it means someone else is condemned in his/her place who did not commit the act. Ricœur's answer to this aporia is to dissociate in a radical way the agent from the act, and this 'dissociation expresses an act of faith, a credit addressed to the resources of self-regeneration' (*MHF*: 490). Reinscribing the unbinding of the agent from his/her act within the theological discourses of faith links it to Derrida's theological and messianic turn. However, Ricœur, by linking it to the resources of self-regeneration, signals a radical departure from Derrida in relation to subjectivity and the self.

Ricœur, like Derrida, draws on religious and philosophical discourses to articulate his solution to the paradox of the unbinding of the agent from the act. By referring back to the ways the 'Religions of the Book' deal with forgiveness and repentance, which he also finds 'inscribed in the Abrahamic memory', he seeks to link forgiveness to self-transformation (*MHF*: 490). Rather than conceiving of forgiveness as being a transaction, Ricœur places it within recognition and the structure of the gift, where 'the antecedence of the gift is recognized at the very heart of the inaugural gesture of repentance' (*MHF*: 490–491). It is the human and inter-subjective dimensions and an emphasis on the responsibility of human agents, which distinguishes Ricœur's approach to forgiveness. However, like Derrida, he accepts a theological dimension to the dilemmas that forgiveness presents us with, but offers different answers to the ontological questions, which do not reduce being to substance and presence.

Unlike Derrida, who constructs being as presence, Ricœur refers back to Aristotle's metaphysics and to the polysemy of the term 'to be', where Aristotle 'accords preference to being as act and power, in contrast to the preference for an understanding in terms of substance that prevailed in metaphysics up to Kant' (*MHF*: 491). Using Kant's argument that 'the original disposition to the good' is fundamental, Ricœur asserts that giving forgiveness means that the guilty person is 'considered capable of something other than the offences and his faults' (*MHF*: 493). This is expressed in the utterance 'you are better than your actions' (*MHF*: 493). This means that imputability demands that one admits fault and suffers the ravages of moral guilt. Forgiveness, however, by enabling the unbinding of the actor from the act does not obliterate the memory of the act, but reinscribes it within memory as recognition while allowing for a re-beginning rather than total effacement and forgetting. Ricœur, in his closing remarks on forgiveness, places recognition at the centre of memory and forgetting. He differentiates between memory and forgetting in order to associate memory with recognition, happiness and event. He considers recognition 'to be the small miracle of memory, but also admits that this miracle 'can … fail to occur', and that '[e]very act of memory (*faire-mémoire*) is … summed up in recognition' (*MHF*: 495). The complex interplay between memory, forgetting and recognition are constitutive of history and forgiveness.

Ricœur, in discussing the role of history and memory, argues that each has different functions. History's project is truth, while memory's is faithfulness. Moreover, history 'has a responsibility to the dead of the past, whose heirs we are' (*MHF*: 499). When dealing with the uses of the discourses of forgiveness in connection to history and memory, Ricœur questions both the means used and aims pursued. He argues that forgiveness in the form of amnesty does violence to both history and memory, because 'the spiritual stakes of amnesty' are 'silencing the non-forgetting of memory' (*MHF*: 501). He sees the institutional uses and abuses of forgetting as 'the symptom of a stubborn uncertainty affecting the relation between forgetting and forgiveness on the level of its deep structure' (*MHF*: 501). Ricœur acknowledges that the relationship between memory and forgetting is very complex, both at the level of human actors and collectivities. The issues involved entail being able to strike a balance between forgetting, memory and reflection. However, this is part of an ongoing problematic, which requires us to be ceaselessly vigilant against misappropriation, misinterpretation, misrepresentation, misuse, misconception, misrecognition and abuse.

Ricœur cautions against the hubris of wishing for a notion of forgetting that verges on total amnesia, but also against a notion of memory that remembers everything. He conceives of a notion of 'memory lacking forgetting' as being 'the ultimate phantasm, the ultimate figure of this total reflection' (*MHF*: 413). He aims for a balance and ongoing negotiation between remembering and forgetting, and advocates for a notion of forgiveness connected to reflection and repentance. He distinguishes two forms of forgetting which are in constant struggle: one achieved through the 'effacement of traces' and the other through the 'forgetting kept in reserve' (*MHF*: 501). Ricœur explains the differences between forgetting and memory in order to articulate the institutional uses and abuses of both. Using historical examples and traversing through numerous religious, poetic and philosophical discourses as well as socio-cultural practices, he argues that it is necessary to recognize that at times 'the political rests on the forgetting of the unforgettable', and the use of amnesty can be justified because a society has to establish some form of concord and cannot go on eternally hating itself (*MHF*: 501). However, it is important for the philosopher to point out the 'purely utilitarian, therapeutic character' of many amnesties, including those of the French Republic (*MHF*: 501). On this point, he concurs with Derrida's assessment. Ricœur at the same time, urges us to 'listen to the voice of the unforgetting memory' which is 'excluded from the arena of power by the forgetful memory bound to the prosaic refounding of the political' (*MHF*: 501). In this way 'the thin wall separating amnesty from amnesia can be preserved' (*MHF*: 501).

Ricœur resolves the crisis, which results from balancing the two forms of forgetting, that is, forgetting through the effacement of traces against the forgetting kept in reserve, 'within the horizon of a happy memory'(*MHF*: 501). This schema is based on a different conception of the intra and inter-relationship between, memory, forgetting and recognition. Unlike Derrida, Ricœur recognizes the necessity of the theatre and staging of amnesia for political and therapeutic purposes, as long as this is simply a necessary gesture to refound the political rather than an attempt to wipe out the unforgivable. However, like Derrida, he does not consider the forgiveness that emanates through these processes to be pure and authentic.

Ricœur locates memory within the structure of recognition, happiness and event. He argues that memory is connected to recognition, while forgetting is not. Thus, one speaks of a happy memory, but one does not speak of a happy forgetting. Moreover, '[t]he arrival of memory is an event' (*MHF*: 502). In contrast, '[f]orgetting is not an event' but 'something that happens or that someone causes to happen', and it is then that we 'recognize the state of forgetfulness we had been in' (*MHF*: 502). Ricœur, as he had done with promise and forgiveness, wants 'to set aside the idea of symmetry between memory and forgetting' (*MHF*: 502). He is acutely aware that once forgetting is linked to forgiveness 'forgetting has its own dilemmas' (*MHF*: 502). On the one hand, memory, because it has the task to faithfully preserve the past from the ravages of oblivion, is in constant struggle against forgetting. On the other hand, forgiveness requires forgetting, while keeping faith with the exhortation never to forget, especially when concerning unforgivable crimes. These two competing demands, between memory and forgetting, mark the receding horizon of forgiveness that gives forgiveness its sense of incompletion.

As we have seen, for Ricœur at the heart of forgiveness there is the prior recognition of fault, loss, and debt, owned by the actors involved. The questions arise: How does one deal with loss and wrongs which are irreversible and go on forever and often extend 'back to far-distant epochs?' (*MHF*: 502). Can such loss or wrongs be measured? In these cases can the debt ever be repaid, forgotten or forgiven? What is the role of forgetting, memory, mourning and forgiveness in these implacable situations?

Ricœur identifies three figures of loss: 'the inextricable, the irreconcilable [and] the irreparable' (*MHF*: 503). He goes on to clarify that '[t]he admission that loss is forever would be the maxim of wisdom worthy of being held to be the *incognito* of forgiveness in the tragedy of action' (*MHF*: 503). Recognizing that human action and its tragic dimensions are part of the human condition leaves room for repentance, consolation and forgiveness. In order to solve the impasse of irreparable loss, Ricœur aims for '[a] subtle work of unbinding and binding' which now is 'to be pursued at the very heart of debt' (*MHF*: 503). This subtle work involves, 'on one hand, being released from the fault, on the other, binding a debtor who is forever insolvent' (*MHF*: 503). Ricœur introduces a radical notion of '[d]ebt without fault. Debt stripped bare. Where one finds the debt to the dead and history as sepulcher' (*MHF*: 503). In other words, both binding and unbinding an agent from his/her act recognise that forgiveness does not efface the debt but only the fault. The debt to history and the dead remain in the form of sepulchre as the work of 'forgetting in reserve'. The question arises, if forgiveness is possible within a more symmetrical relationship between memory and forgetting. For Derrida, forgiveness within Ricœur's schema, because it is connected to the subjectivist modalities of memory and forgetting, would be implicated in doing violence to the other as it would eliminate its irreducibility.

For Ricœur, the asymmetry between forgetting and memory in relation to forgiveness lies in the 'irreducible equivocalness' between the two poles of forgetting: 'forgetting through effacement and forgetting kept in reserve', rather than the irreducibility of the other (*MHF*: 503). It is in the space of this irreducible equivocalness that 'the most secret mark of forgiveness can come to be registered' (*MHF*: 503). In order to give us a better understanding of the complex relationship between memory and forgetting in relation to forgiveness, Ricœur embarks on an investigation of the possibility of what he calls *ars oblivionis* (art of oblivion) that would be comparable with the *ars memoriae* (the art of remembering and commemoration). He draws on various traditions and schools of thought to come up with three ways the *ars memoriae* could be exercised by various actors, institutions and societies in relation to the strategies of forgetting and remembering. Firstly, he rejects any forgetting which is based on effacement and the 'ruinous competition between the strategies of memory and forgetting' (*MHF*: 504). What he proposes instead, is 'the possibility of a work of forgetting, interweaving among all the fibers that connect us to time: memory of the past, expectation of the future, and attention to the present' (*MHF*: 504). Unlike Derrida's work on forgiveness which relies on a prophetic tradition where everything is future, Ricœur injects all the modalities of time within forgetting. In this way he preserves the past, present, and future, without privileging the other and the 'to come'. Secondly, Ricœur raises the possibility of a kind of forgetting which 'outsmarting its own vigilance, as it were, forget itself' (*MHF*: 504). As a result of forgetting itself, forgetting can commemorate its own forgetting. As paradoxical as this may sound, it has relevance to the need of the theatre of forgetting that preserves what one cannot forget. This is necessary so one is not paralysed into inaction or falls victim to what Ricœur has called the phantasm of total memory and recall. Thirdly, Ricœur proposes a different type of forgetting which follows

> the path of a forgetting that would no longer be a strategy, nor a work, an idle forgetting. It would parallel memory, not as the remembrance of what has occurred, nor the memorization of know-how, not even as the commemoration of the founding events of our identity, but as a concerned disposition established in duration. If memory is in fact a capacity, the power of remembering (*faire-mémoire*), it is more fundamentally a figure of care, that basic anthropological structure of our historical condition (*MHF*: 504–505).

Instituting care at the centre of memory gives the modalities of forgetting and remembering an anthropological rather than prophetic or messianic dimension. Care mediates between all modalities of forgetting, remembering and forgiveness, as well as time. Ricœur goes on to explain that '[i]n memory-as-care we hold ourselves open to the past, we remain concerned about it' (*MHF*: 505). Forgetting the past is not an option nor is an interminable remembering. For Ricœur the '*ars oblivionis*' is part of the vigilance of memory within time itself, and '[i]t can only arrange itself under the optatives mood of happy memory. It would simply add a gracious note to the work of memory and the work of mourning. For it would not be work at all' (*MHF*: 505). His notion of carefree memory marks the 'horizon of concerned memory, the soul common to memory that forgets and does not forget' (*MHF*: 505). By making the soul the common ground of memory and forgetting, Ricœur toys with the theological and philosophical ideas of immortality. Memory, both as part of our mortality and immortality, watches over the forgetting and non-forgetting. The interminable play between forgetting and memory is mediated by care which partakes both in the capacity to forget and not forget. Forgiveness marks the space of both forgetting and memory mediated by love. By introducing the notion of love, Ricœur places the problematic of forgiveness within Platonic and Christian discourses rather than the injunctive, messianic discourse of the other in Derrida. Ricœur declares that '[u]nder the sign of this ultimate *incognito* of forgiveness, an echo can be heard of the word of wisdom uttered in the Song of Songs: "Love is as strong as death."' (*MHF*: 506). He affirms that love is stronger than death and concludes that 'the reserve of forgetting … is as strong as the forgetting through effacement' (*MHF*: 506). However, by elevating forgiveness to the heights of love he makes the strength of forgetting kept in reserve as the ultimate safeguard against the treachery of forgetting through effacement and through acts that do violence to the other. Forgiveness as unbinding is effected through love, which is embedded in recognition, intersubjectivity and reflexivity.

Derrida's concept of death, unlike Ricœur's, comes from the other, is anterior to any constitution of the subject and marks its emergence. For Derrida, love is narcissistic and his Narcissus is a blind Narcissus and thus devoid of reflexivity (see *MB* and *PO*: 199). In other words, the self-reflection and recognition of the myth of Narcissus are never instituted within Derridean forgiveness based on the concept of the utterly other. In Derrida the ruse of Narcissus never comes to an end, and the other resists all reflexivity and processes of interiorization. For Ricœur, forgiveness is embedded in the complex modalities of forgetting and memory. Love comes to mediate between the three and effect a notion of forgiveness which is theological, but also within the structure of reflexivity, reciprocity, recognition, agency, selfhood and horizontality. Ricœur locates forgiveness and love within inter-subjective relations. However, Derrida, by eliminating intersubjectivity and reflexivity, leaves a notion of a solipsistic narcissism that admits no self-understanding or relation of the self as other. Ricœur's notion of imputability within Derrida's schema is inadmissible. The subject and the self are aligned with doing violence to the other.

7.5 Concluding Remarks

Derrida, in this later phase of his work, applies his philosophy of alterity to concrete situations of violence to the other. The application of deconstruction to ethico-political concerns is based on the notion of the utterly other which is charged with instituting a new thinking that eliminates violence to the other. Because the construction of the other is inscribed within a messianic and futural structure, and outside any categories associated with subjectivity, Derrida's philosophy of alterity ignores all processes, institutions and systems associated with the construction of otherness involving human actors. Moreover, Derrida's dis-embodied and de-subjectivised other side-steps the issues associated with intersubjectivity, self and other. His shift towards an ethic of unconditional hospitality and forgiveness goes a long way in re-defining the parameters of his thinking with regard to a non-violent relation to the other. However, his persistence in eliminating the subject and the self leaves no space for modes of thinking and acting which involve engaged, situated and embodied human actors, who are grappling with the vagaries and tragedies of human life, and operate within frameworks of reflexivity, recognition and horizontality.

In contrast to Derrida's other directed and messianic thinking steeped in immanence, Ricœur has instituted a thinking that takes into account the long tradition of the deconstruction of the subject, but does not jettison the subject. Ricœur deals with the questions of forgiveness, self, other, intersubjectivity, memory, recognition, and reflexivity, within a model that allows for horizontality, reciprocity, agency, self as other, and inter-subjective modes of engagement within concrete situations. By emphasizing the contingent lives of human actors, and by recognizing the role played by love and care, Ricœur re-inscribes the question of subjectivity within a radical mode of thinking that retains the positive links to the Western tradition, including the hermeneutic and phenomenological philosophical traditions.

In the next chapter, I will turn to Derrida's great work *The Animal That Therefore I Am* in order to map out the final trajectory of Derrida's thought on violence to the other where the other is constructed as ahuman inscribed in the abyssal gaze of the animal as the utterly other.

8. Violence to the Other: Limitrophy, Animot, Divanimality, the Abyssal Limit, and the Ends of Man

Derrida's messianic turn and his insistence on a non-originary concept of the other which is beyond any subjectivist categories of Western metaphysics, leads him to a philosophy which aims to dislodge and go beyond the oppositions human/animal, life/death. This radical turn is encapsulated in four texts published in English under the title *The Animal That Therefore I Am*. The title itself is a rewriting of Descartes' famous formulation of subjectivity, 'I think, therefore I am', and signals a complete break with all forms of thought based on Cartesian philosophies of subjectivity. In this chapter, I will deal extensively with these very complex and multilayered texts, because I consider them to mark the last phase of Derrida's work on the 'violence to the other' in relation to the animal as absolute other.

At this point it is important to give some background to the four texts. In 1997 a ten day conference was held in Cerisy on Derrida's work titled 'The Autobiographical Animal' – a title which Derrida chose himself. During this conference Derrida delivered a ten hour seminar titled *The Animal That Therefore I Am*. Only the introduction to this seminar, comprising the first two texts, was published in the conference proceedings with the title *The Animal that Therefore I Am (to be continued)*. In 2003 Derrida makes good his promise, 'to be continued', when the third text, near the end of this seminar, titled *And Say the Animal Responded*?, is included in the special issue of *Les Cahiers de L'Herne*, dedicated to him and published in 2004. The fourth text, on the question of the animal in Heidegger, titled "*I don't know why we are doing this*", is a transcription of the last oral lecture Derrida gave as a response to the issues raised and discussed. The text retains a great deal of its informality, as it was an outline rather than a completed and written out text. Taken together these four texts represent the centrality of the problematic of 'The Animal' as other in Derrida's work.

Much has been written about these texts regarding their radicality as well as their difficulty, the reference to an animal holocaust, and Derrida's famous or infamous description of the cat (see Berger and Segarra, 2011). The main charge against these texts has been summed up by Gongton's critique that 'the text does not, and indeed *cannot*, tell us unequivocally how to proceed, how animals *ought* to be conceptualized, treated, or thought in relation to humans' (Gongton, 2009: 191). What Gongton and most critics fail to take into account is that Derrida's discourse on 'The Animal' seeks to institute a new, radical thinking based on the wholly other, which is beyond the prevailing ontological and deontological paradigms and established discourses based on prescriptive notions of ethics and socio-political praxis.

Derrida in these four texts reveals the various modalities of violence to the animal as other, and gestures towards a radical post-subjectivist and post-humanist notion of the other as ahuman. He re-inscribes the other within more injunctive ethics and messianic discourses, and aims to deconstruct and go beyond all forms of thought based on the grand duality of Western metaphysics, man/animal. Derrida's project is to institute a new radical philosophy based on the wholly other, which eliminates 'violence to other' and breaks away from all forms of subjectivist thought and praxis.

Derrida's underlying strategy is to posit the question of the animal not in relation to Man from the perspective of Man, but the question of Man from the perspective of 'The Animal', and thus dethrone the superiority and mastery of man over the animal. This entails a radical rethinking and overturning of the entire edifice that underpins the construction of what is proper to Man and the position of 'The Animal' as the other. By positing the question of Man from the point of view of the animal, Derrida arrives at a radical re-articulation of the relationship between human and animal, life and the world. In order to signal a radical departure from any form of thinking that does violence to the other, he introduces in these texts a number of new concepts such as *limitrophy*, *animot*, *animort*, *divanimality*, *zooto*biographical, zooauto-bio-biblio-graphy, zoosphere, *auto-motricity*, *and divanimality*, and re-introduces the notions of *oto*biography, hospitality, the gaze, the trace and *différance*, among others. These concepts connect to his earlier problematics but also point to a more futural, transgressal and abyssal structure of a philosophy of limitrophy.

Derrida's first step is to radicalise the idea of the limit. Hence, he is not simply interested in questioning the limit between Man and Animal by looking for discontinuities in the line that constitutes the division, but seeks to change the ways we think about the limit. His new concept of *limitrophy* aims to introduce a different logic and experience of the limit which is 'properly *transgressal*' and has an abyssal structure (*TAT*: 29). He declares that *Limitrophy* is his subject, not only in relation to 'what sprouts or grows at the limit, around the limit, by maintaining the limit', but also in relation to 'what *feeds the limit*, generates it, raises it, and complicates it' (*TAT*: 29). His interest is not in effacing the limit 'but in multiplying its figures, in complicating, thickening, delinearizing, folding, and dividing the line precisely by making it increase and multiply' (*TAT*: 29). The dividing line between man and animal cannot be instituted within this abyssal structure which escapes any attempts to fix its infinite transgressal effects.

The idea of the abyssal limit and Derrida's questioning of the very limits that mark the division between life and death, will inform all his texts. Derrida's new concept of *Limitrophy* announces his formulation of a plural concept of limit regarding the living that goes beyond our conception of the human and the duality of human/animal. He argues that beyond the human there is not just the opposition of 'The Animal' or 'Animal Life' but a 'heterogeneous multiplicity of the living' and 'a multiplicity of organizations of relations between living and dead' (*TAT*: 31). By relativising the division between the living and the dead, he dissolves their limits. Furthermore, this new conception of the living and dead consists of

> relations of organization or lack of organization among realms that are more and more difficult to dissociate by means of the figures of the organic and inorganic, of life and/or death. These relations are at once intertwined and abyssal, and they can never be totally objectified (*TAT*: 31).

The relations between different spheres of life are marked by heterogeneous multiplicity, and their relations are inscribed within the abyssal structure of the limit. As such they resist objectification and allow for unending inter-relations between different realms. Derrida's approach is to deconstruct the discourses and practices relating to 'The Animal', which try to limit and objectify these relations, and demonstrate their ultimate failure.

Derrida's second step is to embark on the immense task of deconstructing the opposition man/animal within different spheres by deconstructing the anthropomorphic, anthropocentric and anthropo-theomorphic constructions of 'The Animal', which he links to the question of the wholly other. He begins his various deconstructions of the duality man/animal by demonstrating the centrality of the question of the animal in philosophical, religious, theological, scientific, political, ethical, cultural, mythical, literary and other discourses. He identifies in them a common thread: that of defining what is proper to Man in opposition to 'The Animal'. In the process of defining what is proper to Man, they assign or deny 'The Animal' certain faculties, capacities and attributes. By constructing the animal world in the singular as 'The Animal', and by denying it what they attribute to humans, they exclude it from what is proper to Man and define the limits between Man and 'The Animal'. This exclusion underpins the violence to the animal as wholly other, and derives from a philosophical thinking where the subject-Man hold sway over the animal.

The subjugation of 'The Animal' enabled Man to wage a relentless and pitiless war against the animal species and the living in general, especially in the last two hundred years. This ongoing war has been disavowed and dissimulated by man, and represents for Derrida an entrenched expression of the violence to the other. Thus, Derrida's target in these diverse discourses is Man and the entire edifice of a thinking based on the primacy of Man, which places 'The Animal' under his control and in the service of his well-being.

Derrida sets in motion the deconstruction of the foundations of the various discourses on 'The Animal', in order to announce a radical re-inscription of the question of 'The Animal' in relation to the question of Man within his philosophy of alterity. He declares that the question of the animal as the wholly other and its relation to Man, has been fundamental to his thinking and its presence marks his entire philosophical oeuvre. His aim in these four texts is to show that in every discourse in relation to the animal, especially with Western metaphysics, there is a recurrence of the same dominant schema which defines Man's superiority over the animal as being proper to man. However, Derrida points out, within the structure of what is proper to man, there is an originary fault, a default, that undoes this propriety of man and makes possible 'his very becoming-subject, his historicity, his emergence out of nature, his sociality, his access to knowledge and technics' (*TAT*: 45). This originary default is prior to man's emergence as subject and dissolves the division between man and animal.

Derrida goes on to demonstrate how this default, of what is proper to man as opposed to the animal, becomes the deconstructive lever of all forms of anthropocentric thought and ethics within numerous discourses, including, among others, the philosophical discourses of Plato, Aristotle, Descartes, Kant, Levinas, Lacan and Heidegger. Derrida's aim is to continuously expose this default in a number of important philosophical and other texts by deconstructing their dualities, such as speech/truth, reaction/response, lie/pretence and so forth, upon which they base their construction of what is proper to Man. He does this by pointing out the moments of negation and disavowal of the animal in them. Furthermore, while these texts deny the animal what they attribute to Man, they do not finally succeed in eliminating the 'animality' of their texts. The animal comes to unsettle and undo the texts and expose their underlying subjectivism, even in thinkers who claim to have overcome and go beyond it.

I will now turn to the first text, where the question of 'The Animal' in relation to Man is posited in terms of the gaze of the other in order to unseat notion Man from its privileged position. The question of subjectivity, self, and other, will again be central to Derrida's project of his radical thinking regarding 'violence to the other'.

8.1 Under the Gaze of the Other

In the first text titled, *The Animal That Therefore I Am (more to follow)*, Derrida begins the decentring of man within different domains, including Cartesian philosophy, by raising the philosophical question of 'The Animal' as the utterly other, and subjecting Man to its gaze. Throughout this work Derrida analyses the discursive modalities of 'The Animal', 'therefore', 'to follow', and 'I am', from the perspective of the animal. He explores the interrelations between these four modalities in order to expose the violations to the other and to re-articulate the 'I', 'The Animal', and 'to follow' within a new kind of thinking. He aims to arrive at a notion of the other which is post-human, but also post-animal, and goes beyond the divisions man/animal, life/death.

Derrida begins his discussion of the violence to the other by analysing the construction of the duality Man/animal. He implicates entire systems of thought and practices in the construction of Man in opposition to 'The Animal', and critiques the fundamental principles upon which the edifice of what is proper to Man is based. He argues that the entire spectrum of philosophy based on Western metaphysics, but also mythical, literary, religious, ethical, scientific, economic, political, socio-cultural and other discourses have developed an extensive list of what is proper to Man. This list is almost interminable and includes, among other things, nudity, shame, gaze, seeing, *logos*, speech, reason, language, sociality, consciousness, evil, history, time, laughter, dissimulation, clothing, writing, autobiography, death, the subconscious, and suffering. Within these discourses Man was given certain capacities, including the capacity to make promises, respond, lie, pretend, say I am etc. In contrast, 'The Animal' is deprived of the capacity to respond, lie and make promises. It lacks language, writing, consciousness and many of the other attributes which are the exclusive provenance of Man. When these qualities are given to the animal through fabulization, the animal is simply made human from the point of view of Man, thus eliminating its irreducible alterity.

Derrida demonstrates how various philosophical discourses and thinkers partake in the construction of the list of what is proper to Man as opposed to 'The Animal'. By identifying some of the central questions philosophers raise in relation to the animal, such as if the animal can respond and see the way humans do, they exclude the animal from an entire field of philosophical knowledge and ethics. Derrida takes nudity and its connection to shame as a primary example of the exclusion of the animal from the moral codes, self-knowledge and self-reflection that define man. The animal is taken, by philosophical and religious discourses, to be naturally nude, and as such has no need to dress itself. The question arises, if the animal can be given the attributes of nudity and shame and thus become constitutive of the spheres of morality, self-reflection and self-knowledge. Through an examination of the notion of nudity, Derrida demonstrates that although philosophers and thinkers raise different questions and use different definitions, these are fundamentally underpinned by the idea of lack in relation to the animal. This is illustrated by analysing the discourses of major thinkers and philosophers. For example, in relation to Being, Heidegger questions 'if the animal *has time*', if it shares the finitude of man as death, and if the animal has world (*TAT*: 22). Lacan questions the role of the animal as the other in relation to speech, consciousness and the construction of the subject. In relation to definitions, Aristotle defines the animal as *alogon*, that is, lacking *logos*, while Levinas defines the animal as a non-human and lacking the human face and gaze. Bentham diverges from this tradition and raises the question of animal suffering. Bentham's questioning of suffering being only the attribute of Man goes to the heart of Man's relation to the animal as other, which Derrida unremittingly deconstructs.

Defining 'The Animal' in terms of lack of attributes, capacities and faculties in relation to Man marks the limit between man and animal, and places the animal in a position of inferiority. This has led to man's infinite superiority over the animal life which, Derrida argues, 'has its property the fact of being at one and the same time *unconditional* and sacrificial' (*TAT*: 20). The consequences of the unconditional and sacrificial superiority of man are multiple and detrimental to animal life. It justifies putting the animal under the control of man and subjugating it. In many religious traditions, it provides even theological justifications for making animals sacrificial offerings. It permits and rationalizes the violent treatment of animals through unfettered commercialization and industrialization processes. It leads to the indiscriminate slaughter, exploitation and extermination of animal species, and allows scientific and other types of invasions into animal life by humans on a global scale.

However, in spite of the immeasurable violence of man against the animal, man continues with his disavowal of these practices. Consequently, for the past two hundred years, the forms of violence committed by man against the animal life have intensified and accelerated to an unprecedented level. Derrida is emphatic that

> [n]o one can deny seriously any more, or for very long, that men do all they can in order to dissimulate this cruelty or to hide it from themselves; in order to organize on a global scale the forgetting or misunderstanding of this violence, which some would compare to the worst cases of genocide (there are also animal genocides: the number of species endangered because of man takes one's breath away) (*TAT*: 25-26).

Derrida shifts the centre of gravity from the human to the animal and attributes to man the genocide of animals as the ultimate form of dissimulated and disavowed forms of violence to the other.

Derrida's analyses of the situation regarding the violence committed by man against the animal are striking and poignant. He regards the treatment of animals as pathological, pathetic and unbearably cruel. Using the Greek word 'pathos' and referring to its connections to passion and shared suffering among the living, an appeal is made to our sense of compassion and responsibility to the other. Here the other is the nonhuman whose suffering is exposed though the circulation of animal images. Derrida writes in relation to the countless images that portray the suffering of animals:

> If these images are 'pathetic,' if they evoke sympathy, it is also because they 'pathetically' open the immense question of pathos and the pathological, precisely, that is, of suffering, pity, and compassion (*TAT*: 26).

The place given to the interpretation of this compassion relates to 'the sharing of this suffering among the living, to the law, ethics, and politics that must be brought to bear upon this experience of compassion' (*TAT*: 26). What Derrida aims in his oeuvre is to call us to our responsibilities and obligations towards 'the living in general', and to the 'fundamental compassion' which, if taken earnestly, 'would have to change even the very cornerstone … of the philosophical problematic of the animal' (*TAT*: 27). Derrida's task is to effect this change.

Derrida, by connecting the question of the animal to the pre-ontological concept of the other, seeks to expose and dismantle the philosophical foundations that deny and rationalize the violence to 'The Animal'. To this end, he continues to unveil the violence to the other by positing the question of the animal in terms of the ontological categories 'I', 'I am', 'who', and 'what', and by defining the discursive modalities of 'to follow' and 'therefore'. He begins with an exploration of the possible meanings of the phrase on the title of his work, where an offering is made of 'more to follow' (*TAT*: 3). He gives the phrase 'to follow' a number of meanings, both from the perspective of the animal and human, such as 'It follows, itself; it follows itself. It could say "I am," "I follow," "I follow myself," "I am (in following) myself" (*TAT*: 3). He proceeds to articulate the implications of each one of these for the meaning 'to follow'.

To begin with by making both Man and animal interchangeable, Derrida eliminates any order of succession and dissolves the ontological limits that define man and animal. He clarifies that the process of answering these ontological questions from the perspective of the animal means

> [p]assing across borders or the ends of man I come or surrender to the animal, to the animal in itself, to the animal in me and the animal at unease with itself, to the man about whom Nietzsche said … something to the effect that it was an as yet undetermined animal, an animal lacking in itself (*TAT*: 3).

Derrida announces the end of Man as the privileged locus of the question of Man. By making man and animal undetermined and inscribed by lack, he radicalizes both the question of the animal and man. In addition, by making man surrender to the animal, he makes alterity the defining factor of man's constitution in all domains, including the philosophical questions of what and who is man. The task now is to dismantle the philosophical question of Man in relation to the animal within Western thought. In this endeavour, Derrida's philosophical affinities lie with Nietzsche rather than Heidegger. Derrida, following Nietzsche and going against the philosophies which attribute only to man the capacity to make promises, gives both man and animal the ability to make promises and surrenders man to the promise and gaze of the animal. By overturning the order of hierarchy and by breaking the limits that define the relations between man and animal, his answers regarding the meaning 'to follow' are formulated in a prophetic discourse. He writes, 'since all of time and for what remains of it to come we would therefore be in passage toward surrendering to the promise of that animal at unease with itself' (*TAT*: 3). Man surrenders to the animal as other.

The fundamental questions of Western metaphysics 'what?', 'who?' and 'whom?' are posited and answered by Derrida in terms of the gaze of the utterly other. He subjects Man to the piercing and injunctive gaze of the animal as the wholly other, and in the process he overturns the ways one arrives at knowledge and self-knowledge. He argues that '[s]ince time, therefore. Since so long ago, can we say that the animal has been looking at us?' (*TAT*: 3). The answer, as to what animal and who this animal is, is given emphatically by Derrida: 'What animal? The other' (*TAT*: 3). Under the gaze of the other there is no possibility for the subject to even posit the epistemological questions of 'what' or 'what am I?'. The question of the subject cannot be posited in terms of the ontological question 'who?', 'who am I?', or in the accusative case of

'Whom?', without submitting to the gaze of the other. The possibility of positing the subject in relation of the subject's other, or the subject as other, is eliminated. All forms of subjectivity and otherness are determined or are, at best, effects of the other. If there are any doubts about the elimination of the subject in Derridean deconstruction his assertion 'Who am I therefore? Who is it that I am (following)? Whom should this be asked of if not of the other?' puts those at rest (*TAT*: 5–6).

The ontological questions of 'Who I am' and 'Who I am following', are raised and answered through the face to face encounter with the other and under the gaze of the animal as utterly other. The gaze of the other is defined as '[t]he gaze of a seer, a visionary or extra-lucid blind one' (*TAT*: 4). This formulation of the gaze echoes Derrida's preoccupation with the notion of the gaze and sight in relation to the other in many of his earlier works, especially in the *Memoirs of the Blind: The Self-Portrait and Other Ruins* and *Memoirs for Paul de Man*. The concept of the gaze in this work, as a kind of blindness, links to the notion outlined in his conversation on photography with Gerard Richter, published in English as *Copy, Archive, Signature: A Conversation on Photography*, where Derrida takes up again the question of the other, the gaze and seeing in relation to photography. As in this previous work on blindness and the gift, he argues that

> I give myself to the other precisely there where I cannot give myself to myself, cannot see myself seeing, in a way. Nor can I see myself or know myself as giving. I can see myself as seen, but cannot see myself seeing (*CAS*: 32).

The other marks the absence of identity as self-relation and being as presence. Self-presence cannot be instituted within the concept of gift and giving. Blindness is at the centre of the self in its relation to itself, self-knowledge and reflexivity. Derrida defines this experience as an 'experience of the gift, of what cannot return to me' (*CAS*: 32). Gift as no-return to a defined being repeats his elimination of the subject and any related ontological categories.

Derrida, in the last phase of his work, continues with a more radical formulation of the gaze of the utterly other in relation to the animal, which becomes central to his deconstruction of subjectivism and subjectivist ethics of Western metaphysics and other thought systems. He uses nudity as the starting point in order to institute a different ethics that is ahuman, post-human and post-animal. He subjects the naked Man to the gaze of the animal in order to examine the ethical relations between them, and institute an ethics of responsibility that would derive from the other. Being naked in front of the other (the animal), which Derrida takes to be a basic premise of ethics and morality, engenders in Man the feeling of shame. However, there is a paradox in this schema. Man attributes to the animal a natural nakedness and thus no shame, yet the shame Man feels derives from the animal. Although Derrida makes nudity and shame proper to man, he relativises them both in terms of the gaze of the animal as a wholly other. When man is naked and face-to-face with the other (in this case the cat) looking to see in the direction of his sex, Derrida asserts that '[*t*]*o see*, without going to see, without touching yet, and without biting, although that threat remains on its lips or on the tip of the tongue'(*TAT*: 4). However, within this scene

> [s]omething happens … that shouldn't take place – like everything that happens in the end, a lapsus, a fall, a failing, a fault, a symptom (and 'symptom,' as you know, also means 'fall': case, unfortunate event, coincidence, what falls due [*échéance*], mishap). It is as if, at that instant, I had said or were going to say the forbidden, something that shouldn't be said. As if I were to avow what cannot be avowed in a symptom and, as one says, wanted to bite my tongue (*TAT*: 4).

Derrida re-inscribes the ideas of the gaze in relation to the animal as seeing without seeing, symptom as fall and lack. Man standing naked and face to face with the animal as the wholly other, marks the non-space where shame, prohibition, nudity, self-knowledge and vision are articulated. He aims to answer the questions, why one is overcome by shame for being naked in front of the animal and why one is ashamed of being ashamed, from the point of view of the animal. He writes, '[a]shamed of what and before whom? Ashamed of being as naked as a beast' (*TAT*: 4). Since the animal has been considered as being naturally naked, and as such has no need to dress itself, it has been given no sense of shame. By subjecting the naked man to the gaze of the naked animal, entails the becoming animal of man. Man by being ashamed of his nakedness, when face to face with the animal, means that man is given his sense of shame, and consequently ethics, by the animal. Thus any ontological questions regarding man and the origins of ethics have to be re-thought from the point of view of the animal's gaze as the wholly other which plays at and exceeds the limits that define both the human and the animal.

The treatment of nakedness and shame in relation to the animal as the wholly other will also become the starting point to radicalize further the notion of consciousness, reflexivity, self-knowledge and evil. Derrida argues that in many philosophical texts there is an underlying assumption, but never mentioned, that 'the property unique to animals, what in the last instance distinguishes them from man, is their being naked without knowing it' (*TAT*: 4–5). This implies that animals are 'without consciousness of good and evil', and that they 'wouldn't be naked because they are naked' in their natural state (*TAT*: 5). This position has led to the situation that '[i]n principle, with the exception of man, no animal has ever thought to dress itself' (*TAT*: 5). Consequently, clothing and shame are considered as being 'proper to man, one of the "properties" of man', with shame deriving from a notion of fall (*TAT*: 5). The notion of fall and its connections to shame will become fundamental in Derrida's deconstruction of an ethics of animal sacrifice and violence to the other.

Derrida overturns the questions of being with, consciousness, ethics and knowledge as being proper to man. In order to radicalize the idea of being, he raises the question whether the animal is deprived of being able to see the nakedness of man, and how the notion 'to follow' relates to it. He posits the question of the subject in terms of 'who I am following', and places the 'I' under the gaze of the animal as absolute alterity in order to deconstruct a number of dualities such as before/after, front/back, human/animal. Furthermore, he aims to critique the Heideggerian 'with' and Heidegger's notion of being as gathering rather than dissociation. Consequently, he re-inscribes the notions of next to and with from the perspective of the animal, and makes the subject/Man both subject and object of the other's gaze. He argues

> The animal is there before me, there next to me, there in front of me – I who am (following) after it. And also, therefore, since it is before me, it is behind me. It surrounds me. And from the vantage of this being-there-before-me it can allow itself to be looked at, no doubt, but also – something that philosophy perhaps forgets, perhaps being this calculated forgetting itself – it can look at me. It has its point of view regarding me. The point of view of the absolute other, and nothing will have ever given me more food for thinking through this absolute alterity of the neighbor or of the next(-door) than these moments when I see myself seen naked under the gaze of a cat (*TAT*: 11).

The animal represents the point of view of the absolute other as neighbour whose absolute alterity means that it remains outside any modality of appropriation, mastery, and being with. Inscribing the animal with absolute alterity and point of view, frees the other from any relation to man that seeks to escape the gaze of the other. The animal as the wholly other inescapably surrounds the subject, and subjects it to its bottomless gaze. The bottomless gaze demonstrates 'the naked truth of every gaze, when that truth *allows me to see and be seen* through the eyes of the other, in the *seeing* and not just *seen* eyes of the other?' (*TAT*: 12). Derrida goes on to clarify his notion of seeing as being 'those seeing eyes, those eyes of a seer whose color must at the same time be *seen and forgotten*' (*TAT*: 12). Here Derrida aligns himself with Levinas' construction of the other, but deviates from him because the other bears no relation to a human face. The animal is part of the structure of the wholly other, and as such it is independent of subjectivity based on human consciousness. The other sees without seeing. In this way the injunctive power of the gaze becomes part of the all-seeing, abstract other that bears no relation to a concrete subject.

Derrida continues exposing the violations to the other in relation to the animal within philosophical discourses, by critiquing and overturning philosophy's construction of *logos*. He begins by examining the ways philosophy has treated the question of response in relation to the animal in order to radicalize the notion of *logos*, speech and language. He argues that philosophers from Descartes to Lacan, although they have given the animal 'some aptitude for signs and for communication', they 'have always denied it the power to *respond* – to *pretend*, to *lie*, to *cover its tracks* or *erase* its own traces' (*TAT*: 33). This means that the animal is excluded from the field of purposeful and intentional speech which is the privilege of man. Derrida raises the question of speech and language by putting Man in the place of the animal and argues

> [b]ut whether it is fictive or not, when I ask, 'The animal that I am, does it speak?' the question seems at that moment to be signed, to be sealed by someone. What does it seal? What claim does it make? Pretence or not, what does it seem to translate? What this animal is, what it will have been, what it would, would like to, or could be is perhaps what I am (following) (*TAT*: 33).

In other words, the discourse on the animal's ability to respond is predetermined by the limit that marks the division between man and animal.

This limit is based on the idea that the animal cannot respond in terms of speech and by using linguistic signs. Thus, it leaves no traces or its traces can be effaced. Derrida, by placing himself in the place of the animal and questioning whether he possesses the attribute of speech and language, makes speech and language part of the animal. He questions the idea of lack of response upon which the limit between man and animal is based, and argues that one 'cannot treat the supposed animality of the animal without treating the question of the response, and of what *responding* means. And what *being erased* means' (*TAT*: 33).

Derrida posits the problematic of response anew. He raises the questions, if the animal can respond, and if so to whom does it respond and how. He re-introduces the concept of trace in order to question the indivisible limit between man and animal, and to signal his deconstructive gesture towards all concepts connected to Man, including the capacity of response. By making the trace constitutive of the animal, he makes the animal's traces both erasable and inerasable. Derrida argues '[t]he fact that a trace can always be erased, and forever, in no way means – and this is a critical difference – that someone, man *or* animal, I am emphasizing here, *can of his own accord* erase his traces' (*TAT*: 33). Both animal and man come under the ineffable power of the trace. Human and animal traces are interchangeable and part of the structure of the Deridean trace. This implies that the animal's traces will remain, even when all attempts are made to erase the trace of the animal. The trace is anterior to speech, language and response and, finally, to *logos*.

Derrida continues to expose the violence to the animal as other within philosophy, by pointing out philosophy's linguistic and conceptual construction of the animal and animal life under the singular 'The Animal', and its exclusion from philosophy proper and the ontology of Man. Derrida argues that the use of the singular 'The Animal', homogenizes all animals and represents a linguistic and conceptual violation which denies the plurality, heterogeneity, and multiplicity of animal life. He sees this refusal by philosophy to question the principles upon which the limit that marks the human and the animal is based, as encompassing the entire philosophical tradition of Western metaphysics, and has its roots in the privileging of the human above the animal. He asserts,

> that never, on the part of any great philosopher from Plato to Heidegger, or anyone at all who takes on, *as a philosophical question in and of itself,* the question called

> that of the animal and of the limit between the animal and the human, have I noticed a protestation *based on principle*, and especially not a protestation that amounts to anything, against the general singular that is *the animal* (*TAT*: 40).

Using the singular 'The Animal' marks the limit between the human and the animal as being single and indivisible. This constitutes a 'violation to the other' with numerous and grave consequences. A very fundamental consequence is that it results in the homogenization of all non-human living things 'that man does not recognize as his fellows, his neighbours, or his brothers' (*TAT*: 34).

The brotherhood of Man, as constituted within philosophy and different domains, does not include the animal as neighbour. Consequently, the animal is excluded from the duties of and rights to hospitality. Derrida by making 'The Animal' part of man's fellows, neighbours and brothers, radicalises the Heideggerian being with, Levinas' definition of the neighbour as a human face, and the notion of hospitality. For Derrida the 'being with', hospitality, the face of the other, and brotherhood, includes and extends to 'The Animal'. He notes that '[o]ne cannot speak – moreover, it has never been done – of the *bêtise* or bestiality of an animal' but only of Man (*TAT*: 41). The fundamental question that Derrida asks is, 'why the ultimate fallback of what is proper to man' relates to 'a property that could never in any case be attributed to the animal or to God', but nevertheless 'comes to be named *bêtise* or bestiality' (*TAT*: 41). By questioning the proper and property as being constitutive of man, Derrida unseats Man from his privileged position. Making bestiality a category that is inclusive of man, animal and God, radicalizes the notion of the limit. Consequently, what constitutes the limit that defines the animal and the human and the ontological positing of being, as well as the theological conception of God, has to be rethought. Animality, or bestiality, partakes of human and divine and exceeds both. This is a very radical turn that Derrida takes, because the other is not God as understood within theological discourses. As we shall see, Derrida's concept of *divanimality* signals a more radical conception of the wholly other and aims to dissolve these long held divisions.

Derrida continues his critique of the subjectivism of various philosophical discourses, and aims to re-define philosophy's ontological question 'I am' from the point of view of the animal as absolute alterity. He identifies the positing of the ontological question 'I am' within Western metaphysics, based on the point of view of Man, as 'violence to the other'. In order to expose this violence, he critiques and deconstructs the ipseity within which the 'I am' is constructed, and explores 'what ties the history of the "I am," the autobiographical and autodeictic relation to the self as "I," to the history of "The Animal," of the human concept of the animal' (*TAT*: 34). As in his previous deconstructions, Derrida is relentless in his treatment of the 'I' and the self in all its modalities, ranging from consciousness and memory to life itself. He critiques the privileging of the confessional mode in relation to the 'I' and the self within Western thought, and its connections to the production of the truth of the human subject in opposition to the animal. The autobiographical 'I' and the self come under heavy fire as they are charged with the fatal malady of auto-immunity and auto-affection as auto-infection. The 'I', closed and asphyxiated within itself and within its own self-generating automaticity, admits no alterity. However, alterity is what prevents this auto-infection and enables the movement of the trace of the other to fissure subjectivity as self-presence. Derrida's forceful critique with regards to self and autobiography needs to be quoted at length. He argues

> Autobiography, the writing of the self as living, the trace of the living for itself, being for itself, the auto-affection or auto-infection as memory or archive of the living, would be an immunizing movement (a movement of safety, of salvage and salvation of the safe, the holy, the immune, the indemnified, of virginal and intact nudity), but an immunizing movement that is always threatened with becoming auto-immunizing, like every *autos*, every ipseity, every automatic, automobile, autonomous, auto-referential movement. Nothing risks becoming more poisonous than an autobiography, poisonous for oneself in the first place, auto-infectious for the presumed signatory who is so auto-affected (*TAT*: 47).

The writing of the self as 'I', is based on the conception of life as auto-referential and anthropomorphic. Such a conceptualization of life is inadmissible within Derrida's notion of the other. For Derrida, as argued in his earlier works, autobiography can only be written as death of the solipsistic 'I'. This represents a more radical turn in Derrida's construction of the other, because he abandons any reference to the human confessional 'I' and to the autobiography of the self. As in his earlier work, he replaces the autobiographical with the *oto*biographical, and in order to take account of the animal within a radical continuum that constitutes both life and death, human and animal, he replaces the autobiographical with the *zoo*tobiographical and finally autobiography with zooauto-bio-biblio-graphy (*TAT*: 34). The self is eliminated in its autobiographical and narrative dimensions. Identity, based on a notion of the subject as 'I', is seen as a form of solipsistic auto-affection. Derrida injects the animal and animality within the auto and the biographical, and subjects both to the structure of the trace of the other.

Derrida re-introduces the concept of the trace, to include both the animal and man. By making the animal as absolute other, constitutive of the trace and of all modalities of subjectivity, Derrida conceives of himself as an animal and his texts as animal texts within both life and death. In this way he locates his written texts and thought within what he calls zoosphere and he aims to institute

> the crazy project of constituting everything thought or written within a zoosphere, the dream of an absolute hospitality and an infinite appropriation. How to welcome or liberate so many animal-words [*animots*] *chez moi*? In me, for me, like me? (*TAT*: 37).

He locates his animal texts within a zoosphere, which he calls a 'paradisaical bestiary', and explains that the zoosphere project has been at the forefront of his thinking since his early works. The zoosphere is the space of infinite appropriation and absolute hospitality of all spheres of life as well as of everything written or thought. The absence of Man entails a concept of the other as ahuman, which does not mean simply replacing the human with the animal. In order to avoid replacing anthropocentric and anthropomorphic discourses of and on the animal, Derrida introduces his new concept of the *animot*. This concept denotes a more radical formulation of the other because it combines multiple functions, and aims to go beyond the established models of thinking in relation to Man and animal.

To begin with, Derrida wants to dissociate his thought of the other in relation to the *animot* from any traditional forms of fabulization and mythical narratives of animals that take the form of the human and make them subject to man. He argues that the history of fabulization 'remains an anthropomorphic taming, a moralizing subjection, a domestication' of animals (*TAT*: 37). Furthermore, it is '[a]lways a discourse *of* man, on man, indeed on the animality of man, but for and in man' (*TAT*: 37). Liberating the *animots* (animals) from the anthropomorphic violence to the other, means a philosophical, ethical, political, linguistic and hermeneutic break with all forms of thinking and praxis that are based on the limits that define what it proper to Man, especially the ontology of Western metaphysics.

Discussing the plethora of animal references (*animots*) in his own texts, Derrida locates them within his deconstruction of Western metaphysics and his construction of a thought based on the trace and the utterly other. As in his discussion of religion, where he speaks of the 'machine like return of religion', Derrida evokes '*the animal machine*', but for a different purpose. He explains that the animal machine is like a virus that obsesses and invades all his writings. He defines it as '[n]either animal nor nonanimal, neither organic nor inorganic, neither living nor dead, this potential invader is *like* a computer virus' (*TAT*: 39). Its function is to be 'lodged in a processor of writing, reading, and interpretation' but not limited to them (*TAT*: 39). Furthermore, 'it would be an animal that is capable of deleting (thus of erasing a trace, something Lacan thinks the animal is incapable of) (*TAT*: 39). Derrida goes on to assert that

> [t]his quasi-animal would no longer have to relate itself to being *as such* (something Heidegger thinks the animal is incapable of), since it would take into account the need to strike out 'being.' But as a result, in striking out 'being' and taking itself beyond or on this side of the question (and hence of the response) is it something completely other than a species of animal? (*TAT*: 39).

Derrida departs from the Heideggerian concept of being by striking out being, and not simply writing it under erasure. Being is inscribed by the concept of the quasi-animal, and cannot be thought of in terms of Heidegger's '*as such*'. Within this schema, all ontological concepts and thought would be subject to ongoing processes akin to those of a 'computer virus', which infects all forms of life and non-life as well as all interpretative paradigms, reading and writing. The dichotomy of human/animal is struck out, and the striking out of 'being' takes us to what is other than a species of animal or human. The new concept of *l'animot* inscribes this new, radical turn in Derrida's thought, which is antithetical to all systems of closure and determined forms of life.

Derrida's concept of the *animot* is central to the last phase of his work. It echoes his earlier concept of *différance* and has a number of functions. Firstly, *animot* acts as a graphic and linguistic inscription of alterity that fissures the connections between the plural and the singular, grapheme and phoneme, signified and signifier. Because the word *animot* in French when spoken is identical to the sound of *animal*, for both singular and plural, the deconstruction of the concept's identity and meaning, are effected through the grapheme. This graphic intervention within the linguistic structure of the concept is the silent and ongoing undoing of the signified by the signifier. Derrida explains that his new concept of *l'animot* aims 'to forge another word in the singular' which is 'close but radically foreign, a chimerical word that sounded as though it contravened the laws of the French language' (*TAT*: 41).

Secondly, *l' animot* deconstructs the construction of identity as auto-affection, and severs its connections to self-presence. The hybrid word *animot* becomes a silent substitute 'for what you hear', thus fissuring the primacy of the voice and its connection to identity and self-presence. As a result, the grapheme – *archewriting* – comes to deconstruct the division between the *autos* and the other.

Thirdly, *l'animot* deconstructs the limit between human and animal within philosophy, and announces Derrida's new thinking. Echoing Nietzsche's *Ecce Homo* or the Christian suffering of Christ, Derrida exclaims: *Ecce animot*. His substitution of Homo with the *animot*, signals his affinities with the Nietzschean critique of the subject, but also his own philosophical project based on the new thinking of the infinite opening to the absolute other outside violence and suffering.

Fourthly, *l'animot* proclaims the hybrid and chimerical as being constitutive of the irreducible multiplicity of mortals that gives no primacy to the human. Derrida describes *animot* as being '[n]either a species nor a gender nor an individual', and in this way the concept is outside and beyond these anthropocentric and species bound categories (*TAT*: 41). He defines *animot* as 'an irreducible living multiplicity of mortals', which is not 'a double clone or a portmanteau word', but 'a sort of monstrous hybrid, a chimera waiting to be put to death by its Bellerophon' (*TAT*: 41). The *animot* has no connection to any species, it is genderless and ahuman. Being a monstrous hybrid it cannibalizes the singular, valorises the ephemeral, and admits the irreducible multiplicity of mortals. Mortality and life are subject to the interminable trace of the chimerical and hybrid nature of the *animot*. Derrida explains that '[b]y means of the chimera of this singular word, the *animot*, I bring together three heterogeneous elements within a single verbal body' (*TAT*: 47). Firstly, *animot* allows the 'plural *animals* [to be] heard in the singular' thus fissuring any attempt to institute a singular origin (*TAT*: 47). Secondly, it does away with the idea of 'The Animal', written in the 'general singular, separated from man by a single, indivisible limit' which does violence to the animal as absolute other (*TAT*: 47). Finally, *animot* allows for a vision where the plurality of 'living creatures' 'cannot be assembled within the single figure of an animality that is simply opposed to humanity' (*TAT*: 47).

Drawing upon the mythical, religious, theological, literary and other domains, Derrida continues with exposing the violence to the other, in order to re-define the meaning 'to follow', 'to see', hospitality and ethics. The Greek mythical story of Chimera, and the biblical story of the fratricide of Cain, will become the launching pads for the final countdown against modes of thinking that do violence to the other. Through these stories, Derrida announces the construction of a radical ethics, based on the other, and a new thinking of the living and the world. He begins with the overturning of the question of man and animal, by subjecting both to the hunt as a modality of 'to follow' and 'to see'. He uses the mythical story of Chimera, and its killing by Bellerophon, to reinscribe the notion 'to follow'. Chimera is the mythical hybrid animal which is constituted by multiple animals, and therefore is outside the norm. Bellerophon is the one who follows Chimera in order to kill it. He represents the hunter, the one who persecutes and hunts Chimera down, by pursuing, tracking, taming, and finally succeeding in his aim. Derrida argues that Bellerophon 'would say: I am (following), I pursue, I track, overcome, and tame the animal' (*TAT*: 42). In this sense 'to follow' the animal, as a modality of the hunt, is to eliminate the threat and its hybrid monstrosity. Thus, any animal which defies the single attribution allowed, is hunted down or forced to be only one animal. In the mythical context of Chimera, 'to follow' is inscribed by the modalities of the hunt. This means that at the heart of the relation between man and animal, there is hunting and killing of the animal in order to eliminate its plural origin. However, for Derrida, it is not only the animal that is subject to the modalities of the hunt.

Derrida takes the story of Cain's and Bellerophon's fratricide, Bellerophon killed his brother, before killing Chimera, in order to re-inscribe the hunt as a modality of 'to follow' within the human domain. Derrida aims to analyse the complex inter-relations between the hunter and the hunted, ‘to follow’, the fall, and to see, in order to demonstrate that, depending on the perspective one adopts, both animals and humans can share the same fate. The questions that arise in relation to the hunt as a modality of ‘to follow’ are: Who is following whom? Who is the hunter? Who is the hunted? Who follows? Who is the persecutor and who is the persecuted? What follows? Where do man and the animal fit in, and what are the tangles and webs they traverse in their relation to the notions of the fall, ‘to follow’, and ‘to see’?

Derrida takes the Biblical story of Abel and Cain from the religious domain, to illustrate the connections between the fall of Man and the animal. He demonstrates that the animal is at the core of religion and ethics based on the notion of the fall and ‘to see’. In the biblical story the animal is to be tamed, raised, and sacrificed, because God prefers the sacrifice of the animals raised by Abel, the herdsman, to the agricultural fruits of the earth offered by Cain, the agricultural worker. However, Derrida argues, God prefers the sacrifice of the very animal ‘that he has let Adam name – *in order to see*’ (*TAT*: 42). The freedom accorded to Adam, or Ish, by God to name the animals, ‘was only a stage “*in order to see*,” in view of providing sacrificial flesh for offering to that God’ (*TAT*: 42). The animal, within this religious tradition, becomes connected to ethics, sacrifice and knowledge. However, the naming of animals is a power given by God to Man, and thus the animal forms part of the sacred which is expressed in language. In other words, the animal is constitutive of the ethics of responsibility, and each animal’s sacred linguistic singularity is part of ‘to see’. For Derrida, the failure of Man to address his responsibility to the animal constitutes a fall. In this way he dissociates the fall of Man from theological discourses associated with the original sin.

Derrida identifies a number of complex relationships between the biblical story of fratricide, violence to the other, and fall. He argues that the killing of Abel by his brother Cain is the second original sin, fall or fault. This fault has more serious consequences in relation to violence to the other than the first original fall of disobeying God’s orders that resulted in the expulsion of Man from paradise. Derrida uses the Biblical story of Cain and his admission of killing his brother ‘after failing to sacrifice an animal to God’ to introduce the notion of ‘*excessive* fault’ within the idea of limit (*TAT*: 43). For Cain such fault is ‘unpardonable, not simply wrong but excessively culpable, *too* grave’ (*TAT*: 43). This is expressed in Cain's address to Jehovah, when he declares that his 'fault is too great to bear' (*TAT*: 43). Derrida makes excess a necessary condition and a kind of default when he asserts that 'a wrongdoing [is] always excessive, in its very essence' and 'a form of default in the face of an imperative necessity [*le de'faut devant le "il faut"*]' (*TAT*: 43). For Derrida, any wrongdoing and recognition of the violence to the other belong to excess and exceeding of limits. It is from this economy of excess that the new philosophy of *limitrophy* and the new ethics based on the other derive.

In the Biblical story of Cain the excessive fault becomes connected to evil and the hunt that involves the hunter and the hunted. Cain's excessive fault obliges him to flee and turn into a wonderer. He becomes the hunted down, the expelled, the persecuted, the one who is chased out, the criminal, the shamed, and the one who has to dissimulate himself and hide his nakedness under a veil. Derrida identifies the construction of God as a hunter and this is also expressed in language. He writes, 'Jehovah's language is indeed that of a hunter' (*TAT*: 43). Cain by killing his brother Abel succumbs to temptation and falls into a trap set for him by God. The hunted Cain 'becomes prey to the evil *lurking* in the shadow like an animal' (*TAT*: 44). Man, like a beast, becomes the hunted animal and is turned into a human beast. The ethics based on the idea of excessive fault is at the core of the biblical story of the hunt.

Derrida also uses Cain's story to expound the multiple modalities of 'to see' and the hunt, outside a subjectivist model. Derrida argues that the fratricide of Cain and his persecution, demonstrate the 'paradoxes of this manhunt' which 'follow one after the other as a series of experimental ordeals: "in order to see"' (*TAT*: 44). This formulation of 'to see', unconnected to the subject's self-knowledge and even consciousness, aims to institute an injunctive concept of the other, and dislodge the capacity of man to make promises. Although Cain is a hunted criminal and a fugitive, he comes under the protection of God. The unconditional promise that no one is permitted to kill him, in order to avenge his brother's death, is given by God. The idea of promise, as being a capacity allowed only to man, becomes relativised as God's promise to the hunted and persecuted Cain is inscribed in the injunction that no harm should come to him. Derrida explains that God

> promises this human beast protection and vengeance. *As if* God had repented. *As if* he were ashamed or had admitted having preferred the animal sacrifice. *As if* in this way he were confessing and admitting remorse concerning the animal (*TAT*: 44).

By linking the question of the animal to promise and the absolute other as God, Derrida makes God responsible for the fate of the animal. Nudity, repentance, remorse and shame as the basis of religious ethics, are not only experienced by humans but also by God for wishing for and allowing the animal to become a sacrificial offering to Him. God and animal become relativised and part of the structure of the injunctive construction of the wholly other.

Within this schema, ethics is beyond any ultimate theological point of reference that relies on an anthropomorphic and anthropocentric notion of God. The protection of the other, and revenge upon those that would bring harm to the other, is a sacred duty ordained by God. The notion of unconditional hospitality becomes connected to an injunction against harming the animal/human as absolute other. This means that Derrida radicalizes the notion of unconditional hospitality and protection offered to the persecuted, when he asserts that God promises to take 'revenge seven times on anyone who kills Cain, that is to say, the murderer of his brother, he who, after this second original sin, has covered the nakedness of his face, the face that he lost before Him' (*TAT*: 44). Derrida, through his concept of the wholly other, collapses the distinction between human and animal, God and animal, God and human, and institutes a thinking based on the faceless wholly other and unconditional hospitality to the persecuted.

In the case of the myth concerning Bellerophon and Chimera, the same kinds of injunctions apply with regard to the persecuted and the sacred law of hospitality. Bellerophon's story shows two important cases of the inviolability of the sacred law of hospitality that no guest should be harmed. In the first case, Bellerophon as a guest is not put to death by his host in order to avenge the honour of his wife, whose accusations against him were, nevertheless, false. In the second case, Bellerophon escapes death because his current host, whose guest he is, does not carry out an order from Bellerophon's offended previous host to execute him. The order for Bellerophon's execution is contained in the letter from the first host, which Bellerophon himself delivered to the current host without knowing its contents. In both cases the strict laws of hospitality, which give unconditional asylum to a guest and prohibit anyone from harming him/her, have been applied.

Through his deconstruction of the stories of Cain and Bellerophon, Derrida contends that all ethics are based on the other. Thus, the ideas of shame, fault, fall, nakedness, and ultimately ethics, derive from collapsing the distinction between man and animal and making them subject to the wholly other defined as *l'animot*. Derrida ends the first text with the radical re-positioning of the 'I' in relation to the animal, by linking them both to animality, which he defines as 'the life of the living' (*TAT*: 49). The auto-affection of the solipsistic 'I', is replaced with *auto-motricity*. He defines *auto-motricity* as 'a spontaneity that is capable of movement, of organizing itself and affecting itself, marking, tracing, and affecting itself with traces of its self' (*TAT*: 49). Derridean *auto-motricity* is anterior to self-relation and constitutive of both the living and animality. It is anterior to the 'discursive thematic of an utterance or of an *ego cogito*, more so of a *cogito ergo sum*' (*TAT*: 50). However, 'between this relation to the self (this Self, this ipseity) and the *I* of the "I think," there is, it would seem, an abyss' (*TAT*: 50). Derrida re-introduces the notion of abyss, to re-think the relation of the 'I', 'I think', self, and the limit, between man and animal. His aim is to pluralize and exceed the concept of the limit itself between all these notions. The Cartesian positing of the subject in terms of 'I think', which links it with 'therefore' in order to arrive at the 'I am' within consciousness, is rejected by Derrida. Derrida's positing of the 'I' in terms of *auto-motricity* links it to an abyssal structure. *Auto-motricity* is what characterizes all living life, and is constitutive of the animality of both man and animal.

Derrida closes this complex text by returning to the first question which he posited regarding the animal, that is, to rethink the question of man from the perspective of the animal. As we have seen, he subjected the naked man to the gaze of the animal, and questioned the assumptions that the animal lacks the capacity to respond, and nudity is 'natural' to animals but not to man. In order to answer the question of man being naked under the gaze of the animal, Derrida introduces the concept of the mirror. Using the concept of the mirror, he aims to deal with the problematic of reflexivity, self-narration, self-relation and self-reflection. Derrida's mirror has the image of man and animal (cat) naked reflected in it, and both are looking into their and each other's reflection. By making the animal as the wholly other part of the reflection process and nudity, Derrida makes the animal part of his interminable narcissistic reflection. What breaks this interminable self-relation and self-reflection is the reflection of the animal. The play on nakedness and self-reflection is caught in the mirror of reflection, for both man and animal. Derrida raises the question if there is animal narcissism and if the animal as other constitutes the primary mirror of all reflection. He posits anew the question of the animal and his ideas should be quoted at length. He argues:

> The animal in general, what is it? What does that mean? Who is it? To what does that 'it' correspond? To whom? Who responds to whom? Who responds in and to the common, general, and singular name of what they thus blithely call the 'animal'? Who is it that responds? The reference made by this what or who regarding me in the name of the animal, what is said in the name of the animal when one appeals to the name of the animal, that is what it would be a matter of exposing, in all its nudity, in the nudity or destitution of whoever, opening the page of an autobiography, says 'here I am.'
> 'But as for me, who am I (following)?' (*TAT*: 51).

Derrida inverts the question of the animal and self-reflection. He makes the gaze and eyes of the animal the primary mirror of man. It is through this primary mirror that the question of Man and animal can be raised. The recognition of the self in its ontological and deictic dimensions expressed as 'here I am', is posited through the animal and belongs to it. One appeals to the name of the animal when one attempts to respond to the ontological questions of 'what', 'who' and to 'whom'. The response to the questions of 'who am I' and 'who I am following' can only be achieved through the other.

8.2 *Animot*: the trace and scent of the other

In the second text, titled "*But as for me, who am I (following)*?", Derrida again raises the question of the 'I am' and, more specifically, the autobiographical 'I' in relation to the animal. In this text he introduces his concept *animot* and re re-introduces the notion of the trace as scent, in order to radicalize the notions of the subject, self, 'to follow', animal and world. As in his earlier work, he conceives of the trace as being 'always that of another', but the trace now follows the Heracletian notion of the unity of opposites expressed in his enigmatic pronouncement 'the upward-downward path' (οδός άνω κάτω). Thus, for Derrida, the trace demonstrates that by following 'the consequence or direction of this double arrow (it is a matter of the scent, and the scent one smells is always the trace of another), the animal becomes inevitable, and, before it, the *animot*' (*TAT*: 55). The *animot* is anterior to the question of the animal and the positing of the subject in their particularity and corporeality. Derrida, by introducing the notion of the scent into the trace, moves away from his notion of spectre of his earlier work. Like spectre, the sent denotes a presence which is not a presence. However, the scent, since it partakes of both animal and Man, escapes the dichotomy Man/animal and embodied notions of subjectivity. This conception of man, in relation to the other and the subject, breaks away from Descartes' and Levinas' anthropomorphism, anthropo-theomorphism, anthropocentrism, and constructions of subjectivity.

The complex interplay between trace, *animot* and scent unsettle the certainties of what defines man. Derrida by injecting the concept of the *animot* in Levinas' chiasmus, and within the Cartesian and 'Greco-Judeo-Christiano-Islamic' tradition he represents, aims to inscribe within philosophy and any other discourse the 'trace of another as animal, as *animot*' (*TAT*: 55). In every positing of the 'I' within the Cartesian *cogito ergo sum,* and consequently in every autobiography, Derrida introduces the structure of 'I am dead,' (*TAT*: 56). The self and the 'I' for Derrida are effects of the *animot* as other. Consequently, the positing of the 'I am' entails the death of the 'I', and the questions of self-reflection and ethics, have to be rethought. However, the insistence of defining man in terms of the Cartesian cogito means that, within philosophical discourses and within the discourse of positive sciences of animal behaviour, 'the question of whether an animal can see *me* naked, and especially whether it can see *itself* naked, is never asked' (*TAT*: 59). By problematizing the concept of self-reflection in relation to man, Derrida critiques all discourses based on reflexivity. By endowing the animal with the possibility of self-reflection, self-relation, relation with the other, and self-identification, he deconstructs the absolute limit between man and animal. The ability of the animal to recognise itself as another, endows it with a kind of 'hetero-narcissist "self as other"', and this 'hetero-narcissism is erotic' (*TAT*: 60). This is evident in the animal's courtship rituals, where seduction and exhibition are used to lure the partner into reproduction displays. Moreover, Derrida argues, the animals' displays of 'modesty or shame, in the sense of some sensitivity to nakedness', would mean that these categories 'would no longer be limited to the human and foreign to the *animot*' (*TAT*: 60). The consequences of such a position, in relation to the animal within human life, living animals and the world, are too numerous to deal with in this work.

Derrida considers nakedness, shame, guilt, hiding, dissimulation, simulation, fault, reticence, modesty and death as being fundamental to any development of ethics. By attributing these to the animal, he radicalizes them, and breaks away from the subjectivist ethics that underpin their constructions. To this end, he analyses a number of texts where the animals' attributes, experiences, and behaviours are described. Taking the lead from his earlier questioning of whether animals have a notion of nakedness, he concludes that animals possess modesty and thus 'have a sense of nakedness' (*TAT*: 61). In addition, the *animot*, which is now defined as 'the animality of certain animals', has the capacity to show 'undeniably guilty behavior' by 'hiding or putting its tail between its legs after committing a fault', but also when sick 'or at the point of death, both of which would be felt as faults, as what must not be shown' (*TAT*: 61). Derrida complicates the issue by questioning if one can conclude from the above behaviours that the modalities of 'hiding of oneself' relate to modesty as expressed by different types of dissimulation that both Man and animal partake. His concepts of *animot* and *animort* make the dichotomy irrelevant.

The *animot*, as a non-substitute for the animal, defines all living life in a different way to that upon which the division between life and death is based. Derrida, in order to differentiate the *animot* from non-living life, introduces the notion of *animort*, which he defines as the 'nonanimal as nonliving, in fact, as dead [*le mort*]?' (*TAT*: 62). The next step for Derrida is to raise fundamental questions about what is proper to the animal in the same manner as that of what is proper to man, including dreaming. He proceeds by raising a number of questions that are fundamental to many systems of thought, beginning with the Cartesian 'I think' and ending again with the concept of the mirror. He argues,

> 'Does the animal think?' 'Does the animal produce representations?' a self, imagination, a relation to the future as such? Does the animal have not only signs but a

> language, and what language? Does the animal die? Does it laugh? Does it cry? Does it grieve? Does it get bored? Does it lie? Does it forgive? Does it sing? Does it invent? Does it invent music? Does it play music? Does it play? Does it offer hospitality? Does it offer? Does it give? Does it have hands? eyes? etc.? modesty? clothes? and the mirror? (*TAT*: 63)

He acknowledges the immensity of all these questions in relation to 'their history, their presuppositions, [and] the complexity of their stakes' (*TAT*: 63). Derrida, by raising these questions, does not aim to produce yet another series of discourses condemning the treatment of animals or simply give back to the animals what subjectivist systems of thought deprive it of. His aim is far more radical, because he targets all forms of thinking with regard to the animal, ranging from the Cartesian subject to the law of hospitality. He seeks to produce a musical key that would change the tone of all this questioning, rather than construct a discourse on animal liberation, animal rights, and opposition to the homogenization and suppression of animal diversity. The function of this key would be 'to indicate a tonality, some high notes that change the whole stave', which would alter the ways we question what is proper to the animal (*TAT*: 63). Changing the entire spectrum of what is proper would require new questioning and responses, and finally a new discourse on the animal and Man.

Derrida places the new discourse on the animal within futural messianic discourses of 'to come'. The future, in this last phase of his work, is announced as a kind of dreaming which takes place 'in the depths of an undiscoverable burrow to come' (*TAT*: 63). However, this dreaming contains a kind of *schizis* that consists of incompatible and contradictory commands, injunctions, and impossible tasks. The schizoid structure of the future dream contains a new, somewhat inhuman, language, which acts like an unheard of music that does not aim to make him

> the representative or emancipator of an animality that is forgotten, ignored, misunderstood, persecuted, hunted, fished, sacrificed, subjugated, raised, corralled, hormonized, transgenetized, exploited, consumed, eaten, domesticated (*TAT*: 63).

Derrida clarifies, in a very powerful way, that his new language would involve creating 'an unheard-of grammar and music', that would 'create a scene that was neither human, nor divine, nor animal' (*TAT*: 64). Eliminating all the subjectivist and humanist discourses that have dominated religion, theiology, theology, politics, economics, law, ethics, socio-cultural practices, science, consumption, commercialization, and ultimately all discourses that underpin Western metaphysics and Western thought, is nothing short of a total revolution. This new thinking would be based upon a linguistic overturning which would lead to the institution of a new, radical hybrid language. Derrida explains, very forcefully, that the purpose and function of this new hybrid language, of which the concept of the *animot* is an example, would be to denounce

> all discourses on the so-called animal, all the anthropo-theomorphic or anthropo-theocentric logics and axiomatics, philosophy, religion, politics, law, ethics, with a view to recognizing in them animal strategies, precisely, in the human sense of the term, stratagems, ruses, and war machines, defensive or offensive manoeuvres, search operations, predatory, seductive, indeed exterminatory operations as part of a pitiless struggle between what are presumed to be species (*TAT*: 64).

Derrida, in the last phase of his work, is very clear that the project of deconstruction aims to sever all connections with all discourses that engage in the perpetuation of the modalities of violence to the other. This would extend to language itself. In other words, Derrida's adoption of more messianic discourses moves closer to utopia thinking rather than the earlier injunctive construction of the other. This is evident when he specifies the type of dreaming, '[a]s though I were dreaming, I myself, in all innocence, of an animal that didn't intend harm to the animal' (*TAT*: 64).

In order to construct this new concept animal-*animot* outside the circle of violence to the other and enact the revolutionary project of deconstruction, Derrida posits again the question of being in terms of the pre-ontological question of 'following' from the perspective of the animal. This pre-ontological question of 'following', as the persecution and seduction of the other, is anterior to the question of being and engenders the 'I'. Derrida contends that

> before the question of (the) *being* as such, of *esse* and *sum*, of *ego sum*, there is the question of following, of the persecution and seduction of the other, what/that I am (following) or who is following me, who is following me while I am (following) it, him, or her (*TAT*: 65).

Derrida's positing of being as nonbeing, produces a non-subjectivist, ahuman notion of the 'I' and self. He argues, very emphatically, that

> [t]he being standing in place of nonbeing, this *milieu* that derives from nothingness, is me, the most cunning of animals, on the other side of vertigo, but of the same vertigo of the animal abyss, since it is I, the Self who self-reflects and says '(as for) me I am,' and 'beast I am.' (*TAT*: 66–67).

The Cartesian of 'therefore I am', is replaced by the 'beast I am'. The pre-originary structure of the seduction of the other, inscribes the self-engendering act of the 'I' as simply part of an interminable 'following'. Thus, for Derrida, the 'self-engendering act of the "I am,"' as a form of 'autobiographogenesis, is in its essence an act of seduction' (*TAT*: 67). Within Derrida's radical philosophy '[b]eing becomes seduction, that is, the ruse of the most *rusé* of animals' (*TAT*: 67). It follows that the Cartesian 'I am', becomes 'the seduction of a seducer' (*TAT*: 67). He articulates the pre-originary act of seduction within of series of followings as the '[o]ne who says: I am He who is, who follows you and whom you are (following), who is (following) after you with a view to seducing you and to have it be that, coming after, you become one who follows me' (*TAT*: 67). The emergence of the 'I' is an act of seduction by the other, and the two are engaged in an incessant dance between being a follower and being followed. The 'I am' and the autobiographical 'I' become part of 'The Animal' question, and autobiography is given over to *zootobiography*. The bestiality of both Man and animal effect the collapse of the division between them.

Derrida goes on to analyse Richard de Fournival's *Bestiaires D'Amours* (*Bestiary of Love*), in order to further animalize the image of self and make autobiography as the privileged form of self narration part of animality. In de Fournival's work man becomes an autobiographical animal. However, being a Christian, when engaged in a confessional narrative, de Fournival confesses 'the sin of confession' and acknowledges the 'narcissism that is involved in writing on oneself, even in order to avow and to show oneself in one's nakedness. Naked as a beast' (*TAT*: 69). The confessional narrative entails that the denuded self is on narcissistic display. For Derrida, this is another dimension of the modalities of the nakedness of man which man denies to the animal, because the animal is thought of as being naturally naked. However, in every confession there is an avowal of narcissism, and as a result

> one admits that guilt, and even the lie and perjury, are lodged within veracity itself, within the heart of promise, in the naked and intransitive simplicity of the 'I am,'

> which already conceals its transitive interest, the following of an 'I am following': I am (following) someone else, I am followed by someone else, I pursue a desire or a project, I hunt and chase myself at the same time, I do, me (*TAT*: 69).

Derrida's formulation of the 'I' and the self, as in his earlier work, aims to deconstruct all modalities of the truth of the self within confessional narratives. Confession is taken to be the truth of the self, yet within this truth and the promise of telling the truth there is an admission of sin, guilt, lie and perjury. In other words, Derrida takes confession to be the space where the truth of the 'I am' and 'to follow' cannot be instituted for this would involve a paradoxical disavowal of the truth of the self outside confession.

The next philosophical issue that Derrida tackles is the capacity of response which is denied to the animal. In order to radicalize and pluralize the idea and the locus of response, Derrida analyses Porphyry's works where the animal is given response capacities. Derrida takes the place and adopts the perspective of the animal, and argues that as an animal 'I hear, I listen, I respond, I respond to a question but also to an invitation or a command, I obey' (*TAT*: 85). Furthermore, he argues that '*I present* myself in response to a call, an interrogation, an order, a summons, or an injunction' (*TAT*: 85). By attributing to the animal the capacity to respond to a question, command or invitation, Derrida dissolves the limit that marks the division between animal and Man. In addition, he inscribes the presentation of the self as an affirmation of the 'I', within *animot's* capacity to respond outside speech. Derrida goes on to argue

> *I present myself* is at the same time the first autobiographical gesture and the gesture of all the 'Here-I-am's' in the history of the law. Now, even when it is mute, Porphyry's *animot* seems capable of what I *do* when I *say* upakouō. It is capable of doing what I say I am doing even if, for its part, it doesn't say so (*TAT*: 85).

The *animot* becomes a subject, even in its autobiographical dimension, by obeying the call, interrogation, order, summons and injunction of the animal as other. This schema echoes Derrida's earlier formulations, where the 'I' cannot posit itself as such, nor can it posit itself as other, because it cannot take the place of the other. The 'I' of auto-affection admits irreducible hetero-affection, which includes the animal. This means that the limit between the human and the animal cannot be established as a 'simple and linear differentiation of the human from the animal' (*TAT*: 95). As a result, Derrida argues, 'the question of the "I," of "I am" or "I think,"' need 'to be displaced toward the prerequisite question of the other: the other, the other me that I am (following) or that is following me' (*TAT*: 95). The problem becomes, how the other will be determined and within what logic in order to allow the law of the heteronomy of the other to displace the anthropocentrism and logocentrism of systems of thought whose logic, Derrida admits, his own discourse is following and operates within (*TAT*: 95).

The Derridean other requires the displacement of the Cartesian subject constructed in terms of 'I', 'I am' and 'I think'. This displacement of anthropocentric systems of thought will be effected through his concept of the *animot* which, as we have seen, has been used to radicalize the philosophical, linguistic and conceptual constructions of the animal. The function and power of the *animot*, in relation to all philosophical systems based on Cartesian subjectivity, are announced by Derrida. He argues that even though the *animot* is

> disavowed, foreclosed, sacrificed, and humiliated by them, and in the first instance with respect to what is closest to them, within themselves, on the edge of the infinite vertigo of the 'I am' and of 'I am who I am (following) and by whom I am followed as much as preceded.' Their 'I am' is always 'I am after the animal even when I don't know it.' And this disavowal of foreclosure is just as powerful when they don't speak of it or when they speak of it in order to deny to the *animot* everything they attribute to the human (*TAT*: 113).

Within the Derridean structure the question of the subject is intricately connected to that of the animal and the *animot*. The pre-originary *animot* is constitutive of all human and animal life, and constantly displaces the subject. The positing of the 'I am' has no privileged or fixed locus nor order of hierarchy, because it is embedded within what precedes and what follows it as well as whom it follows and by whom it is followed. The formulation of the other as *animot* from the perspective of the animal, aims towards 'the thinking of the other, of the infinitely other who looks at me', and privileges 'the question and the request of the animal' (*TAT*: 113). By linking the question and request of the animal to the infinitely other, Derrida places at the centre of his philosophical thinking a conceptualization of being in terms of the Heideggerian 'who is Man' and 'what is being'. However, through the deconstruction of the dichotomy human/animal, Derrida aims to answer these questions through his concept of the *animot*.

As we have seen, the *animot*, as the Wholly Other, marks the linguistic, philosophical and ethical departure from the discourses which construct and support the dichotomy human/animal. However, it is important to point out that for Derrida the *animot* cannot be mastered or subsumed under the theological discourse that makes God a non referent, nor can its effects be absorbed within the Heideggerian *es gibt*. The *animot*, as an inscription of the other, is beyond being (*epekeina tes ousias*). As such it negates the need for presence and temporal finitude. The other's infinity means that there is no hierarchy in what question comes first, before or after. Derrida further clarifies that the question of the other is asked

> Not in order to put it in front of that of man, but in order to think that of man, of the brother and the neighbour from the perspective of an animal question and request, of an audible or silent appeal that calls within us outside of us, from the most far away, before us after us, preceding, and pursuing us in an unavoidable way, so unavoidable that it leaves the trace of so many symptoms and wounds, of stigmata or disavowal within the discourse of whomever seeks to remain deaf to that appeal (*TAT*: 113).

The question of man, thought from the perspective of an animal question and request, subverts and overturns the question of Man. The question and request of the animal, as infinitely other, is pre-originary and constructed as an appeal, which is within man and surrounds man. Here the call of the other is less injunctive but more haunting. The appeal of the other is anterior to the subject but also posterior to it. It announces itself outside the necessary predicates upon which the question of Man rests. In other words, before one can posit any question in relation to being and beings, one needs to consider the source of both the question and its positing being the other. The call, as request of the other, can be silent or audible, but always inescapable. It is both internal and external to the subject without depending on it, leaves a trace, and comes from far away.

Derrida, as in his earlier work, deals with the notion of the gaze and the call of a de-subjectivised other as an appeal that is not locatable, temporalized or particularized. Even if one remains deaf to the appeal of the other, its trace will remain as a symptom, wound, disavowal, or stigmata. The notions of symptom and stigmata are of particular importance.

The first signals a move away from the psychoanalytic and psychological conceptions of the subject in its relation to alterity. The second signals a turn towards more mystical, thaumaturgical, theological and messianic discourses. This means that even if the subject remains deaf to the appeal of the other, its effects will always be felt and experienced. The other becomes a presence with no presence, and the subject and the self are inscribed by its ineffaceable traces.

Derrida ends the second text, titled "*But as for me, who am I (following)?*", by arguing that his new ethics cannot simply rely on the subjection of the subject to the other in order to break with the 'Cartesian tradition of an animal without language and without response' (*TAT*: 118). He concludes with the enigmatic statement that '[i]t takes more than that', and goes on to argue that 'even within a logic and ethics of the unconscious, which, without renouncing the concept of the subject, would lay claim to some "subversion" of it' (*TAT*: 118). Derrida has spent much effort and ink to renounce the concept of the subject but in this very last phase of his work he wishes to resurrect it, albeit within a structure of subversion. After arguing for the elimination of all forms of subjectivity and the independence of the other from any subjectivism, this is a strange admission. However, one should not be carried away by such statements and ignore Derrida's ferocious critique of the subject and the self in favour of a philosophical thinking based on the desubjectivised other.

8.3 Radical Alterity: Divanimality and another thinking of life

In the third text, titled *And Say the Animal Responded?*, Derrida takes up the Lacanian positing of the problematic of the subject in terms of reaction and response. In critiquing Levinas' ethics and conceptualization of the subject, Derrida advocates for an ethics which recalls 'the subject to its being-subject, its being-host or -hostage, that is to say, its being subjected-to-the-other, to the Wholly Other or to every single other' (*TAT*: 119). This is an important formulation of Derrida's notion of the other in relation to subjectivity and the subject. Derrida's subject is both host and hostage to the other and is subjected to the Wholly Other, both as general and particularistic other. If the subject in his work on hospitality and forgiveness is holding the other hostage, now the subject is held hostage to and by the other. Hence, Derrida's ideas regarding the relation between subject and other take a final turn towards asymmetry and non-relation. This means that the subject and any inter-subjective relations are eliminated. The only relation that is permitted between the subject and the other, is based on the absolute alterity and irreducibility of the Wholly Other. Consequently, any remnants of subjectivism, even within post-subjectivist thinkers such as Lacan and Heidegger, are savagely deconstructed by Derrida.

Derrida begins with Lacan's essay *The Subversion of the Subject* in order to critique his conception of the other, and locate him within Cartesian subjectivism. Deploying a strategy of deconstruction similar to the one adopted in his essay *The Politics of Friendship*, Derrida deconstructs a number of dualisms, among them Lacan's distinction between reaction and response and their connections to responsibility. Derrida takes one of Lacan's seminal references to the Other in order to pinpoint the place where Lacan unwittingly constructs a notion of the other 'as the one from whom "the subject receives even the message that he emits"' (*TAT*: 126). Derrida takes this phrase as the deconstructive lever of Lacan's text, and aims to question the distinction between '*responsibility* and *reaction*, and all that follows from it' (*TAT*: 126). For Derrida, Lacan's adherence to subjectivism, prevents him from taking his insight about the other to its radical conclusion, and thus eliminate all traces of subjectivity. Unlike Lacan's solution of connecting reaction and response to the notion of subjectivity, Derrida dissolves the dichotomy between the two by re-introducing his concept of *différance*.

Différance would re-inscribe the duality of reaction and response and therefore the

> historicity of ethical, juridical, or political responsibility, within another thinking of life, of the living, within another relation of the living to their ipseity, to their *autos*, to their own autokinesis and reactional automaticity, to death, to technics, or to the mechanical [*machinique*] (*TAT*: 126).

Derridean *différance* bears no relation to any paradigm based on the structure of the solipsistic subject, to which Lacan falls victim. Alterity comes to fissure any notion of the self, autonomy and life conceived within historicity and temporality. Derrida aims for an ethical, juridical and political responsibility dissociated from the ipso-centrism of Western metaphysics. Derrida's other requires another thinking of life and of the living, where the *auto* in all its forms, including the *autos* as auto-affection, are abandoned. This non-subjectivist thinking entails a different political, ethical and juridical notion of responsibility which moves away from concepts of the self connected to human actors.

Derrida goes on to clarify that his new thinking entails a locus for radical alterity that breaks away from 'every identification of an image of self', but also from 'every fellow living creature' and 'every fraternity or human proximity', and finally from 'all humanity' (*TAT*: 132). The place of the Other is ahuman, and as such

> the ahuman or at least the figure of some – in a word – *divinanimality*, even if it were to be felt through the human, would be the quasi-transcendental referent, the excluded, foreclosed, disavowed, tamed, and sacrificed foundation of what it founds, namely, the symbolic order, the human order, law and justice (*TAT*: 132).

The radical place of alterity breaks with self-image, identity and humanity. Derrida's formulation of the other as ahuman and anti-foundational, demonstrates his hostility to any form of human subjectivity and reciprocal relation between self and other. This implies that neither the human nor the animal can constitute the radical place of alterity, upon which Derrida aims to base his new politics, ethics and philosophy. The other is severed from any notions of subjectivity, and is independent of any living entity. Derrida introduces his new concept of *divinanimality*, which signals a more radical abandonment of positing the question of being in terms of the human, animal, or God. The other, even when posited through the human, cannot become foundational, while at the same time founds the human and symbolic order, law, and justice. Since the entire foundation of human life, experience and social structures exclude *divinanimality* by privileging the human over the animal, the question for Derrida becomes one of dismantling this model.

Derrida re-introduces the notion of the trace in relation to the animal, to critique the anthropocentrism and phallogocentrism of Western thought and to further develop his concept of the other. The trace has the same function as in Derrida's earlier deconstructions, but in this case applied to both animal and human. Derrida defines the inherent properties of the trace as 'always being erased and always capable of being erased [*Il appartient à une trace de toujours s'effacer et de toujours pouvoir s'effacer*]' (*TAT*: 136). Although the Derridean trace can be erased and has the capacity to erase itself, its effacing is impossible. The trace remains beyond the mastery and the power of either God, human, or animal. This means that no one has the ' *power* to erase *it* and especially not to "judge" its erasure, even less so by means of a constitutive power assured of being able to erase, performatively, what erases itself' (*TAT*: 136). The trace cannot be repressed, and remains outside the performative function of language and power structures. However, it is subject to destruction and death, and its erasure subject to judgement.

Derrida concludes his discussion of the trace with a new and important element in his thought. He speaks of the spurious opposition between the imaginary and the symbolic, which underpins the anthropocentric and phallogocentric 'reinstitution of the superiority of the human order over the animal order, of the law over the living, etc.' (*TAT*: 136). He argues that the wounded reactions to the three traumas of humanity, namely, the reaction to the Copernican ideas and to Freud's 'decentering of consciousness under the gaze of the unconscious', cannot be equated with the Darwinian trauma (*TAT*: 136). What Derrida alludes here is a very radical rethinking of the entire project of philosophy. He aims to institute a parallel Darwinian 'revolution' into philosophy. If Darwinism meant the death of God as a creator, Derrida is announcing the death of philosophical thinking, politics and ethics based on Western metaphysics. This leads us to Derrida's Deconstruction of Heideggerian metaphysics. Although for Heidegger the task was to name being without objectifying it, for Derrida being becomes subject to the structure of the trace, and, finally, it is struck out.

8.4 Radical Otherness: Striking out being

In the final text, titled "*I don't know why we are doing this*", Derrida deconstructs Heidegger's seminar '*The Fundamental Concepts of Metaphysics: World, Finitude, Solitude*', which he gave in 1929–1930. In this work Derrida takes aim at his closest philosophical ally, Heidegger. He argues that, even though Heidegger's primary target in this essay and in *Being and Time* is Descartes, Heidegger's discourse in relation to the animal 'remains, in spite of everything, profoundly Cartesian' (*TAT*: 147). In other words, Derrida dismisses Heidegger's critique of Cartesianism in *Being and Time* and his attempts to go beyond the humanism and subjectivism of Western metaphysics. Derrida, in his critique of Heidegger's treatment of the animal, aims to give back to the animal what Heidegger deprives it of, that is, the other '*as such*', world, finitude and the experience of death. Furthermore, he aims to articulate a conception of alterity that inscribes both animals and humans within a different conception of the living. In this way he seeks to depart from Heidegger's conception of being, world, finitude and solitude.

Heidegger attempts to answers the question of 'What is man' in conjunction with the question of 'What is world'. The question raised by Derrida is: what is the position of the animal as the utterly other within Heidegger's radical schema in relation to his answers to these questions? To understand the significance of Heidegger's radical philosophy, upon which Derrida draws heavily, but also its shortcomings one needs to understand his conception of the world in relation to man and the animal. The position of the animal in Heidegger's conception of the world would lead Derrida to ultimately re-evaluate Heidegger's radicality regarding the problematic of alterity and subjectivity.

Derrida's first point of attack is Heidegger's conception of being in relation to the animal. For Heidegger, Derrida argues, the animal has 'a relation to the being [*l'étant*] but not to the being as such' and the '*as such*' (*TAT*: 142). Although in Heidegger the '*as such*' does not depend on *logos* – language –, his final curtain call regarding the animal is within the logocentric discourse of Western metaphysics which privileges Man. Derrida acknowledges that Heidegger's attempts to re-define the essence of Man outside consciousness and reason through his idea of the awakening of attunement, radicalized our conception of man, the living and the world. However, Derrida argues, Heidegger fails to accord the animal the same categories he accords Man. This failure is most evident when discussing his concepts of finitude and world. Heidegger institutes a 'limit between animal and human' by arguing that 'only the human is "finite" in the sense of finitude', while the animal is not finite in the same sense (*TAT*: 151). Thus for Heidegger the animal 'doesn't have finitude just as it doesn't have speech, just as it doesn't die "properly,"

properly speaking, etc.' (*TAT*: 151). This formulation is problematized by Derrida because, although man shares with the animal the fate of being mortal, for Heidegger the animal does not experience death in the same way as Man. This Derrida argues is a result of Heidegger's conception of the world in relation to being.

Derrida takes issue with Heidegger's concept of the world in relation to Being, animal, and the world. For Heidegger there are three conceptualizations of the world corresponding to inanimate (material) things, animal and Man. Derrida quotes Heidegger's definition of man, that 'man is not merely a *part of the world* but is also master and servant of the world in the sense of "*having*" world' (*TAT*: 153). Heidegger's three famous theses 'the stone is worldless [*weltlos*], the animal is poor in world [*weltarm*], man is world-forming [*weltbildend*]' determine the ways the animal has world and what type of world it has (*TAT*: 153). Heidegger's formulation homogenizes animal life and conceives of the animal as being poor in world, while man has the capacity to master and change the world. This model can provide the continuous justification for the sovereignty and superiority of man over the animal.

Furthermore, Heidegger takes finitude and death as marking the difference between inanimate beings, man, and animal. Contrary to what Heidegger had maintained in his previous work, in this seminar he claims that what distinguishes the animal from the stone is that 'the animal can die' while the stone 'cannot die' (*TAT*: 154). Derrida takes his cue from this statement to problematize the concepts of death and life, and to re-affirm his philosophical position that the division between life and death is problematic. Against Heidegger's doubt that places death within what is proper to Man, Derrida's concept of the *animot* re-inscribes the notion of death within a notion of the world that places death and life beyond temporality. Since death, for Derrida, is inscribed in the living subject, anchoring the subject upon presence is the mirage of auto-immunity. The death of the subject conceived of as auto-affection, is the precondition of the emergence of any form of subjectivity. Subjectivity and the self, and any modalities of identity, are fatally wounded by alterity-*animot*, which, paradoxically, inscribes all modalities of life and non-life.

Derrida takes from Heidegger the radical construction of being outside *logos*, but aims to go beyond Heidegger's divisions of the world into inanimate, animal and Man. This is a project which is both radical and problematic, especially when it comes to the question of the subject in its concrete manifestations. Derrida concludes his critique of Heidegger, and thus his onslaught on any vestiges of Cartesianism, by defining the differences between Nietzsche and Heidegger, and by attributing to the former the importance of perspective. He argues that Nietzsche, as opposed to Heidegger, would have rejected Heidegger's notion of '*as such*' in relation to being. Adopting a Nietzschean approach, he affirms that

> the relation to a being, even the 'truest,' the most 'objective,' that which respects most the essence of what is such as it is, is caught in a movement that we'll call here that of the living, of life, and from this point of view, whatever the difference between animals, it remains an 'animal' relation (*TAT*: 160).

For Derrida, every living being is subject to the movement of life. All relations are animal relations, and there is no privileging of particular relation to a being or subject. In other words, Derrida introduces the chimera-*animot* into life itself, which encompasses all beings and being as such. Such position means that animal and human, life and death are part of the interminable movement of the living. This is a position closer to the Heracletian eternal change and constant flow of life and antithetical to any stabilization processes and closed systems. It is not surprising then that Derrida ends by setting out a different strategy to that adopted by Heidegger in relation to being.

Derrida's strategy is to pluralize the 'as such'. This process would not simply consist in giving back to the animal what humans deprive it of, but also 'in marking that the human is, in a way, similarly "deprived," by means of a privation that is not a privation, and that there is no pure and simple "as such"' (*TAT*: 160). Derrida concludes that this project would postulate 'a radical reinterpretation of what is living', 'but not in terms of the "essence of the living," of the "essence of the animal."' He acknowledges that his radical approach means that 'the stakes are so radical that they concern "ontological difference," the "question of being," the whole framework of Heideggerian discourse' (*TAT*: 160). In other words, through his deconstruction of Heidegger's conception of being, Derrida aims to go beyond the Heideggerian radicalization of phenomenology, and institute a new conception of being based on the utterly other, which he inscribes through his concept of the *animot*. His anti-essentialist concept of the other is marked by infinitude and is beyond the division of life and death, human and animal. It is self-referential and generative of all modalities of life and death. The question becomes if such a philosophical model can side step the question of Being, being and beings and their interrelations by simply appealing to the notion of the self-referential concept of the other, which is beyond ontology. This is a radical project not only in terms of ontology's fundamental questions, but also of the entire thinking upon which our political, ethical, legal and socio-cultural ideas are based.

In order to identify in a concrete way of how Derrida sees the project and future of deconstruction, I will turn to his last interview given to Le Monde's Jean Birnbaum in 2004. In this interview he outlines his political project in a forceful way, but concerning his impending death he declares, paradoxically, that he has not yet learned how to live.

8.5 Post-globalization politics and ethics: Europe, sovereignty, fundamentalism and messianic vision

I will take Derrida's last interview he gave to Le Monde's correspondent Jean Birnbaum in 2004, two months before his death, as the closing statement of the last phase of Derrida's work. This interview merits extensive examination because in it Derrida outlines his political project in more concrete terms. He places himself clearly in the camp of the critics of current forms of globalization, religious fundamentalism, Euro-centrism, American global dominance, and the dominance of media discourses and their resulting intellectual morass. He assesses critically the function and role of international institutions, and warns against the global ascendancy of neo-liberal agendas and the capture of the political system and processes by special interest groups and politico-economic lobbies.

During this interview, Derrida expresses his continuous insistence that the project of deconstruction is non-Eurocentric, and remains critical of all forms of Euro-centrism to the very end. However, one would be misunderstanding the entire project of deconstruction, if deconstruction is seen as separate from the European intellectual tradition which gave it birth and provided its philosophical basis upon which the critique of

Western metaphysics was launched. Derrida, as he has done previously, acknowledges the influence and importance of European thought, and is unwilling to jettison the positive parts of the European intellectual, socio-cultural and political legacy (Derrida, 1992). He explains that from the beginning of his work, including 'deconstruction itself', he has 'remained very critical with regard to Eurocentrism, to its formulation in modernist form, in the work of Valery, Husserl, or Heidegger, for instance' (*LMI:* 12). He asserts that deconstruction is 'a project that many have taken, rightly so, as an act of defiance toward all Eurocentrism.' (*LMI*: 12). However, Derrida in the same breath affirms that '[w]hat I call "deconstruction," even when it is directed against something European, is European, is a product of Europe, a reflection of Europe on itself as experience of a radical otherness.' (*LMI*: 14). In other words, what marks his philosophy and politics, is radical otherness whose formulation escapes the shortcomings of the Eurocentric Western metaphysics, which he aims to overcome and go beyond (see also Derrida, 1992). However, Derrida in his closing statements makes Europe the moral and political guardian of human rights, justice and equality, and of all radical elements of the project of deconstruction.

Derrida expresses his anxieties regarding the prevailing political, media, economic and religious discourses, and the global landscape. He clearly articulates his fears of the domination of what he terms 'media intellectuals', who simply uncritically repeat the 'doxa' in the service of particular interests. Consequently, he calls for a 'rigorous war against the doxa', media intellectuals, and general discourses 'pre-formatted by the media, who are themselves under the control of politico-economic lobbies, and often editorial and academic as well.' (*LMI:* 6–7). In the demise of public discourse he implicates the shadowy forces of unelected political and economic lobbies, and their alliances with the global media conglomerates. Derrida is not afraid to expose their destructive impacts and cautions us against the mediatised discourses which have permeated academia and publishing, and whose main purpose is to give legitimacy and repeat the doxa. In other words, Derrida is troubled by the colonization of the public sphere, (to use a Habermasian term), by dominant political and economic lobbies, and their discourses. Hence, his insistence on the necessity of the opening to the other fits well with his critique of the current political and economic systems in play, which, as we have seen, are involved in what Derrida calls 'violations to the other'. However, whether his answer of a new thinking based on the wholly other will deliver the desired outcomes is debatable since it dispenses with the subject, self, and notions of agency. Who are the political and economic actors that would question the prevailing doxa if not situated, embodied, concrete subjects that operate within frameworks of recognition, equality, horizontality, reflection, reciprocity and critical inter-subjective engagement?

As in his previous work, Derrida's answer to these problematics is to gesture towards a futural politics, ethics and the law, and a different economic model. His hope is for a new Europe 'to come' which is not captive to neo-liberal agendas, but shoulders its responsibilities 'in the name of the future of humanity, in the name of international law', and declares this to be 'my faith and my religion' (*LMI:* 12). Within this messianic, but at the same time secular model, he articulates his vision of Europe and the world. He envisages a future Europe which maintains all the radical and revolutionary ideas it has generated since the Enlightenment, such as Human Rights and adherence to principles of justice and equality. It is a Europe which will 'unite against the politics of American global dominance', but 'also against Arab-Muslim theocratism, unenlightened, and without a political future' (*LMI:* 12). However, he acknowledges the plurality within these blocks, and urges us to 'ally ourselves with the opposition within them' (*LMI:* 12).

Derrida further articulates his vision of Europe, not as a 'military superpower, protecting its markets and acting as a counterweight against other geopolitical blocs', but instead 'a Europe that would sow the grain of a new post-globalization politics' (*LMI:* 12–13). However, Derrida's critique of globalization has more to do with its economic imperatives, such as 'cheaper, better, more for less, from anywhere', increased levels of inequality and 'the race to the bottom', rather than objecting to any form of global, overarching bodies which ensure multi-polar rather than mono-polar international relations.

Although Derrida's thought in the last phase of his work takes a turn towards more messianic and theological thinking, Derrida wishes to locate his political project within secularism. Thus, he does not abandon secularism, but instead radicalizes the concept of politics itself by injecting immanence in the form of 'à venir', or 'to come', disconnected from eschatological or teleological thinking. Consequently, Derrida, right to the end, adheres to a futural form of secular politics and announces that ‘[t]his movement is coming’ and it is unstoppable. In respect to Europe he goes on to clarify that, for him, Europe is ‘a post-globalization Europe, transforming the concept and the conventions of sovereignty and international law’ (*LMI:* 13). Derrida’s future vision of Europe rejects current processes of globalization, and is not conceived in terms of its currently formulated conventions of nation-states and sovereignty. Instead, it will be a Europe ‘independent of NATO or the UN’, whose military power would be ‘neither offensive nor defensive’, but ‘would firmly enforce the resolutions of a reconstituted UN (for example, and with utmost urgency, in Israel, but also elsewhere)’ (*LMI*: 13).

Since Derrida locates deconstruction’s project within secular frameworks based on the thinking of the utterly other, in this last interview, he cautions against the threat posed by fundamentalist forms of religious thought and what he called the ‘*machine-like return of religion*’. He approaches the question of religion in his last interview in a more concrete way, in order to articulate his concerns about the rise of Christian fundamentalism in the United States and what he calls unenlightened ‘Arab-Muslim theocratism’ (*LMI:* 12). He entrusts Europe to be the ‘site from which we can reflect best on certain aspects of secularity, for example, or social justice, which are European legacies [...]’ (*LMI*: 13). Addressing issues of social justice within a secular framework and hoping for an independent Europe, in terms of its military power and obligations, and making Europe the enforcer of Human Rights and UN resolutions, signals a desire to stay within the European political legacy of secularity.

It is within this secular, political, and ethical schema that Derrida wishes to locate the ongoing, radical and revolutionary character of his own writing. He argues that ‘[i]f I had invented a writing it would have been as an endless revolution’ (*LMI:* 8). He connects his own legacy to his concept of the trace and states that ‘[t]he trace I leave to me means at once my death, to come or already come, and the hope that it will survive me’ (*LMI:* 8).

8.6 Concluding remarks

In the last phase of Derrida's work, the question of the other, and its relations to the subject and the self, is a central concern. Derrida aims to break away from systems of thought and praxis implicated in the 'violence to the other', and to institute a new, radical thinking which would eliminate all modalities of violence to the other. The other is conceived of as a pre-ontological, de-subjectivised and ahuman category, which is constructed within an injunctive and messianic framework which is beyond being and notions of subjectivity and the self. Within Derridean deconstruction the subject and the self are in a non-relation to the other.

During this phase, Derrida continues to privilege the singularity of radical otherness, and to valorise dissociation and separation rather than the Heideggerian being with and gathering. As in his earlier work, Derrida's project of deconstruction aims to open the space of alterity by displacing the subjectivism and humanism of Western metaphysics, and break away from all systems of thought and knowledge where the subject Man holds sway. The subject and the self within Derrida's philosophical schema are subject to the other, and are obligated to answer the call of the other within a more haunting, injunctive and imperative framework. The hearing and the response to the call, which always comes from and belongs to the wholly other and never to a subject, inscribes the subject before its emergence. The question becomes: 'who' responds to the call of the other and in what manner? Derrida's answer is that the subject responds, even when it does not respond, cannot fail but to respond to the call of the other. By placing the wholly other beyond being (*epekeina tes ousias*), Derrida is left off the hook. He simply does not have to deal with the question of being posited in the ontological terms of 'what' and 'who is Man'. He posits the question in terms of 'to Whom' and answers it with the philosophy of the de-subjectivised, injunctive, ahuman, post-animal, and post-human Other. Within this schema, the conscious or unconscious subject and all its associated categories are eliminated, and a futural and messianic philosophy of the other is instituted. The subject, before positing itself as a subject, is already inscribed by the trace of the other, which, in the last phase of Derrida's work, is conceived of as ahuman. The trace of the other is ineffaceable, even when it can be erased, and remains outside notions of power and mastery. Thus, the other, in its latest inscription as *animot*, severs all connection to the subject and becomes a quasi-transcendental category whose workings are already inscribed in its non-originary origin that cannot be instituted, because it constantly erases or effaces itself. However, through this process of erasure, the trace remains.

To this author Derrida's thought of the other is like a fugue composed of variations on the same theme but with different stress each time. The pre-ontological injunctive power and the call of the wholly other cannot be answered by a subject constructed or connected to any post-subjectivist or subjectivist categories. The response to the other and our responsibility to the other come from the other as does everything else, including faith, justice, knowledge, reason, self, I, ethics, politics, law, economics, and finally our search to the answer 'Who is it that I am (following)'? For Derrida the answer is, 'the other'.

Derrida's philosophical model, in the last phase of his work, is based on the radical re-inscription of the concepts of hospitality, life, death and the world. His concept of the *animot* is the inevitable conclusion as he tries to radicalize the entire spectrum of our thinking, and shift the emphasis from our subjectivist and humanist preoccupations to the infinite opening to the other, who escapes the traps of the modalities of violence to the other. However radical Derrida's thinking proves to be, the problematic of embodied, inter-subjective relations among concrete human actors remain, and cannot be entirely sidestep by an appeal to a pre-ontological, quasi-transcendental concept of the other and a philosophy of *limitrophy*.

9. Conclusion: The Self: Particularity, Reflexivity and Recognition

The construction of the self and other and their intra- and inter-relationship present scholars with many problems and challenges. Whereas the post-Kantians and the post-Hegelians try to maintain some notion of universality, the communitarians want to save the individual and situate him/her within a predominantly social realm. And while the Habermasians wish to maintain a communicative interactivity between self and other, others try to effect a compromise between universalism and individualism. Some feminists seek to preserve the idea of difference and the gendered subject and self, while others are happy to enter the critique of identity politics. Consequently, some entertain the idea of a deconstructed subject, and see the desubjectivised, disembodied, disembedded, decentered and fractured self as a way or a means of purging the subject of its metaphysical residues. But others, who take up the challenge of deconstruction and the critique of the identity politics, nevertheless want to hold on to universalism and a specific brand of ethics, without abandoning the idea of the subject and the self.

Various attempts have been made to anchor the subject and the self on to something that is beyond the self. For Derrida, it is the other; for Taylor, it is transcendental demands that emanate from beyond the self; and for Ricœur, it is an otherness of the self within a reformulated subjectivity. Instead of attempting to canvas all of these alternatives at this point, I propose to conclude by drawing attention to those which, in being critical of Derrida's thought, depart from it productively. In doing so, I argue that when conceiving of the subject and the self we need to take into account the long history of the death of the subject as a foundational ground for modern Western thought. This ends not in a rejection of the self, but in a reformulation of it along the lines mapped out in particular by Ricœur and Taylor. To conceive of the other as being devoid of situatedness – and the concomitant demands of recognition, reflexivity and narrativity – is to neutralise it in the process of universalising it. Intersubjectivity cannot be resolved by jettisoning the subject and the idea of horizontal and symmetrical relationships. Nor can the question of how the self relates to the other be answered by eliminating the notion of identity.

9.1 Benhabib: situating the self between the universal and the particular

In *Situating the Self* Seyla Benhabib argues for a postmetaphysical and interactive universalism, based on the 'vision of an embodied and embedded human self whose identity is constituted narratively' (Benhabib, 1992: 6). Although she agrees with Ricœur that one cannot ignore the narrative construction of the self, she collapses the notions of 'embodied self' and 'narrativity'. Ricœur, on the other hand, wants to separate the embodied self from his notion of selfhood. Benhabib aims to reformulate 'the moral point of view as the contingent achievement of an interactive form of rationality rather than as the timeless standpoint of a legislative reason' (Benhabib, 1992: 6). Reason and morality thus become part of an interactive and intersubjective framework. Benhabib wants a narratively constructed self, whose morality is based on a notion of interactive rationality, and which relates to a concrete rather than a transcendental other.

Because Benhabib's point of view is feminist, she criticises a philosophical tradition that rests on the paradox of the disembedded and the disembodied self. Her feminism obliges her to construct subjectivity in a way that neither disregards context nor eliminates the embodied self. Benhabib's construction of the self results in a parallel construction of the other, which is based on a distinction between the generalised and the concrete other. She argues that

> the standpoint of the generalised other requires us to view each and every individual as a rational being entitled to the same rights and duties we would want to ascribe to ourselves. In assuming the standpoint, we abstract from the individuality and concrete identity of the other (Benhabib, 1992:158–159).

She goes on to argue that

> the standpoint of the concrete other, by contrast, requires us to view each and every rational being as an individual with a concrete history, identity and affective-

> emotional constitution. In assuming this standpoint, we abstract from what constitutes our commonality, and focus on individuality (Benhabib, 1992:158–159).

This results in a relation with the other which

> is governed by the norms of *equity* and *complementary reciprocity*: each is entitled to expect and to assume from the other forms of behaviour through which the other feels recognised and confirmed as a concrete, individual being with specific needs, talents and capacities. Our differences in this case complement rather than exclude one another. The norms of our interaction are usually, although not exclusively private, non-institutional ones. They are norms of friendship, love and care (Benhabib, 1992:158–159).

This syncretic or hybrid point of view attempts to reconcile the universal with the particular, the rule with the exception, and equality with equity. On the one hand, she adopts the Habermasian view of the universalism of discourse ethics; on the other hand, as a feminist she tries to get beyond procedural ethics, by introducing friendship, love and care into the norms of interaction with others. Although such an ethics moves in the direction of Derrida, it does not have the injunctive and interrogatory power of the Derridean other. In rejecting the idea of a disembedded and disembodied self, and insisting on the importance of narrative in the construction of the self, Benhabib departs radically from Derrida's ontologically disembodied conception of the self and other. Benhabib's refusal to abandon the concept of identity, and her insistence on distinguishing the generalised from the concrete other, constitute a critical break from, and an alternative to Derrida's concept of the other. Her notion of an intersubjective engagement between self and other represents a powerful alternative to Derrida's view that ethics is founded on submission to and answering of the call of the other.

9.2 Ricœur: oneself as another

Paul Ricœur tackles the question of self and other in a way that both relates to and departs from Derrida's conception of it. Ricœur is a thinker who tries, like Derrida, to exit the phenomenological tradition, although he sees some positive aspects in Husserl's 'uncompromising refusal to hypostatise collective entities and his tenacious will to reduce them in every instance to a network of interactions' (Ricœur, 1991: 224). Unlike Derrida, Ricœur does not want to eliminate subjectivity and agency, but to reformulate agency as critical. The minimal criteria for Ricœur's notion of human action involve being able to 'identify [it] through the projects, intentions, and motives of agents capable of imputing their action to themselves' (Ricœur, 1991: 224). In other words, imputability is central to any conception of self and other as well as ethics. While avoiding Derrida's de-subjectivised and de-individualised concept of the other, he also keeps his distance from those reifications of a generalised other which are expressed in the mode of collectivities. He therefore cautions us against abandoning the idea of reciprocity in intersubjective relations.

Minimal criteria for judging human actions have to be retained, because if they are 'abandoned . . . one begins again to hypostatise social and political entities, to raise power to the heavens, and to tremble before the state' (Ricœur, 1991: 224). Ricœur thus wants to salvage from phenomenology a theory of action and agency that can be grounded on individual autonomy and built into intersubjective relationships. At all times it must be capable of being monitored rationally, and it must be able to resist reification into either rationalist or collectivist fantasies. Ricœur's theory allows questions to be asked of both individual responsibility and the conditions of ideal communication. In other words, Ricœur appropriates Husserlian intersubjectivity for a theory of critical agency, in which the ego is no longer the Husserlian monadic ego. Instead, it becomes responsive to the other within a model of intersubjectivity that allows the other to be independent. Rejecting the phenomenological view that the relationship between the 'I' and the other is analogical, Ricœur substitutes a dialogical or even dialectical relationship that retains linkages with reflexivity.

In *Oneself as Another* Ricœur deals directly with the problematic of the other in relation to subjectivity, self, and narrative identity. Here he shows the importance of distinguishing identity as sameness (*idem*) from identity as selfhood (*ipse*). Unlike Derrida, he does not abandon the concept of identity. Instead, he articulates its complexity in terms of its reflexivity, intersubjectivity and recognition (*ipse*) rather than its sameness (*idem*) through time. Ricœur still maintains the importance of narrative identity as both a stabilising and transformative task (Ricœur, 2004). By distinguishing the 'I' from both the 'self' and 'selfhood' (where the latter presupposes reflection rather than a timeless concept of identity), he is able to think of identity as existing outside the confines of the same (where the 'same' is conceptualised as the certainty of the cogito's self-positing). Ricœur proposes a notion of otherness that does not exclude the self (in its reflexive modality of selfhood) but questions the notion of identity within a framework of difference.

For Ricœur, 'oneself' is that entity which can conceive of itself reflexively 'as another'. In other words, Ricœur makes the other part of the positing of the subject, but in a way neither dependent on nor derived from the subject. The self cannot articulate its own identity unless it is capable of conceiving itself and placing itself in the position of the other and therefore positing itself as other: the engagement of self with the other is thus both internal and external to self and self-identity. Because the reflexive mode of the self is maintained and incorporated within the modality of otherness, subjectivity as self-reflexivity is not 'written off'. The writing of the subject as other is a precondition of the subject's identity. Derrida fails to grasp this reflexive and intersubjective capacity of the self. The Derridean other does not include the self because it is beyond the self. The relations between the self and the other, therefore, are dissymmetrical. By 'writing off' both the subject and the self, Derrida 'writes off' the other as the positing of the self as other. The result is a quasi-transcendental and other-worldly construction of the other which is beyond both human and animal. It cannot answer the question of how the self relates to the other except in a messianic and post-ethical manner.

There is a dialectic between self and other-than-self and Ricœur aims to explore the otherness that is constitutive of selfhood. He does so by means of an analytic-hermeneutic procedure which opens up the problematic of the self in terms of a 'who' rather than an 'I' (*OA*: 19). 'To say *self* is not to say *I*', he writes. 'The *I* is posited – or is deposited' (*OA*: *1*8). What is important is the confrontation between identity as sameness (*idem*) and identity as selfhood (*ipse*). Unlike *idem*-identity, *Ipse*-identity includes otherness. Consequently, 'with the question Who? . . . the self returns just when the same slips away' (*OA*: 128). Derrida also posits the question of the subject in terms of 'Who?', of course. But he does so in order to demonstrate the indebtedness of the subject to the other, and to construct the subject in terms of a call that answers affirmatively to the other. The 'I am' of the subject and of the self is replaced with the answer to the call of the other as a passive reply. In Ricœur, by contrast, the 'Who?' refers to that problematic of attestation which opens up the relationship between self and other.

Ricœur offers two kinds of models of otherness. The one which derives from Levinas and is based on externality he rejects, because the injunction is 'primordially attestation, or the injunction risks not being heard and the self not being affected in the mode of being-enjoined' (*OA*: 355). The other model derives from Heidegger, who

> relates the otherness of the call to strange(r)ness, and to the nothingness of thrown-being, fallen or deteriorated, and finally reduces the otherness of conscience to the encompassing otherness of being-in-the-world, which we centered . . . around the flesh[;] there is a strong temptation to compare, by contrast, the otherness of the injunction to that of other people (*OA*: 352–253).

Ricœur rejects this model because Heideggerian attestation is either 'primordially injunction' or runs the risk of 'losing all ethical and moral significance' (*OA*: 355). Derrida's model of otherness shares with Levinas' the ethical primacy of the other, and with Heidegger's the notion of the call. But it departs from both by maintaining the injunctive power of the other, which is achieved by separating the other from its being-in-the-world. In rejecting these models, Ricœur proposes a third modality of otherness: '*being enjoined as the structure of selfhood*', which is connected with self-attestation but not reducible to it. Ricœur's model of otherness constitutes selfhood in terms of experience of others, but makes the other irreducible to such experience. Thus otherness is never completely external to the self, nor can its irreducibility be absorbed – either by elevation or negation – into the ontology of the self-present subject.

The Derridean other is a 'limit-concept', which points in the direction of the messianic and the prophetic hence the characterization of his philosophy as *Limitrophy*. As such, it is aporetic in relating the subject to self and otherness. Yet one cannot underestimate the force of a thinking that moves at the limits of such aporias, constructed always as a future that has not yet come and that has not yet been thought. This is not only the strength and the radicality of Derrida's thought, but also its weakness. For by refusing to ground his thought in ontology and to make the other subject to any ontological categories, Derrida has signalled the limits of its possibilities. But he has also drawn attention to the insurmountable difficulties of overcoming those limits which the Western tradition – in 'becoming subjective' – has placed on the problematic of irreducible alterity.

9.3 Taylor: the other, injunction and intersubjective recognition

Taylor aims to show the multiple sources of the modern self, and to define a concept of the self which is shaped in part by the other. Here the notion of recognition becomes important. Taylor's thesis is that 'our identity is partly shaped by recognition or its absence, often by the *mis*-recognition of others' (Taylor, 1995: 225). The historico-sociological preconditions for the modern concern with recognition are modernity's assertion of the equal dignity of each and every citizen, and the individualisation which typifies modern social identities. We are all under the imperative to construct an identity, and comforted by the democratic sentiment that each identity is equally worthy of respect. Modern politics thus becomes a struggle to have that identity recognised, and to shelter it from its misrecognition. These historico-political vectors occur in a philosophical context in which it is argued that even individualised identities are shaped through dialogical relations with the other, and that intersubjectivity – as described phenomenologically – is the locus in which the political struggle for recognition takes place. This is why Taylor can argue, without apparent paradox, that 'inwardly generated identity gives a new importance to recognition', because one's 'own identity crucially depends on [one's] dialogical relations with others' (Taylor, 1995: 231).

From a Derridean standpoint, this kind of statement is manifestly paradoxical. For according to Derrida, the notion of an inwardly generated identity derives from the idea of how subjectivity is connected to self-presence: it cannot be seen as the product of a dialogical relation with others, especially not, significant others. Moreover, because the Derridean other is beyond any kind of intersubjectivity, it no longer refers to concrete, significant, particular or even generalised others. Since the relation of self to other is asymmetrical, the other takes the form of an injunction without appeal, or indeed without any kind of subjective co-determination. The patent connection here between Derrida's work and Kafka's novels is referred to by Derrida himself, who acknowledges their common inheritance. As rival models of the self-other relation, Derridean 'verticality' is anathema to Taylorian 'horizontality'. The 'other' is not an over-arching horizon, which relativises the determinations of the subject and makes difference possible. On the contrary, what is envisaged is a displacement and fusion of horizons, designed to overcome the arrogance of Eurocentric constructions of the modern subject and modern culture.

9.4 Epilogue

Derrida understands the metaphysical subject as a self-reflexive presence, according to which the self relates both to itself (in auto-affection) and to the other (by absorbing it within the ontology of the same). This results from the construction of Being as self-presence within Western metaphysics. In the course of deconstructing presence, Derrida produces a series of meditations on non-presence, all based on the concept of the other. Deconstruction is thus an impersonal reflexive mode, in which there are neither actors nor subjects. He conceives of the other in such a way that the self comes to be constructed as answerable to the other within a relationship of asymmetry and the later phase of his work within a relationship of violence to the other.

In opening up a space for the other, Derrida emphasises its injunctive and interrogative power. The Derridean other thus becomes the linchpin of an ethics that is not only post-subjectivist but also post-deconstructive. As the new *a priori*, the other points towards a transcendental limit, but does so without the negative and subjectivist aspects of Western metaphysical thought. But since these developments constitute a radical departure from subjectivism, we still need to maintain a narrative construction of the subject – a point of *restance* or identity of the subject, which is connected to a reflexive and interactive engagement with the other. For if the other is thought of as determining the subject's relation both to itself and to the other, and this other is a 'limit-horizon' (ungrounded within the world and a 'world-horizon'), then the only position available to the subject is submission to the demands and to the call of the other.

Ever since Descartes, the self has been posited in relation to itself within self-consciousness. But it is doubtful that the self has ever been conceived of as grounded only within a subjective metaphysics of presence. In Descartes, an appeal to God ensures the ultimate validity of reality; in Kant, the *Ding-an-sich* is the unknown and unknowable residue of the real; and whereas Nietzsche appeals to a quasi-biological and trans-subjective will-to-power, Heidegger regards Being as the ground from which both Being and being-there emerge. The Derridean appeal to the other follows a venerable metaphysical tradition of thinking at the limits of both the subject and the concept. Derrida's exit from that tradition is an exit that was prepared for by the tradition itself, and the turn to the subject today is always made in a post-metaphysical direction. This is why those new theories of the subject and the self which include narrativity, expressivity, reflection and recognition also incorporate the other and make room for a 'right of difference', instead of surrendering it to the imperial sway of the subject. From this perspective, Derrida resembles a general who continued to fight old and successful wars, even though the important battles are being now fought elsewhere.

Nevertheless, Derrida's conception of the neutralising and generalising other has many radical and important implications for our ethics, politics and the law. In particular, both his emphasis on the right to difference and his notion of otherness as an injunction can serve as critical foils against utilitarian defences of cultural diversity and neo-liberal definitions of the social bond. If they do the job imperfectly, it is because Derrida's notion of the other ignores – to use Benhabib's categories – the universality of the generalised other, and reifies the particularity of the concrete other. We need a notion of the other that takes account of Benhabib's, Ricœur's and others' treatment of the 'concrete other'. As I have argued, a workable concept of the self must be capable, as Ricœur suggests, of that reflexivity which is required in order to conceive of the other. And it also requires that intersubjective recognition which comes from the other in the symmetrical manner outlined by Taylor.

In Derrida, the other casts a long shadow over both the subject and the self, so much so that they become non-existent: in the night all cows are black. The other, however, can neither be overshadowed nor jump its own shadow; it therefore acquires a hypostasis that might relegate it to those shadows which move in the night. But in the dark there are no shadows unless the moonlight illuminates the contours of those subjects who can be both themselves and other than themselves. Since there is reflection, one needs to explore the nature of this self-relation and self-reflection. Derrida demonstrates the negative aspects of self-relation by assimilating self-reflection to the narcissistic model of auto-affection. But there is another kind of self-reflection that allows for irreducible alterity as a moment not simply of undifferentiated affirmation, but also of particularity, reflexivity and recognition.

Bibliography

Works by Jacques Derrida

(1973), *Speech and Phenomena, And Other Essays on Husserl's Theory of Signs*, trans. David B. Allison, Northwestern University Press, Evanston.

(1976), *Of Grammatology*, trans. Gayatri Chakravorty Spivak, The Johns Hopkins University Press, Baltimore and London.

(1978), *Writing and Difference*, trans. Alan Bass, Routledge and Kegan Paul, London and Henley.

(1979), *Spurs Nietzsche's Styles, Éperons Les Styles de Nietzsche*, trans. Barbara Harlow, The University of Chicago Press, Chicago and London.

(1980), *The Archeology of the Frivolous, Reading Condillac*, trans. and intro. by John P. Leavy, Jr, University of Nebraska Press, Lincoln and London.

(1981), *Positions*, trans. and annotated by Alan Bass, The University of Chicago Press, Chicago and London.

(1981), *Dissemination*, trans. Barbara Johnson, The University of Chicago Press, Chicago and London.

(1982), *Margins of Philosophy*, trans. with additional notes by Alan Bass, Harvester Press, Sussex.

(1983), 'The Time of a Thesis: Punctuations' in *Philosophy in France Today*, ed. Alan Montefiore, Cambridge University Press, Cambridge.

(1984), 'Deconstruction and the Other', in Richard Kearney, *Dialogues with Continental Thinkers: The Phenomenological Heritage*, Manchester University Press, Manchester.

(1985), *The Ear of the Other, Otobiography, Transference, Translation*, Christie McDonald ed., trans. Peggy Kamuf, Schocken Books, New York. Both the 1985 and 1988 editions were used in the book.

(1986), *Glas*, trans. John P. Leavy, Jr., and Richard Rand, University of Nebraska Press, Lincoln and London.

(1987), *The Truth in Painting,* trans. Geoff Bennington and Ian McLeod, The University of Chicago Press, Chicago and London.

(1987), *The Post Card, From Socrates to Freud and Beyond*, trans. Alan Bass, The University of Chicago Press, Chicago and London.

(1987), 'Ulysses Gramophone: Hear Say Yes in Joyce', in *A Derrida Reader: Between the Blinds*, Peggy Kamuf ed., Harvester Wheatsheaf, New York and London, 1991.

(1988), *The Ear of the Other, Otobiography, Transference, Translation,* Christie McDonald ed., trans. Peggy Kamuf, University of Nebraska Press, Lincoln and London. Both the 1985 and 1988 editions were used in the book.

(1988), *Limited Inc*, Gerald Graff ed., trans. Samuel Weber and Jeffrey Mehlman, Northwestern University Press, Evanston.

(1988), 'The Politics of Friendship', *The Journal of Philosophy*, no 11, November, pp. 632–644.

(1988), 'Like the Sound of the Sea Deep Within a Shell: Paul de Man's War', trans. Peggy Kamuf, in *Memoirs for Paul de Man*, Rev. ed., trans. Cecile Lindsay, Jonathan Culler, Eduardo Cadava, and Peggy Kamuf, Columbia University Press, New York.

(1989), *Edmund Husserl's Origins of Geometry: An Introduction*, trans. Peter Leavey, Jr., University of Nebraska Press, Lincoln and London.

(1989), 'Introduction: Desistance', in Lacoue-Labarthe, *Typography: Mimesis, Philosophy, Politics*, Christopher Fynsk ed., Harvard University Press, Cambridge, Massachusetts, London.

(1989), *Memoires for Paul de Man*, rev. ed., trans. Cecile Lindsay, Jonathan Culler, Eduardo Cadava, and Peggy Kamuf, Columbia University Press, New York.

(1989), *Of Spirit, Heidegger and the Question,* trans. Geoffrey Bennington and Rachel Bowlby, The University of Chicago Press, Chicago and London.

(1989), 'How to Avoid Speaking: Denial', trans. Ken Frieden, in Budick Stanford and Iser Wolfgang eds., *Languages of the Unsayable: The Play of Negativity in Literature and Literary Theory*, Columbia University Press, New York.

(1991), From *Psyche, Inventions of the Other*, in Derek Attridge ed., *Acts of Literature*, Routledge, London.

(1991), 'At This Very Moment in This Work Here I Am', in Peggy Kamuf ed., *A Derrida Reader: Between the Blinds*, Harvester, Wheatsheaf, New York and London.

(1991), 'Letter to a Japanese Friend', in Peggy Kamuf ed., *A Derrida Reader: Detween the Blinds*, Harvester, Wheatsheaf, New York and London.

(1991), 'Inventions of the Other', in Derek Attridge ed., *Acts of Literature*, Routledge, London.

(1991), '"Eating Well," or the Calculation of the Subject: An Interview with Jacques Derrida', in Eduardo Cadava, Peter Connor & Jean-Luc Nancy eds., *Who Comes After the Subject?*, Routledge, New York and London.

(1992), *The Other Heading, Reflections on Today's Europe*, trans. Pascale-Anne Brault and Michael B. Nass, Indiana University Press, Bloomington and Indianapolis.

(1992), 'Passions: An Oblique Offering', trans. David Wood in David Wood ed., *Derrida: A Critical Reader*, Blackwell, Oxford and Cambridge, Mass.

(1992), *Given Time: I. Counterfeit Money*, trans. Peggy Kamuf, The University of Chicago Press, Chicago and London.

(1992), 'Given Time: The Time of the King', trans. Peggy Kamuf, *Critical Inquiry*, no.18, Winter, pp.161–187.

(1993), *Memoirs of the Blind: The Self-Portrait and Other Ruins*, trans. Pascale-Anne Brault and Michael Naas, The University of Chicago Press, Chicago and London.

(1993), *Circumfession*, in Geoffrey Bennington, *Jacques Derrida*, trans. Geoffrey Bennington, The University of Chicago Press, Chicago and London.

(1993), *Aporias*, trans. Thomas Dutoit, Stanford University Press, Stanford California.

(1994), *Specters of Marx, The State of the Debt, the Work of Mourning, and the New International*, trans. Peggy Kamuf, Routledge, New York and London.

(1995), *The Gift of Death*, trans. David Wills, The University of Chicago Press, Chicago and London.

(1995), *Points . . ., Interviews, 1974–1994*, Elisabeth Weber ed., trans. Peggy Kamuff & others, Stanford University Press, Stanford California.

(1995a), *On the Name*, Thomas Dutoit ed., trans David Wood, John P. Leavey, Jr and Ian McLeod, Stanford University Press, Stanford California.

(1995), '"There is No *One* Narcissism" (Autobiographies)', in *Points . . ., Interviews, 1974–1994*, Elisabeth Weber ed., trans Peggy Kamuf and others, Stanford University Press.

(1996), 'Remarks on Deconstruction and Pragmatism', in Chantal Mouffe ed., *Deconstruction and Pragmatism*, Routledge, London and New York.

(1996a), 'As if I Were Dead: An Interview with Jacques Derrida', in *Applying: To Derrida*, John Brannigan ed., Ruth Robbins and Julian Wolfreys, Macmillan Press, London.

(1996b), *Archive Fever: A Freudian Impression*, trans Eric Prenowitz, The University of Chicago Press, Chicago and London.

(1998), *Monolingualism of the Other; Or, The Prosthesis of Origin*, Mieke Bal and Hent de Vries eds, trans Patrick Mensah, Stanford University Press, Stanford, California.

(1998), 'Faith and Knowledge: the Two Sources of "Religion" at the limits of Reason Alone', in Derrida Jacques and Gianni Vattimo eds, *Religion*, Polity Press, Cambridge U.K.

(2001), 'I have a Taste for the Secret', in *A Taste for the Secret*, Derrida Jacques and Maurizio Ferraris, Giacomo Donis and David Webb eds, trans Giacomo Donis, Polity Press, Cambridge. U.K.

(2001), *On Cosmopolitanism and Forgiveness*, trans. Mark Dooley and Michael Hughes with Preface of Simon Critchley and Richard Kearney, Routledge, New York.

(2004), *Jacques Derrida: 'I am at War with Myself'*, Interview given to Jean Birnbaum, Le Monde, August 19, Studio Vision, New York (e-resource).

(2005), *On Touching – Jean-Luc Nancy*, trans. Christine Irizarry, Stanford University Press, Stanford, California.

(2005a), *Paper Machine*, Mieke Bal and Hent de Vries eds, trans. Rachel Bowldy, Stanford University Press, Stanford, California.

(2008), *The Animal that Therefore I Am*, Marie-Louise Mallet ed., trans. David Wills, Fordham University Press, New York (e-book).

(2010), *Copy, Archive, Signature: A Conversation on Photography*, Richter Gerard ed., trans. Jeff Fort, Stanford University Press, Stanford, California.

Other Works Cited

Appadurai, Arjun, (1996), *Modernity at Large: Cultural Dimensions of Globalization*, University of Minnesota Press, Minneapolis.

Attridge, Derek, ed., (1991), *Acts of Literature*, Routledge, London and New York.

Badiou, Alain, (2006), *Polemics*, trans. and introduction Steve Corcoran, Verso, London and New York.

Bannet, Eve Tavor, (1989), *Structuralism and the Logic of Dissent: Barthes, Derrida, Foucault, Lacan*, University of Illinois Press, Urbana and Chicago.

Bataille Georges, (1985), *Visions of Excess: Selected Writings, 1927–1939,* edited and with an introduction by Allan Stoekl, trans. Allan Stoekl with Carl R. Lovitt and Donald M. Leslie, Jr., University of Minnesota Press, Minneapolis.

Bataille Georges, (1991), *The Accursed Share: an Essay on General Economy*, trans. Robert Hurley, Zone Books, New York.

Baudrillard, Jean, (2008), 'The Vanishing Point of Communication', in Clarke, David B, Doel, Marcus, Merrin, William and Smith, Richard G., *Jean Baudrillard: Fatal Theories, Routledge*, Hoboken.

Baudrillard, Jean, (2008a), 'On Disappearance', in Clarke, David B., Doel, Marcus, Merrin, William and Smith, Richard G., *Jean Baudrillard: Fatal Theories, Routledge*, Hoboken.

Baudrillard, Jean, (2000), *The Vital Illusion*, edited by and Julia Witwer, Columbia University Press, New York.

Baudrillard, Jean, (1996), *The Perfect Crime*, trans. Chris Turner, Verso, London.

Baudrillard, Jean, (1983), *Simulations*, Semiotext(e), New York.

Bauman, Zygmund, (1991), *Modernity and Ambivalence*, Polity Press, Cambridge.

Bauman, Zygmund, (1995), *Life in Fragments: Essays in Postmodern Morality*, Blackwell, Oxford and Cambridge, Mass.

Beardsworth, Richard, (1996), *Derrida and the Political*, Routledge, London and New York.

Beck, Ulrich, Anthony Giddens, and Scott Lash, (1994), *Reflexive Modernisation, Politics, Tradition and Aesthetics in the Modern Social Order*, Polity Press, Cambridge.

Benhabib, Seyla, (1992), *Situating the Self: Gender, Community and Postmodernism in Contemporary Ethics*, Routledge, London and New York.

Berger Anne and Sagarra Marta, eds, (2011), Demenageries: Thinking (of) Animals after Derrida, Rodopi, Amsterdam.

Bernasconi Richard Simon Critchley, eds, (1991), *Re-Reading Levinas*, Indiana University Press, Bloomington and Indianapolis.

Bernet, Rudolf, (1982),'Is the Present Ever Present? Phenomenology and the Metaphysics of Presence', in *Husserl and Contemporary Thought: Research in Phenomenology*, Vol. 12, pp. 85–112.

Bernet, Rudolf, Iso Kern and Eduard Marbach, (1993), *An Introduction to Husserlian Phenomenology*, Northwestern University Press, Evanston, Illinois.

Bernet, Rudolf, (1994), 'Derrida-Husserl-Freud: The Trace of Transference', *Southern Journal of Philosophy*, vol. 32, Supplement, Spindel Conference: Derrida's Interpretation of Husserl, The University of Memphis, Memphis, Tennessee.

Birmingham Peg, (1997), 'Toward and Ethic of Desire: Derrida, Fiction, and the Law of the Feminine' in Holland Nancy ed., *Feminist Interpretations of Jacques Derrida*, Pennsylvania State University Press, University Park, Pennsylvania.

Blanchot, Maurice, (1981), 'Literature and the Right to Death', in *The Gaze of Orpheus and Other Literary Essays*, trans. Lydia Davis, Station Hill Press, New York.

Blanchot, Maurice, (1988), *The Unavowable Community*, trans. Pierre Jorris, Station Hill Press, New York.

Bloom Harold, Paul de Man, Jacques Derrida, Geoffrey Hartman and J. Hillis Miller, (1979), *Deconstruction and Criticism*, Routledge and Kegan Paul, London.

Boyne, Roy, (1990), *Foucault and Derrida: The Other Side of Reason*, Unwin Hyman, London.

Brannigan John, Ruth Robbins and Julian Wolfreys, eds, (1996), *Applying: To Derrida*, Macmillan Press, London.

Buber, Martin, (1970), *I and Thou*, trans. Walter Kaufman, T. & T. Clark, Edinburgh.

Budick, Stanford & Wolfgang Iser, eds, (1989), *Languages of the Unsayable: The Play of Negativity in Literature and Literary Theory*, Columbia University Press, New York.

Cadava, Eduardo, Peter Connor & Jean-Luc Nancy, (1991), *Who Comes After the Subject?*, Routledge, New York and London.

Canclini Garcia, (1995), *Hybrid Cultures*, University of Minnesota Press, Minneapolis.

Caputo, John, D., (1997), *The Prayers and Tears of Jacques Derrida: Religion without Religion*, Indiana University Press, Bloomington and Indianapolis.

Cassese Antonio, (1990), *Human Rights in a Changing World,* Polity Press, Cambridge.

Cassese Antonio, (1995), *Self-determination of Peoples: a Legal Reappraisal*, Cambridge University Press, Cambridge and New York.

Castells Manuel, (2000), *The Rise of the Network Society*, 2nd edition, Blackwell, Oxford.

Castells Manuel, (2000b), *End of Millennium*, 2nd edition, Blackwell, Oxford.

Castells Manuel, (2009), *Communication Power*, Oxford University Press, Oxford.

Castoriadis, Cornelius, (1989), 'The State of the Subject Today', *Thesis Eleven,* 24, pp. 5–43.

Castoriadis, Cornelius, (1991), 'Power, Politics, Autonomy', in *Philosophy, Politics, Autonomy*, Oxford University Press, New York, pp. 143–174.

Chun Allen, Ned Rossiter, and Brian Shoesmith (eds), (2004), *Refashioning Pop Music in Asia: Cosmopolitan Flows, Political Tempos, and Aesthetic*, RoutledgeCurzon, New York.

Critchley, Simon, (1992), *The Ethics of Deconstruction Derrida and Levinas*, Blackwell, Oxford & Cambridge, Mass.

Critchley Simon, (1997), *Deconstruction in a Nutshell*, Fordham University Press, New York.

Culler, Jonathan, (1983), *On Deconstruction: Theory and Criticism after Deconstruction*, Routledge, London.

Davis, Colin, (2010), *Critical Excess: Overreading in Derrida, Deleuze, Levinas, Zizek and Cavell*, Stanford University Press, CA.

De Bloois Joost, (2010), 'The Last Instance: Deconstruction as General Economy', in Houppermans, Sjef; Sneller, Rico; van Zilfhout, Peter, eds, *Cultural Theory After Derrida*, Rodopi, Amsterdam [electronic resource].

De Rosnay Joël, (2006), *La Révolte du Pronétariat: Des Mass Média aux Média des Masses*, Fayard, Paris.

Dews, Peter, (1987), *Logics of Disintegration: Post-Structuralist Thought and the Claims of Critical Theory*, Verso, London, New York.

Dews, Peter, (1995), *The Limits of Disenchantment: Essays on Contemporary European Philosophy*, Verso, London, New York.

Diderot, Denis, (1994), 'The Paradox of the Actor', *Selected Writings of Art and Literature,* Penguin, Harmondsworth.

Eagleton Terry, (1981), *Benjamin, or Toward a Revolutionary Criticism*, New Left Books, London.

Ellis, John M., (1989), *Against Deconstruction*, Princeton University Press, Princeton, New Jersey.

Evans, Claude J., (1991), *Strategies of Deconstruction: Derrida and the Myth of the Voice*, University of Minnesota Press, Minneapolis, Oxford.

Fagan, Madeleine, Ludovic Gloieux, Indira Hâsimbergović and Marie Suetsugu eds, (2007), *Derrida: Negotiating the Legacy*, Edinburgh University Press, Edinburgh.

Falk, Richard, (1995), *On Humane Governance: Toward a New Global Politics*, Polity Press, Cambridge.

Featherstone, Mike, (1990), *Global Culture: Nationalism, Globalization and Modernity*, Sage Publications, London.

Feder, Ellen; Rawlinson Mary and Zakin Emily, (1997), *Derrida and Feminism: Recasting the Question of Woman*, Routledge, New York and London.

Ferry, Luc and Alain Renaut, (1990), *French Philosophy of the Sixties: An Essay on Antihumanism*, trans. Mary H. S. Cattani, MIT Press, Cambridge, Mass.

Flichy, Patrice, (2007), *The Internet Imaginaire*, trans. Liz Carey-Libbrecht, MIT Press, Cambridge, Massachusetts.

Foucault, Michel, *Madness and Civilization: A History of Insanity in the Age of Reason*, (1973), trans. Richard Howard, Vintage Books, New York.

Frank, Manfred, (1989), *What Is Structuralism*?, trans. Sabine Wilke and Richard Gray, University of Minnesota Press, Minneapolis.

Frank, Manfred, (1992), 'Is Self-Consciousness a Case of *présence à soi*? Towards a Meta-Critique of the Recent French Critique of Metaphysics', trans. Andrew Bowie, in David Wood ed., *Derrida: A Critical Reader*, Blackwell, Oxford and Cambridge Massachusetts.

Freud, Sigmund, (1973), *New Introductory Lectures on Psychoanalysis*, Vol 2, trans. James Strachey, Penguin Books, London.

Fukuyama, Francis, (1992), *The End of History and the Last Man*, Penguin, Harmondsworth.

Fukuyama Francis, (1999), *The Great Disruption: Human Nature and the Reconstitution of Social Order*, Free Press, New York.

Fukuyama Francis, (2007), *After the Neocons: America at the Crossroads*, Profile, London.

Fynsk, Christopher ed., (1989), *Typography: Mimesis, Philosophy, Politics*, Harvard University Press, Cambridge, Mass. and London.

Gadamer, Hans-Georg, (1975), *Truth and Method*, The Seabury Press, New York.

Gasché, Rodolphe, (1986), *The Tain in the Mirror: Derrida and the Philosophy of Reflection*, Harvard University Press, Cambridge, Mass. and London.

Gasché, Rodolphe, (1994), *Inventions of Difference: On Jacques Derrida*, Harvard University Press, Cambridge Massachusetts and London.

Congdon Matthew, (2009), 'Derrida and Other Animals', review, Telos, Fall 2009, pp: 185–191.

Grosz, Elizabeth, A., (2005), 'Derrida and Feminism: A Remembrance', *Differences: A Journal of Feminist Cultural Studies*, Fall2005, Vol. 16 Issue 3, pp: 88–94.

Grosz, Elizabeth, A., (1994) *Volatile Bodies: Towards a Corporeal Feminism*, Allen and Unwin, St. Leonards, N.S.W.

Gutman, Amy ed., (1994), *Multiculturalism, Examining the Politics of Recognition*, Princeton University Press, Princeton.

Habermas, Jürgen, (1979), *Communication and the Evolution of Society*, trans. T. McCarthy, Beacon Press, Boston.

Habermas, Jürgen, (1987), *The Philosophical Discourse of Modernity*, trans. Max Pensy, Polity Press, Cambridge.

Habermas, Jürgen, (1990), *Moral Consciousness and Communicative Action*, trans. Christian Lenhardt and Shierry Weber Nicholsen, MIT Press, Cambridge, Mass.

Habermas, Jürgen, (1994), *Theory of Communicative Action*, Vol. 1, trans. Thomas McCarthy, Beacon Press, Boston.

Hägglund Martin, (2008), *Radical Atheism: Derrida and the Time of Life*, Stanford University Press, Stanford, CA.

Hart, Kevin, (1989), *The Tresspass of the Sign: Deconstruction, Theology and Philosophy*, Cambridge University Press, Cambridge.

Hart, Kevin, (1995), 'Impossible Marx', *Arena Journal*, no.5, pp.185–209.

Hartman Geoffrey H., (1981), *Saving the Text: Literature/Derrida/Philosophy*, The Johns Hopkins Press, Baltimore.

Harvey, Irene, (1986), *Derrida and the Economy of Différance*, Indiana University Press, Bloomington.

Haverkamp, Anslem ed., (1995), *Deconstruction Is/in America: A New Sense of the Political*, New York University Press, New York and London.

Hegel, Georg W. F., (1979), *Phenomenology of Spirit*, trans. A. V. Miller, Oxford University Press, Oxford.

Heidegger, Martin, (1978), *Being and Time*, trans. John Macquarrie and Eduard Robinson, Basil Blackwell, Oxford.

Heidegger, Martin, (1982), *On the Way to Language*, trans. Peter D. Herts, Harper and Row, San Francisco.

Heidegger, Martin, (1987), *Nietzsche*, Vol. III, *The Will to Power as Knowledge and as Metaphysics*, ed. and trans. David Farrell Krell, Harper Collins, London.

Held, David, (1995), *Democracy and the Global Order, From the Modern State to Cosmopolitan Governance,* Polity Press: Cambridge.

Hill, Leslie, (2007), *The Cambridge Introduction to Jacques Derrida*, Cambridge University Press, Cambridge (e-book).

Hofstadter, D., (1979), *Gödel, Escher, Bach: An Eternal Golden Braid,* Harper & Row, New York.

Holland Nancy ed., (1997), *Feminist Interpretations of Jacques Derrida*, Pennsylvania State University Press, University Park, Pennsylvania.

Honneth, Axel, (1995), *Struggle for Recognition: The Moral Grammar of Social Conflicts*, trans. J. Anderson, Polity Press, Cambridge.

Houppermans Sjief, (2010), *Cultural Theory After Derrida*, Rodopi, Amsterdam [electronic resource].

Howells, Christina, (1999), *Derrida: Deconstruction from Phenomenology to Ethics*, Polity Press, Cambridge.

Howells, Christina, (2007), 'Satre and Derrida: The Promise of the Subject, Chaque fois unique, la fin du monde', in Fagan Madeleine, Ludovic Gloieux, Indira Hâsimbergović and Marie Suetsugu, eds, *Derrida: Negotiating the Legacy*, Edinburgh University Press, Edinburgh (e-book).

Husserl, Edmund, (1960), *Cartesian Meditation: An Introduction to Phenomenology*, trans. Dorion Cairns, Nijhoff, The Hague.

Husserl, Edmund, (1962), *Ideas: General Introduction to Pure Phenomenology*, trans. W.R. Boyce Gibson, Collier Books, New York.

Husserl, Edmund, (1964), *The Phenomenology of Internal Time-Consciousness*, Martin Heidegger ed., trans. James S. Churchill, Indiana University Press, Bloomington and London.

Husserl, Edmund, (1970), *The Crisis of European Sciences and Transcendental Phenomenology: An Introduction to Phenomenological Philosophy*, trans. David Carr, Northwestern University Press, Evanston.

Husserl, Edmund, (1977), *Logical Investigations*, trans. J. N. Findlay, 2nd ed. vol. 2, London and New York.

Husserl, Edmund, (1991), *On the Phenomenology of the Consciousness of Internal Time (1893–1917)*, trans. John Barnett Brough, Kluwer Academic Publishers, Dordrecht, Boston, London.

Hutnyk, John, (2005), 'Hybridity', *Ethnic and Racial Studies*, Vol. 28, No. 1, pp.79–102.

Irigaray Luce, (1985), *Speculum of the Other Woman*, trans. Gillian C. Gill, Cornell University Press, Ithaca.

Irigaray, Luce, (1993), *An Ethics of Sexual Difference*, trans. Carolyn Burke and Gillian C. Gill, Cornell University Press, Ithaca, New York.

Irigaray, Luce, (1995), 'The Question of the Other', trans. Noah Guynn, *Yale French Studies*, no 87, pp. 7–19.

Irigaray, Luce, (2008), *Conversations*, Continuum International Publishing Group, London.

Irwin, Jones, (2010), *Derrida and the Writing on the Body*, Ashgate, Farnham.

Jay, Martin, (1993), *Downcast Eyes: The Denigration of Vision in Twentieth-Century French Thought*, University of California Press, Berkeley.

Johnson, Barbara, (1994), *The Wake of Deconstruction*, Blackwell, Oxford and Cambridge, Mass.

Johnston, Christopher, (1993), *System and Writing in the Philosophy of Jacques Derrida*, Cambridge University Press, Cambridge.

Kamuf, Peggy ed., (1991), *A Derrida Reader: Between the Blinds*, Harvester Wheatsheaf, New York and London.

Kant, Immanuel, (1956), *Critique of Practical Reason*, trans. Lewis White Beck, Bobbs-Merrill, Indianapolis.

Kearney, Richard, (1984), *Dialogues with Continental Thinkers: The Phenomenological Heritage*, Manchester University Press, Manchester.

Keenan Thomas, (1997), *Fables of Responsibility: Aberrations and Predicaments in Ethics and Politics*, Stanford University Press, Stanford, California.

Kierkegaard, Søren, (1968), *Fear and Trembling* and *The Sickness Unto Death*, trans. Walter Lowrie, Princeton University Press, Princeton.

Kraidy Marwan, (2005), *Hybridity, Or the Cultural Logic of Globalization*, Temple University Press, Philadelphia.

Krupnick, Mark, (1983), *Displacement: Derrida and After*, Indiana University Press, Bloomington.

Lacan, Jacques, (1977), *Ecrits: a Selection*, trans. Alan Sheridan, Tavinstock, London.

Lacoue-Labarthe, Philippe, (1989), *Typography: Mimesis, Philosophy, Politics*, Christopher Fynsk ed., Harvard University Press, Cambridge, Mass. and London.

Lawlor, Lenard, (1992), *Imagination and Chance: The Difference between the Thought of Ricœur and Derrida,* SUNY Press, Albany, New York.

Lentricchia, Frank, (1980), *After the New Criticism*, University of Chicago Press, Chicago.

Levinas, Emmanuel, (1969), *Totality and Infinity: An Essay on Exteriority*, trans. Alphonso Lingis, Duquesne University Press, Pittsburgh.

Levinas, Emmanuel, (1978), *Existence and Existents*, trans. Alphonso Lingis, Martinus Nijhoff, The Hague.

Levinas, Emmanuel, (1981), *Otherwise than Being or Beyond Essence*, trans. Alphonso Lingis, Martinus Nijhoff, The Hague.

Levinas Emmanuel and Richard Kearney, (1986), 'Dialogue with Emmanuel Levinas', in *Face to Face with Levinas*, Cohen, Richard A. ed., State University of New York, Albany.

Lewis, Michael, (2008), *Derrida and Lacan: Another Writing*, Edinburgh University Press, Edinburgh.

Llewelyn, John, (2008), *Margins of Religion: Between Kierkegaard and Derrida*, Indiana University Press, Bloomington, IN.

McCance, Dawne, (2009), *Derrida on Religion: Thinker of Difference*, Equinox, London and Oakville.

McCarthy, Thomas, (1990), 'The Politics of the Ineffable: Derrida's Deconstructionism', in *Hermeneutics and Critical Theory in Politics and Ethics*, Michael Delly ed., MIT Press, Cambridge, Mass.

McCarthy, Thomas, (1991), *Ideals and Illusions: On Reconstruction and Deconstruction in Contemporary Critical Theory*, MIT Press, Cambridge, Mass.

MacIntyre, Alasdair, (1985), *After Virtue: A Study of Moral Theory*, 2nd ed., Duckworth, London.

Magliola, Robert, (1986), *Derrida on the Mend*, Purdue University Press, West Lafayette, Indiana.

Mathews Gordon, (2000), *Global Culture/Individual Identity: Searching for Home in the Cultural Supermarket*, Routledge, New York.

Marx-Scouras, Danielle, (1996), *The Cultural Politics of Tel Quel*, Pennsylvania State University Press, University Park.

Mattelart Arnaud, (2007), *La Globalization de la Surveillance: Aux Origines de L'Ordre Sécuritaire,* La Découverte, Paris.

Michelfelder, Diane P., and Richard, E. Palmer, eds., (1989), *Dialogue and Deconstruction: The Gadamer-Derrida Encounter*, State University of New York Press, Albany.

Mjaaland Marius T., (2008), *Autopsia: Self, Death, and God after Kierkegaard and Derrida*, Walter de Gruyter, Berlin [electronic resource].

Moghissi Haideh, (2007), *Muslim Diaspora: Gender, Culture and Identity*, Taylor and Francis, Hoboken.

Montefiore, Alan ed., (1983), *Philosophy in France Today*, Cambridge University Press, Cambridge.

Mortley, Raoul, (1991), *French Philosophers in Conversation: Levinas, Schneider, Serres, Irigaray, Le Doeuff, Derrida*, Routledge, London and New York.

Mouffe, Chantal ed., (1996), *Deconstruction and Pragmatism*, Routledge, London and New York.

Nagel, Thomas, (1986), *The View from Nowhere*, Oxrord Univerity Press, New York.

Nancy, Jean-Luc, (1991), *The Inoperative Community*, trans. Peter Connor, Lisa Garbus, Michael Holland and Simona Sawhney, Peter Connor ed., University of Minnesota Press, Minneapolis and Oxford.

Nancy, Jean-Luc, (1992), 'Elliptical Sense', trans. Peter Connor, in David Wood ed., *Derrida: A Critical Reader*, Blackwell, Oxford and Cambridge, Mass.

Norris, Christopher, (1990), 'Limited Think: How not to Read Derrida', *Diacritics,* 20.1, pp.17–36.

Norris, Christopher, (1990b), *What's Wrong with Postmodernism*, Harvester, Wheatsheaf, New York and London.

Norris, Christopher, (1994), *Truth and the Ethics of Criticism*, Manchester University Press, Manchester and New York.

Noys, Benjamin, (2010), *The Persistence of the Negative: A Critique of Continental Political Theory*, Edinburgh University Press, Edinburgh.

O'Connor, Patrick, (2010), *Derrida: Profanations, Continuum*, London and New York.

Plato, (1989), *Symposium*, trans. by Woodruff Paul and Nehamas Alexander, Hackett Publishing Company, Indianapolis.

Platon, (1991), *Symposion*, Trans Elektra Andreade, Kaktus Editions, Athens (bibliographical reference transliterated from Greek).

Rapaport, Herman, (2002), *Later Derrida: Reading the Recent Work*, Routledge, London.

Rapaport, Herman, (1991), *Heidegger and Derrida: Reflections on Time and Language*, University of Nebraska Press, Lincoln and London.

Rawls, John, (1972), *A Theory of Justice*, Oxford University Press, Oxford.

Reynolds, Bryan, (2009), *Transversal Subjects: From Montaigne to Deleuze after Derrida*, Palgrave Mcmillan, New York.

Ricœur, Paul, (1991), *From Text to Action: Essays in Hermeneutics, Vol. II*, trans. Kathleen Blamey and John B. Thompson, Northwestern University Press, Evanston.

Ricœur, Paul, (1992), *Oneself as Another*, trans. Kathleen Blamey, University of Chicago Press, Chicago and London.

Ricœur Paul, (2004), *Memory, History, Forgetting*, trans. Kathleen Blamey and David Pellauer, University of Chicago Press, Chicago and London.

Rorty, Richard, (1979), *Philosophy and the Mirror of Nature*, Princeton University Press, Princeton.

Rorty, Richard, (1989), *Contingency, Irony, and Solidarity,* Cambridge University Press, Cambridge.

Royle, Nicholas, (2009), *In Memory of Jacques Derrida*, Edinburgh University Press, Edinburgh.

Ryan, Michael, (1982), *Marxism and Deconstruction: A Critical Articulation*, John Hopkins University Press, Baltimore and London.

Sallis, John, ed., (1987), *Deconstruction and Philosophy: The Texts of Jacques Derrida*, University of Chicago Press, Chicago.

Sandel, Michael J., (1982), *Liberalism and the Limits of Justice*, Cambridge University Press, Cambridge.

Sartre, Jean-Paul, (1948), *Anti-Semite and Jew*, trans. George J. Becker, Schocken Books, New York.

Sartre, Jean-Paul, (1991), *The Psychology of Imagination*, Citadel Press, New York.

Sneller Rico, (2010), 'A Contemporary *Maskil Sarfat?* Derrida and the Provence Cabbala', in Houppermans Sjief, *Cultural Theory After Derrida*, Rodopi, Amsterdam [electronic resource].

Spivak, Gayatri Chakravorty, (1983), 'Displacement and the Discourse of Woman', in Mark Kuprick ed., *Displacement: Derrida and After*, Indiana University Press, Bloomington.

Taylor, Charles, (1989), *Sources of the Self: The Making of the Modern Identity*, Harvard University Press, Cambridge, Mass.

Taylor, Charles, (1991), *The Ethics of Authenticity*, Harvard University Press, Cambridge, Mass.

Taylor, Charles, (1992), 'The Politics of Recognition', *Multiculturalism: Examining the Politics of Recognition*, A. Gutmann ed., Princeton University Press, Princeton.

Taylor, Charles, (1995), *Philosophical Arguments*, Harvard University Press, Cambridge, Mass., London.

Thomassen Lasse ed., (2006), *The Derrida-Habermas Reader*, Edinburgh University Press, Edinburgh.

Thomassen Lasse, (2007), 'Derrida vs Habermas Revisited', in Fagan Madeleine, Ludovic Gloieux, Indira Hâsimbergović and Marie Suetsugu, eds, *Derrida: Negotiating the Legacy*, Edinburgh University Press, Edinburgh.

Turkle Sherry, (2005), *The Second Self: Computers and the Human Spirit*, MIT Press, Cambridge, Massachusetts.

Turkle Sherry, (1997), *Life on the Screen: Identity in the Age of the Internet*, Phoenix, London.

Van Zilfhout Peter, (2010), 'Traces of Nihilism', in Houppermans Sjief, *Cultural Theory After Derrida*, Rodopi, Amsterdam [electronic resource].

Walzer, Michael, (1987), *Interpretation and Social Criticism*, Harvard University Press, Cambridge, Mass.

Wolfreys Julian, 1998, *Deconstruction: Derrida*, Macmillan Press, London.

Wolin, Richard, (1992), *The Terms of Cultural Criticism: The Frankfurt School, Existentialism, Poststructuralism*, Columbia University Press, New York.

Wolin, Richard, ed., (1993), *The Heidegger Controversy: A Critical Reader*, MIT Press, Cambridge, Mass., London.

Wood, David, (1987), 'Following Derrida', in John Sallis ed., *Deconstruction and Philosophy*, The University of Chicago Press, Chicago and London.

Wood, David, (1989), *The Deconstruction of Time*, Humanities Press International, Atlantic Highlands, New Jersey.

Wood, David, ed., (1992), *Derrida: A Critical Reader*, Blackwell, Oxford and Cambridge, Mass.

Zizek, Slavoj, (1993), *Tarrying with the Negative*, Duke University Press, Durham.

Zizek, Slavoj, (1997), 'The Abyss of Freedom', in Zizek & F.W.J. von Schelling, *The Abyss of Freedom/ Ages of the World,* University of Michigan Press, Ann Arbor.

Bibliographical Appendix

The literature concerning the controversy surrounding deconstruction and Paul de Man is considerable, but see:

Hartman, Geoffrey, (1988), 'Paul de Man, Fascism, and Deconstruction: Blindness and Insight', *The New Republic*, 7 March 1988, pp. 26–31.

Todorov, Tzvetan, J. Hillis Miller (1988), *TLS,* 17–23 June 1988, p. 676, p. 684.

Miller, Hillis J., (1988), *TLS,* 17–23 June 1988, p. 676, p. 685.

Chase, Cynthia, (1988), *TLS*, 8–14 July 1988, p.755.

Eagleton, Terry, (1989), 'The Emptying of the Former Self', *TLS,* 26 May–June 1 1989, pp. 573–574.

See also, *TLS*, 13–19 May 1988, p. 541; 26 August – 1 September 1988, p. 931; 23–29 September 1988, p. 1047.

See also *TLS,* 11–17 November, p.1251; 24–30 June, p. 705; 8–14 July, p.755; 15–21 July, p. 781, 1988.

Norris, Christopher, (1988), 'Paul de Man's Past', *London Review of Books*, 4 February 1988, pp. 7–11.

See letters of reply of Norris, Christopher, Culler, Jonathan, and Ayer, A. J., *London Review of Books*, 21 April 1988, p. 4.

See also letters by Claude Rawson, Glen Frankfurter and Cushing Strout, in *London Review of Books*, 2 June 1988, p. 4.

McCannell, Juliet Flower and Christopher, Norris, (1988), *London Review of Books,* 7 July 1988, p. 4.

See also letters of reply of Derrida, Jacques and Norris, Christopher, in *London Review of Books*, 4 August 1988, p.4.

See also letters in *London Review of Books*, 17 March, p.4; 31 March, p. 4; 5 May, p. 4; 19 May, p.4; 7 July, p. 4; 15 September, p.4, 1988.

Kermode, Frank, (1989), 'Paul de Man's Abyss', *London Review of Books,* 16 March 1989, pp. 3–7.

Donaghue, Denis, (1989) 'The Strange Case of Paul de Man', *The New York Review of Books,* 29 June 1989, pp. 32–37.

Griswold, Charles L., Jr., (1989), 'Deconstruction, The Nazis and Paul de Man', *The New York Review of Books*, 12 October 1989, p.69.

See also Letter to the Editors of Grisworld, Charles, L., Jr., in *The New York Review of Books,* 12 Octtober 1989, p. 69.

See also Letter to the Editors of Bell, Daniel, in *The New York Review of Books,* 29 September 1989, pp. 75–76.

See also *New York Times*, 1 December 1987, p. B1.

Also *THES*, 11 December, 1987, p. 11.

Jay, Gregory S., (1988) 'Paul de Man: The Subject of Literary History', *MLN*, 103.5, December 1988, pp. 969–994.

Wiener, Jon, (1988), 'Deconstructing de Man', *The Nation*, 9 January 1988, pp. 22–24.

See also letters of reply from Jack Sheinkman, Micah L. Sifry, Hans Robert Jauss, and Jon Wiener in *The Nation*, 4 June 1988, p. 774.

Hirsch, David H., (1988), 'Paul de Man and the Politics of Deconstruction', *Sewanee Review*, 96, Spring 1988, pp. 330–338.

Simpson, David, (1989), 'Going on about the War without Mentioning the War: The Other Histories of the "Paul de Man Affair"', *Yale Journal of Criticism*, 3.1, Fall 1989, pp.163–173.

Christensen, Jerome, (1990), 'From Rhetoric to Corporate Populism: A Romantic Critique of the Academy in an Age of High Gossip', *Critical Inquiry,* 16, Winter 1990, pp. 438–465.

Stern, Frederick C., (1990), 'Derrida, de Man, Despair: Reading Derrida on de Man's 1940s Essays', *Textual Practice*, 4.1, Spring, pp. 22–38.